Zoroastrians in Britain

Zoroastrians in Britain

*The Ratanbai Katrak Lectures,
University of Oxford 1985*

JOHN R. HINNELLS

CLARENDON PRESS · OXFORD
1996

Oxford University Press, Walton Street, Oxford OX2 6DP
Oxford New York
Athens Auckland Bangkok Bombay
Calcutta Cape Town Dar es Salaam Delhi
Florence Hong Kong Istanbul Karachi
Kuala Lumpur Madras Madrid Melbourne
Mexico City Nairobi Paris Singapore
Taipei Tokyo Toronto
and associated companies in
Berlin Ibadan

Oxford is a trade mark of Oxford University Press

Published in the United States
by Oxford University Press Inc., New York

© John R. Hinnells 1996

All rights reserved. No part of this publication may be reproduced,
stored in a retrieval system, or transmitted, in any form or by any means,
without the prior permission in writing of Oxford University Press.
Within the UK, exceptions are allowed in respect of any fair dealing for the
purpose of research or private study, or criticism or review, as permitted
under the Copyright, Designs and Patents Act, 1988, or in the case of
reprographic reproduction in accordance with the terms of the licences
issued by the Copyright Licensing Agency. Enquiries concerning
reproduction outside these terms and in other countries should be
sent to the Rights Department, Oxford University Press,
at the address above

British Library Cataloguing in Publication Data
Data available

Library of Congress Cataloguing in Publication Data
Zoroastrians in Britain: the Ratanbai Katrak lectures, University of Oxford 1985
John R. Hinnells.
Includes bibliographical references and index.
1. Zoroastrianism–Great Britain. 2. Great Britain–Religion–20th century.
I. Title.
BL1535.G7H56 1996   295'.0941–dc20   95–635
ISBN 0–19–826193–4

1 3 5 7 9 10 8 6 4 2

Typeset by J&L Composition Ltd, Filey, North Yorkshire
Printed in Great Britain on acid-free paper by
Bookcraft (Bath) Ltd., Midsomer Norton

*This book is dedicated to
Dastur Dr Kaikhusroo M. JamaspAsa,
High Priest of the Anjuman Atash Bahram, Bombay
and
Dastur Dr Sohrab H. Kutar,
late High Priest of the Zoroastrians of Europe—
two holy men and noble Zoroastrians
from whom I have been privileged to learn much*

PREFACE

I was greatly honoured to be invited to deliver the Ratanbai Katrak lectures at the University of Oxford in 1985. It was a daunting prospect to follow my own teacher, Prof. Mary Boyce, whose research for the previous series of lectures justly received such acclaim (Boyce 1977). This was devoted to traditional Zoroastrianism as it was maintained still in the 1960s in the most conservative villages in Iran, where it has been established for some two and a half millennia; and it suggested to me, by way of contrast, a study of how Zoroastrians have been faring in the modern diaspora, far from either of their old homelands of Iran and the Indian subcontinent. My seven lectures considered the Zoroastrians in India (mostly Bombay), Pakistan (mostly Karachi), Hong Kong, Britain, and on the North American continent; that is, within a number of different religious environments—Hindu, Muslim, Chinese culture, a secular society, and one with high-profile evangelical and fundamentalist Christians. The research involved me in almost 100,000 miles of travel to stay with, and research the records of, communities in these different places. Later research was conducted in East Africa and I subsequently visited Australia to study the Zoroastrian communities there. The global-survey questionnaire associated with this research has acquired gargantuan proportions, with over 1,700 responses yielding approximately 80,000 pages of computer printout (for a preliminary study, see Hinnells 1994a). The material on the British community alone grew unexpectedly in size, because of the quantity of Association records found in the attic at Zoroastrian House in London, there was a good response rate to the survey questionnaire and Manchester University generously funded a research assistant to undertake an extensive programme of structured in-depth interviews (detailed in Ch. 6). The Katrak trustees and the publishers, therefore, kindly agreed to my proposal to publish the material on Britain as a separate volume.

The British Zoroastrians merit a book. The history of Parsi

travel to Britain dates back to the early eighteenth century; numbers visiting and settling reached a level whereby a formal Association was established in 1861, making this the oldest of the formally constituted South Asian communities in Britain. It may also be considered to be a microcosm of this macrocosm because its members include people from rural and urban India, from Pakistan and East Africa, a control group from Iran, and now a substantial proportion of people born in Britain. Because records have been preserved, it is possible to write the history of this community, and this provides a unique opportunity to study the long-term trajectory of settlement for a British South Asian minority. In the broad field of the study of religion there is an increasing interest in the study of diaspora communities. The Zoroastrians provide an excellent case-study. The world's oldest prophetic religion now has a more global dispersion than at any other time in its history, but the scattered communities are small enough for it to be possible to become personally acquainted with a substantial proportion of their members. I hope, therefore, that this work will be of interest to people studying both ethnic minorities in Britain and international diaspora religions.

The British Zoroastrians are probably the largest Zoroastrian community outside Iran and the Indian subcontinent and they have played an international role on many occasions. As the number of Zoroastrians declines dramatically in the old (or 'sending') countries so the diaspora groups can be expected to play an increasingly significant role in the future of the religion. Since they have been ignored in all publications on the 'Good Religion', the time is right for a study of them. The British Zoroastrians are distinctive in many ways, both in terms of their history and demography. They were among the first Indians to travel to Britain in the nineteenth century for education, for business, and to settle. Their diaries and the books they produced for the British provide an unrivalled insight into aspects of Anglo-Indian relations of the period. They also have a political significance in that two Zoroastrians were elected Members of Parliament at Westminster in the nineteenth century, and a third entered the House of Commons in the 1920s. The pioneering role of these individuals has received inadequate attention in previous studies of Zoroastrians. As Chapter 6 will try to show, the educational and social structure of the community makes it a particularly interesting group which has contributed more to British society than has been appreciated. There is a large body of literature on ethnic minorities in Britain, but relatively few writers have studied the role of religion in the various communities; because of the remarkably generous help given to me by Zoroastrians for almost a quarter of a century, I have been privileged to observe and record the practice and evolution of the noble religion of ancient Iran in modern Britain.

A study of Zoroastrians in Britain is an appropriate subject for the Katrak lectures. The lectureship was founded in 1922 by Dr Nanabhai Naoroji Katrak (1858–1945) in memory of his wife Ratanbai. A similar lectureship was started in 1926 at the Sorbonne in memory of his second wife, also named Ratanbai. Dr Katrak thereby undertook two typically Zoroastrian benefactions, creating a memorial not in stone but with a charity and supporting scholarship. In making the first-named endowment in Britain he reflected the generally positive Parsi attitude to Anglo-Indian relations. I hope and believe that he would have approved of a project to study his co-religionists in this country. As a medical man Dr Katrak was noted for a book on Indian medicines and for his work with cholera victims. He was also a member of the Bombay Municipal Corporation and worked to improve the city's sanitation. Throughout his life he was deeply committed to his religion. As well as being active in various religious societies and involved in a number of conferences, he served for sixty-one years as a trustee of one of Bombay's chief fire temples, the Anjuman Atash Bahram, where his portrait now hangs. The present high priest of that temple, Dastur Dr Kaikhusroo M. JamaspAsa, has been a source of inspiration for much of my own work and this book is dedicated to him as a token of deep respect and affection. He has been my mentor and guide not only on the travels mentioned in the first chapter, but also in my journey through Parsi studies. We have long been engaged in a joint book on 'The Parsis in British India: Their History and Religion'. Dastur JamaspAsa kindly agreed to my postponing my part of that project in order to undertake the Katrak lectures. Neither of us then thought that this work would take so long, the time involved being extended both by the mushrooming of the research and a succession of medical problems. I am grateful to him and to the Katrak trustees, for their patient forbearance and hope that this volume is acceptable as I move on to the next. The book is also dedicated to the first high priest to be formally recognized outside the old countries, Dastur Dr Sohrab H. Kutar, a medical doctor and priestly inspiration to his community in London. These two holy men have made me realize why, in practice as well as in theological terms, Zoroastrianism is referred to by its adherents as the Good Religion. Through honouring them, I also honour the benefactor and Mrs Katrak.

I am deeply conscious of my indebtedness to many people. As always I wish to express my profound thanks to my teacher and friend, Prof. Mary Boyce whose scholarship is matched only by the love she has and conveys for the subject. I am deeply grateful to all my Zoroastrian friends. Anyone who has encountered Zoroastrian communities will readily appreciate that my decades of contacts with Parsis in Britain and around the world have been times of great happiness because of the generosity and love of 'the good life' for which Zoroastrians are known. My only regret is that my contacts with the Zoroastrians of Iran were curtailed at the end of the 1970s. I hope that I have done them justice, even though my links with them are less close. I am grateful to the leaders of the various Zoroastrian organizations who have given me unrestricted access to their files and allowed me to quote from them. A research project which has involved such extensive global travel and survey work is necessarily dependent upon research funding. It is a pleasure as well as a duty to record my thanks to my old university, Manchester, for the travel grants and for the funding for Dr Rashna Writer to spend a year collecting the interview data used in Chapter 6. It was, of course, a pleasure to work with and learn from Dr Writer. Generous help was also give by the universities of Oxford and of Hong Kong, by the British Academy, the Spalding Trusts, the World Zarathushtrian Trust Fund, and by individual Zoroastrians, notably Tahamtan and Godafrid Aresh, the Rivetna family, Minoo and Coomi Treasureywala. I hope they find this first return on their investment acceptable. The computer analysis of the survey and interview data could not have been done without the Mehta family and to them I owe a particular debt of gratitude.

In my studies of the living Zoroastrian community I have

laughed and learned with many. The danger of mentioning some is the unwitting omission of others, but worthy of special mention are: Cyrus P. Mehta, the first Zoroastrian I met and who first suggested to me that I write an article on British Zoroastrians, for unfailing help for nearly a quarter of a century, and his late wife Dina for all her kindness; successive leaders of the Zoroastrian Trust Funds of Europe, notably Shahpur F. Captain; Dr (Mrs) S. Kutar; Rusi Dalal; the secretary at Zoroastrian House, Mr Modi; Malcolm Deboo, who worked as librarian for many years and helped me chase much information; Dr Rashna Writer, research assistant with the Interview Schedule and friend; Burjor and Zarin Avarai, good friends and noble Zoroastrians. To them all, named and unnamed, I express my deepest gratitude for their friendship and help. A number of people have kindly taken the time to read the manuscript, namely Mary Boyce, Richard Gombrich, Rusi Dalal, Shahpur F. Captain, Roger Ballard, and Belinda Baker. They have saved me from many errors and I am very grateful to them, though the responsibility for any mistakes which remain is my own. Ms Nora Firby has, as always, given frequent invaluable professional help, mostly on bibliographical matters, but in other ways also.

One is schooled to avoid the personal 'I' in scholarly writing. However, in this book it seemed essential to break with this custom. In part this is because many of the judgements are based on personal contact and observation, rather than on archives or survey figures. It seemed important to make clear where the basis of a judgement is subjective and to record insights given to me orally by individuals.

At various points in the text reference has been made to my research on other Zoroastrian communities which were included in the 1985 Katrak lectures. I hope circumstances will allow me to publish that material more quickly and have referred to that work as 'the subsequent Katrak volume'. As British Zoroastrians themselves do not use diacritical marks, I have not done so in this book. Many personal names are quoted in the body of the text. Their significance is commented on when known. The reason for including the others is so that in subsequent research on Zoroastrian diasporas the information is available to see where people were involved in different communities, as for example the Cama and Dinshaw families were. Normally people have been referred to by the surname or family name. There are some idiosyncrasies. In one or two instances where I have known a revered figure personally I have felt compelled to write as I spoke to them: for example, the late Mr Jehangir Moos, an outstanding worker for the community for whom I have too much respect to call simply 'Moos'. It is for the same reason that some people are called by both given and family names. I hope the reader will not find these small irregularities distracting.

I wish to express my profound gratitude to Miss Nora Firby for compiling, with her usual care, the index to this volume.

Last, and certainly not least, I wish to thank the doctors who have kept me at work and above all my family for their support and love.

J. R. H.

CONTENTS

Abbreviations		xv
1.	Introduction	1
	(a) A Brief Overview of Zoroastrian History	1
	(b) South Asians in Britain	27
	(c) Some Questions of Terminology	44
2.	Zoroastrian Perspectives on Contacts with the British	50
	(a) Iranian Zoroastrians and the British	50
	(b) Anglo-Parsi Relations in India	53
	(c) Parsis and the British in Pakistan	58
	(d) Parsi Experiences in East Africa	60
	(e) British–Zoroastrian Religious Interaction	67
	(f) Conclusion	74
3.	Early Zoroastrian Arrivals in Britain	77
	(a) The Earliest Arrivals	77
	(b) Nineteenth Century Parsi Travellers' Diaries	88
	(c) Zoroastrian Literature for the British	97
	(d) Conclusion	102
4.	A Century of Zoroastrian Associations in Britain (1860s–1960s)	107
	(a) The Founding of the London Association	107
	(b) London and the Iranian Zoroastrians	111
	(c) The Incorporation of the Association	114
	(d) The Parsi Social Union	117
	(e) Broacha House, Edinburgh	119
	(f) Growing Numbers, Problems, and the Need for a Zoroastrian House	121
	(g) Personalities and Politics within the Community	125
	(h) London: An International Centre	132
	(i) The Post-War Situation	133
	(j) The London Funeral Ground	134
	(k) A New Zoroastrian House and Community Religious Needs	138

(l)	Zoroastrian 'Boundaries'	142
(m)	The World Zoroastrian Organization (WZO)	144
(n)	Local Zoroastrian Associations	148
(o)	Conclusion	150

5. Zoroastrians in British Politics ... 155
   - (a) Dadabhoy Naoroji (1825–1917; MP 1892–1895) ... 156
   - (b) Muncherji Bhownagree (1851–1933; MP 1895–1905) ... 174
   - (c) Shapurji Saklatvala (1874–1936; MP 1922–1923, 1924–1929) ... 194
   - (d) Zerbanoo Gifford (1950–) ... 218
   - (e) Conclusion ... 221

6. British Zoroastrians Approaching the Third Millennium ... 227
   - (a) Some Observations on Research Methods ... 227
   - (b) A Broad Demographic Picture ... 230
   - (c) Religion and a Sense of Identity ... 233
   - (d) Zoroastrians and the British ... 235
   - (e) Does being a Zoroastrian Conflict with being British? ... 238
   - (f) The Country of Birth and the Preservation of Heritage ... 241
   - (g) Decade of Arrival and Religious Practice ... 243
   - (h) Contacts with the Old Country ... 245
   - (i) Differences between the Generations ... 246
   - (j) Some Gender Issues ... 249
   - (k) Intermarriage ... 250
   - (l) Transmitting the Tradition: The Social Context ... 255
   - (m) Transmitting the Tradition: Religious Knowledge ... 258
   - (n) The Practice of the Religion ... 261
   - (o) British Zoroastrians in International Perspective ... 272
   - (p) Conclusion ... 275

7. Conclusion ... 279
   - (a) Zoroastrians in Britain: An Overview ... 279
   - (b) Zoroastrians and other South Asian Religions in Britain ... 296
   - (c) Another Comparison ... 303
   - (d) The Study of Diaspora Religions ... 305
   - (e) The Future for British Zoroastrians ... 309

Bibliography ... 311

Glossary ... 321

Index ... 325

ABBREVIATIONS

AGM   Annual General Meeting
EIA   East India Association
CIE   Companion of the Indian Empire
FEZANA   Federation of the Zoroastrian Associations of North America
ICS   Indian Civil Service
ILP   Independent Labour Party
INC   Indian National Congress
IPP   Indian Parliamentary Party
JCOI   *Journal of the K. R. Cama Oriental Institute* (Bombay)
NOLZA   North London Zoroastrian Association
PD   *Parliamentary Debates* (Hansard, the official record of Parliamentary proceedings)
PP   *Parsi Prakash* (see Bibliography)
WZO   World Zoroastrian Organization
ZS   Zoroastrian Studies (an educational body in Bombay)
ZTFE   Zoroastrian Trust Funds of Europe

1

Introduction

The Zoroastrian community is the oldest of the Asian communities in the United Kingdom. The first travellers came in the eighteenth century and the formal Association was established in 1861. The community therefore has a longer trajectory of settlement than any other Asian group in Britain. It is also a microcosm of the macrocosm of South Asian migration in that its members have come not only from India (both cosmopolitan Bombay and rural Gujarat) but also from Pakistan. Further, it has a substantial proportion of Parsi Zoroastrians who settled first in East Africa and then felt compelled to leave that continent and migrate on to Britain in the 1960s and early 1970s. Some of its members migrated directly from the original Zoroastrian homeland, Iran, about the time of the Revolution in 1979. Before studying the British community it is necessary first to give a brief overview of Zoroastrian history and teaching and then to locate the story of Zoroastrian migration to Britain in the context of other groups who came from Asia in the twentieth century, the laws which governed that entry, and their experiences within Britain.

(a) *A Brief Overview of Zoroastrian History*

Zoroastrianism is the name given to the religion of the Iranian prophet Zarathushtra, or as he is known in the West, Zoroaster. There has been much debate over his date. The earlier consensus placed him in the seventh–sixth centuries BCE but in the last twenty years more scholars have argued for an earlier dating of approximately 1200 BCE. When Cyrus the Great established the Persian Empire in the sixth century BCE, Zoroastrianism became the official religion of what was then the largest empire in the world, stretching from north India to Asia Minor, Greece, and Egypt. The Jews, when liberated from exile in Babylon by Cyrus, therefore lived under Zoroastrian protection. There were no examples of religious intolerance in that empire. Zoroastrianism was, thus a major world religion at the time of the great era of Greek philosophy, at the time when Buddhism and Jainism grew in India and when Confucius' teaching was spreading in China. The first empire under which Zoroastrianism held sway, that of the Achaemenids (named after an eponymous ancestor), was overthrown in the fourth century by Alexander, referred to in the West as 'the Great', but in Iran as the 'accursed', hated because he destroyed the splendours of Persian rule and killed the priests. Under him and his successors (the Seleucids) Iran was subject to western influences, but in the second century BCE Iranian traditions reasserted themselves under a new empire, that of the Parthians (named after the province in north-east Iran where they first enter the light of history). In the first century BCE the Parthians sought to re-establish the boundaries of their Achaemenid predecessors and moved westwards throughout the fertile crescent and into Asia Minor. In the second century BCE the Parthians expanded westwards, conquering Media, Babylonia, and Mesopotamia. In 54 BCE they inflicted a heavy defeat on the Roman general Crassus at the battle of Carrhae and pressed westwards capturing Jerusalem in 40 BCE. The Jewish king, Herod, managed to escape, obtain Roman reinforcements, and recaptured Jerusalem two years later. Zoroastrianism was, then, a powerful religion in the world at the time of Jesus and in the areas into which the early Christian Church spread, just as it was in northern India at the same time.

In the third century CE there was an internal rebellion in Iran and the Sasanians (again named after an eponymous ancestor) assumed power, returning control of the Iranian plateau to the people from Persia in the south-west of the country. The Sasanians, like the Parthians before them, were the main opponents to stand against the might of the Roman Empire, and thereafter they confronted the forces of Christian Byzantium until the rise of Islam. The Sasanian period is the time when the Persian Empire is generally thought to have been at its most splendid in terms of magnificent palaces and royal wealth. In religious terms it was important as a time when priestly authority was maintained, theological ideas were articulated, and a canon of scripture was established.

The seventh century saw the end of the imperial phase of Zoroastrian history as Islam conquered Iran and over the following 1,200 years gradually reduced Zoroastrianism to the religion of a tiny, oppressed, and persecuted minority forced to retreat into the relative safety of the more obscure villages around the desert cities of Yazd and Kerman. When the tax on unbelievers was first imposed it did not seem a heavy burden compared with the charges of the old monarchy, but gradually that burden grew until it ground Zoroastrians into abject poverty. The imposition of Arabic resulted in the loss of both the traditional language and of many treasures in the oral tradition. Over the centuries the laws became increasingly oppressive and Zoroastrians were deprived of many rights in their homeland. At various times there were forced conversions and persecutions. In the twentieth century Zoroastrians enjoyed greater freedom under the Pahlavi dynasty (1924–79). When the Iranian Parliament was established in 1906 they were allocated one Member of Parliament and were given opportunities to flourish in commerce and the professions. In the 1960s and early 1970s they were allowed to rise to positions of important government office, such as oil minister and deputy Prime Minister. As their wealth increased and the sense of security developed, so increasing numbers migrated from the desert towns to the great metropolis of Tehran where many of the ancient customs were eroded as the 'modern generation' adapted to city life. An unknown, but not insubstantial, proportion converted to Baha'ism which presented itself as the modern fulfilment of religions, increasing a trend in religious conversion that began in the nineteenth century. When the Shah fell from power in 1979 and Iran became an Islamic Republic under Ayatollah Khomeini, many Zoroastrians feared a return to earlier harsh conditions and left the country. Reports on the present condition of the community in the homeland vary. Generally it seems that although its members have not experienced the extremes of previous centuries they nevertheless feel themselves to be vulnerable to attack, especially from extremists; they also feel restricted by Islamic legislation in terms of dress, social life, education, career, and indeed in their basic inequality before the law. The number of Zoroastrians in Iran is unknown. In the 1960s there were estimated to be approximately 16,000 but in the 1990s the government of the Islamic Republic have stated that there are 90,000 Zoroastrians in Iran. To many outsiders an increase of 400% seems implausible, but some explain it to be a result of Iranians returning to their Zoroastrian roots (from the Baha'ism, for example).

In the tenth century CE a Zoroastrian base was founded in India. As conditions had worsened in Iran a small group had set out in the ninth century as the pilgrim fathers of the faith to seeking a new land of religious freedom. The text which relates this story, the *Qissa-i Sanjan*, tells how they settled first in north Gujarat, at Diu, and then sailed south, settling in the tenth century at a place they named Sanjan after their home town in Iran. Until the arrival of the British in the seventeenth century these Zoroastrians, known as the people from Pars (that is, Persia), or Parsis, lived in relative peace and obscurity. Under British rule they grew in power, becoming by the mid-nineteenth century leading businessmen; they flourished as middlemen in trade and through their immense success in western education became influential in politics. Over the decades they migrated to Bombay leaving their centres in Gujarat as places for the poor, elderly, and infirm. The Parsis consider that in the course of the twentieth century they have lost something of their standing in Indian society, but even in independent India they retain a significance out of all proportion to their numbers. Since 1947 they have held high office in the armed forces, the diplomatic and civil services and have been elected to the national Parliament. Their typical perception of India and Hinduism is that they have been shown exceptional tolerance and given security; they believe that they have not had to forsake any of their important religious traditions, nor been compelled to assimilate. They believe that they have contributed much to their adopted land through their achievements and their charities. Since the nineteenth century scholarly discovery of the common Indo-Iranian parentage of Zoroastrianism and Hinduism, there has been something of an emphasis on their shared religious values.

In the nineteenth century wealthy Parsi traders sought out new lands for business opportunities. First they travelled to China, as part of the opium trade and to import tea, silks, and ivory. Communities grew up in Canton, Shanghai, and Hong

Kong but in the Communist take over of China in 1947 resources were centred on Hong Kong. The first Parsi visitor to Britain was in the seventeenth century but it was the nineteenth century before there was a steady trickle of business men and students. By 1861 the numbers, though still small, merited the establishment of the formal Association.

Also in the early to mid-nineteenth century Parsis travelled to Sind and the North-West Provinces of India and helped to develop the trading-centres there, notably Karachi. Although some left after Partition, and the establishment of the Islamic state of Pakistan in 1947, the majority remained and there is a well-established community of Zoroastrians to this day. Later in the nineteenth century Parsi traders and professionals sought out new opportunities in East Africa, first on the island of Zanzibar and then on the mainland, during the building of the East Africa railway from Mombasa through to Nairobi and beyond. These various communities flourished, especially after the Second World War, but with the policy of Africanization in the 1960s and Idi Amin's expulsions from Uganda in the early 1970s, most East African Parsis emigrated to Britain, though a few went to Canada.

In the 1960s and 1970s growing numbers migrated westwards from the Indian subcontinent first to Britain, then to the USA and Canada, and from the 1980s to Australia.

At the approach of the third millennium, therefore, Zoroastrians are more dispersed around the globe than at any other time in their history. But in numerical terms they are a declining community. In India numbers peaked in 1941 at 114,890. By 1961 they were declining at the rate of 10% per decade (down to 100,772) but in the decade 1971–81 the rate accelerated to 20% and at the end of the decade numbers were down to 71,630 with most (50,053) in Bombay. Briefly, the reason for this numerical decline is an ageing population caused by late and low marriage rates, resulting in small or no families; high educational and career expectations have caused many to delay or avoid marriage. In Pakistan also there has been a decline in numbers. There is no precise census data comparable to that from India but informed community estimates suggest that the peak of 5,000 has dropped to approximately 2,000 in the 1990s. The Pakistan Parsi population is also an ageing one, but out-migration has had a proportionately higher effect here than in India. In East Africa numbers have shrunk from a total of 500 in each of the main centres (Zanzibar, Mombasa, Nairobi) in the post war years to about 40 in the late 1980s. In Hong Kong there are approximately 150 Zoroastrians but the numbers may be expected to decrease after the return of Hong Kong to Chinese rule in 1997. In the 'old countries', therefore, Zoroastrians are a diminishing population. This gives their diaspora communities all the more importance in the history of the religion, for it is only here that numbers are growing because of further migration, and being young populations, the birth-rate exceeds the death-rate. As London has the largest Zoroastrian population in any city of the diaspora that Association, and the related groups in Britain, have a particular significance both in terms of past history and of future prospects. (See above all Boyce 1978*a*, and for the early period Boyce 1975, 1982, 1991; Kulke 1974 for the Indian history; on Iran, Boyce 1977, 1992: Chs. 8, 9 Amighi 1990; on the Iranian and Indian Zoroastrians in the dispersion, Writer 1994 and Hinnells 1994*a*).

Zoroastrian Literature

The reconstruction of the historical development of Zoroastrian teaching has been a matter of scholarly controversy which it is necessary to outline briefly. The traditional Zoroastrian belief is that the whole of the holy book, the *Avesta*, was revealed through Zoroaster. In the middle of the nineteenth century, a German orientalist, Martin Haug, identified just one proportion, the *Gathas*, as the words of the prophet. The rest was seen as later priestly elaboration, albeit incorporating some very ancient liturgical texts, the *Yashts*, which provided an insight into Zoroaster's background. The 'classical' Zoroastrian theology of the Middle Persian (Pahlavi) texts, written down in the eighth to tenth centuries CE, was seen as a priestly elaboration far removed from the visionary teaching of the prophet. Thereafter, the quest of Zoroastrian scholarship and of westernized Zoroastrians alike was to seek to understand the pure teaching of the prophet independent of later doctrinal 'corruption'. Such a perspective, for example, lies behind a book still quite widely used (Zaehner 1961). But in the course of twentieth century studies various scholars, notably Lommel (1930) and Boyce (1977, 1993), have argued for a greater degree of continuity between the *Gathas* and the later texts. Boyce in particular emphasized the immense faithfulness with which the priestly word is preserved in both Iranian and Indian traditions, because of the importance attached both to memory and to the sound of words uttered in prayer, as Zoroaster's words had been. Many of the Middle Persian texts were only committed to the recording of a venerable oral tradition. Boyce argued that western scholars, mostly coming from a Protestant-Christian background, devalued the religious insights which the Zoroastrian priesthood had into its priestly founder's message (Boyce 1978*b*). Something of these scholarly debates is reflected in contemporary orthodox and liberal Zoroastrian discussions concerning the authority of the priestly tradition and whether the *Gathas* are the sole source of religious authority.

Zoroastrian Belief and Practice
A brief word is necessary on the place of Zoroaster in the living faith. As noted above, most western academics date Zoroaster to approximately 1200 BCE. Many orthodox Parsis date him around 6000 BCE. For them the important point is his place as the first of the great prophets of world religions. Tradition relates that his wondrous nature was evident from the outset, for he is the only child to have laughed and not cried at birth. Recognizing his religious importance, the forces of evil sought to destroy the baby, and his father and others were inspired to try to kill him, but each time he was miraculously saved. When he grew up he became an officiating priest and one day while engaged in his duties he saw the Bounteous Immortal, Vohu Manah, the Good Mind, and was led into the presence of Ahura Mazda. The message that he took back to his people was at first rejected and the established priests at the royal court plotted to have him imprisoned. Then, and throughout his early life, he was the victim of the assaults of evil, but he remained steadfast in his commitment to his divine calling. When the king's favourite horse was taken ill, Zoroaster was brought into the royal presence and healed the animal on the condition that the king accepted the Good Religion, which he did; thereafter the teaching of Zoroaster became the official religion of the realm. According to later tradition he was murdered by invaders while

at prayer when he was 77, but this has been shown to be a misunderstanding of older traditions (Boyce 1993: 14–16; for an account of the popular beliefs about Zoroaster, see Hinnells 1985*b*: 92–7). Zoroaster, it is believed, was chosen by Ahura Mazda to receive his revelation concerning the Good Religion and to preach it to mankind. The hand of God may be seen in his life through the miracles that happened, and he was the foreordained turning-point in the history of religion, but there is no doctrine of the divinity of Zoroaster in the ancient texts. There is, however, a sense that he is not simply like other men and a number of orthodox Parsis in India want to stress the uniqueness of his stature, seeing him as a highly developed manifestation of the divine nature; almost, as it were, as an *avatar*. Iranian Zoroastrians typically see him simply as the great prophet who brought the revelation directly from God.

The starting-point for an understanding of central Zoroastrian teaching is the doctrine of creation. God (Ahura Mazda in the *Gathas*, Ohrmazd in Pahlavi literature) is the eternal, wholly good creator. Zoroastrians, traditionally, do not believe that God can be at once all-powerful, all-good, and all-loving because of the reality of evil in the world as manifested in such phenomena as the suffering of the innocent. Evil, therefore, they attribute to a wholly independent source of evil, (Anra Mainyu in the *Young Avesta*, Ahriman in Pahlavi literature) which, or who, has existed from eternity, and over whom Ahura Mazda currently does not have control but who He will eventually conquer. The myth merits brief elaboration. It is as little known to British Zoroastrians as medieval thought is to British Christians, but the values it enshrines are still powerful and the following exposition emphasizes those common ideals (for further details, see Hinnells 1985*b*: 42–70).

Ahura Mazda dwelling in light and goodness was aware of the existence of evil and produced creation as the battle-ground in which to overcome Anra Mainyu. First He created the world in unseen, intangible, 'spiritual' (*menog*) form and then fashioned this in 'material' (*getig*) form. The point is that in Zoroastrian thought the material is not opposed to the spiritual, but is its complement, indeed in some sense its fulfilment. Anra Mainyu (literally 'the Destructive Spirit') is characterized by the will to kill, destroy, and defile. He, therefore, assaulted the Good

Creation, inflicting smoke on the pure fire, and violence, suffering, misery, disease, and ultimately death on the creatures (both animal and human) which Ahura Mazda had created to be by nature perfect, without need, sinless, eternal. All the evils which afflict humanity and the material world are therefore the work of Anra Mainyu. But as Anra Mainyu attacked the perfect material world of Ahura Mazda, so he became ensnared within it and the history of the world is the history of the battle between good and evil. With the coming of the prophet, Zoroaster, who brought the Good Religion from Ahura Mazda, the human population learned the ways of truth and, in an optimistic spirit, Zoroastrians believe that although all humans have free will to follow or reject the Good Religion, ultimately all will choose good so that evil will be defeated and ejected from existence. Teachings on the 'end of the world' are also important, both because of the understanding they encapsulate regarding human nature and destiny and because they are thought to have influenced Jewish, Christian, and Islamic teaching (Boyce 1991: ch. 11). The term 'end of the world' is not a Zoroastrian one, for the world is God's; its end would therefore be His defeat. Instead Zoroastrians speak of the renovation of existence (*frashokereti*), that is the time when the Good Creation will be restored to the perfect state which existed before the assault of evil. The difference after the renovation is that evil will then be destroyed and therefore no longer able to assault Ahura Mazda's world. He will then become not only all-good but also all-powerful.

Before relating the myth of the renovation it is necessary to explain the myth of the soul's fate after death, because the two doctrines are inextricably linked. It is believed that after death the soul lingers around the body for three days, meditating on its thoughts, words, and deeds. These are then weighed in the scales of justice. If the good outweigh the evil then the soul is led across the Bridge of Judgement (Chinvat Bridge) by a beautiful damsel, the sum of its thoughts, words, and deeds, and is conducted to heaven where it is rewarded according to its merits. If, however, the evil predominate, the soul is led by an ugly old hag, the personification of its nature, to the Bridge which becomes ever narrower and the soul falls into hell where it is punished according to its crimes. A significant feature, therefore, of Zoroastrian teaching is that everyone, rich or poor, man or woman, is rewarded according to their own thoughts, words, and deeds. There is no possibility of saving grace, or of one person dying for others. The *Gathas* seem to imply that the damned are annihilated, but in the Middle Persian texts at least, this time in heaven and hell is not, however, eternal. This first judgement is evidently one in the spirit because the body can be seen to remain on earth. The doctrine of the resurrection is therefore central to traditional Zoroastrian thought, both because it involves the restoration of the divinely created body and because it facilitates the second judgement. This takes place after the renovation. Prior to the renovation the forces of good and evil pair off in mortal combat. The earth is shaken in the tumult, so that earthquakes break out. The conflict is cosmic because the cosmos is the divine creation, so the sun, moon, and stars do not give their light. The proper order of human society will be overthrown by this final onslaught of evil, and basic human values will be destroyed so that children do not respect parents, nor students their teachers. After the triumph of the heavenly forces, a saviour will be born who will raise the dead and introduce the final judgement scene. Because of the resurrection, the dead can now be judged in the body, unlike the first judgement which was concerned with the soul; the soul then returns to heaven or hell for appropriate reward or punishment. But once punished in body as in soul then the corrected person can proceed to dwell with Ahura Mazda in perfection. Now that evil has been expunged from the universe heaven and earth can combine in what is literally the best of both worlds for eternity. (The apocalyptic tradition developed over the millennia from the time of the prophet to medieval times and down to the present; see Boyce 1993: 169–70.)

This myth highlights various Zoroastrian values: the religious importance of the interconnectedness of material and spiritual worlds, of the body and soul; the world is not seen as the material prison of a spiritual self, but rather as the divinely created snare for evil; everyone has personal responsibility for their own thoughts, words, and deeds; the emphasis on the fundamental goodness of human nature; the conviction that all suffering, misery, disease, and death are alien to Ahura's creation—there is traditionally no concept of suffering being sent by Ahura to test people, nor of death as being due to the divine will.

Introduction

TABLE 1. *The Amesha Spentas*

Scriptural (Avestan) form	Later form	Meaning	Creation protected	Ritually represented by
Ahura Mazda (or Spenta Mainyu)	Ohrmazd (Spenag Menog)	Lord Wisdom (Holy Spirit)	Mankind	The priest
Vohu Manah	Vahman	Good Mind	Cattle	Glass of milk
Asha (Vahishta)	Ardvahisht	(Best) Righteousness, Truth	Fire	Ritual flame
(Spenta) Armaiti	Spendarmad	(Holy) Devotion	Earth	Ground of ritual setting
Khshathra (Vairya)	Shahrevar	(Desirable) Dominion	Sky (conceived of as stone or metal)	Pestle and mortar
Haurvatat	Hordad	Wholeness	Water	Consecrated water
Ameretat	Amurdad	Immortality	Plants	Haoma and other plants (e.g. flowers)

There is another dimension of traditional Zoroastrian theology which merits brief exposition because of its impact on the contemporary tradition. The primary creations of Ahura Mazda were the Amesha Spentas, the Bounteous (or Holy) Immortals. These are always seven in number, though the 'names' within that number vary slightly according to whether or not Ahura himself is included within the seven, as he most commonly is in living practice. Although their 'names' may make them appear to be mythological beings, and mythological imagery is associated with them, the meaning of those 'names' and their role in Zoroastrian thought is essentially abstract (the distinction between mythical and abstract thought is not really applicable to Zoroastrian teaching). Each of these forces is represented by, and manifest within, one of the seven creations into which the Good Creation is traditionally divided. The Amesha Spentas are listed with the main variant spelling and their associated creations in Table 1. With the exception of Spenta Mainyu these beings represent both human and divine qualities; they are the meeting-point between the human and divine. Ahura Mazda can be approached, or prayed to, through any of these powers. Each one of them is represented by a token in important rites (e.g. a beaker of milk represents Vohu Manah) and when invoked in purity and with true devotion they are thought be powerfully present in worship. Beneath them in the spiritual hierarchy are a number of 'worshipful beings' (*yazatas*). Generally they are the divinities of pre-Zoroastrian tradition, but conceived as the creations of, and subordinate to, Ahura Mazda. The two figures most commonly encountered within the living tradition are Mithra (the power of Contracts, Compact or Agreement) and Sraosha (Obedience). Many Zoroastrian friends have commented to me that the Amesha Spentas and *yazatas* play a role in Zoroastrianism comparable to that of the archangels and angels in Christianity. So although Zoroastrians commonly assert that they are monotheists, there are nevertheless various spiritual powers whose aid is invoked. There are three ways in the living tradition in which these forces are most commonly encountered: in worship, because of their presence through invocation; because they préside over one of the five liturgical divisions of the day (*gahs*); and because one of the months of the year, or the days of the month, is named after them. When the name of the month and the day of the month coincide, as for example the day of Mithra in the month of Mithra, the fifteenth day of the seventh month, this is a festival (or *jashan*) day special to that power. Mithra is also important in that the symbol of priesthood, the mace (*gurz*) and the temple itself are associated with the name of Mithra (temples are known as *dar-i Mihrs*, courts of Mithra, and also in India by the Gujarati term *agiary*, 'house of fire'). The background theological or historical explanations are rarely understood, the point here is simply that these benign powerful forces remain part of living practice. None, however, erode the primacy of the creator Ahura Mazda, to whom is dedicated in due honour the first day, the first month, and absolute personal allegiance.

There is another dimension of Zoroastrian life on which the theology impacts directly. Because Zoroastrians believe that life in the material world is the good creation of Ahura, then conduct in that life is strictly directed. Fundamentally, the guiding principle is to ally oneself with the good and distance oneself from evil, although with the emphasis on the doctrine of free will Zoroastrians do not doubt that many people do not follow that principle. Allying oneself with the good has two dimensions: ethical and devotional. In ethical terms Zoroastrians are expected to act so that order (Asha—see Table 1) is the guiding principle behind all thoughts and actions, this is manifested in life affirming attitudes. It is sinful to deny the body or to abuse it, for both actions fail to honour the divine creation. Marriage and having children is a religious obligation because the army of Ahura Mazda is thereby expanded. In the Pahlavi literature the Aristotelian principle of the Golden Mean is used to express a fundamental Zoroastrian principle: virtue is defined as the mid-point between opposing vices, so the married state is the virtuous mean between the extremes of celibacy and debauchery. As 'the good' is defined in terms of balance, so sin is identified with 'excess and deficiency'; as fasting is a sin, so is gluttony: both abuse the body (Zaehner 1961: chs. 13–14). Again, few Zoroastrians know the texts and formal philosophy just as few Christians know formal medieval theology. However, the attitudes to life, family values, what might be described as 'the work ethic', the enjoyment of the good things of life, and generally the lack of an emphasis on asceticism (there have been some exceptions in Hindu India) all reflect an attitude which historically was formed by this theology.

The attitudes to good and evil have one direct and powerful effect on the great majority of Zoroastrians, especially in India but also in Britain, and this concerns the purity laws. Such laws are common in many religions, but in Zoroastrianism they have both a clear and explicit theological foundation and a strong living power (Boyce 1977: ch. 5). Because death is conceived as the ultimate weapon of evil, and is associated wholly with it, any dead matter is seen as the presence of evil. This is conceived of not only in spiritual but also in material terms, which is logical in a religion which emphasizes the necessary interconnectedness of the material and spiritual worlds. 'Evil is present in all dead or decaying matter, but above all in a corpse, because that represents the (temporary) victory of evil over the most important of the divine material creations, the human body.' The more righteous the deceased, the more polluting his or her corpse, because the greater the triumph of evil. From the moment of death the corpse must be kept apart from that which is pure, for example the living. It must be touched only by 'professionals', that is, full-time corpse-bearers, or *nasasalas* whose profession involves regular contact with pollution and so entails low social status. The disposal of the corpse is an important matter. Since the material world, the earth, is a sacred creation the burial of such pollution is doctrinally wrong because it would involve the defilement of the sacred. As the waters are similarly sacred, burial at sea is equally wrong. Since the fire is not simply the symbol but the very presence of the creative force of life and is spoken of in the texts as 'the son of God', cremation, according to tradition, involves desecration. Hence the Zoroastrian funeral involves exposure of the dead to vultures in a *daxma*, or as the British in India called it, a 'Tower of Silence'. In ancient times bodies were simply exposed in a desolate place for consumption by wild animals. Since Islamic times at least the *daxma* has been a round structure, or walled enclosure, open to the sky. In concentric circles oblong spaces are marked out in which the corpse is exposed. Vultures normally take less than half an hour to devour the flesh, the body-juices drain away in channels to a central pit, the bones are bleached in the sun and when powdery are also disposed of in the pit into which nowadays acid is poured. Zoroastrians believe that Ahura Mazda created nothing without a purpose and vultures, and other carrion-eating creatures, are thought to have been created for the specific purpose of disposing of dead matter.

Non-Zoroastrians are commonly revolted at the practice and sensational articles have often been published in the West which have caused deep offence to Zoroastrians. As I have been taken around funeral grounds in Bombay and other centres in Gujarat by one of the High Priests it is appropriate to give a more informed account than is generally available. I confess that before my first visit I shared the common western revulsion, though I would not then have admitted it. In practice I found them deeply moving places. Even in noisy, polluted, crowded, traffic-dominated Bombay the funeral grounds exude an atmosphere of naturalness, peace, and calm, because the natural habitat of the jungle is more evident than the industrial life of the city as creepers, trees, and plants encircle the bungalows (*bunglis*) where the corpse is taken and prepared for the funeral and for its last journey to the tower. Animals and birds—peahens and other creatures—flourish. In the great metropolis of Bombay it is impossible to follow the ancient tradition of a *daxma* being in a barren place apart from the good creations. Where this tradition can be followed in Gujarat, the lonely isolation of the *daxma* does not generate the ghoulish atmosphere implied by sensational western reporters; it is a quiet place where the proper respect and care can be taken to treat the soul with dignity and prayerful support and at the same time the living world is protected from evil.

The body is removed to the funeral grounds as soon after death as possible. Specially adapted vans, with all-metal fixtures are used, because wood, being porous, is thought to absorb the pollution. The buildings in the funeral grounds are designed to meet the ritual needs, where the body can be washed and clad in the sacred shirt (*sudre*) before the prayers begin. The body is laid in a clearly marked-off area, into which no-one except the *nasasalars* enter because it is a place of intense pollution. Before a burning light representing the divine forces which hold evil at bay, and accompanied by the dog, the priest begins the prayers which last up to the moment of the funeral. A dog is brought into the room, partly because dogs are thought to have special vision which enables them to see forces humans cannot. A dog is something of a holy animal in Zoroastrianism, for it typically displays the religious qualities of obedience and loyalty. It also protects people, as here at the time of death. For the last rites the bereaved women pray in the *bungli*, while the men wait outside, but it is the men who form a procession, walking in pairs to protect each other against the presence of evil, and accompany the deceased to the *daxma*. There, watched by the priest, the men take their leave of the deceased and the *nasasalas* carry the corpse into the tower. As the corpse is exposed, further prayers begin which last about twenty-five minutes—that is, as long as it normally takes the vultures to perform their task. At home and in the temple further prayers are said and the mourners wash before re-entering the outside world. There are several important rites to be celebrated during the first three days after death, when traditionally the soul is believed to be meditating on the balance of good and evil in its life before it crosses the Bridge of Judgement. These rites conclude with the *uthumna* ceremony when a charitable bequest is commonly announced in memory of the deceased.

From a Zoroastrian point of view, the rite of exposure is a natural process, because it involves humans providing food for the birds at death as animals provide food for people in life; it is ecologically sound because it does not make ever-increasing demands for land as burials do; it is swift and hygienic, unlike cemeteries which Zoroastrians have traditionally found repulsive. Much western reporting of Zoroastrian funerals is not only crude and sensational but also offensive. Another personal experience may illustrate this. A British publisher produced a book on world religions with the chapter on Zoroastrianism written by myself. The publisher chose and published the illustrations without any consultation. When the book appeared, there was a photograph of a partly devoured corpse in a *daxma*, obviously taken with a powerful telephoto lens by a non-Zoroastrian (ordinary Zoroastrians do not enter the *daxma*; only the *nasasalas* and neither they nor any other Zoroastrian would take such a photograph). When I protested forcefully to the publisher that this was grossly offensive to Zoroastrians and utterly insensitive, the reply was simply: 'But this does happen, how can they object?' It is unlikely that such a response would have been given to Catholics or Muslims if they had objected to a photograph of a worm eaten corpse. The parallel is precise because burial is religiously significant for these groups (because of the doctrine of the resurrection), as the *daxma* is for Zoroastrians. Small minorities rarely have the power to command respect for even their most sensitive feelings.

The purity laws are important in life as well as at death. Anything leaving the body is considered dead, for example cut finger-nails, hair, urine, or blood. Blood is the life-force within the body, but dead when it leaves. 'The holy' is that which is close to the form in which God created it, the impure is that which is tainted by the presence of evil. So, for example, a menstruating women is the locus of evil. There is no sense of a menstruating woman being immoral, far from it. Traditionally a woman is seen as the key to the fight against evil, for it is she who gives birth to the children who are the new recruits in the army of Ahura Mazda. The battle of creation is re-enacted at the birth of each child. Just as Anra Mainyu sought to destroy life at the beginning of creation, so he does within the womb, the place where individual material life begins. The monthly bleeding was traditionally interpreted as the emission of dead matter from the scene of the conflict between the forces of good and evil. Similarly, for all the great holiness of the moment of birth, the afterbirth (and presumably the frequency of death associated with birth in antiquity) meant that the period immediately following the birth was a time when pollution was powerfully present and had to be strictly controlled through the isolation of the new mother. So also a menstruating women is the hapless victim of the assault of evil and is, therefore, polluted. She has to be kept apart from the holy, for example from a practising priest or the sacred fire. Indeed a woman during menstruation would not attend any religious function.

As blood is dead when it leaves the body, so, too, is the breath – again a life force when it is inside the divine creation. It is, therefore, important that when a priest is ministering to the holy fire in the ritual he should not pollute it with his impure breath. To prevent this he wears a mouth veil, the *padan*. A strict Zoroastrian would not blow out the flame of a candle (but would nip it) or of a match (rather he would flick it). In modern thought smoking is often interpreted as blasphemous because it involves defiling fire through breath and spittle – though it has to be said that some westernized Zoroastrians do smoke.

Anything which is associated with death or decaying matter is polluting. So for example, flies are seen as especially impure, indeed are part of the evil creation, because they collect on dead meat. In the ancient myths the fly often symbolises death and in practice killing flies (and other deadly creatures such as snakes) is considered meritorious. For similar reasons, it is virtuous to preserve the purity of the home by keeping it clean. When a housewife sweeps and cleans the house she is traditionally thought to keep the danger of pollution away from her family. After she has completed this task each morning it is customary for her to carry the small household fire (with incense or sandalwood) from room to room to spread both the sweet smell and divine blessings throughout the home. If someone is staying with a strict Zoroastrian family, it is courteous to ask the host how cut nails or hair should be disposed of – putting them down a flushing toilet might be thought to pollute the sacred creation of water. Some orthodox families I have stayed with in the course of this research keep an area of sand (not sacred earth) outside the house where such remains can be burned. Even Zoroastrians who are not doctrinally strict may well find cut hair and nails repulsive. For the religiously minded the point of the purity laws is that they are battle orders against evil and its weapon of death; they are part of the war each Zoroastrian must wage on behalf of the good. It has been said that cleanliness is not next to godliness in Zoroastrianism, but part of it. Modern Zoroastrians argue that the purity laws really do protect life, for they accord with scientific views on hygiene. Once again, the ancient logic is rarely known, but the practice remains strong.

How important is it to know the ancient traditions in order to understand living practice? A historian would naturally assert that it is very important. But in Derbyshire (where I come from), and elsewhere, part of the old tradition of drawing curtains when a funeral passed was to keep out the demons of death. At weddings, bridesmaids were dressed like the bride to attract the demons of barrenness away from her so that she might remain fertile. The fact that people no longer hold such beliefs does not rob the customs of all value as tokens of either respect in the one case or happy support in the other. The fact that Zoroastrians may not know the explanations behind the presence of the dog, the burning of the lamp, and so on does not mean that they do not find such traditions comforting. Practices hallowed by time can provide an outlet for grief, or appropriate sharing in joy.

The subject of the purity laws is, especially for Parsis, related to the subject of who is, and is not, a Zoroastrian. Here it is difficult to assert with confidence what the ancient tradition was. For Iranian Zoroastrians the tradition is clear—a Zoroastrian is someone who has undergone the initiations (*sedra pushun*, i.e. what in India is known as *sudre kusti*) and consciously professes the faith. The position is more complex for Parsis, who form the great majority among British Zoroastrians. The following focuses mainly on the nineteenth and twentieth centuries. The question of conversion to Zoroastrianism has surfaced in Iran only in the last few decades (Amighi 1990: 283–90) and even now it is rare because of the Islamic tradition that apostasy can, in theory at least, be punished by death. In India the issue was virtually never discussed because the caste traditions meant that there was a widespread assumption that a person is born into a religion and does not choose one. It has become a matter of great debate among Parsis in twentieth century India because as a result of westernization, intermarriage has occurred more and a number of Parsis have sought to have their spouse initiated. There was a test case in the Bombay High Court in 1906, when one of the great luminaries, Tata, married a French lady (Suzanne Brier), had her initiation performed, and the wedding blessed by Zoroastrian rites. Despite his standing (and immense charities) the leading Parsi institution (and administrator of the great bulk of Parsi charity) the Bombay Parsi Punchayat publicly condemned Tata, established a committee of experts, and then went to court against him. The ruling has been quoted by all subsequent disputants on this subject, including British Zoroastrians. Unfortunately it was not really a clear ruling (partly because it is not obvious whether the crucial statements are legally authoritative or simply part of unbinding summary) and so has been claimed by both sides of the debate (Writer 1994: 129–49). There is also, of course, the fundamental question of whether a Bombay High Court ruling early in the twentieth century should have authority in independent India or the diaspora. Most Indian born Zoroastrians think that it should. Basically the two judges argued that although in theory one might distinguish between Parsi as a racial term and Zoroastrian as a religious term, in practice the two had become synonymous in India; in a society dominated by caste no one could convert into a 'race' and therefore conversion into (Parsi) Zoroastrianism was impossible. People might practice Zoroastrianism in private but the only people who could claim in law to be Zoroastrian were those born of a Zoroastrian father (i.e. descent is through the father, not the mother as in Judaism). In community debates some have argued that this means that a man who has married out of the community can have his children initiated, but in practice the traditional priests, which means nearly all of them both in India and Britain, argue that as Zoroastrianism has always emphasized the equality of the sexes, such a discriminatory practice is wrong and therefore no children of any intermarriage can be initiated. In India there has been effectively no debate about the initiation of spouses and certainly not of anyone else. Because intermarriage is a more common phenomenon in the diaspora (including Britain) than in India, it is a subject of frequent debate and of importance there (see Ch. 6). However the arguments are rarely understood by outsiders, it is worth outlining the arguments which have been advanced against intermarriage and conversion.

Missionary religions such as Christianity and Islam teach that there is a right and a wrong faith, and that the right faith is necessary for salvation. Conversion is, therefore, a necessary practice. In ancient Iranian religion there was the idea that Zoroastrianism is not simply 'the Good Religion' but the 'best religion' and it is one for which over many centuries Zoroastrians have suffered and died. But most modern Zoroastrians believe that there is truth in all religions; hence there is not the same necessity for conversion. Further, they argue that religion is intimately related to personality. Parsis commonly believe that people are born into the religion that God thought appropriate for them. In India many Parsis, under Hindu influence, accept the idea of rebirth (it is not part of historical Zoroastrianism); they therefore generally argue that one is born into the religion appropriate for that stage of the soul's development. There is widespread acceptance that religion is 'in the blood' or something to do with the genes. It is what you are, not simply what you believe. To change religion, many argue, inevitably causes psychological damage and an individual should, therefore, be religious in the tradition into which he or she was born. There is a strong Zoroastrian aversion to evangelism because it is associated with persecution, an understandable view in the light of their experience in Islamic Iran. Parsis often argue that more people have been tortured and killed in the name of religion than in any other cause. Further, they often allege, mixed-faith marriages leave children in a religious vacuum, and lead to irreligion and that such marriages are associated with a higher rate of divorce. There is also a strong conviction, especially but not only, among the orthodox that as the tiny community is under the threat of numerical decline, intermarriage will hasten the end of the world's oldest prophetic religion. It is very widely believed that intermarriage must inevitably lead to the dilution of the traditions of the community. There is effectively no call for proselytizing, but some western-educated in India, and some of the liberal persuasion in the diaspora, argue that since intermarriage is inevitable and increasing, if the spouses and offspring are excluded, this will speed the community's extinction and an infrastructure has therefore to be evolved, if not for conversion then for the acceptance of the families of intermarrieds. They argue that Zoroaster must have accepted converts for the religion to grow and if the terms 'Parsi' and 'Zoroastrian' are synonymous in India, they are not in the West and hence religious conversion must be accepted. The argument rages on. Orthodox Parsis deny Zoroaster converted people but insist he only called his fellow Iranians to be more religious and asked no-one to change their religion. They point to the fact that it was only during the 'heretical' (Zurvanite) phase of imperial Iranian history, the Sasanian times, that there was evidence for Iranians seeking to convert people to Zoroastrianism. Reference is often made, with pride, to the example of Cyrus the Great when he established the Persian Empire and released the Jews from exile in Babylon. He did not seek to make them Zoroastrians but encouraged them to return to the homeland and gave funds for the building of the Jewish temple so that they could practice the religion which they were born into. That is the proper religious role-model in the opinion of many orthodox Parsis. Since Mrs Tata's initiation at the start of the century, there has been only one public initiation of a white person, an American in New York in the 1980s. That provoked an international storm of protest and has not been repeated, although it is said to have been done in private in the U.S.A. There is no known case of a white Anglo Saxon being initiated in Britain.

It is important to conclude this account of Zoroastrian belief and practice with a description of the daily religious life of the ordinary Zoroastrian in the Indian subcontinent, not only because this is part of the memory of most British Zoroastrians, but also because it is what is seen on visits back to the old country and represents part of community lore about the practice of the religion, even for those born in Britain.

Traditionally there are only two formal religious Zoroastrian duties: to observe the seven great festivals (New Year, *No Ruz*, and the six seasonal festivals or *gahambars*) and to say the daily prayers associated with the sacred shirt and cord, the *sudre* and *kusti*. The *gahambars* have remained an important part of Iranian

Zoroastrianism, especially in the region of Yazd (Boyce 1977: ch. 2), though less so in Tehran (Amighi 1990). They embody a whole range of Zoroastrian duties: temple worship and sacrifice, joyful giving, and sharing of food or labour in the preparation of meals for the whole community. Each is a five-day festival and they provide times of welcome rest from the hard toil of daily life. Left-over unconsecrated food is given in charity to the poor Muslims, or animals. In India the festivals were preserved into the early twentieth century but after Independence the government restricted large community meals because of the wastage of food in a land where many knew poverty. The festivals therefore declined in importance, especially in Bombay where their agricultural basis had less significance.

The history of the *sudre-kusti* prayers is almost the reverse of that of the *gahambars* for they are not so widely practised in Iran but are in India even though few may pray five times daily as was the custom. In Iran such visible badges of the religion were not emphasized because minorities were vulnerable and oppressed. In India, however, the concept of the sacred cord as the marker of a religious person is common. It may be assumed that the brahmin cord and the Zoroastrian *kusti* both derive from ancient Indo-Iranian tradition, but what is restricted to priests in Hinduism is the mark of all members of the religion in Zoroastrianism, quite possibly a reform introduced by Zoroaster himself as Boyce suggests (Boyce 1978: ch. 2). The *sudre*, or shirt, is a white cotton garment worn next to the skin at all times (except when bathing), like a vest. It is invested with much symbolic significance: it is the armour of faith protecting the Zoroastrian against evil, or reminding him or her (for it is worn by men and women alike) of the duty to fight spiritually for goodness. The *kusti* is a long belt woven from lambs wool and is spoken of, among other things, as the sword-belt of faith. At the five appointed times of the religious divisions of the day (*gahs*) Zoroastrians wash, because physical cleanliness is a necessary part of purity in a religion which emphasizes the importance of the body as well as the soul. They face the light, untie the *kusti*, and commence the traditional prayers which take approximately five minutes. In these they reject evil, contemptuously flicking the ends of the *kusti* as Anra Mainyu is spurned, and resolving to work for good as they firmly tie the knots with resolution (Mistree 1982: ch. 14).

The prayers are said in the ancient language of the *Avesta*, for this is the language of revelation when Zoroaster saw Ahura Mazda, and therefore the right medium for communication with Him. (Orthodox Parsi teachings on the importance of Avesta in prayers are more complex and are outlined below.) The *kusti* prayers are said before many important deeds from going to temple, on a journey, or any important occasion. They constitute the core practice for Zoroastrians from the Indian subcontinent. For Iranian Zoroastrians the words of prayer are more important than the objects, the *sudre* and *kusti*. For Parsis they are inseparable.

For Parsis the first ritual donning of the *sudre* and *kusti* at *naujote* is a momentous occasion. The term is generally understood as meaning new, or second, birth that is the birth into the religion. (Among Iranian Zoroastrians the rite is known as the *sedra pushun*, putting on the *sedra*, because *nozad*, the equivalent term to *naujote*, is used for priestly initiation.) Initiation is the moment when young persons take on themselves the responsibilities of the religion. In Zoroastrian thought human beings are by nature good. Sin involves conscious rejection of the good and is therefore possible only when someone is old enough to know the difference between right and wrong. Consequently initiation takes place just before puberty and not in infancy. Since a baby cannot sin, there is no need for anything like infant baptism. Initiation is not a means of grace which gives salvation, it is acceptance of religious duties and initiation into the army of God. Because the *naujote* is seen as entry into the community rather than as a means to personal salvation the rite is commonly celebrated in a public fashion. It can be performed in the home or temple, but most commonly takes place in a public place, or *baag* (used also for weddings), which in India has the rooms for taking the necessary bath, for changing, for prayer, and for feasting. The rite begins with a purificatory bath (*nahn*) to cleanse from the pollution of the outside world where evil is mixed with good. Traditionally, the child then takes a sip of *nirang*, consecrated cow's urine, which has been used in Zoroastrianism and Hinduism since ancient times as a cleansing agent, although nowadays, especially in the diaspora, pomegranate juice is used instead. The child enters the ritual room dressed in white pyjama trousers and a shawl over the upper part of the body. He, or she (the rite is the same for either gender) is then invested with the *sudre* and *kusti* and says the associated prayers for the first time publicly in the presence of the priest, family, and friends. This has always been an occasion of great joy, but with the awareness of decreasing numbers, and especially in the diaspora, it is of yet greater moment. Like most Zoroastrian rites it is associated with the happy sharing of food.

Temples were not part of the early religion, for it was in large measure a nomadic tradition in which prayers were said not in man-made structures but before the divine creations of fire (e.g. in the form of the sun) and water. In imperial Iran the tradition of temple-building began, but the heart of even the most splendid royal temple remained a simple room housing the living flame of the fire. Under Islamic rule temples were eventually compelled to be small, inconspicuous structures in which the fire had often to be hidden from public gaze, even of the faithful, in case a Muslim entered and defiled it. Until the nineteenth century there were very few Parsi temples in India. The rites were mostly carried out in the home using the household fire. Even some of the temples did not have a permanently burning fire; the priest simply took his fire from home. But as Parsis became wealthy in the nineteenth century they began to employ servants, who were rarely Parsi, so that the home could not have the purity necessary to maintain a permanently burning ritual fire. Hence temples were important as places where the necessary purity could be maintained. The community now had the wealth to build temples and so they proliferated (Hinnells 1985*a*). Twentieth century Parsis have, therefore grown up with a community memory, extending back generations, of worship in a temple. They are central to much of the living religion in the Indian subcontinent.

When Parsis go to pray in a temple they are essentially undertaking a pilgrimage to stand before the fire and receive divine blessing (a pilgrimage which may take place on a daily basis). The practices are the same for men and women, apart from the restrictions on menstruating women. Cleansing him/herself physically by washing in the outer precinct, and spiritually by saying the *sudre-kusti* prayers, the worshipper passes through an outer hall, decorated with pictures of the heroes of the faith, where people may sit and talk, or consult the priest.

Naturally there are paintings of the prophet, but also photographs of leading figures and benefactors. They are commonly garlanded and it is usual for the worshipper to touch the pictures as they pass, drawing inspiration from the great examples of the religion. With head covered as a sign of respect, and shoes left outside so that no impurity is taken into the presence of the holy, the worshipper proceeds alone to the prayer-room. There the fire stands within a sanctuary marked off by floor-to-ceiling walls with a doorway for the priest to enter and windows for the faithful to see through. The worshipper takes a piece of sandalwood, lays it in a silver ladle in the sanctuary doorway, so that the priest may later offer it to the fire, takes a pinch of ash from the fire left in another ladle, kneels and touches the forehead to the floor in obeisance, but then stands to offer prayers to God. There are no set times to offer the prayers, though many people like to be there at the turn of one of the five *gahs* when the fire is 'fed' by the priest in the *boi* or *maatchi* ceremony. But even if many people are present there is no sense of congregational worship, each person prays to Ahura Mazda alone, just as the religion consistently emphasizes individual responsibility. The priest is there not as one who offers sacrifice, but as a man whose life is dedicated to the maintenance of the level of purity necessary for direct contact with the physical presence of the divine. The robes he wears are white, symbolic of that purity, and are basically those of priests in ancient Iran. He wears a white turban so that no loose (therefore dead) hair may pollute the fire and during the rites wears a white mouth-mask (*padan*) to prevent his breath (again dead because it has left the body) from polluting the fire. Outsiders seeing photographs of an officiating priest often comment that he looks like a western surgeon, an analogy Zoroastrians generally like because the priest tends the spirit as the doctor cares for the body and both are the good creations of God. Also, as many Zoroastrians explain the purity laws in terms of modern hygiene, they think the analogy has several levels of interpretation.

There is more to a temple than individual prayer before the fire. There are a number of other rooms in which the 'higher' or 'inner' ceremonies are performed. These are generally performed by the priests on behalf of the lay people, although there are no restrictions, other than the purity laws, on attendance. Such ceremonies include those offered on behalf of the deceased after funerals, but there are a range of such rites. They do not require exposition here because they are not part of the ordinary British Zoroastrian (or even Indian Zoroastrian's) experience. The temple precinct, particularly the well-endowed ones in India, may also include other areas. Almost all have accommodation for the priest for his use during the period of his temple duty so that he may live apart from the pollution which is inevitably encountered in the outside world. Temples usually have wells from which pure water is drawn for the rituals and a pomegranate tree grows so its leaves can be used in the liturgy. Some of the larger temples keep a cow so that its urine (*gomez*) may be consecrated (*nirang*) and then be used as a spiritual cleansing agent – an idea which presumably developed from the fact that cow's urine has a high ammonia content and can be used like a disinfectant to cleanse the body. Many large temples also have assembly halls where lectures, initiations, or weddings can be held. A temple can, therefore, encompass a complex of rooms or buildings. All make provision for the worshippers to wash and cleanse themselves physically and have external areas for preparatory purificatory prayer so that they may enter the holy precinct in a state of purity.

It is important to say something about the Zoroastrian understanding of the nature and purpose of religious ritual and beliefs concerning the fire.

The prevailing Zoroastrian understanding of religious rites is that they are concerned with the actualization of religious power. The holy Avestan words when recited in purity with devotion by a religiously qualified person (a priestly initiate who must be the son of a priest) then the spiritual realities to which the words relate, notably the Bounteous Immortals, become 'really' present. At many rites the representations of the seven creations are present (man, earth, fire, water, plants, cattle (in a beaker of milk), metals). As the priest gazes intently upon that creation, and recites mindfully the powerful words invoking the presence of the associated being, so those heavenly forces are praised and pleased and they dwell within the world and strengthen it. Few Zoroastrians may articulate their beliefs in this way, though one of the three senior high priests from Bombay has done (Kotwal and Boyd 1977) but all have a strong sense of the intense holiness of the place and the experience. Ordinary Zoroastrians tend to speak of the aura of the fire and of its power. There are many layers to the symbolism of the fire: the idea of light, of the divine formless icon, of life-giving warmth; but in worship there is another and overwhelming idea. This is best explained by another personal experience and by leaving the final words to my mentor the High Priest, Dastur Dr Kaikhusroo M. JamaspAsa. Dastur JamaspAsa took me on a tour of religious sites in Gujarat. We travelled from village to village and from town to town for several days, mostly in silence. Whenever we passed a temple he went in for a few moments to pray. When he came out it was impossible to miss a sense of difference about him. After a few days I could not help but ask a very western and naïve outsider's question: 'Kaikhusroo, can you put into words how you feel in the prayer-room?' He answered simply, but powerfully, 'I stand in the presence of God.'

(b) *South Asians in Britain*

British Zoroastrians, especially those who have arrived from Iran, commonly express forcefully their sense of difference from the Asian population in Britain. One anecdote may illustrate the point. Originally I envisaged titling this book *Asians in Britain: The Zoroastrian Experience*. Without exception every Zoroastrian with whom I discussed this title objected to it on the ground that (even) the Parsis are not Asians, but really (the original) Persians or Iranians. However, although some 'outsiders' may categorize Parsis as Europeans or as being from some Mediterranean land, as community members often relate, to many in Britain the Parsis are not distinguishable from others who have migrated from the Indian subcontinent. The arrival of Parsis in Britain has generally been as part of a wider movement of people. Their entry has been subject to the same immigration laws and their settlement has been affected by the same Race Relations Acts and by the historical forces which gave rise to the legislation. Many have also been subject to the same experience of discrimination. A central theme of this book is the distinctiveness of the Zoroastrians, but the British community cannot be understood without being set in the wider context of Asian immigration into Britain and the associated debates. There is a huge body of literature relating to the subject but this book is not the place for a comprehensive review and discussion. The following is a brief overview of those aspects of the literature relevant to the study of Zoroastrians in Britain.

There is a popular image that immigration to Britain is essentially a post-1945 phenomenon and that it threatened the perceived homogeneity of the British 'island race'. In a famous speech in April 1968 a member of the then Tory Cabinet, Enoch Powell, saw the threat from the large numbers of Black immigrants as being so great that he forecast, that in the now (in)famous lines: 'As I look ahead, I am filled with foreboding. Like the Roman, I seem to see the River Tiber foaming with much blood' (*Observer*, 21 April 1968).

In the build up to the 1979 general election in 1978, the then leader of the Tory Opposition, shortly to be elected Prime Minister, Margaret Thatcher, expressed in a television interview views on the perception of the threat of migration which she reasserted later in a newspaper article:

Some people have felt swamped by immigrants. They've seen the whole character of their neighbourhood change . . . Of course people can feel swamped. Small minorities can be absorbed—they can be assets to the majority community—but once a minority in a neighbourhood gets very large, people *do* feel swamped. They feel their whole way of life has been changed. (*Observer*, 25 February 1979, quoted in Solomos 1989: 83)

One aspect of this perceived homogeneity is the widespread popular assumption that a race consists of distinct physical types preserved by in-breeding. Typically the British race is thought of as being of unified linear descent of the Germanic/Anglo-Saxon stock, perhaps with some Celtic input, although the 'Irish question' has often led to the exclusion of this latter element from discussion (Miles 1993: 109; Rich 1990: 13 ff.). Such views on race are not, of course, unique to Britain. They have, for example, been a central part of much Parsi discussion on community survival and the debate on intermarriage, notably in the breeding programme called for by Desai (1948).

In fact immigration to Britain has occurred for millennia,

from the time of the Roman invasion which introduced soldiers and traders of many nations, indeed, Fryer (1984: 1) points out that as the Romans brought some Africans, the latter were here before the Saxons! Thereafter came Saxons, Vikings, Normans, followed by various European groups—Jews, gypsies, and Irish people, to name a few. It was not only White Europeans who came. From the seventeenth century wealthy British families brought back from their own Asian travels servants or 'pets' and Blacks were sold, essentially as slaves, in Britain (Holmes 1988: ch. 1; Fryer 1984: ch. 2; Visram 1986: ch. 1). From the late eighteenth century Asians were employed as seamen, or Lascars, some of whom left their ships in British ports and settled. The caricature of these groups was that they not only lived in poverty but also led lives of crime and sexual immorality, that they slept with white prostitutes and fathered a half-caste population which would reproduce the failings of their fathers and sinful mothers, thus threatening in acute form the 'purity of the race'. They were also seen as taking away the jobs of Whites and depending on British charity (Fryer 1984: ch. 3; Rich 1990: ch. 6; Visram 1986: ch. 3). In the nineteenth century powerful stereotypes emerged of the people from the subcontinent either as peddlers, or as Hiro (1992: 108) puts it, the 'coolies of the empire'. Wherever cheap manual labour was needed, Indians were used as indentured labour in conditions often not far short of slavery. One factor in the British perception of Asians and Africans was the mentality of empire, and the associated ideas of an order of racial hierarchies, which upheld the conviction that it was the 'White man's burden' to govern and guide subject nations because of the polarity which separated members of an 'advanced' from those of a 'backward' race, and divided a superior from a subject people. All these were prominent elements in Victorian thinking and were exemplified in some of the writings of Rudyard Kipling (Rich 1990: ch. 1).

There were some variations between the stereotypes of different races, for example between Africans and Asians. Negroes were sometimes caricatured as 'nearer the brute; nor can one wonder at their proved incapacity to evolve for themselves any approach to civilization' (W. Archer writing in 1917, quoted in Rich 1990: 66). The point to elaborate here is the stereotyping of people from the Indian subcontinent. In addition to the images already mentioned, of the cheap exploitable labourer, there was also a dimension (owing much to the reports of missionaries) of the heathens worshipping many gods, monstrous idols, and 'the personifications of their own vices', and hence being in need of fatherly care and evangelical zeal (Pailin 1984; Sharpe 1965; Mitter 1977). In contrast to the image of the poor labourer some circles of British society were struck by the flamboyant wealth of visiting Indian princes who were thought to care little about the poor of their own country. Such princes became the centre of some fanciful interest among nobility and indeed royalty (Vadgama 1984). The Mutiny of 1857 was a great shock to the British image of relations with the people of India resulting in the British withdrawing more into their enclosed clubs and caricaturing the Indians as devious and untrustworthy (Kincaid 1938: ch. 7). With growing industrialization in Britain, India and the rest of the Empire was seen as a source of raw materials, but the inhabitants were not themselves valued, often being stereotyped as physically weak, naturally subservient to rulers, but bullies to those under their own control (Rich 1990: 27–9). After the World Parliament of Religions in Chicago in 1893, some knowledge began to circulate among liberal intellectuals of the mystical teaching of prominent Hindu teachers, a process stimulated by the growing body of more balanced scholarly study of 'oriental religions' (Sharpe 1985). So just as the West commonly polarized Indian society into extremes of wealth and poverty, it also polarized the religion of India into the naïve superstition of the masses and the abstract mysticism of a few gurus.

The interwar years were not a time of substantial migration from Asia and Africa, although a few settled in the West following their service in the First World War. The main problem was the poor image of seamen and the political reactions to them in various ports around the country. There was some Irish immigration and in the 1930s some European Jews sought to enter the country, but their passage was obstructed by government policy. As far as British self-perceptions were concerned, there was less emphasis on German ancestry following the First World War, less stress on imperial duty but more importance placed on loyalty to the Crown. There was some government concern that Communists and Indian 'radicals' would recruit among the Indian students studying in Britain and some welfare concerns for them during the depression. Among the student body early in the century were a number of future leaders both from Africa (e.g. Kenyatta) and India (e.g. Gandhi and Nehru. Holmes 1988: part III; Visram 1986: chs. 7–8). These fears of Communist recruitment were intensified by an awareness that some Indian students had experienced particular difficulties during the Depression.

With the onset of the Second World War a significant development was the recruitment of forces from around the Empire and the arrival of Black American soldiers to be based in Britain. Although the aid of all allies was needed, this did not result in the same attitude to, or treatment of, all. For example, the segregation practised in the American forces was preserved in Britain with some towns being open to Whites off-duty and others to Blacks. Blacks and Asians were not given serious opportunities for promotion, so reinforcing the image that they were there to serve, not to take any share in power (Holmes 1988: part IV).

After the war there was an urgent need for a supply of male manual workers to replace those who had died, in order to rebuild British industry. Workers were actively recruited from Europe, from camps for displaced persons, notably political refugees. They came as European Voluntary Workers (EVWs) for fixed term employment in areas where there was no available British work-force. In practice many later settled and were joined by their families. Many Poles, Irish, Italians, Germans, Austrians, and various other Europeans peoples were recruited. In the 1940s there was relatively little recruitment from the colonies, except for a few soldiers who settled after their war-time service and some doctors who migrated because of the opportunities created through the establishment of the National Health Service (Solomos 1989: 41–4).

Migration from the West Indies began in the early 1950s and a few years later from the Indian subcontinent (although some Sikhs had settled earlier in the decade; Helweg 1986). The motivations behind the migration varied. Some of the 'push' factors were poor employment prospects in the Caribbean, the building of dams which swept away villages in the Punjab and the problems of Partition. The attractions, or 'pull factors', were often the reverse side of the coin of motivation: the search for money to maintain families in the old country; the idealized picture the migrants had of life in the mother country. Migration was relatively easy prior to 1962 because Commonwealth membership entailed the right of people to live and work anywhere within its boundaries. Typically, the Asian migrants were single young males who were willing to work long and unsocial hours in order to raise funds to send home. They were generally confined to the low paid manual-labour sector of the employment market or in the dirty jobs which Whites did not want. Even well-qualified persons were restricted to such labour. They lived as frugally as possible sharing not only rented housing but even beds used in rotation during shift work. Such a pattern of life inevitably reinforced British perceptions of Asians as living in poverty and squalor. Chain migration was common: people followed friends and relatives who had already made the journey and established a base and who could therefore help in finding accommodation and employment. The result of this chain migration was that whole villages would be deprived of most of their young men. Residence in Britain was generally seen as temporary, undertaken until such time as the overseas funds were no longer needed. The migrants cherished the so-called 'myth of return' (Anwar 1979) and since the stay in Britain was not seen as permanent, families remained in the old country. The history of Asian migration to Britain has been fundamentally affected by the changing political climate and legislation, which will be discussed below. The numbers of people coming from the subcontinent began to grow in 1960 but increased substantially in 1962 when new legislation was introduced to restrict entry. There was a rush, especially of wives and families, to enter before the restrictions became effective. This changed the nature of the community totally. There was no longer a serious expectation of return: settlers had come to stay. The Indian population in Britain therefore grew and became permanent. The families also ensured that the men paid closer attention to community traditions with regard to dress, smoking, drink, and religion. It might be said that instead of groups of Indian or Pakistani men they became communities of Hindus, Sikhs, and Muslims (Ballard 1977).

The pattern of migration was not uniform, Hindu and Sikh

women came earlier than Muslim wives. Whereas West Indians tended to settle in big cities, especially London, Asians dispersed more widely, for example to areas where the textile trade was strong—north Manchester, Bradford, and Leeds. They settled also in areas associated with car manufacture, notably in the west Midlands and Coventry. In addition a large proportion settled in Leicester and in London. Chain migration meant that different groups of Asians settled in particular regions; Gujaratis congregated in Leicester whereas people from Pakistan settled in south Lancashire and the south-east. The different religious groups acted differently. Muslims and Sikhs tended to build religious centres—mosques and gurdwaras—quite quickly whereas the tradition of home worship meant that Hindus were not so anxious to build temples but concentrated rather on Indian cultural centres. The term 'Hindu' is not only a western label in origin, it is also something of an external label for many of the communities so designated since members are linked not by strictly religious issues but rather by such secular concerns as language or a particular region of origin (notably Gujarat and Punjab) or by caste divisions. There is then, no such single phenomenon as the 'Asian community' in Britain (Knott 1986*b*).

A different and important group of South Asians arrived in Britain in the late 1960s and early 1970s from East Africa following the process of Africanization in various countries, notably Kenya and then in 1972 from Uganda when Amin forcibly expelled all Asians. Typically, East African Asians came as whole families. A substantial proportion were successful businessmen and those who were able to bring their money with them could move more quickly, if not straight away, to the leafy suburbs rather than to the cheaper housing of the inner cities favoured by the early workers. Furthermore, the East African Asians (many of them Gujaratis) had preserved more of the nineteenth century Indian traditions than their co-religionists who stayed on in British India (Bhachu 1985; Robinson 1986). The interaction between Asians already in Britain and those who came via Africa has not always been smooth.

The parliamentary leaders of both the Conservative and Labour parties, and the mass media, decided that immigration control was necessary because of the increased number of Commonwealth immigrants in the 1950s (Miles and Phizacklea

1984). When such proposals became public they had the immediate effect of provoking more permanent settlers to come, for the reasons noted above. There have been a number of Acts in the twentieth century relating to immigration, starting with the Aliens Act of 1905. Prior to this there had been essentially no state controls over people entering and leaving Britain (although in 1813 and 1823 Acts had restricted the rights of 'alien' seamen to settle), but in 1905 immigration officials were given powers to stop the entry of 'undesirable immigrants'. 'Undesirable' covered lunacy, a criminal record, and in particular those without financial means to support themselves. The last of these conditions was judged largely by the method of arrival. If the immigrants arrived in a cabin on board a ship they were assumed to have the necessary finances. If, however, they travelled 'steerage' (the cheapest accommodation) on an immigration vessel, and could not show how they would support themselves, entry was forbidden. Such refugees were seen as competing with the indigenous population for jobs and housing. Admission was promised to those whose sole motive was to escape religious or political persecution. Whether the Act was covertly targeted at Jews is a matter of debate (Gainer 1972). In 1914 tighter immigration controls were imposed because of wartime concerns. These controls were amended in 1919 in the Alien's Restriction Amendment Act and in 1920 by an Alien's Order, particularly with regard to seamen and certain Chinese groups (Holmes 1988: 111–14; Miles 1993: 144–62).

The governments in the dominions were establishing their citizenship laws (e.g. Canada in 1946), and the British government produced its own British Nationality Act in 1948. This preserved something of the old idea of 'subjects' as opposed to aliens and distinguished between British subjects and Commonwealth citizens, the latter still being considered citizens of the United Kingdom and Colonies and therefore having the right of settlement in Britain (Parry 1957; MacDonald 1983: 8–19). Throughout the 1950s governments contemplated the possibility of imposing much stricter immigration controls but decided that such a step was inconsistent with the public proclamations regarding the nature of the Commonwealth and Britain's position in it. Riots in the 1950s (notably Notting Hill in 1958— ironically caused by Whites, not Blacks) and fears of growing immigration numbers in the early 1960s provoked the government to introduce radical legislation in 1962 (Saggar 1992: 69–73, 96–106). Entry was permitted only to holders of Labour Employment Vouchers, their direct dependants, and students committed to leaving the country at the completion of their studies. In practice this reinforced chain migration because those already in work in Britain could help to obtain work for relatives and friends with their own employers. Various events and a growing public mood of antagonism towards Black immigrants through the 1960s increased pressure for further restrictions. For example, Labour's Shadow Home Secretary, Patrick Gordon-Walker lost his safe parliamentary seat in Smethwick in 1964, and then in a by-election lost an even safer seat, vacated especially for him, because he was seen as 'soft' on immigration. There was, then, widespread public anxiety regarding immigration. Whether there should have been, and whether the press and the politicians handled the situation wisely, are different issues (Solomos 1989: 44–58). In 1968 the Second Commonwealth Immigrants Bill was enacted, with the particular concern to restrict Asian immigration from East Africa and in 1971 the Tory government introduced an Immigration Act which severely curtailed the rights of Commonwealth citizens to enter Britain (Macdonald 1983: 1). It was constructed so that it targeted Black Commonwealth citizens. In 1981 the British Nationality Act, which made yet tighter the controls restricting the entry of such citizens and then the imposition of visa controls in 1985 to restrict visits for people from South Asia and certain African states, effectively closed the door to new immigration. There is then a long history of legal restrictions seeking to bar entry to Asians, among whose number Parsis would be counted by government (Sachdeva 1993; Saggar 1992: 78–135; Fryer 1984: 381–99; Holmes 1988: 260–70; Hiro 1992: 233–60; Rich 1990: 167–204).

In the 1960s–80s there was what successive governments presented as a counterbalancing legislative programme of Race Relations Acts designed to make discrimination on the grounds of colour illegal (1965 in public places; 1968 extending the legislation into housing and employment; 1976 establishing more proactive antidiscrimination law. Cashmore and Troyna 1983). From the 1950s the Labour party, notably the MP Fenner

Brockway and successive party conferences, had called for laws to prohibit racial discrimination. The 1965 Act, rather than criminalizing discrimination, sought to establish a process of conciliation when problems had (already) occurred. Although this was a weaker stand than many had called for, it did lay a foundation for stronger legislation later. In the 1966 Local Government Act note was taken of the difficulties of towns and cities where large-scale settlement had occurred and Section 11 Funding was given to support moves to aid immigrants, such as additional teaching resources in schools. The 1969 Local Government Act attempted to deal with inner-city deprivation and one criterion for measuring need was the presence, on a large scale, of Commonwealth immigrants. There was, therefore, an attempt in various forms not only to restrict immigration but also to deal with the problems that immigration had been seen as causing. In the House of Commons the then Junior Home Office Minister, Roy Hattersley (later Deputy Leader of the Labour party) made a much-quoted remark which has been seen as the epitome of the Labour party's rationale on immigration. He said: 'Integration without control is impossible but control without integration is indefensible' (quoted in Sagger 1992: 90). This is not the place to judge the allegation that this combination of measures placed the point of discrimination at the point of entry rather than in housing or employment.

This brief history of immigration, the related laws, and the general 'mood' of the country provides the back cloth against which Zoroastrian experiences have to be understood. Since Zoroastrians rarely settled in the deprived inner-city areas some aspects of this race relations and local government (as opposed to immigration) legislation are not as important for this study as the overall history of settlement. From the late 1970s all political parties, but especially the Tory party, distanced themselves from what they saw as the earlier 'liberal' policies, partly because of the fears (real or imagined is not at this point the question) raised at the prospect of 'overwhelming' Asian immigration following the flight of Asians from East Africa. It was against this background that support grew for the extreme right-wing National Front and in which context Mrs Thatcher made the comments quoted above. During her period in office the public profile of the National Front declined as successive measures were introduced to tighten yet further controls on immigration. These were the general attitudes at the time when the survey used below was started. The period 1980–5 witnessed a number of riots and disturbances in inner-city areas (Solomos 1989: chs. 6, 9) such as Brixton, Handsworth, Toxteth, Tottenham, and elsewhere. The ensuing debate focused on the problems of policing areas where crime and violence were evident and to some extent on the social deprivation which in the view of many (e.g. Lord Justice Scarman who produced a powerful report on the Brixton troubles in 1981) was the underlying cause of the problems. The point here is not what the real causes were, but what effects the riots and the public debate had on the perception of race relations. The government and tabloid press both blamed 'outsiders' for the difficulties and Blacks in particular were blamed for much of the violence, including that on Asians. The survey used in Chapter 6 was in the early stages of preparation at the end of this period of inner-city rioting.

Studies of South Asian Religions in Britain

The body of literature on South Asians in Britain is substantial. Most of it concentrates on the problems faced by the various communities: prejudice and difficulties in housing, education, and employment. The problems are real ones. Unfortunately the strong focus on them results in the perception of South Asian people as 'problems'. Relatively few books take seriously the religious dimension of the life of the communities. There are, however, some and it is important to refer to these as part of the overall context for the study of Zoroastrians in Britain. The University of Leeds Community Religions Project has facilitated a number of publications (e.g. Barton 1986; Bowen 1988; Kalsi 1992) and there have been a number of others (Bowen 1981). But the works which are most relevant to the study of British Zoroastrians are Knott (1986*a* and 1991), Burghart (1987), Jackson and Nesbitt (1993), and Banks (1992). Most of them focus on specific communities—Knott (1986) on Hindus in Leeds, Jackson and Nesbitt on the nurture of Hindu children in Coventry and Banks on Jains both in Gujarat and Leicester. One factor, among others, which makes these publications relevant to a study of the Parsis is that something like two-thirds of British Hindus and an even greater proportion of Jains ultimately come from Gujarat. Some came through direct migration and others migrated via East Africa, thus following the same route as Parsis from the same part of the subcontinent. Their experiences are, therefore, comparable. Burghart's book is a collection of studies on various aspects of different Hindu communities in Britain. These publications are not merely descriptive reports but raise wider issues relevant to this research and it is therefore worth indicating briefly the themes from their studies which may be considered appropriate in this particular context. Obviously these may not be the same issues that the authors themselves considered most significant in their work.[1]

Knott (1986 and 1991) discusses the factors which result in what an external observer might consider to be change in the religious tradition, although Hindus themselves may wish to affirm the eternal nature of the message. These she considers to be: (i) The external pressures to unify the diverse traditions within the Hinduism, for example Gujarati and Punjabi beliefs and customs regarding deities, forms of worship, and so on. One such pressure is the outsider's perception of Hinduism as a single phenomenon. Another is the need to unify in the face of what is sometimes seen as an alien world and another the emphasis in British education (at university as well as school) on the 'Great' or Sanskritic tradition, which does not always equate very closely to the daily religious life of the majority of Hindus (Knott 1986*a*: 53, 57, 83, 88, 115; Burghart 1987: 226). (ii) Certain practical problems which force change: the physical constraints of buildings converted from another use, be it a home or a church hall (Knott 1986*a*: 154; see also Bowen 1987: 25; Banks 1992: 183); the difficulty of observing Hindu festivals when the British calendar and working day does not harmonize with that in India (Knott 1987: 171). (iii) The pressure on the priesthood to change. British Hindu priests are usually part-time and are therefore unable to maintain the necessary purity. Further, not all priests are trained traditionally and even fewer in western style religious education so they find it difficult to articulate the

---

[1] Lewis 1994 on Muslims in Bradford unfortunately came into my possession too late to include in this discussion, though see Ch. 7, Sect. (*b*).

rational, as opposed to the practical, dimension of the religion. (iv) The difficulty of perpetuating a religion from a continent where it is a fundamental part of daily life in a culture where religion is typically seen as an optional aspect of life (Knott 1986*a*: 73; Bowen 1987: 25; Menski 1987: 198f; Burghart 1987: 1 f.; and see Banks 1992: 178, 198). (v) The frequent search by young, western-educated people for rational explanations of standardized, or streamlined, rituals (Knott 1986*a*: 48, 53, 57). (vi) The apparently inevitable trend towards the institutionalization of religion in Britain, often according to alien western norms such as youth groups and formal religious education classes (Jackson and Nesbitt 1993: 179; Knott 1987: 166, 178; Banks 1992: 184). (vii) The fact that some seek a religion which is seen as being more intellectually respectable, or scientific. Banks, for example, points to the emphasis among some educated Jains on an explanation of dietary laws as leading to a healthy body, on the practice of meditation and austerities leading to a healthy and peaceful mind, and on *ahimsa* as leading to a peaceful society (1987: 207–10). Similarly Knott (1987: 179) notes how many educated middle-class Hindus stress the Hindu traditions associated with Gandhi, namely vegetarianism, *ahimsa*, and the emphasis on *bhakti* as set forth in the *Gita*. There are, in short, a range of external and internal pressures for religious change.

Jackson and Nesbitt (1993) discuss the pressures for change, but an important emphasis in their work is the level of enjoyment and fulfilment Hindu children receive from a great diversity of Indian practices, which is far greater than most scholars appreciate. They highlight such activities as seeing and participating in worship both in daily home life and at festivals in the temple; and seeing grandmother praying at the home shrine. But above all they emphasize the visual and performing arts—the iconography, dance, music, dressing up, videos (not only religious ones but also of family events in India), and Indian films, for example the epic film of the *Ramayana*. These two authors bring out vividly the pleasures of Hindu extended family life, of socializing with kin in the evening and at weekends, of youth festivals, and the atmosphere of meetings when holy men come on visits from India. In view of the common emphasis on British Asians' problems with employment, housing, and education,

Jackson and Nesbitt's work provides a much-needed counterbalance to a substantial body of literature. They also stress that what is learned in these diverse ways is appropriate behaviour (for example family duties or the appropriate ritual actions) rather than the philosophy of the religion. One interesting example in the context of this study is the way Hindu children find comfort in the sacred mantras they hear, even though they are not given the rational explanation associated with western religious education. The consequence of this last point is that there can be a dissonance between the children's experience of Hinduism and what is related by teachers at school, even when the study of 'world religions' is not mere tokenism—something which embarrasses many Hindu children (Jackson and Nesbitt 1993: 33).

The different forces experienced by British Asians of pressures for change and the love of the tradition, understandably result in contrasting attitudes to the desirability or necessity for change in the religion. These often build on the existing internal divisions (Knott 1986a: 35; 1987: 158, 162) and may be exacerbated when the groups have their own buildings, for then leadership gives more community power. The role of community leaders is particularly important. They commonly affect both the community's internal self-perception and present the community image to the outside world (Banks 1992: 167–70); but often these leaders are not professionally religious in terms of the priesthood, traditional learning, or asceticism (in the case of Jains). Many hold their position due to their business success or high professional standing. Their voice is sometimes presented as not that of the mystic or the scholar (implying forms of extremism), but the 'authentic' voice of the practitioner. This image of the ordinary lay person presenting the 'real' religion is reinforced in some western publications, not least those associated with interfaith dialogue and religious education committees (Knott 1986a: 74–6; 1987: 159, 162; Burghart 1987: 9; Bowen 1987: 15, 25).

Some leaders and outside scholars, look towards the evolution of a specifically British Hinduism, British Islam and so on, and speculate on what form these will take. But, as Knott observes, Islam (for example) in Britain is a complex phenomenon because it is the sum of the way of life of each of its adherents, Pakistani, Bangladeshi, Indian, and some Middle Eastern elements. It is also something which is being continually formed not a 'once-for-all' event (1991: 94 f.). It evolves in reaction to external events such as the Iranian revolution; conflict in the Middle East or between India and Pakistan; the (perception of the) growth of fundamentalism and of events in Britain, such as the Rushdie affair or changes in the law. Knott in the same article (pp. 100-5) lists seven issues meriting attention in research on the 'maturation of . . . religions in Britain'. They are: (i) The transmission of sacred and 'native' languages. (ii) Religious nurture in the home and the community. (iii) The sense of individual identity—what does it mean to say 'I am a Hindu', and so on? (iv) The sense of group identity—the extent to which the group incorporates outsiders, be they other Asians or non-Asians. What can Hinduism be on other soils, as it is by definition of the land and of the people of Bharat? (v) Leadership and the provision of religious leaders appropriately trained in terms of the old country and able to meet the religious educational needs of the young people brought up in Britain. (vi) Universalization—will an overarching form of Hinduism emerge which incorporates the different groups and which approximates more to the 'great tradition' reflected in most academic studies? (vii) The impact of western ideas about religion (e.g. the centrality of doctrine or the growth of secularization) on South Asian religions in Britain.

Before addressing the subject of the Zoroastrians in Britain it will be helpful to conclude this introduction with a brief picture of the demography of the South Asian population in Britain as it is in the 1990s and therefore as it has become after the research behind these publications discussed above.

South Asians in Britain in the 1990s

It is notoriously difficult to give precise numbers of South Asians in Britain because there has been no question on race or ethnicity in censuses until the 1991 Census. In round figures it would be reasonable to suggest that the sort of numbers involved are as follows. In 1947 there were approximately 7,000 Asians in Britain; in 1971 numbers had increased to approximately 650,000; by 1981 to a little over a million and 1,479,600 by 1991, making them about 2.7% of the total population (Jones 1993: 12; Owen 1992-3 (i); Ballard and Kalra 1994). Jones's study looked at the changing patterns of education and employment among Britain's ethnic minorities in the 1980s. Owen looked at settlement patterns, age, family, housing, and economic characteristics, based on the 1991 Census data. Ballard and Kalra considered population size, household patterns, class, and social activity. Together these studies provide a broad background of South Asian experiences against which those of the British Zoroastrians have to be seen and a picture of the overall situation at the time when this research was undertaken.

People from India compose the largest group (840,000, including approximately 220,600 who came from East Africa), with 476,600 from Pakistan. Whereas the Afro-Caribbean community is thought to be decreasing in size, the South Asian population is expected to double over the next forty years if there is no significant change in the birth-rate or immigration policy. The biggest growth in numbers of immigrants in the 1980s was from refugees from sub-Saharan Africa and in percentage-growth terms from people from Japan. As far as South Asians were concerned, the immigration was due mainly to reunification of families. The broad demographic picture of the South Asian population is of a young community, but there are differences between the nationalities. Half of the people from Pakistan and Bangladesh are under the age of 20 and the average age of people from India is 30 (Owen 1992–3: no. 2). The first two groups are still predominantly male, but the Indian population is now roughly balanced between the genders. About half of the Indian and Pakistani population were born in Britain. Whereas only 6% of White households consist of extended families, about one-quarter of Indian and half of Pakistani families consist of more than the small nuclear family (Owen 1992–3: no. 4). Only 5% of Asian men and 2% of Asian women are married out of the community. The average number of dependent children is four times as high in 'ethnic minority' communities as in the White population (Jones 1993: ch. 2), but the number of dependants of retirement age was substantially lower than among the White population.

It is not generally appreciated that a higher proportion of South Asian than of White youth proceeds to higher education. Of Asians aged 16–19, 56% remain in education, compared with 37% of Whites, even though fewer Asians are in the professional and managerial classes from which universities draw most of their applicants (Jones 1993: ch. 3). Whereas 10% of Whites are graduates, 15% of Indians are. Among educated Asians, 64% gained their qualification in the UK and half were UK-born. So the popular stereotypes of Asians as undereducated or as having 'questionable' Asian degrees are unfounded. In terms of gender, a higher proportion of Indian and African Indian than Pakistani or Bangladeshi women have formal qualifications. It is the African Asian community in particular which is well qualified educationally, with 75% of its men aged 16–19 in education and 56% of its women (compared with 36% and 38% of White young men and women respectively).

Ballard and Kalra (1994: ch. 5) show that the high educational levels are translating into employment levels, with an increasing proportion of members, especially in the Indian community, entering professional and managerial classes. Because of the higher levels of educational involvement, fewer Asian than White young people are economically active, but in the age-group 45–64 slightly more Asian than White men are economically active (83% compared with 81%; Jones 1993: ch. 4; Owen 1992–3: no. 4). Among the women, African Asian women have the same rate of economic activity as Whites (69%), but fewer Indian women (57%) and only 23% of Pakistani/Bangladeshi women are so active. Overall, Jones concludes, African Asian and Indian women have economic activity rates and qualification levels nearer to those of White women, and there is far less difference between the positions of men and women within these particular ethnic groups (p. 158). More Asian than White males are self-employed (13% compared with 9%; p. 65). Jones's overall conclusion is that Indian and African Asian male employees 'whose highest qualification is "A" level or above are more likely to be in the top (Professional, manager, or Employed) category than are whites' (p. 71). African Asians and Indians tend to be in the professions rather than in the senior management of large organizations. Pakistani and Bangladeshi men are not so well represented in the higher level of employment. The Asian labour force tends to be more polarized than the White labour force. It is well represented in the high professional levels, but it also has a high proportion among the less well qualified and the Asians' level of employment is lower than that of Whites. The levels of unemployment among Indian men is approximately the same as that of Whites, but it is higher among Pakistanis and Bangladeshi (see also Ballard and Kalra 1994: ch. 5). The substantive point of Jones's study for this book is that it demonstrates the falsity of the White stereotype of Asians as poorly qualified and restricted to the lower end of the employment scale. Education is highly prized, widely sought, and a means to better employment, especially for the Indian and African Asian population, both men and women. (Panayi 1994: 2 f.) is right to reiterate the point made by Khan (1979: 3) that it is wrong to study Asians in Britain simply as problems.

(c) *Some Questions of Terminology*

The consequence of introducing race relations legislation was the need for a public definition of 'race' in order to define what was meant by 'racial prejudice'. In the 1960s, and later, 'race relations' for many people meant Black–White relations. The fact that out-migration from Britain regularly exceeded immigration was not normally referred to in public discussion and indicates that the problem was not really as stated, that of scarcity of land for housing or employment for people. Another point which was ignored was that many more Irish than Afro-Caribbean or South Asian people entered the country without restriction, even though the Republic of Ireland was not part of the Commonwealth. In terms of percentage growth the increased immigration in the 1980s was from Japan (129.8%) and Turkey (124.5%, mostly Kurdish refugees) (Owen 1992–3: no. 5). The clear indication is that colour, not population size, was the problem. Further, the level of immigration into Britain was far below that into the United States, France, Germany, or the Gulf States (Glazer and Young 1983: 3 f.; Banton 1983: 334). The media sometimes implies that South Asian countries 'export' so many of their people that they swamp other nations. In fact only 1% (approximately 8.6 million) of the South Asian population lives overseas, compared with about 30% (approximately 350 million) of Europeans (Clarke, Peach, and Vertovec

1990: 1). These indicators strongly suggest that the public outcry from the 1960s onwards has not been based on the rationale proclaimed publicly. The problem lies more in the hidden agenda: the conception of a homogeneous island race.

The concept of race has changed over the centuries and differs in various countries (Banton 1987; Rex 1986). It is popularly taken to indicate significant and clearly demarcated biological differences between peoples, for example between Jews, Anglo-Saxons, Asians, and Negroes. In the nineteenth century 'race' was used to denote a group of persons of common descent. There was debate on whether humanity developed from one ultimate line of descent, or several. After Linnaeus's classification of plants, writers began to think in terms of 'genus' and 'species', so the debate over Black versus White races focused on whether these categories represented different species of one genus, or different subspecies. Darwin's theories on evolution modified the concept, and the concern grew for the preservation, or development, of the 'healthy race' as exemplified both in some imperial attitudes and in Nazi philosophy. There is, in fact, no scientific evidence to justify the commonly asserted stereotypes of racial characteristics based on alleged biological differences. The 1968 Race Relations Act interpreted race as 'a group of persons defined by reference to colour, race, nationality, or ethnic or racial origins'. Essentially this leaves much of the question of the definition of race open, since it uses the term race within the definition and does not distinguish the concept clearly from 'ethnicity'. Words generally mean what people want them to mean. In the context of this book the terms 'race' and 'ethnicity' are important from two perspectives: (*a*) that of British Law and public debate; (*b*) the internal Zoroastrian (which has mostly meant Parsi) debates notably on intermarriage and conversion. For these purposes 'race' can be used to refer to boundaries drawn around peoples on the perception of biological differences. 'Ethnicity' in contrast will be used to refer to the sense of cultural distinctiveness, a sense typically worked out in consciousness of a distinctiveness from other groups and commonly in some sort of conflict with them (Parkin 1970: 119, and see the discussion in Amighi 1990: 2–24). This usage is consistent with a House of Lords judgement in the Mandla *u* Lee case where the principal judgement defined an ethnic group as having two essential features: (*a*) a long shared history of which the group is conscious as distinguishing it from other groups and the memory of which it keeps alive; and (*b*) a cultural tradition of its own, including family and social customs and manners, often but not necessarily associated with religious observance (Robilliard 1984: 4 ff., and see Rex 1986: 18–22). It is possible that different 'races' do not have different cultures (Lyon 1972–3). Thus 'race' will be used where the emphasis is on perceived biological differences and 'ethnicity' when the focus is on 'cultural' qualities which in theory an individual may reject or accept (though different members of a group would use different aspects of their culture to define their identity) (Ballard and Kalra 1994: 4, and see also Ballard 1994*b*). An illustration of how these different terms would relate to internal Zoroastrian (Parsi) debates is the published arguments of the three Bombay high priests who objected to the proposal of the then Indian Prime Minister, Mrs Gandhi, for an 'Adoption of Children Bill' in 1980. The intention was to give adopted children the full rights of their new parents. The high priests argued that a child adopted by Zoroastrian parents but born of non-Zoroastrians could not be considered a Zoroastrian, however it was brought up. Here the priests were arguing that 'Zoroastrian' refers to the race, not the cultural upbringing (or ethnicity) of the child (Hinnells 1987). It is essential to recognize, however, that these terms remain ambiguous. Different people draw different boundaries around their group, and may change those boundaries in various situations. 'Race' and 'ethnicity' are therefore fluid concepts determined not by any objectively defined essence but as a result of social processes. (Ballard 1994*a*: 1–34).

Other terms also require comment, namely 'acculturation', 'assimilation', and 'integration', although they are not as controversial as those already discussed. By 'acculturation' in this book is meant the acquisition of characteristics of another's culture, here specifically the extent to which Zoroastrians have acquired traditional British values, norms, or ideals. Clearly it is possible that an individual may acquire such values in one aspect of his/her life (e.g. language) but not in another (e.g. attitudes to marriage). The issue is more complex because an individual may drop his/her customs at some stages in life and return to them, or indeed may drop them in some contexts and companies but not in others at the same stage of life. Acculturation is not therefore a static condition. It may be helpful to think of some people as 'bi-cultural'. 'Assimilation' denotes a process whereby an individual or group either adopts the values and so on of the majority, or drops parts of their own culture, across a broad spectrum. In short, the group or individual becomes more akin to the dominant group, but distinctiveness is not necessarily completely lost (Krausz 1972: 250). 'Integration' refers to the degree of change in received traditions necessary to observe the law and fundamental social requirements such as attendance at school between the ages of 5 and 16 and the payment of taxes. (For a general discussion of these and related terms, see Cashmore 1984.)

Another term that is used frequently in the book but which has to be questioned is 'community'. The term does not correspond to any clearly definable formal body. In a real sense there is no Zoroastrian community in Britain. There are the formal memberships of different associations as indicated in Chapter 4, but even these hardly constitute homogeneous groups with clearly defined boundaries and a powerful unified sense of identity. There are various factions, subgroups (not simply orthodox/reform but also Bombay, East African, and Iranian Zoroastrians), and many non-active members as well as non-members who keep in erratic contact. There is no clearly delineated national Zoroastrian community. But there is a sense among most Zoroastrians of 'we Zoroastrians' against 'them', the non-Zoroastrian world. Even if the historian considers this entity to be mythical, it is nevertheless a powerful myth which affects the sense of self-identity among many Zoroastrians. The term therefore has value, even if the above qualification is necessary.

There are other terms meriting brief discussion. 'Black' is commonly used as an umbrella term to include all non-whites, that is, to include both Afro-Caribbean and Asian; others restrict Black to the former group only. I have adopted the latter practice because in my opinion a single term devalues the distinctiveness and rich traditions of each group. I have also used 'White', which could be subject to the same objection. However, in the context of this book it is clearly a reference to one comparatively distinct group (despite its varied ingredients) of people claiming Anglo-Saxon or European descent. The terms 'East' and 'West' are being questioned increasingly, and rightly so because they are such relative terms. Britain is, for example, east of America which is east of Australia. However, in Zoroastrian discussions, as in so many others, the 'West' is used as shorthand for the mainly White, European-language dominated, economically developed nations. It is a convenient label in this context for Britain, the USA, Canada, and Australia, the lands of the new Zoroastrian diaspora.

The term 'diaspora' merits comment. In view of the long history of settlement of Zoroastrians in Britain it seems inappropriate to describe it as an 'immigrant' religion. Nor is 'religion in migration' appropriate; since virtually none of the Zoroastrians in Britain envisage emigrating, it is wrong to refer to their religion as still being in a state of migration. The term 'diaspora' is convenient because it indicates a community with a strong sense of living away from the old country of the religion. Most labels have weaknesses when examined carefully, and there has been debate concerning 'diaspora' (see Clifford 1994) but the term 'diaspora religion' seems appropriate for British Zoroastrians because its gives importance to the Zoroastrians' own perspective of not being in a state of migration, yet living away from the Iranian homeland. The term may not be so appropriate for the Parsis in India, since that has become a homeland for many of them. It may, however, be appropriate not only for Zoroastrians, but also Hindus, Sikhs, and other 'Asian' religions in Britain.

Some terms used specifically about the Zoroastrians require comment. The terms 'orthodox', 'reform', and 'liberal' are commonly used by Zoroastrians. There are various 'litmus tests' by which an individual's orthodoxy might be ascertained, notably the attitudes to purity in connection with menstruation, or attitudes to intermarriage and conversion. In popular parlance the scale tends to be described as running from orthodox, through liberal to reform. Liberal is commonly associated with modifying teachings and practices (not only on the issues mentioned but also on doctrines or the language of prayer) whereas reform is viewed as supporting significant changes: for example, actively encouraging non-Zoroastrians to convert (e.g. offspring and spouses in intermarriages). These are not fixed categories, what is thought of as orthodox in, say, New York may be liberal in Bombay. Relatively few Zoroastrians (especially in Britain in comparison with some American communities) choose to describe themselves as 'reformists'. I have attempted to use the words as members of Zoroastrian House in London would use them.

2

Zoroastrian Perspectives on Contacts with the British

Zoroastrians, like any migrating racial or religious group, do not arrive in a new country with a mind blank of all perceptions of the land. Any group has its own communal memory, a set of historical perspectives about themselves and others which may not necessarily coincide entirely with those of an outside historian. Before studying the Zoroastrians in Britain it is, therefore, important to consider the presuppositions the various Zoroastrian groups had concerning their contacts with the British. Zoroastrians in each of the old countries have different histories of Anglo-Zoroastrian relations. This chapter is not concerned with a conventional historical account of the respective Zoroastrian communities but rather with the Zoroastrians' communal perspectives on their history and on Anglo-Zoroastrian contacts.

(a) *Iranian Zoroastrians and the British*

Whereas there is a substantial body of Parsi literature regarding relations with the British there is no such material produced by Iranian Zoroastrians. Nevertheless, it would be wrong to assume that migrants from the religion's homeland arrived without some presuppositions.

The earliest western contacts with Zoroastrians in Islamic Iran were through seventeenth century European travellers, most of the important accounts being written by Frenchmen (Fr. Gabriel de Mans; Fr. Gabriel de Chinon; Tavernier; Chardin; Thevenot). The travellers were interested more in commerce than religion. Their perceptions of Zoroastrians were often conditioned by the attitudes of the Muslim population. Zoroastrians were compelled by the rulers to live in poverty and considered to be 'infidels' (*guebres*), 'fire-worshippers', and polytheists. In so far as European travellers were interested in the Zoroastrians, it was as potential interpreters of Persepolis and the Achaemenid inscriptions for the light that might thereby be shed on biblical history. Because the villagers were unable to help in this academic quest, the travellers concluded that they were ignorant peasants. The Zoroastrian experience of Muslim authorities made their leaders wary of outside enquiries, another apparent marker of Zoroastrian ignorance. Not all travellers were unsympathetic to the Zoroastrians, but they were not as well informed, or as close to them personally, as the travellers to Bombay and Gujarat were to the Parsis. The descriptions of the Iranian Zoroastrian tradition generally focused on beliefs and practices that were thought to be strange, notably the death ceremonies, rituals concerned with fire, and the teaching on evil (Firby 1988: ch. 1). Few Iranian Zoroastrians were aware of travellers' reports of their community, but there has been a great sensitivity to adverse external accounts.

At the turn of the ninteenth and twentieth centuries three more sensitive descriptions of the Zoroastrian community were written, by Browne (1893: chs. 13–14), Malcolm (1905: 44–53), and Jackson (1906: chs. 23–4). Browne and Jackson were both scholars specializing on Iran, and Jackson was a Zoroastrian specialist from Columbia University, New York. Their emphasis was on the oppression suffered and courage shown by Zoroastrians, and a more informed attitude was shown to the religion. Jackson's account perhaps betrays some paternalistic attitudes to the villagers, possibly influenced by the attitudes he encountered on his visit to Parsis in Bombay. These accounts did something to alert the outside world to the fate of the Iranian Zoroastrians, but their impact was not very great.

In 1963–4 Prof. Mary Boyce from London University spent a year living in the Zoroastrian village of Sharifabad near Yazd (Boyce 1977). The impact of her theories on the study of Zoroastrian literature was discussed in the previous chapter. The relevant point of her argument here is that these remote villages had faithfully preserved the ancient traditions which could legitimately be used to illuminate some of the obscurities of the older sources. Boyce's scholarly stature is widely respected within the Zoroastrian community; nevertheless some of the educated westernized Tehrani Zoroastrians (mostly in America rather than Britain) thought that by focusing on the remote rural population she presented an image of a fossilized or superstitious tradition to the outside world. It is sad that a scholar whose respect for her subject is evident can nevertheless be suspected of undermining the image of the community because she focuses on what she is convinced is a courageous, stalwart, and historically significant portion of it. Her experiences highlight the extreme sensitivity of Zoroastrians, particularly those from Iran, conditioned as they are by centuries of mockery and misrepresentation from outsiders, both Muslim and European.

Britain also has a powerful political image in Iran as a (former) imperial power, and this played a part in forming the perceptions of those who migrated. The seventeenth and eighteenth century travellers were generally those who also visited India. The Ottoman Turks prevented access to Iran from the eastern Mediterranean, so most travellers journeyed round the Cape and reached Persia via the Indian Ocean. This was one reason why British interests in Persia were often represented through Bombay. The original British imperial concern in the region was to block Napoleon. Later the aim was to use Iran as a buffer to restrict Russia's interests in India. Commercial interests grew when oil was discovered in 1908. The Anglo-Persian Oil Company (later to become BP) was formed and took 75% of the oil revenues. After the First World War the British took considerable political interest in the region, notably in the new Pahlavi dynasty which came to power in 1924. Britain was also thought to have been influential in determining the succession in the 1940s and to have been involved with the CIA in the restoration of the Shah after his overthrow by Mossadeq in 1953, so she is seen by many Iranians as a power which manipulates the economies and politics of other countries for her own interests (Avery 1965; Keddie 1981). She was also thought of as a nation with considerable industrial and educational resources from which successive Iranian diplomatic missions sought to benefit (Wright 1985, 1977). From the 1960s, however, Britain was evidently a fading power as the Americans became increasingly powerful both economically and politically. Iranian links with Europe were with France rather than Britain. By the 1980s Britain's image was, then, largely one of faded glory, though of a nation with some residual political influence (Arjomand 1988; Ghods 1989; Chehabi 1990).

There is also a specifically Zoroastrian dimension to the Iranian image of Britain. The Bombay-based Society for the Amelioration of the Conditions of the Zoroastrians in Persia (founded in 1854) fought hard for many years, mainly through its Iranian representative Maneckji Limji Hataria (Boyce 1969), to lift the crushing economic burden of the poll tax (*jizya*) from the shoulders of its co-religionists and to ease their general condition in the face of great oppression. Hataria received some support not only from Parsis but also from the British ambassador in Tehran, Sir Henry Rawlinson, and from some British MPs (including, but not only, Naoroji and Bhownagree) in personal audiences and petitions (see below, Ch. 4, Sect. (*b*)). There is, therefore, an element in the image which sees Britain as a supporter of the oppressed (Browne 1893: 426), but the dominant image is of a calculating imperial power which manipulated other countries' fortunes for its own benefit. There is also the suspicion that the British, like most westerners, are badly informed about Zoroastrianism in general and about modern Zoroastrians in Iran in particular. Whether those images are justified or not is a different question.

(b) *Anglo-Parsi Relations in India*

The Parsis commonly believe that they were pivotal in the establishment of British power in western India. The first British trading vessel arrived in 1608 at Surat, then the chief port in the region. The Portuguese were already a strong commercial presence and the British required local aid in obtaining the permission from the Muslim ruler to set up their trading base. After initial difficulties this was granted in 1612. But problems developed over the years with the Muslim authorities, and so in 1701–2 the ambassador, Sir William Norris, went to the court of Aurangzeb. He took with him as negotiator the Parsi Rustom Maneck.[1] Rustom had gained substantial negotiating experience

---

[1] There are differences between Modi 1929 and White 1979 on the date of the embassy to Aurangzeb. This text follows White, who bases his dating on the East India Company records, whereas Modi utilizes the evidence of what he recognizes as the rather unhistorical Perian *Qissa-i Rustam Manock* and gives a date of 1710.

with his previous employers, the Portuguese, before becoming Chief Broker to the British in approximately 1698, first in Surat, and then in Bombay. The ambassador proved something of an embarrassment, discourteously leaving the court before he was expected to, and without diplomatic clearance, for which offence Rustom had to pay a fine. Despite these problems, Rustom successfully negotiated the required trading agreements and protection for the British. The story of his relations with the British is a long and complicated one, for he became embroiled in internal British rivalries and was almost certainly the object of plots from (non-Parsi) rival brokers so that his fortunes fluctuated before his final triumph in establishing a great personal fortune through trading for the British (Modi 1929; White 1979). Zoroastrians see Rustom as a successful and crucial negotiator on behalf of the British at a time when the latter were struggling to establish themselves in India. He is also viewed as a prototype of the many Parsis who followed as middlemen in trade with the British. The story of the Maneck family does not, however, end here, for Rustom's sons followed him as Brokers for the British. They were treated unjustly by the officials of the East India Company in Bombay, and so one of them came to Britain to seek redress; in this he is seen as a forerunner of others who travelled west, as will be discussed in the next chapter.

By the middle of the seventeenth century the British were looking for a new base because of the decline of Surat. The port was silting up and Hindu–Muslim rivalries were causing trading difficulties. Bombay appeared to those in the region to offer the solution because it formed a natural harbour and, being almost uninhabited, was free from local tensions. Eventually the Portuguese ceded the seven islands which formed Bombay to the British as part of the dowry of Catherine of Braganza on her marriage to Charles II in 1662. The local Portuguese were, however, reluctant to relinquish control and the British hold on the islands was tenuous for about sixty years. In order to administer the islands they sought to attract minority groups to migrate there. Many who came were Parsis. Eventually Bombay became the commercial capital of India, but at the end of the seventeenth century its unhealthy climate and vulnerability to attack made its acquisition appear a doubtful blessing. Parsis believe that they were crucial in helping the

British to secure control. One Parsi family known to have settled in Bombay prior to British rule was that of Dorabji Nanabhai. He had negotiated with the 'natives' on behalf of the Portuguese. The British confirmed him in office and gave him responsibility for raising taxes. His son, Rustomji Dorabji, is considered by Parsis to have saved the British garrison in Bombay. In 1692 a plague broke out and killed most of the British. In the same year the Muslim naval forces attacked Bombay. Rustomji raised a local army from the native fishermen, repelled the invaders, and took charge on behalf of the British until support came from Surat . In recognition of his services he was given the title of *patel*, lord or chief (David 1973; for a general history of Bombay, see *Gazetteer* 1909 and for the role of the Parsis, Hinnells 1989). Rustomji's significance for Parsis is not only that he saved Bombay for the British, but also that he and his father were consulted by the British about 'the manners, language and customs of the people' of the islands (Karaka 1884: ii. 49). In other words, he was a mediator between rulers and ruled—a role which Parsis believe they played increasingly in succeeding centuries.

The economic *raison d'être* for Bombay was its dockyard. This was built and run by the Parsi Wadia family and so the community consider that they were at the heart of the commercial development of Bombay. Lowji Wadia was brought by the British from the Surat dockyard in 1736 to build the new Bombay development and his family ran it until the 1880s. The ships built by him and his descendants achieved worldwide renown (A. Wadia 1955). From this economic base the Parsis were instrumental in developing the sea-borne trade of Bombay: they were the major non-European ship-owners and they opened up the China trade, which formed the foundation of much Bombay wealth in the mid-nineteenth century. Bombay flourished when the subcontinent was opened up to private traders in 1813 and after the opening of the Suez Canal in 1869. Central to this growth was the industrial revolution in Bombay, notably in the textile trade and the building of mills: these enterprises were pioneered by the Parsis, as were the banking and insurance services which supported the industrial growth. In the twentieth century it was a Parsi, J. N. Tata, who pioneered the emergent steel industry of the country. In these and countless other ways the Parsis see themselves as having been crucial to the economic development of India's commercial capital (Kulke 1974).

In the ninteenth century Bombay became one of India's great centres of western learning through the growth of schools and colleges and the foundation of the university in 1857. Not only were Parsis among the first to attend these institutions, they were also leaders in establishing them. Outstanding among the benefactors was Sir Jamsetji Jijibhoy, who established a trust fund in 1842 which by 1864 was running twenty-one schools with 3,049 pupils. He also built an art school, and medical and religious foundations. Various Parsis funded diverse parts of the university and the first Indian to become a professor was Dadabhoy Naoroji, who became professor of mathematics at the age of 27 in 1852. In the 1860s it has been estimated that although the Parsis represented only 6% of the population they occupied half of the places at the various centres of education in Bombay. The reason why the community took such an active part in this development was partly because education has been a Zoroastrian priority from ancient times and partly because it was seen to open up social and professional opportunities for minorities in British India. Through their educational achievements Parsis came to occupy leading positions in the professions, notably law and medicine. As a result of 'drinking deeply at the well' of western learning, numerous Zoroastrians internalized many of the values of the West. So Parsis were noted for their patronage of the theatre, not least Shakespeare, their knowledge of western literature, and their hobbies. In particular they enjoyed English sport, above all cricket, and by 1900 two histories of Parsi cricket had been written. In social concerns Parsis, for example Malabari, who is discussed below (Ch. 3, Sect. (*b*)) were leading campaigners for women's rights, notably education and the resolution of the problems associated with banning the remarriage of widows in a society where child marriage was common (Hinnells 1978*a* and 1980). The Parsis, therefore, see themselves as leading figures in education and as a significant liberalizing force among the people of British India.

After 1857 the political climate in India changed dramatically. Following the Mutiny, responsibility for the administration of India was taken away from the East India Company and assumed by Parliament in the person of the Secretary of State for India and by the Crown in the person of the 'deputy monarch' or Viceroy. Thereafter a new type of politician was needed in India, one who could argue in Britain on British terms. Local influence was no longer sufficient; a western education became the key to political power in India. Because of their educational achievements Parsis came to the fore. They were leaders in the movements which prefigured the Indian National Congress (i.e. the Bombay Association and the Bombay Presidency Association) and went on to play an important role in the first twenty formative years of the Indian National Congress (INC). Three individuals are especially noted in this context, though there were many others. Foremost is Dadabhoy Naoroji, popularly known as the 'Grand Old Man of India', who was elected president of the INC on three occasions (his role as the first Indian MP at Westminster is discussed in Chapter 5). Pherozeshah Mehta was commonly referred to as the 'uncrowned king of Bombay' as he dominated the city's politics for almost thirty years around the turn of the century. Dinshah Wacha was secretary of the INC for twenty-three years (Dobbin 1972; Natesan 1930). The Parsi community therefore sees itself as having played a significant role in the emergence of national politics in India and as having been responsible for the 'moderate' phase, when what was sought was the reform, not the removal, of British rule.

Although the Parsis commonly consider that their standing in the economic and political life of India has declined in the twentieth century, they nevertheless justifiably believe that they have continued to play an important part in the nation's history. In industrial terms they point to the giant firm of Tatas, and to South Asia's largest private company, Godrej Brothers. As well as leading figures in the armed forces (Parsis have occupied the post of head of each branch of the armed forces since Independence), law (including the post of India's highest law-officer, Solicitor-General), and diplomacy (including ambassadors, e.g. Palkivala, ambassador to Washington), they have also produced politicians, including several in Mahatma Gandhi's entourage (e.g. Minoo Masani, a leading opposition spokesman). Since Indira Gandhi was married to a Parsi (Feroze Gandhi—another member of the Mahatma's circle), some claim that Sanchay and especially Rajiv (who is said to have resembled his father) were Parsis. Many would also point to leading figures in the sciences (notably Homi Baba, the pioneer of atomic research in India) and the arts (above all the conductor Zubin Mehta, currently conductor of the New York Philharmonic and of Israel's national orchestra). The community thus sees itself as making a continuing contribution to the nation out of all proportion to its numbers (Nanavutty 1980: chs. 6–9).

(c) *Parsis and the British in Pakistan*

The compiler of the early history of the Parsis in Sind, Jehangir Framroze Punthakey (1919), wrote in his introduction: It is said about Bombay, that Parsis are the makers of the Bombay of today. And likewise I say about Karachi, that the makers of Karachi of today are also Parsis.' Most Zoroastrians living in Karachi at the end of the twentieth century would express the same sentiment.

Precisely when the first Parsi travelled to Sind is unknown, but the beginning of the modern settlement dates back to the early 1820s in Hyderabad and shortly afterwards in Karachi. It was during the First and Second Afghan Wars from 1839 that Parsi firms began to move to the province in any numbers, mainly as suppliers and contractors to the British forces and as agents of British firms. The Karachi *anjuman* became the major Parsi gateway to the region's trade. Although some of the early arrivals were professionals (Naoroji Fardoonji came as a Surveyor in the Public Works Department in 1847), most came as businessmen (e.g. in the liquor trade notably D. P. Minwalla and H. Ghadialy in 1839) and diversified into numerous businesses wherever the British needed agencies. One of the most important figures of the community's history, Edulji Dinshaw, rose to prominence as a landowner when he utilized his profits from the Second Afghan War to buy land. He and his descendants have been particularly noted for their considerable charitable donations, especially to non-Parsis, a tradition maintained into the 1990s. Two examples may illustrate the point. In 1884 the Vicerene, Lady Dufferin, collected funds to build a hospital in the city. From the whole population of the city she collected

Rs 10,000. Edulji Dinshaw, personally, gave Rs 85,000. Later the family endowed an engineering college which has now been given the status of a full university by government. Although Parsis have donated to numerous types of causes, they have contributed especially to medicine and education. Within the city, as well as in the community, there is respect for, and pride in, their munificence. There is, then, a sense that the Parsis were part of the very foundation of Karachi.

Parsis have been involved in Pakistani politics and commerce since Partition. Jamshed Nusserwanji Mehta (1886–1952) was often referred to as the 'maker of modern Karachi'. He became a member of the Municipality in 1918 (aged 32); he was a councillor for six years and was then President of the Municipality for 13 consecutive years and the first Lord Mayor of the city. His fame was based above all on his concern for the deprived of all communities and on his total integrity (*Nusserwanji* 1954). Parsis have often been close to leading Pakistani politicians. This position goes back to the very birth of the nation. Mohammed Ali Jinnah, the founder of Pakistan, was married to a Parsi, the daughter of an old family friend, Sir Dinshah Petit of Bombay, and his political mentor was the Parsi politician, Sir Pherozeshah Mehta. Similarly, the doctor who cared for Jinnah throughout his final illness, so that he could press his cause successfully with the British, was a Parsi (Wolpert 1984). After the foundation of the state of Pakistan the early cabinet meetings of Prime Minister Liaquat Ali Khan were commonly held in the hotel of a Parsi, Dinshah Avari. Avari went on to become a leading hotelier in Pakistan, owning what was originally intended to be the Karachi Hilton, and is now known as the Avari Towers. He also jointly owned the Lahore Hilton. His son, Behram, became a Member of Parliament in Islamabad. In the Pakistani political world another leading figure is Jamshid Marker, successively Pakistan ambassador in Paris, Washington, and the United Nations; that he held these posts when conflicting parties were in power indicates the widespread respect he commanded. In the world of business another leading family are the Cowasjis, who were major figures in Pakistan's shipping industry. Other Parsis have held high office in the military (two brigadiers, two naval captains) and even in the legal profession with a Supreme Court Judge, Justice Rustom

S. Sidhwa (who, out of the panel of three, argued for the innocence of President Bhutto), an unusual position for a non-Muslim in an Islamic state. In 1994 he was elected a member of the United Nations-sponsored tribunal, based in The Hague, to try accused war criminals of former Yugoslavia.

The community in Karachi thus considers itself to have been an important element in the development of Pakistan both during the period of British rule in Sind and after Independence. It has tended to be successful businessmen who stayed on in Pakistan, so that the family names mentioned above are still prominent in Karachi society. It is, therefore, quite a well-established group with two schools, two temples, and two Towers of Silence, housing-colonies, hospitals, and dispensaries, social clubs and a library—a remarkable achievement for a community which at its largest (in 1911–40) numbered only approximately 4,000–5,000 persons. There is relatively little acculturation with the Islamic majority and the result is, in the community's own estimate, a traditional Zoroastrian group.

Counterbalanced against this pride in past achievements, some Parsis are concerned for the vulnerability of the minority Zoroastrian community in the face of a perceived threat from increasing Islamic fervour. This is felt more outside the security of the well-to-do Karachi community, for example in Lahore. Many young people have concluded that their education and career opportunities are greater overseas. These twin forces of fear and aspiration have led over a third of the 1940 population to emigrate from the country which their elders believe they helped to establish.

(d) *Parsi Experiences in East Africa*

The South Asian presence in the region

Doubtless South Asian traders have travelled to East Africa for many centuries (Gregory 1971: 5–15). The modern period of the history of such contacts can be dated back to the early nineteenth century. The subject is a large and complex one. From the perspective of East African Parsis who migrated to Britain the discussion can be restricted to three areas: Aden, Zanzibar, and Kenya.

Aden was developed by the British as a base from which to rule the Indian Ocean and many Indian traders followed them. From here contacts were maintained with various East African centres. The port came to prominence as the supply point for the Abyssinian campaign. From 1840 so many workers came from India that it became more of an Indian than an Arab town and its affairs were scrutinized by the Bombay legislature (Gavin 1975).

Zanzibar grew as a trading centre when the Sultan of Oman, Seyyid Said, moved his capital from Muscat to the island in 1840. He brought with him many Indian merchants. It is estimated that there were approximately 5,000 in 1860 and in 1872 a regular steamer service was opened between Zanzibar and Bombay (Mangat 1969: 7–9). Zanzibar was originally involved in the slave-trade, but this was later replaced by trade in cloves and the organization of caravans in search of ivory. Indian funds played a major part in this trade (Mangat 1969: 87; Marsh and Kingsworth 1972: 64 ff.; Hollingsworth 1960: ch. 3). The island flourished economically after the opening of the Suez Canal. In 1870 Sultan Barghash came to power, following a period of exile in Bombay where he developed a respect for both British administration and Indian traders and professionals. The presence of both races subsequently grew in Zanzibar, especially after the Second World War. There were approximately 20,000 South Asians there by 1962, but almost all left because of the violence in 1963 and the revolution a year later (Tinker 1977: 119–22; Ghai and Ghai 1970: 99; Ogot and Kieran 1974: 308f.; Lofchie 1965).

Throughout the nineteenth century traders restricted themselves mainly to the coastal belt of what became Kenya, but from 1896 the British began to recruit Indian labourers (mainly from Karachi) and professionals (mainly from Bombay) to build the East African railway from the port of Mombasa in order to open up the hinterland as far as Uganda for trade (Mangat 1969: 32–49; H. S. Morris 1968).

For the next seventy years one of the central themes of Kenyan history is the interaction of the White, Indian, and Black races. From the Indian perspective, the problem was that they outnumbered the Whites 3 : 1 and paid 25% of the taxes whereas the Whites contributed only 6.5%. Yet Whites occupied 11,000 square miles of fertile upland areas and the Indians were restricted to 11 square miles of swampy, mosquito-infested, infertile land. The British presented themselves as the paternalistic protectors of the defenceless Black man and the Indians as exploiters of the Blacks—unscrupulous, dishonest, and dirty. White recruitment from South Africa did nothing to ease the problems of racial/colour prejudice (Hollingsworth 1960: 79–104; Mangat 1969: 22, 66, 100 f.). After Independence in the 1960s various African states absorbed this image of the Indians and saw them as refusing to mingle with the majority population, as draining away African wealth, and as occupying a disproportionately high level of administrative responsibility in the civil service, the professions, and business. The number of South Asians in East Africa grew from approximately 30,000 in 1900 to 364,713 in 1963. The process of Africanization in the 1960s was, therefore, founded on a pervasive image of Indian exploitation of Blacks (Tinker 1977: 119–58; Mangat 1969: 147–77; H. S. Morris 1968: 137–76; Bharati 1972: 105–13; Ghai and Ghai 1970: ch. 4).

From the Indian point of view the situation looked very different. Indian capital and manpower had been crucial to the development of British interests in Africa, yet Indians experienced injustice and discrimination. After the Second World War Indians played an important role in the growth of education, the professions, and the commerce of Africa but when they sought simply to preserve their identity (as they saw it) and refused to intermarry, then they were excluded from key positions and were finally forced to leave the country. The perspectives on relations in East Africa differed considerably from one community to another. The significant point in this context is that the East African Asians felt forced to migrate from countries they had helped develop.

The Parsis in East Africa

Parsis believe that they were pioneers in opening up nineteenth century Indian trade in East Africa as they had been elsewhere. The leading Parsi family in the East Africa trade was the Cowasji Dinshaws. Cowasji (1824–1900) was largely responsible for the development of the port, roads, and telegraphic communications of Aden when it became an important coaling station on the steamer route to Asia (Gavin 1975). He also built up his own shipping line for trade with East Africa and was agent for a number of British companies and the army during the extravagant (and, therefore, for him lucrative) Abyssinian campaign (1867–68). He was consul for several countries and when royalty called at Aden he presented the address of welcome. He was the recognized leader of the Parsi community, founding (with typical Zoroastrian charity), schools, a dispensary, a funeral ground, and a fire temple (1854). His son, Hormusjee, was especially active in expanding the East Africa trade but spent the latter part of his life back in Bombay where he was involved in political work, notably with the Indian National Liberal Federation, being associated with Sir Pheroze Sethna and, significantly for this book, Sir Muncherji Bhownagree. Hormusjee was knighted in 1922 (Joshi 1939).

The first Parsi to arrive in Zanzibar was M. A. Mistry in *c*.1845 and twenty-six other individuals are known to have come in the 1870s–1890s. A number of them came with Sultan Bhargash, notably the Darukhanawala brothers, Sorabji and Bomanji, who were medical officer and municipal planning officer respectively. A third brother came later as an engineer. Bomanji campaigned among Bombay Parsis for his co-religionists to trade with Zanzibar and in 1884 he brought a priest to the island. A burial ground was opened in 1883, an indicator of the community's long-term intention to settle. The Darukhanawala brothers persuaded the Cowasji Dinshaws to transfer their base from Aden to Zanzibar in 1884 and thereafter the Dinshaws dominated community life. They employed most Parsis, and endowed most of the charitable trusts, including the fire temple consecrated in 1895. One problem for such small communities is that they can easily become dependent on a single powerful benefactor, as did the Zoroastrians of Zanzibar. When the Cowasji Dinshaw firm was liquidated in 1953, the Zoroastrian Anjuman of Zanzibar was founded with 184 members to run community affairs, but almost all left after the revolution and there are, at the time of writing, only two Parsi families on the island. The fire no longer burns in the temple, though many records remain (Kased n.d.).

The history of the Parsi settlement on the East African mainland is less clear because the sources are oral not written.[2] The first Parsi known to have come was Jehangir Bhedwar, who built the port when the steamers began to arrive around 1870. He and Sorabji Mistry constructed several government buildings, including the old law-court, the customs house, the treasury building, the railway station, the Anglican cathedral, the general post office, and the National Bank of India. Mombasa Parsis can, therefore, justly claim to have been instrumental in the early development of the city. Most of the community came as engineers, bankers, surveyors, accountants, and contractors with the building of the East African railway. The Association dates from 1897 and by the Second World War numbers had grown to approximately 250. They were still a middle-class professional group consisting of lawyers, doctors, and company managers with few, if any, poor Parsis. Mostly they came as single male workers who eventually returned to their homes and families in India. While they were in East Africa, according to Bharati (1972: 88), they were not really regarded as part of the Indian community. After the general Asian exodus in the 1960s there are now only approximately fifty Parsis left in Mombasa.

As the East African railway travelled to Nairobi, so Parsis went with it; again, almost all of them were professionals. The first purchase of land for burials was made in 1902 and a tin shanty, the forerunner of a more imposing property, was erected in 1910. Until 1940 there were only fifty or sixty Parsis in Nairobi but numbers later grew to about 250 persons. The death register does not give many details such as dates, but it does record the jobs of the deceased and so provides a picture of the membership of the community. The most common professions listed are accountant, treasury official, merchant, advocate, engineer, doctor, dentist, architect, and real-estate agent. It was,

---

[2] A fuller account of Zoroastrians in East Africa will be included in the Katrak volume. The research on this topic owes much to many individuals, especially to T. Aresh, M. Treasurywalla, and Manchester University for funding a research visit to Nairobi, Mombasa, and Zanzibar; to Nyrmla Singh for collecting the documents when health problems prevented John Hinnells from travelling; to E. J. Austin, Mr Dolassa, D. E. Patel, Rusi Dalal, and many others in East Africa; also to Mr Hoshang Kased for permission to use his extensive unpublished manuscript. I also wish to record my particular thanks to Burjor and Zarin Avari both for their greatly valued friendship and for the insights they have shared into the East African Parsi perceptions.

therefore, a socially respectable group with a high educational level (Salvadori 1990: 22–8).

The history of the three East African centres is, therefore, reasonably similar, and involves the migration of well-educated professionals, important businessmen, and their employees. The largest numbers came after the Second World War, as they did to most South Asian communities in East Africa, but the communities were reduced to minuscule proportions with the dramatic exodus in the 1960s. The Parsi perspective on their history in East Africa is that they were an important element in the commercial and administrative development of both Zanzibar and Kenya (the same could be said for Uganda if that country were as relevant to this study). The Zanzibar community was the most affluent because of the Cowasji Dinshaws (or Adenwallas as they were known for obvious reasons) and consequently was able to fund the religious infrastructure of temple and priest. They thought of themselves as separate from the other Indian communities. Kased in his unpublished manuscript collects European travellers' comments which consistently stress the distinctiveness of the Parsis—that they are lighter in colour, educated, 'civilized', honest, and benevolent. He relates one episode which is worth quoting at some length because it exemplifies the way in which the Parsis in East Africa, and throughout the British Empire, saw themselves in relation to the Europeans.

At the beginning of the twentieth century in German-ruled Dar es Salaam, there were two categories of law: (*a*) *Bezirskgericht*, superior law, which was for all Europeans and some non-European Christians, and (*b*) *Bezirksamt* for Hindus, Muslims, Africans, and originally for Parsis. In September 1903 three Parsis from Dar es Salaam, with the support of the Zanzibar Parsis, wrote to the German Governor, distancing themselves from other Indians and arguing that they were more like Europeans and should, therefore, come under the higher jurisdiction. The letter read:

We now humbly and respectfully venture to urge that members of our, that is the Parsi community, are sufficiently advanced to enjoy the rights and privileges of those tried by Bezirskgericht. Our community though Indian in the sense that we have settled in India for generations is not really Indian because India was not originally our native land, our ancestors having to fly from Persia at the time of the Mahomedan conquest, and also because in our customs, habits, manners and religion our community is different from any other in India.

After quoting German scholars' work on Zoroastrianism it continued:

The main body of our sect, after their flight from Persia, settled in India has prospered much and helped materially in the trade and prosperity of India. It is our hope that in the years to come they may occupy a like position in German East Africa and that a large number of our community may be peacefully settled under German rule.

Your Excellency, from these arguments and for these reasons, will see that our community in India as admitted by the British Government occupies socially and intellectually the foremost position among other communities.

We have the privilege of having a monotheistic religion; the moral code prescribed by our religion is on a par with the ethics of the Christian faith; our customs and habits are in no way repugnant to the cleanliness of body or soul and our laws are adaptable to European jurisprudence. (Kased n.d.: 79–82)

This appeal to be recognized as European rather than Indian in character was successful. A comparable one was made in South Africa in 1906 but that failed. The Parsis' actions are a clear indicator of their proud sense of distinctiveness and of their conviction that their religion marked them out as having a value-system and lifestyle that identified them with the European Christians. Further, they believed that the rulers recognized their distinctive character.

In migrating to Britain in the 1960s, therefore, East African Parsis came with a particular and complex web of preconceptions about the British. They had more reason, perhaps, than their Indian co-religionists to believe the British to be unjust in their dealings with Indians and racially (or more accurately colour-) prejudiced. However, they saw Britain as offering a politically safer haven than was available in Africa and better economic prospects than India. Further, they believed they had a special relationship with the British. Although most Parsis who have migrated to Britain have been educated, the Parsis who came from East Africa were typically well established in their professions or businesses, unlike so many who came from India and Pakistan as students or in the early stages of their careers. Although the Parsi communities in East Africa at the start of the twentieth century generally consisted of single male workers, this was not the case with the community after the Second World War. Consequently most East African Parsis who arrived in Britain in the 1960s came as family groups. A few East African Parsi families had already sent their young people to study in Britain in the early 1960s, foreseeing how African politics might develop.

(e) *British–Zoroastrian Religious Interaction*

In addition to business contacts there has also been a level of religious interaction which merits comment, for this has affected the presuppositions, beliefs, and practices of British Zoroastrians. Zoroastrians and their religion came to the attention not only of travellers but also of missionaries, and to that of one in particular, the Revd John Wilson. He was the first to focus attention on the Parsis and he had a considerable impact on them, though hardly the one he intended.[3] Wilson began his work in Bombay in 1829 (G. Smith 1879). He established a school in the Fort area where many Parsis lived and he sought to attract Parsi children to it. In 1839 two of the boys were baptized and this caused a considerable outcry in the community, even (according to Wilson) threats of violence against him and the boys. The reaction was so strong that it deterred others

---

[3] Subsequent missionaries who wrote about the Parsis were H. G. Briggs (*The Parsis, or Modern Zerdushtians* (Bombay, 1952)) and Murray Mitchell (*The Great Religions of the World* (Edinburgh, 1905)), who had virtually no impact, and J. H. Moulton. The latter is noted mostly for his Greek studies of the New Testament, but he also wrote an important study of *Early Zoroastrianism* (London: 1913) and then in 1913 visited Bombay for a year to stay with the Parsis, and published eight lectures he had delivered to them (*The Teaching of Zarathushtra* (Bombay, 1916)). Moulton then wrote a book which combined a scholarly (though heavily Protestant) account of the Parsis and an appeal to them to convert to Christianity (*Treasure of the Magi* (London, 1917)). He influenced some groups of educated Parsis and his writings were serialized in the Bombay Parsi publication *Journal of the Iranian Association*. However, despite the respect in which he was held he never exerted the same impact on Zoroastrians as Wilson did. I have not been able to trace any evidence of his influence on British Zoroastrians, hence his exclusion from the main text. There were no Christian missions to Zoroastrians in Iran, so this discussion focuses wholly on Parsis.

from similar action. But this event was not as significant in the present context as Wilson's public speeches and writings as exemplified by his book published in Bombay in 1843, *The Parsi Religion as Contained in the Zand Avesta and Propounded and Defended by the Zoroastrians of India and Persia, Unfolded, Refuted and Contrasted with Christianity*. Some of his criticisms of Zoroastrianism had little or no impact. For example, he condemned the Parsis for not believing that man is inveterately sinful, an assessment of human nature with which Zoroastrians have no instinctive sympathy and which they basically ignored. Some of his attacks, however, wounded the community deeply. He argued that because Ohrmazd is not omnipotent, but restricted in power by the evil Ahriman, then God is robbed of his essential glory. Further, he argued that the veneration of the seven creations (man, cattle, fire, earth, sky, water, and plants) made Zoroastrians nature-worshippers and that the beliefs in the Bounteous Immortals and *yazatas* made them polytheists. Next he attacked the holy book, the *Avesta*, as 'destitute of all claims to be considered as a revelation from God, but that it is from beginning to end most singularly despicable as a human composition' (p. 342). In particular he savaged the liturgical emphasis of the *Avesta* and its concerns for the purity laws (he was a typical Protestant, being a member of the Church of Scotland, in his loathing of what he considered to be the 'priestcraft' of ritual). In addition he repudiated the authority of Zoroaster because, he said, there was no historical evidence that the prophet ever uttered a prophecy or worked a miracle. Finally, he was scathing in his condemnation of the mythology contained in the Middle Persian texts (see pp. 7–13 above).

The trenchant criticisms caused distress for many reasons. First, because Parsis had always considered themselves to be liked, and to be respected by, the British, such a public denunciation wounded pride and inflicted some humiliation. Second, it charged Zoroastrianism with many of the features of what Parsis knew Europeans considered to be 'pagan' religion, notably polytheism and nature-worship. Third, doubtless many feared that it would seriously undermine the religion of their educated young, which generally meant westernized, people and it was precisely such people, not the poor in rural areas, who would know of the attack. Fourth, it significantly lowered the standing of the priests because they did not have the linguistic or theological training to refute the charges. What many feared was that Wilson appeared to show that Zoroastrianism was not a religion which could command intellectual respect in the modern world.[4]

There was a flurry of written responses by Parsis but the intelligentsia did not think that they were effective defences. The main reaction on the part of the community was to begin a study programme to equip future priests to withstand missionary criticism. The leading figure was K. R. Cama. On his way back to India from a business venture in London in 1855 (see below Ch. 3, Sect. (*b*)) he stayed in Paris and Erlangen for six months to study Iranian languages and history so that he might teach his co-religionists in Bombay. He ran classes, organized a society, encouraged various publications, and supported the establishment of priestly seminaries where candidates studied the ancient languages (Modi 1932; Hinnells 1978: 42–64; 1983). Educated Parsis had come to consider western learning a necessary part of priestly requirements.

It was a German, Martin Haug, who provided the Parsis with what they saw as their effective intellectual response to Wilson. Haug was made Superintendent of Sanskrit Studies at the (British) Government College at Poona in 1859. In 1860 he produced the first western scholarly translation of Zoroaster's own hymns, the *Gathas*, and a year later he delivered an influential lecture to the Parsis of Bombay which was subsequently published and gave rise to numerous invitations, including one to be a governor of a priestly seminary. In 1862 he published a widely read scholarly work, *Essays on the Language, Writings and Religion of the Parsis*, in which he first elaborated the theories outlined on pp. 6f. above, presenting Zoroaster as an unritualistic teacher of an abstract ethical monotheism worthy of respect in the modern world. A Roman Catholic perspective might have

---

[4] There was, in fact, a great deal which could have been challenged, quite apart from the evident religious bias. Wilson's sources were very uneven. He used the 18th-c. traveller, Anquetil du Perron, placed great trust on Greek and Latin texts and their accounts of Zoroastrianism (he, therefore, thought that the 'heresy' Zurvanism was the original form of Zoroastrian doctrine), but knew relatively little of the Iranian sources. In particular he knew little of the *Gathas*, which at his time had not been isolated as the words of Zoroaster as discussed above on pp. 6f. Many of the features he implied Zoroastrianism lacked and Christianity had, e.g. the miraculous works of the prophet, were later denied in Christian studies.

been more sensitive to the idea of continuing priestly authority and to the devotional power of rituals.

Haug's interpretation held sway for over a hundred years not only in academic circles but also among many educated Parsis. For example, Karaka's *History of the Parsis*, published in London in 1884, a book which seems to be kept in as many Parsi homes as any other volume on the community, quotes Haug twenty-six times, that is three times more often than any other writer. Perhaps the most influential writer to show how the community internalized the Protestant value-system is M. N. Dhalla (1875–1956). He grew up in a priestly home and in his early life was a vocal orthodox writer and speaker. He studied first in Bombay then at Columbia University, New York, under (the Protestant) A. V. W. Jackson and as a result of his studies became a leading reformist. After his Ph.D. he was appointed high priest (Dastur) in Karachi and produced a number of books on Zoroastrian history and theology (published by Oxford University Press in New York; e.g. Dhalla 1938), as well as a devotional prayer book (Dhalla 1942). Dhalla did lecture in Britain on occasions, and taught some of the community leaders in the 1970s. He continues to exercise influence. Because Dhalla wrestled, decades ago, with the sort of intellectual problems which many Zoroastrian migrants to the West now face, his books have been found helpful by many of them. In American and Canadian community newsletters his works are often cited, but his writings are used in Britain also, being sold at functions in Zoroastrian House. They therefore merit a brief discussion here.

It is essential to appreciate that Dhalla was both a devout priest and a scholarly man. At times there appears to have been a tension between these two dimensions of his personality. For example, he sometimes expressed concern about excessive ritualism, yet the many Zoroastrians who remember him frequently refer to his devotional worship at home and in the temple. From his studies at Columbia University he was clearly aware of the texts relating to the doctrines of good and evil that were outlined in chapter 1, the myths concerning the figure of evil, Ahriman, the judgement scene, and the final renovation of the universe; indeed, these appear in his accounts of those texts (1938: chs. 30–45). But he was concerned to emphasize the monotheistic nature of his religion and he appears to have doubted the independent reality of Ahriman, so that the traditional Zoroastrian teaching on death as the evil work of Ahriman was modified and Dhalla sometimes speaks of it as God calling people back to himself. The death of children he explains as being because they were too good to live in this world. Some of the myths are rationalized, for example hell is seen simply as the suffering of the conscience, and many of the myths, notably the apocalyptic tradition, are ignored in the writing produced for the community, such as the devotional work (Dhalla 1942). The abstract interpretation of these myths is common among British Zoroastrians at the end of the century.

Dhalla was not, of course, alone in his intellectual wrestling with his tradition. This is not the place for a detailed discussion of the various writers (Hinnells 1995) but one more merits comment, namely J. J. Modi, who produced the standard, if at times tortuous, account of Parsi rites (Modi 1922). Modi was born of a priestly family but his life was devoted to scholarship. His book offers not only a full account of the rituals but also a rationalization of them for the western-educated by putting forward highly symbolic interpretations of various acts. In particular he was concerned with the purity laws, arguing that their motivation and consequence was hygiene. Here he was following the interpretation of a British writer, S. Laing, a finance minister in India who wrote semi-popular books on science and religion with one specifically on Zoroastrianism (Laing 1887). This justification has become very common among Zoroastrians both in India and Britain and is reproduced in some of the books discussed in Ch. 3, Sect. (*c*).

Although these are the main writers to have influenced British Zoroastrians, there have been subsequent religious developments which have affected the attitudes of the community in Britain and therefore merit brief attention. The influence of Protestant attitudes and western rationalism on the community inevitably provoked a reaction among traditional Parsis who feared that cherished beliefs and practices were being discarded in a trivial fashion. The same process was happening among other Indian communities whose young people were absorbing western education, not least Hindus. For the traditionally minded of each community the western-originated Theosophical Society came as a welcome support of their spiritual heritage

(Farquhar 1914). The founders, Madame Blavatsky and Col. Olcott, moved from New York to Bombay in 1879 and until the centre was transferred to Madras by the new leader, Annie Besant, in 1906 Parsis were prominent among the general membership, office-bearers, speakers, and writers of the Society. Several theosophical beliefs exerted quite widespread influence and continue to do so, notably belief in rebirth, an ascetic tendency which often includes vegetarianism (both of which are consistent with Hindu influence), and an occult interpretation of traditional beliefs particularly with regard to unseen forces and the spiritual 'aura' which is believed to surround a person. People not born into, and practising, Zoroastrianism, especially the purity laws, were said to have an aura which it would be harmful to bring into sacred places (e.g. the temple sanctuary). Western academics and their Parsi students were said by theosophists to appreciate only the superficial linguistic level of texts and not the hidden, occult mysteries. This was applied especially to traditional rituals and prayers in the sacred language which, it was said, attuned the worshipper to vibrations on the ethereal level and should not, therefore, be cast aside as a 'dead' language as the Protestantized reformers argued (Hinnells 1983; Langstaff 1983).

Membership of the Theosophical Society is now rare in Bombay and practically unknown among British Zoroastrians, but many of the ideas, especially the occult ideas associated with the purity laws, continue among those who would describe themselves as orthodox and especially among followers of what might loosely be called a Zoroastrianized theosophical movement, Ilm-i Khshnoom (often interpreted as meaning 'Path of Knowledge'). It was started by Behramshah Shroff who is believed to have received spiritual teaching from secret Zoroastrian masters in Iran (not from theosophy's Tibetan masters). After his stay with them he began preaching in 1907. His teachings closely parallel those of the Theosophical Society, notably rebirth, the 'aura', attitudes to purity, the mystical power of the traditional prayers, and vegetarianism. As there are no distinct rituals, no canon of orthodoxy, and only one temple has been built by his followers, his movement cannot be considered as a separate sect and there is no formal membership so that numbers cannot be estimated. There are two main teachers of the movement in Bombay in the 1980s–1990s and one of them, Mrs Meher Master Moos, has produced numerous books and undertakes many tours of Zoroastrian communities, including that in Britain. Khshnoomic teaching, therefore, has its adherents among diaspora Zoroastrians. The aspects of its teachings which provide a powerful appeal are: the authority of a visionary master; an emphasis on the non-rational, experiential dimension of religion; a legitimation of much-loved traditional practices; a sense of identity for what is seen as a spiritually exalted group, which makes significant demands upon its followers with its requirements for ethical and racial purity (Hinnells 1995).

A very different Bombay Parsi religious movement started in 1977, namely Zoroastrian Studies, or ZS, which both owes much to British contacts and is influential upon British Zoroastrians. The founder, Khojestee Mistree, gave up a successful career as an accountant to study Zoroastrianism at Oxford but pursued his work at London University with Mary Boyce. This was a significant step because Boyce was at that time developing her radical theories, in contrast to those of Haug discussed above, of the great continuity of Zoroastrian teaching (see Ch. 1, Sect. (*a*)). Boyce's convictions coincided with Mistree's own deep commitment to his community's traditions and with his interest in the mystical dimension of religion. Inspired by his studies, the charismatic speaker returned to Bombay to establish a teaching project and to raise interest in spiritual matters among his own community. Since then ZS has run countless courses in India and overseas, not least in London. Mistree has also written a book (1982) elucidating his spiritual understanding, which he integrates with the academic perspectives outlined by Boyce. This book is widely used in Britain as elsewhere, and one of his team, Ava Mehta (formerly a teacher in England), has written a book on Zoroastrianism for children (1988). In these various ways Mistree seeks to recall his community to what he sees as the original teaching on the conflict of good and evil, on the resurrection, the value of rituals, the importance of purity laws, the opposition to intermarriage and conversion. Again the appeal lies in the charismatic personality, a clear, strong, well-articulated teaching and, in this case, consistency with contemporary trends in western scholarship. Mistree appeals to a section of the community eager to rediscover its Zoroastrian roots, not least the young, educated, and middle-class. He also undertakes much charitable work for the poor of the community. Inevitably such a powerful message and personality have provoked some opposition, both in Bombay and Britain, among those such as the Kshnoomists who are interested in the occult and reject western scholarly interpretations, and among the liberals. But his influence has increased in London in the 1990s, as will be seen in Chapter 6. The important point here is that there is a high level of interaction between western, indeed British, scholarship, the Bombay community, and the Zoroastrians in Britain.

(f) *Conclusion*

It is important to appreciate the diversities of people and views within the Zoroastrian community in Britain. Those who came from India or Pakistan are more likely to see themselves as having had close relations with the British than those from Iran; those who have come from East Africa are more likely to have a sense of colour-prejudice; Zoroastrians from Iran and Pakistan are more likely to have a sense of religious oppression. The motivations behind the migrations of the various groups were different. For those who came from India, and for many from Pakistan, the journey was seen as being for their own benefit and to them Britain was mainly a land of educational or career opportunities. For Iranian and East African (and to a lesser extent for some Pakistani) Zoroastrians the point was that Britain offered a safe haven. The nature of the migration also varied. Those who came from India for education came as individuals; those from East Africa and Iran generally came as members of wider families. Iranian Zoroastrians are especially conscious of hundreds of years of persecution and are justly proud of what they have achieved in the twentieth century when they have been allowed some freedom (Shahrokh and Writer 1994). The Parsis, again justly, consider that wherever they have settled, in Zanzibar or Sind, Mombasa or Bombay, they have constituted the educated, westernized, professional classes, the entrepreneurs as well as the social and political leaders. They consider that they have been important cogs in the machine both under British rule and in the independent nations.

Zoroastrians consistently assert that they are loyal to the government of the country in which they reside on whatever continent. But their emotional links with the various countries differ considerably. Although burial grounds were purchased and a temple was built in East Africa, so that there was some sense of a continuing settlement, few Parsis seem to have considered their own stay there to be permanent. They were not emotionally tied to the country. Such ties are closer in Pakistan, but the strongest ties, naturally, are with Iran. That is the original homeland where there is a strong sense of Zoroastrians being the true Iranians, unaffected by the Arab conquest. The situation with India is more complex. For some there is a strong sense of being closely tied with India, a perspective which goes back to at least 1600 when the *Qissa-i Sanjan* was written. It relates that the migration from Iran to India was undertaken on the advice of a wise astrologer priest (i.e. it was 'written in the stars', or fate) and the travellers came to land precisely where they did in western India as an answer to their prayers for deliverance when in peril during a storm at sea. Further, the tradition goes, when they landed the local Hindu ruler gave them permission and land to settle, requiring them to conform to only minimal demands, namely not to carry weapons, and to adopt the local language and dress for women. In return the Zoroastrians assured him of the common beliefs and values of the two religions and promised that they would be like sugar in a drink, invisible but making the whole sweeter (Axelrod 1980; Boyce 1984: 120–3). Some Parsi politicians, notably Dadabhoy Naoroji and Pherozeshah Mehta, have affirmed that they were Indians first and Parsis second. There is, therefore, one dimension to the Parsi perspective on their settlement in India which is very positive. Parsis are conscious that few countries would have extended such security to a minority over such a long period. However, there is also a consciousness among many that ultimately they are not Indian, a theme well illustrated by the case in Dar es Salaam, quoted above, which stressed their Persian origins: 'Our community though Indian in the sense that we have settled in India for generations is not really Indian.' It is remarkable how the Parsis have preserved their sense of identity when they are a tiny minority in such a powerful culture, and have done so for over a millennium.

Another aspect of the identity question is Zoroastrian perceptions of their relations with the British. Again, the Dar es Salaam case represents the Parsi attitude, namely the conviction that because of their customs, social structure, and beliefs, and because their religion is on a par with Christianity, they believe that they are like Europeans. They not infrequently quote the travellers who describe them as being as fair in appearance as the Europeans (Hinnells 1978a). The point is that they not only think that they are like the Europeans, they believe others also consider them to be so. The British connection involves a religious dimension. Not only is Zoroastrianism seen to be on a par with (European) Christianity, it is also seen as the ancient source of the great prophetic religions. Because of their understandable pride, the (verbal) attacks on their religion from Britain caused deep distress. Because Parsis have studied both technology and religion, in the West some of them imbibed western assumptions about the nature of religion in general and of their own in particular. Few, if any, other British South Asian communities have experienced such a profound interaction between their own religion and that of the British before their migration to the UK. The intellectual wrestlings of Dhalla and Modi were the forerunners of the experiences of many who came later. There are, in short, many strands to the network of presuppositions with which Zoroastrians came to Britain.

3

Early Zoroastrian Arrivals in Britain

Probably no other religious or ethnic minority group which has migrated from Asia to Britain has had such a close network of both business and intellectual contacts with the British prior to the period of settlement as the Zoroastrians. What is more, few groups have taken such care to record those contacts. This chapter is concerned with three aspects of that early period of settlement: (*a*) the earliest recorded arrivals; (*b*) the literature some of the early travellers produced for their own community in Bombay, which may have affected the Indian community's perceptions of life in Britain; (*c*) the literature produced by the early Zoroastrians in Britain for the British in order to condition the British perception of their small community. For the purposes of this chapter 'early' means before the Second World War and prior to the arrival of the majority of Zoroastrians. During that early period the arrivals were all from India; hence the subject-matter is necessarily the Parsis and not the Iranian Zoroastrians, who did not settle in Britain until later.

(a) *The Earliest Arrivals*

The first Zoroastrian, probably the first Indian, known to have travelled to Britain was Naoroji Rustomji in 1724. He was the son of Rustom Maneck (Seth) whose relations with the British in India were discussed in the last chapter. Rustom had enjoyed the patronage of the then Governor of Bombay, Charles Boone, but when Boone's period of office came to an end in 1721 his successor, William Phipps, took a very different attitude to

One of my many debts to Dastur Dr K. M. JamaspAsa is for the many long periods he spent translating and elucidating for me the contents of *Parsi Prakash*. I am deeply grateful for all his help.

Rustom and his family. He accused them of profiteering, dishonesty, and indebtedness. He replaced them with their Hindu rival, Vitaldas Parak, put Rustom's sons under house-arrest, and imposed a financial charge on the family for them to be allowed to supply food to the brothers. Appeals on their behalf both by the commander of the naval squadron in the Indian Ocean, Commodore Matthews (who knew the family because it had provisioned the squadron), and the Muslim Governor of Surat, Rustam Ali, were to no avail. Eventually Naoroji decided the only hope lay in a direct appeal to the Court of Directors of the East India Company in Britain and managed to set sail with Commodore Matthews in 1724. He stayed in Britain for almost a year, successfully seeking the support of older Company officials who knew the family. Eventually they convinced the Court that Naoroji's family had been unjustly treated and Phipps, unable to justify his accusations, was compelled to free the other brother. Naoroji was awarded an immediate payment in London of £19,125 (with which he funded the purchase of a shipment of goods to take back) and two instalments in India, each of Rs 188,195, thus repaying the Company debt of Rs 523,427 with interest amounting to Rs 54,213 (Hodivala 1931; Commissariat 1953; White 1979: ch. 3).

Naoroji appears to have made a good impression on the officials he met. Charles Boone wrote to the family in Bombay:

Since Nowrojee's coming to England he hath been very ill, but he has taken great pains in this business, and everybody here hath great value and esteem for him because he has managed this affair to the satisfaction of the Hon'ble Company, and for the good and interest of his brothers and family, therefore you ought to make him a handsome present for his long and fatiguing voyage and good services.
(Commissariat 1953: 244, facsimile of the letter, p. 258)

On his return to India Naoroji acquired considerable standing. Although he was not the oldest brother he became head of the family. In his will he left money for the building of a fire temple, known as the Maneckji Seth Agiary, in the central (Fort) area of Bombay. Another part of central Bombay was named Naoroji Hill after him and the income from this land ensured family fortunes for two centuries. Within the community he was elected as a leader (*akabar*) of the first Parsi Punchayat of Bombay and he had important status among the wider trading community. The significance of this episode is not the impression Naoroji made on the British public, since there is no evidence that he created much of a public image, but rather the twin impressions the affair created among his community in Bombay: first Naoroji acquired significant status from his visit to Britain; second, the British authorities were perceived as powers willing to administer justice over the heads of local officials, if they were convinced of the justice of the case. The latter is a theme which will recur in later discussions of Parsi attitudes to the British, not least that of Dadabhoy Naoroji in his earlier political campaigns.

No other Zoroastrian is known to have visited Britain until the middle of the nineteenth century. There are, however, records of charitable donations made in Scotland and England by Bombay Parsis in the early part of the century. The first was on 21 September 1804, when two Parsis made contributions to the 'Patriotic Fund'; on 30 May 1807, five Parsis contributed to the Scottish Corporation in London; on 7 April 1808, Parsis made a donation to the Aberdeen Society of London and on 10 August 1811, one of the Wadias donated Rs 80 to the Edinburgh lunatic asylum (*PP* I. 99, 108, 117). Benevolence is a fundamental Zoroastrian virtue and has characterized the community wherever it has been, in Iran, India, or the diaspora (Hinnells 1985*a*). Nevertheless, it is remarkable that such a small community should make donations to distant causes before its period of real affluence and before the time when strong westernizing forces had their effect.[1] It is indicative of the community's sense of history and significance that the records of these donations exist. Space does not permit the full documentation of the continued acts of Parsi charity in Britain, but a few points may be highlighted. The focus of charity over the following 150 years tended to be education in various forms, and also medicine and the poor, notably during the Irish famine and at the time when the Lancashire mill-workers were suffering. As will be discussed below, more than one early Parsi traveller commented on the extremes of wealth and poverty in Britain and expressed regret

---

[1] It is noticeable how many of these early donations were to Scottish causes. This is understandable for the mid–late 19th c. because many Parsis studied medicine in Edinburgh. But I know of no reason for this focus at an earlier date.

that more was not done for the less fortunate. The main Parsi donor families to British causes in the nineteenth century were the Cama family (especially D. P. Cama, one of the earliest to settle), Sir C. J. Readymoney, Rustomji Jijibhoy, and B. D. Petit.[2] The nineteenth-century Parsi perception of Britain was, therefore, not simply of a mighty imperial power from which one sought benefits, but also of a society with substantial numbers of poor people who needed benevolent help, which Parsis in India were willing to give.

The main purpose for which Parsis came to Britain in the mid-nineteenth century was education. They were leaders in establishing the industrial revolution in Bombay and Gujarat, especially in the textile trade. A number came not for formal education but to see for themselves how British industry worked. The first was Ardashir Wadia who came in 1840 under the auspices of the East India Company to acquaint himself with the developments in marine engineering. He was a member of the famous Parsi shipbuilding family and prided himself on being at the forefront of technological development in Bombay, having introduced gas lighting into the city in 1835 (A. C. Wadia 1840: ch. 4). As a result of the technical knowledge and social contacts acquired during his stay in London, Wadia was appointed Chief Engineer and Inspector of Machinery at the steam factory and foundry in Bombay, an appointment which excited some English jealousies. In 1841 his cousins, Jehangir Naoroji and Hirjibhoy Meherwanji, came for similar reasons.

---

[2] *To schools*: 27 Dec. 1854 to the fund for poor children's education in memory of Prof. Patton's widow (*PP* I. 653); 14 June 1823, for poor children's education in Scotland (*PP* I. 171); 1 Jan. 1864, Cama Girls School near Castle Newe, Scotland (*PP* II. 87). *To universities and further education*: 2 Nov. 1863, Cama family donated £3,000 to University College London, £1,000 to University College Hospital, London, and £2,000 to the Royal Naval Life–boat Institution) (*PP* II. 75 f.); 12 Dec. 1863, The Honble Rustomji J. J. gave Rs 150,000 for five Indians to study law in Britain (*PP* II. 81); 20 Sept.1893, C. J. Readymoney gave £20,000 to the Imperial Institute (*PP* III. 440); 23 Nov. 1893, M. M. Bhownagree donated a colonnade to the Imperial Institute (*PP* III. 444); 1 Jun. 1895, C. J. Readymoney gave £10,500 for a hall at the Imperial Institute (*PP* II. 433); 17 Sept. 1902, B. D. Petit gave £6,000 to the London School of Tropical Medicine (*PP* IV. 90). *Donations for the poor in Britain*': to the Irish famine, 23 Nov. 1822 (*PP* I. 165), 4 Jun. 1846, and again in 1847 (*PP* I. 474) and 29 Jan. 1880 (*PP* II. 683); to the poor Lancashire mill–worker, 17 Sept 1862 (*PP* II. 45 f.); from D. P. Cama to the Lord Mayor's Poor Box at the Mansion house in London, 1 Jan. 1887 (*PP* III. 201); 21 Jan. 1892 (*PP* III. 404); 7 July 1892 (*PP* III. 410f); 10 Jan. 1894 (*PP* III. 466), 13 Oct. 1895 (*PP* III. 546); 18 Jan. 1896 (*PP* III. 570), 6 Jul. 1896 (*PP* III. 589).

Both of these visits resulted in the publication of diaries relating their experiences for Bombay readers which will be discussed in Section (*b*). The first Indian firm to be established in England was started by the Cama brothers and Dadabhoy Naoroji in 1855, with offices in London and Liverpool. R. B. Desai came in 1857, stayed for seven years to learn about the soap industry, and went back to Bombay to build a factory (*PP* II. 484); R. M. Darukhanawala stayed in Oldham to learn about the manufacture of explosives before returning to Bombay as head of the explosives department of the government artillery depot (*PP* II. 521; no date is given but he died in 1875). Sometimes Parsis came to learn about, and purchase, equipment. For example, N. A. C. Wadia came in 1859 to purchase machinery for boiler improvements and in 1860 Ookerji came to buy a steamer (*PP* I. 797, 827). The most famous such informal student was J. N. Tata. His first visit to Britain was in 1865 when he focused his attention on the Lancashire mill industry and on Manchester's commercial life which experience in due course enabled him to open his Nagpur mills before starting India's steel industry (Harris 1958). These, and other, examples illustrate how 'education' should not always be interpreted in a formal institutional sense. Generally these practical experiences predated the visits of those who came for conventional education. They appear to have facilitated business success back in India.

Extant records suggest that few young people came for schooling, because of the distances which would thereby separate families. The first to come was Dinshawji, son of the businessman Furdonji Limji Panday, who arrived on 29 September 1832. Two years later he was joined by the 8-year-old son of Framji Pestonji Patuck (*PP* I. 253, 274). The experiences of Dinshawji do not appear to have been helpful. After his return to Bombay in 1842 he went to China for business but he is said to have spent his life suffering from mental illness. The sons of Cursetjee Maneckji Shroff (a legal pioneer and prominent social reformer) attended school in England, but their schooling was conducted under the paternal eye of the family friend, Dadabhoy Naoroji (*PP* II. 619; Masani 1939: 91).

University was the main educational attraction which brought Parsis to Britain, and, once Bombay University had been opened in 1857 to provide undergraduate education, they were especially seeking higher degrees. The two main subjects studied were medicine and law. The first medical graduate gained his MD from St Andrews and his FRCS from London in 1861 (Muncherji Behramji Kolah, *PP* II. 7). There were two memberships and one Fellowship of the Royal College of Surgeons in the 1870s and thereafter numbers grew too great to be listed.[3]

A legal training became a significant qualification for political office in the second half of the nineteenth century in India. When, in 1858, the rule of India passed from the East India Company, with its local factories, to the Crown and Parliament, Indian leaders had to argue with the British, in Britain, and on British terms. The best foundation from which to do this was a legal training. Further, the law cast something of the mantle of the rulers onto its professionals. The highest legal training, and the requirement for practising as a barrister, was to study in England. An early incentive in this field was provided by C. J. Readymoney, who donated a prize of Rs 5,000 in 1863 for Parsis to study law in England (*PP* II. 64) and in 1863 the Honble Rustomji Jijibhoy gave funds for five Indians (of any community) to pursue such studies. Some of the earliest Parsi law graduates in Britain became leaders within the community notably Pherozeshah Mehta (1868), and Cursetjee Maneckji Shroff and Limji N. Banaji in 1869 (*PP* II. 305). Five more individuals are named in the *Parsi Prakash* as having completed their legal training in Britain in the 1870s.[4] It was the outstanding students who travelled to Britain. Their work in London typically enhanced their standing when they returned to India. Thus Shroff rose to become the first native judge and Mehta was the dominant figure in Bombay politics at the turn of the century (see above, p. 57, and Mody 1963).

---

[3] In 1873 D. N. Parekh was awarded a gold medal for his medical studies at University College London, in which year R. C. Bahadurji and C. F. Khory became Members of the London Royal College of Surgeons (*PP* II. 452f. 461). The following became LRCPs in the 1870s: 1876, R. N. Khory and C. F. Khory (*PP* II. 572 and 453 respectively); 1877, M. E. Reporter (*PP* II. 589); 1878, E. Maneckji (*PP* II. 633); 1878, H. J. Khambatta (*PP* II. 634); 1879, M. S. Mehta (*PP* II. 665).

[4] In 1871 three unnamed Parsis are said to have passed their law exams (*PP* II. 461); 1878, N. R. Motabhoy (*PP* II. 634); 1880, D. D. Dara (*PP* II. 695). These are minimal figures. Since *PP* does not include Pherozeshah Mehta, one may assume other names are also omitted.

Parsis are understandably proud of the number of educational pioneers in the community. Instances of such leaders include the following: the first Indian girl to go to school, Dosebai Cowasji Jessawalla; the first Indian to study at Oxford (Cursetjee Maneckji Shroff in 1864); the first woman to study at Oxford (Cornelia Sorabji in 1889), and the first Indian to be President of the Oxford Union (Karaka in 1937). One 'first' the community rarely refers to is that it produced the first Indian to study Christian theology at university namely Dhunjibhoy Naoroji at Edinburgh in 1843. He was one of the boys converted by Wilson, as described in Chapter 2. More widely known, and quoted, is that the first Indian to be made a professor at a British university was Dadabhoy Naoroji who was made professor of Gujarati at University College London in 1856, though it is not clear that he had many duties. Very few Zoroastrians in Britain would know all these details, but most would be both conscious and proud of the general fact that their forebears were in the vanguard of Indian students in Britain.[5]

In many ways the pinnacle of respectability was to enter the Indian Civil Service. The British government made it difficult for Indians to enter, precisely because it gave them a say in the running of their own country. This was a focus of much political agitation, not least by Dadabhoy Naoroji, as will be seen below. By holding the examinations only in England, by basing them on the English public-school syllabus, and by putting an age-limit on candidates of 22 (younger than Indians could realistically hope for in view of their lesser educational opportunities), the British reduced the numbers of Indian Civil Servants to a trickle. Nevertheless some Parsis tried. In June 1856 R. H. Wadia arrived in Britain in order to study for the entrance examination. He had allowed himself two and a half years, that is until December 1858, when he would meet the then existing age requirement of 23. However, the age-limit was reduced to 22 and he had to give up. The *Parsi Prakash* includes an account of public reaction:

[5] On Jessawalla, see Jessawalla 1911 and her obituary in *PP* IV. 32 for 11 Jan.; on Cursetji Maneckji Shroff, see Dharukhanawala 1963: II. 759 f.; on Karaka, see Karaka 1938; on Sorabi, see Vadgama 1984: 200 f.; on Dhunjiboy, see Naoroji 1909; on Naoroji, see *PP* I. 701.

There was great interest and excitement among the Natives when the young man left India to come to England, and there is great disappointment among his friends at the result. He has been laughed at for trusting the Government, and it is said that while Government go on changing their regulations in this way no faith can be put on them. (*PP* I. 707 f.)

Wadia then travelled around America, deeply dejected, before joining his father's business back in Bombay, but he died at the age of 34 (death notice, *PP* II. 362).

The first Indian recorded entering the Indian Civil Service was C. R. Wadia, who in 1874 passed the entrance examination at the age of 18 (*PP* II. 496); the following year a second Parsi, C. J. Padshah, was successful (*PP* II. 589). The personal costs involved were enormous: S. C. Cama was sent to England at the age of 12 in 1841 to study for the examinations, but died in Britain at the age of 20 before he could take them (*PP* II. 323). English ailments such as colds and influenza could cause medical problems for people from India as great as those experienced by British travellers in the subcontinent. It was more common for Parsis to enter the Indian Medical Service. The first to do so were S. H. Dantra and C. A. Dalal in 1876, and twelve more passed by 1870 (*PP* II. 625, 684, 698). But in this service 'natives' were distanced from political decisions and were, therefore, not as ruthlessly (though still largely) excluded.

Although most Parsis in the nineteenth century came to Britain for education, either formal or informal, some also travelled for business. Among the first referred to in the *Prakash* are three unnamed gentlemen who departed on 10 January 1859 (*PP* I. 778), but their experiences are not related and many must have suffered this same fate of being omitted from historical records. There are occasional tantalizing references in the *Prakash* to individuals who sought to establish businesses in Britain; L. M. Banaji, for example, is said in his obituary (*PP* 30 June 1902) to have started a business in London in 1862 but it collapsed with the share mania in Bombay in 1865. P. M. Meherhomji is said, in his obituary, to have come to Britain for business with Naoroji in 1858, but no more is known of him. It is Naoroji's first business venture with the Camas in 1855 which is best known. The firm dealt in a range of goods: thread, opium, wine, and spirits. K. R. Cama and Naoroji resigned because they disapproved of the last two commodities. K. R. Cama returned to Bombay where he settled and concerned himself primarily with the religious reform programme mentioned earlier, but his brother, M. H. Cama, stayed on in Britain for business. Naoroji's later political campaigns were supported by subscriptions from India, but in the early period, while he was establishing himself politically, he financed his work through his own import–export business (Masani 1939: Ch. 7). It was started in 1859 with J. P. Kapadia and P. R. Colah, two young protégés whom he brought with him on his second visit. He was joined by another Parsi assistant, E. N. Master, in 1860. Naoroji became a director of the Queen Insurance Company and a guarantor of the Industrial Exhibition of 1862, both indicators that at that time his business was reasonably successful. However, many of his creditors lost money in the Bombay stock market crash in 1865 and this caused Naoroji serious financial problems. Much of his time as a businessman in Britain was spent in the north-west of England, mostly in Liverpool, but he was also a member of the Manchester Cotton Supply Association. He regularly exhorted his countrymen that their main hope for success in the textile trade was to study the Lancashire textile industry at first hand (on the Zoroastrians and the textile trade see, S. D. Mehta 1954: ch. 2).

Most of these early Zoroastrian settlers were young single males but there were also examples of families migrating at an early date. The first family known to have undertaken a tour to Britain was that of Dr B. D. Cooper in 1858 (*PP* I. 759). In 1862 the two daughters of Cursetji Maneckji Shroff came as part of their father's ardent campaign for educating women. Naoroji's family moved to Britain in 1865 and on the same boat came the families of D. R. Colah and J. B. Wadia. Three months later the family of J. B. Vacha sailed from Bombay (*PP* II. 153, 161). In 1868 one of K. R. Cama's daughters, Bhikhaiji, the wife of a longstanding London dweller, D. P. Cama, travelled throughout Britain. Thus from 1858 to 1868 there were several examples of Zoroastrian women not merely coming out in Indian society but indeed travelling the world (Murzban 1917: II. 339 f.).

One pioneering venture in travel to Britain of which the Parsis are proud is that they organized the first Indian cricket team to tour England. The venture is worth more than a passing humorous mention for reasons which will become apparent. The first Parsi cricket club, the Oriental Cricket Club, was founded in Bombay in 1848 and renamed the Zoroastrian Cricket Club in 1850. Thereafter the number of such clubs in the community proliferated. Other communities in Bombay started clubs, but not so many in proportion to their numbers. The intercommunity matches could be very tense, especially those between Parsis and Muslims, to such an extent that the *Hindi Punch* records that they occasionally had to be cancelled. Great pleasure was taken, naturally, in beating the Europeans. In order to learn more about the sport the Parsis began to discuss a British tour as early as 1878, but it was 1886 before it occurred. In one sense the results were disappointing: played 28, won 1, lost 19, drawn 8. But victories had not really been anticipated; the aim was rather 'to learn the game'. The president of the club, Pherozeshah Mehta, in proposing the toast to the departing team, said:

I may say that the object of the team in going to England is a very modest one. Cricket, as you know, is the national game of England. It has taken root among the Parsi community, and as artists go to Italy to do homage to the great masters, as pilgrims go to Jerusalem to worship at a shrine, or as students in the Middle Ages went to the chief seats of learning in places where Science and Philosophy had made their home, so now the Parsis are going to England to do homage to the English cricketers, to learn something of their noble and manly pastime in the very country which is its chosen home.   (Darukhanawala 1935: 61 f.; *PP* III. 183)

Something of the attitude to the tour in Britain may be reflected in the comments of the English *Cricket Chit Chat* of 1887:

A visit of a team of native Cricketers (Parsis) to England is an event of no small significance, not only from the stand-point of cricket, but also from the political point of view. Anything which can tend to promote an assimilation of tastes and habits between the English and native subjects of our Empress Queen cannot fail to conduce to the solidity of the British Empire, and if only for that reason this latest development of cricket, the zeal with which the natives of India are working to secure proficiency in the chief as well as the best of our sports, cannot be overestimated. The Parsi fraternity is the most intelligent, as well as the most loyal of the races scattered over our Indian possessions . . . Their visit to England last summer was avowedly undertaken with an educational object. Their aim was chiefly to improve their cricket. (Patel 1892: 8 f.)[6]

Both of these sources make the assumptions that the Parsis have a special affinity for cricket and for the British value-system it represents (e.g. 'manliness', 'noble') and that the aim of the tour was the 'solidity of the Empire'. The understanding was that they were learning about being British, not just about cricket.

In the middle of the nineteenth century one can see the early signs of what might be described as a prototype Zoroastrian community in Britain. Parsis came as individuals for legal, medical, or technical education, for trade and simply for travel, as well as coming with their families. Even Parsis who stressed their intercommunal concerns, such as Naoroji, seem to have sought fellow Parsis as business partners. Those who came must have been conscious of this potential for a community because in 1861 the Religious Society of Zoroastrians was formed (see Ch. 4). The records suggest that those who came tended to keep in contact with one another rather than disperse (though, of course, it may be that records survive only of those who contacted co-religionists) and that Dadabhoy Naoroji and the Cama family were the two focal points for the attention of travellers in the mid-nineteenth century. Travel to Britain could be an important factor in career or business development and often gave status to the traveller back in India. Those who came were mostly members of the leading families, or they became leading families on their return: the Jijibhoys, Readymoneys, Banajis, Pandays, Shroffs, and Collahs, but perhaps most of all the Camas and the Wadias.

It would be a mistake to assume that it was only the liberals who travelled west. They did, naturally represent the majority,

---

[6] There was a second tour in 1888 with slightly better results on the field: played 31, won 8, lost 11, drawn 12 (Patel 1892: 15). There is a remarkable account of Parsis and cricket written by C. A. Kincaid, a judge in the Indian Civil Service, who argued that the only explanation for the Parsi aptitude for cricket, and for the preservation of their identity in India, must be that they, like the British, had derived their qualities from the Greeks. In the Parsi case he explains this as a result of Alexander the Great's invasion (quite how Greek qualities link to cricket, or how the British inherited Greek traits he does not explain!). The article, written in the Feb. 1905 issue of *East and West*, was reproduced in its entirety in The *Parsi*, Mar. 1905, with the only comment from the editor being that he attributed the Greek influence to the earlier Achaemenid period, not as late as Alexander.

because the liberals tended to be the western educated and westernized individuals. Obvious examples are Dadabhoy Naoroji, Cursetji Maneckji Shroff and Pherozeshah Mehta. But some of the Parsi travellers kept themselves at a cultural distance from their British environment. The earliest travellers, for example the Wadias discussed below, brought their own servants with them to prepare their food so that they would not have to break the purity laws by interdining. Even those who stayed did not necessarily become westernized. The obvious example is M. H. Cama, who was central to the formation of the Zoroastrian Society and its president until Naoroji succeeded him in 1864. He conducted a lengthy literary campaign against his reformist brother, K. R. Cama. Though he was generous in his charitable donations to British causes, such as University College London and the Royal Naval Life–boat Institution, in his religious life he did not wish to depart from his cherished tradition. Similar in some ways was Bai Bhikhaji Cama. Despite her travels, not only throughout Britain but also in America, Japan, and China, in the words of her obituary, she 'lived a simple and native life' (*PP* III. 346 for 13 October 1890). The point is that it was not just the reformers and the non-religious Parsis who travelled to Britain. Travellers also came who held traditional beliefs and adhered to customs and practices of Zoroastrianism. They did not all leave their religion behind in India.

(b) *Nineteenth Century Parsi Travellers' Diaries*

Various Zoroastrian travellers produced accounts of their visits and impressions of Britain.[7] These were often explicitly addressed, as the Wadias put it, to the authors' 'fellow countrymen', but most of them (Malabari's later edition is the exception) were published in London and for private circulation. It is reasonable to assume that the books may have affected the perceptions of the authors' circles of friends, who were the people most likely to be considering travelling themselves, but would probably not have had any influence on the poor of the

---

[7] I wish to record my thanks to Rashna Writer and Ruby Cooper for help in obtaining some of this material at a time when I was unable to travel to the libraries.

community in Gujarat. Perhaps their main value is as first-hand accounts of Parsi travellers' perceptions of Britain.

The earliest account was by Ardeshir Cursetjee Wadia, published in 1840. His visit, noted above, lasted for a little over twelve months (1839–40). His account is essentially a diary of activities with relatively little comment. Although the bulk of his time was spent in making industrial and business contacts (mostly in London, but also in Manchester and, to a lesser extent, Liverpool) he enjoyed an active social life. But he was not overwhelmed by his experiences in Britain. He wrote of his first formal ball: 'I certainly was much gratified with the evening's entertainment; but it was similar to our Bombay balls' (p. 32).

The second account to be written was by Wadia's two cousins, Jehangir and Hirjeebhoy Wadia. They, too, came to study engineering in general and shipbuilding in particular. Their stay was longer—two and a half years—so that they had an even greater range of experiences to relate. Theirs is not a simple diary, but a very readable account of their impressions which displays a nice sense of humour.

The other early travellers are, perhaps, less interesting but they are worth noting nevertheless. Jehangir H. Kothari travelled to Britain in 1883–4 and then journeyed on around Europe and indeed the world, staying in America, China, and Japan. He records little more than what he did, with relatively few observations. A later traveller was B. M. Malabari. He came to study business but is best known as a leading social reformer in India. He arrived in Britain on 17 April 1890. His account is full of observations and reflections on Britain and the British, not always complimentary (for example on the unwillingness of the English to learn languages!).

The initial impression of all travellers appears to have been of the speed, bustle, and crowding in Britain. Kothari commented on London:

Well may they call it great and busy. The continual and most extraordinary bustle and traffic is quite sufficient to bewilder the ordinary stranger; on the footwalks the business people seem to rush along as if for a race; carts, drays, omnibuses and crowds of other vehicles, completely fill the street. It is there that you see that time is money.   (Kothari 1889: 14)

The Wadia brothers also comment:

From the immense number of people, and vehicles of every description, that we saw hurrying along apparently in great haste, and from the increasing noise, we were apprehensive that some public commotion had taken place . . . Every street down which we looked, appeared to be pouring out countless multitudes to swell the throng . . . But we were afterwards informed that this constant tide of human beings was to be witnessed every day for twelve or fourteen hours. (J. N. and H. M. Wadia 1841: 29)

Similarly, they were impressed by the great movement of shipping:

We were greatly surprised to see the amazing number of ships going out and pouring into the Thames, and steamers every now and then running backwards and forwards; we cannot convey to our countrymen any idea of the immense number of vessels . . . colliers, timber ships, merchantmen, steamers, and many other crafts, from all parts of the world, hastening as it were, to seek refuge in a river, which is but a stream compared to the Ganges and the Indus . . . we thought it a great wonder that such a small and insignificant a speck as England appears on the map of the world, can thus attract so many nations of the world to her. (p. 24)

A. C. Wadia commented on how busy things were, but he also drew attention to the dirt around him:

The scene was to me very extraordinary. I had never before witnessed so dense a fog; and the streets and shops were lighted with gas, although it was noon-day . . . Another nuisance of London is the dirty state of the roads compared with Bombay. (A. C. Wadia 1840: 26, 65)

Malabari was struck by the contrast of rich and poor in Britain, and wrote feelingly about the sad condition of the latter:

Poor as India is, I thank God she knows not much of the poverty to which parts of Great Britain have been accustomed—the East end of London, for instance, parts of Glasgow, and other congested centres of life. Men and women living in a chronic state of emaciation, till they can hardly be recognised as human; picking up as food, what even animals will turn away from; sleeping fifty, sixty, eighty of them together of all ages and both sexes, in a hole that could not hold ten with decency; swearing, fighting, trampling on one another; filling the room with foul confusion and fouler air. This is not a picture of occasional misery; in some places it represents the every-day life of the victims of misfortune. (Malabari 1893: 85)

While the crowds, dirt, and poverty thus left some travellers with strong negative impressions of Britain, what impressed all was the technology. Malabari commented on this in British-ruled Aden: 'At every turn, we saw some trophy of the Englishman's practical genius—roads, drives, tunnels and tasks' (1893: 17). The Wadia brothers in particular were impressed with all forms of technology—with steam power for example:

What is there in England that cannot be done by steam? Carriages fly upon iron rail roads heated by coal, wood is sawn by steam, iron is hammered into anchors, and rolled into plates, bars, and wire by steam.

The very fires to get up all these powerful machines are blown up by steam, water is pumped by steam, butter is churned by steam, books are printed by steam, money is coined by steam, ships heedless of wind and tide, navigate the seas by steam, guns are fired by steam, and every article of clothing from head to foot is made by steam. (J. N. and H. M. Wadia 1841: 134 f.)

The railway tunnel under Liverpool was another scientific development which inspired them:

Our countrymen will be astonished when we tell them, that over the tunnel stands a portion of the town of Liverpool, and it seems very extraordinary and curious to imagine our travelling under-ground, while over our heads are moving about horses and men, and in fact every transaction carried on. Here then, again, is a remarkable proof of our frequent assertion that the English are a most wonderful people. (p. 419)

The brothers were convinced they knew the basis of British power:

What has been the principal means of her [Britain] doing this? Why, by knowledge or science put into practice, because knowledge is power; and it is by the power of knowledge alone, and not by the power of arms, that she has so many means of attracting the world to her, and extending the spread of her manufactures. (25)

If technological knowledge was the basis of British power in the eyes of the travellers, then it was British society and above all royalty which fascinated them. Each of the early travellers went to great lengths to see, or be seen by, royalty (A. C. Wadia 1840: 50; Kothari 1889: 17) but it was the Wadia brothers who commented most. One day they took up a position where the Queen was known to walk. She noticed their traditional dress and sent a messenger seeking their names and asking which country they came from. On receipt of their card she 'did us the honour upon reaching the end of the terrace again to look upon us, and what to her was the novelty, our costume'. They were eloquent in their admiration of her regal qualities (pp. 234 f. and 102).

The magnificence associated with royalty and the theatre was a common theme in much of the literature. But that does not mean that the travellers were uncritical of all they saw. Racial prejudice was commented on by the Wadia brothers in 1841.

We would inform our countrymen that the majority of the lower orders in England are very rude in their manners and behaviour towards strangers, whom they do not like to see in their own country.   (p. 109)

There were also several complaints against Londons cab drivers; so Wadia in 1840:

The drivers of the cabs and other public vehicles, are an insolent and imposing set of men, who take ever advantage, especially of foreigners. (A. C. Wadia 1840: 65 see also Malabari 1893: 152)

The theme of racial prejudice was not taken up again by Parsi travellers until D. F. Karaka in the 1930s. He was the son of the Parsi historian, and he was the first Indian to be elected, in 1935, President of the Union at Oxford. He wrote two books of reflections on the British character and his own experiences (1935 and 1938). One of his major themes is that despite India's greater history and longer contribution to civilization, it is treated by the British as barbaric. He believed that British politicians, Churchill in particular, displayed this attitude:

The only sensible thing to do with barbarians when they get out of control is to shoot the louts. This expressed somewhat crudely, is the keynote of Churchillism. Though never officially defined, Churchillism is universally understood.   (Karaka 1935: 89).

He appears to have had mixed experiences at Oxford. On being elected president of the Union he writes: 'It was as if I had crashed into the stronghold of a bigoted tradition' (1938: 41). He felt that he had achieved something 'for my people'.

> But the day for me was spoilt by a paragraph in a leading London paper which suggested somewhat ungraciously, that now that an Indian had been made President of the Union, the office was no longer what it was. I have never forgotten that nor forgiven the man who wrote it . . . But Oxford itself treated me well. (1938: 42)

Karaka had no doubts that the cause of the prejudice he faced was colour, a theme which recurs frequently in his writings.

There was no single Parsi attitude to the British among the early travellers. Several writers assert that British officials were helpful towards Indians in their careers. Thus A. C. Wadia (1840: 57) on hearing of his appointment as chief engineer and inspector of machinery at Bombay, commented:

> I felt very grateful to the Hon. Company; not only as regards myself, for this distinguished proof of their confidence, but also on behalf of my countrymen, as it affords important evidence that the Hon. Court are willing, in every way, to promote the interests of the natives in India, by appointing them, as well as Europeans, to offices of responsibility, in all cases where applicants are known to possess the requisite capabilities.

His cousins expressed a similar point of view:

> we have received from the Honourable Court of Directors, individually and collectively, uniform encouragement, kindness and facility, towards accomplishing our object, and we can assert that there is every disposition to encourage native talent and genius – to give our countrymen situations of honour and trust, and to promote in every way the welfare of the natives. (J. N. and H. M. Wadia 1841: 356)

But not all Parsi visitors to Britain had the same opinion. Naoroji Fardunji, in a paper to the Bombay Association (1853) and to the National Indian Association in London (1874), stressed that 'during my long residence in England I have been deeply impressed with the ignorance that prevails in this country regarding the condition of India' (1874: 3) and said that he wanted to remove this 'apathy'. He then gave a vigorous denunciation of the British rulers who treated Indians as:

a conquered and inferior race... This feeling of superiority and race antagonism, which pervades all classes of Europeans in India, is the chief cause of a great and growing evil. [Indians] are often treated with incivility, harshness and even contempt and personal violence. They are frequently stigmatised as niggers, a nation of liars, perjurers, forgers, devoid of gratitude, trust and good nature... On many occasions the subject race is treated as if they were rude barbarians and inhuman savages... A considerable number of European officers and others belonging to the dominant race are often so reckless in their demeanour in the interior of the country that they have no hesitation in shooting, killing, assaulting and ill treating the Natives, and committing gross outrages... I will quote a few out of a large number of acts of violence resulting in murder and manslaughter. The evil is greatly aggravated in consequence of the offenders being allowed to escape scot-free without any punishment, and in several cases, with inadequate punishment. The code of criminal procedure applicable to the ruling race is different from that to which the Natives are subject... British born subjects have peculiar rights and privileges which often enable them to enjoy immunity from conviction and punishment. (Fardunji 1874: 4–5)

In addition to quoting examples of injustice, Fardunji refers to the opinion of the Advocate-General for India, Sir C. E. Trevelyan, that one of the problems is that the right 'class' of Englishman is not being sent out. He then draws a contrast between his experiences of the British in India and of the British in Britain:

In common with myself those of my countrymen, who come over to this country and mix freely with Englishmen of every grade, are struck with the marked contrast which they observe between the personal demeanour of the British in India and the generality of the people of the United Kingdom. The difference is so great that it is difficult to account for it, except by the fact that the Englishman during his sojourn in India considers himself a superior being belonging to the ruling race, moves in his own proud and limited circle, assumes high airs, lords over the natives of India, whom he treats as an inferior and abject race, and is totally emancipated from all the salutary restraints which are imposed upon him by the usages of the excellent and highly refined society and the influence of public opinion which prevail in this land of freedom and centre of civilization. (1874: 18)

Fardunji was an active reformer in Bombay (Natesan 1930: ch. 3) and he can be assumed to have made his strong views heard there on numerous occasions and not just in his Bombay Association lecture. His impression that the British behaved differently, and more justly, in Britain than they did in India merits comment. Whether this was true it is difficult to say from this distance in time, but a number of older Parsis have suggested to me that when an Englishman rounded the Cape his personality changed. It is possible that the Wadias' experience was not unrepresentative and that the British in Britain behaved differently on the rare occasions in the nineteenth century when they met Indians, and moreover Indians who were leaders in their own industries. But the government's deliberate exclusion of Indians from the Civil Service, together with remarks elsewhere by the Wadias and Malabari, suggest that racial prejudice was faced by nineteenth century Zoroastrian visitors, as Karaka found in the 1930s, and as Zoroastrians in the 1980s and 1990s have mentioned (see Ch. 6).

There were other things in Britain which left them unimpressed. British hobbies seemed strange to the Wadia brothers. They could not understand the English love of gardening and why 'gentlemen should dig the ground with their own hands, and in fact go through all the duties of a gardener merely to pass away their time' (1841: 88). Nor could they see why people enjoyed ballet, commenting after a visit to the theatre that the famous ballerina (Taglioni) was paid highly 'to stand for a long time like a goose upon one leg . . . Had we not seen instances that convinced us the English were clever people, we should have thought them very foolish indeed thus to pay a dancing puppet.' (1841: 102–3). They also questioned the integrity of the press, noting how a newspaper would change its position on an issue, and they regretted that 'the public mind should be excited daily with strong and inflammatory language'. They wished that the editors would 'only write what they *really do think to be right*' (1841: 366, original italics). London did not seem to several of the visitors to be an attractive place, especially in comparison with Paris (A. C. Wadia 1840: 67; Kothari 1889: 21 f.). Malabari found several features of British conduct not to his liking, commenting that marriage was going out of fashion in Britain and that British friendship was as fickle as the weather and not reliable, unlike Asiatic friendship (1893: 66 f. and 119 f.). He attended a Christian church and describes the 'sing-song' responses: 'There seems to be a good deal of drawl in the reading, and a good deal of vocal gymnastics' (1893: 97). The Wadias were also alienated by the divisions within the Christian churches:

Some of them, it is to be regretted, are used to find fault with each others' creed, and to point out the rocks and shoals upon which other sects have split, instead of looking out for the whirlpools into which they are themselves rapidly gliding. Oh, we thought, would that religion in England was not taken up as a trade! Would that charity and brotherly love were preached and acted upon, instead of finding faults with their fellow brethren, and exciting each other to bitter religious hatred, which has for centuries past thrown discord among men and severed the dearest ties of friendship and love in society. (J. N. and H. M. Wadia 1841: 209)

These passages illustrate how mistaken is the simplistic but common, picture of the Parsis as having unquestioning affection for the British establishment. Perhaps the passage which best illustrates the critical, but here humorously critical, views of British society is the Wadias' account of Parliament. First they sought to explain to their countrymen the composition of the House of Lords. After mentioning the great landowners and the bishops they continue:

After sometime admirals of the navy and commanders of the army were made noblemen and sent to the House of Peers, sometimes persons have been made noblemen for lending their lives to the King, sometimes if a person has been very troublesome in the House of Commons and been constantly asking for information not pleasant for the Government to give, he has been made a nobleman; if a minister wanted votes upon a particular measure which he was anxious to carry, a peerage has been conferred upon a person to abstain from voting against the question; and if a man who held a little place in the ministry was found to be of no use, and would not resign his situation, he was made a nobleman and sent to the House of Peers. (1841: 171)

They commented on the length of speeches, even though the outcome of the vote was known in advance and therefore the whole procedure was a waste of time . But it was the House of Commons which impressed them least:

. . . and yet upon the whole we were disappointed. We had expected to have seen the representatives of all the wealth, all the talent, all the resources of the country, better dressed and a different looking set of men. We saw them with their hats upon their heads for the last two or three hours sleeping in all directions, and only opening their eyes now and then, when a cheer louder than common struck upon their ears ... (1841: 182 f.)

In so far as we can judge from these published travellers' accounts, what seemed to have impressed the early Parsi arrivals was that London was a busy international centre of knowledge, industry, and commerce. Britain was a technologically advanced and powerful country. They loved the splendour of royalty and theatre. But their impressions were not all positive. They were struck by the dirt and poverty of the cities. The British, they thought, were clever people, some of whom were willing to help Indians, though others displayed ignorant and prejudiced attitudes. Integrity, they felt, could not always be relied on with regard to newspapers and peerages, marriage and friendship. They were not impressed with the procedure or all the persons in Parliament, nor with Christianity as they experienced it in society.

(c) *Zoroastrian Literature for the British*

This section cannot be concerned with all the literature produced by Parsis for the British, because the Bombay community generated a considerable body of material intended to influence the British in India.[8] The subject here is the material produced by Parsis in Britain specifically for the native British reader. Books on Zoroastrianism were published by outsiders, but they are not relevant to the specific question asked here: what image did the (Parsi) Zoroastrians seek to present of themselves to the white community?

There are seven main publications in this category: Framjee 1858; Naoroji 1862 and 1908; Karaka 1884; Kapadia 1905; A. S. N. Wadia 1912; and Masani 1938. They are quite different

---

[8] This is not the place for an extensive reference, but one indication is given by Morris 1984, who shows how the English-language newspapers founded by Parsis, or those in which they had a significant influence, were used by them to condition the British perceptions of the community in India.

types of publications despite their common aim. Framjee and Karaka are, in fact, the same author. The 1884 work is an expanded version of his earlier one, though with some differences other than expansion. Karaka was an active politician. He was the first Indian chairman of the Bombay Municipality in 1875; a member of the Bombay Legislative Council, and a founder member of the Bombay Presidency Association. He resigned from the last in 1886 (one year after its inception) because he feared that it was in danger of alienating the British by campaigning in the British elections for the Liberals (a step encouraged by Naoroji). He was, therefore, an 'establishment man'. His pro-British attitude is clear in his books; indeed the second is dedicated to the Prince of Wales. The first book was written while he was living in Britain, the second after further visits. Kapadia was not a politician but a lawyer and lecturer at University College London. He was active among British Zoroastrians, especially among the students, as will be seen in the next chapter, and he was concerned to increase knowledge in the West about Asian religion and culture. He was, with L. Cranmer-Byng, editor of the Wisdom of the East series published by John Murray in London. Whereas Karaka's books are concerned with Parsi secular life as much as religion, Kapadia's much smaller book is concerned simply with religion. Little is known of Ardasir N. Wadia. He was a professor of English and History at Bombay's prestigious Elphinstone College in Bombay University and was interested in wider Indian social concerns, as evidenced by his 1913 book (also published in London) *Reflections on the Problems of India*. His political views are somewhat extreme. He opposed education for all because, he argued, not all were able to benefit from it and uneducated people are necessary for menial tasks. Caste, he considered, formalized genetic differences between people and such a social structure he regarded as essential. He was vigorously opposed to calls for independence from Naoroji and others, since he thought that British rule, though not perfect, was better than any other in history (1913: ch. 4). The Parsis, he argued, were close to the British but distanced from Hindus and Muslims (1913: 118). His book on Zoroastrianism, therefore, presents his religion to the educated people of a power with which he was in sympathy, unlike other Asian groups. Little comment is necessary on Dadabhoy Naoroji at this point, as he is discussed elsewhere in this book. At the time of giving his lecture in Liverpool he had held a professorship of mathematics in Bombay, was professor of Gujarati in London, had ventured into business, but had barely started his political career. Sir Rustam Masani was a prolific writer of different types of literature: novels, historical studies of Bombay, the life of Naoroji; he edited various newspapers (e.g. *Indian Spectator*, a paper devoted to presenting Indian political views to the British and started by Naoroji); he was the first Indian to become Bombay's Municipal Commissioner (1922); he held various senior posts in the banking world and finally became Vice-Chancellor of Bombay University. But he retained a lively interest in his community throughout (Karanjia 1970). The common feature of all these authors is their high level of western education; they were all involved in western politics either in Britain or in Bombay and were conscious of the need to project a good community image. Whatever the motives behind the books, it seems unlikely that they were in fact widely read by the British public; nevertheless, they show the features of their religion and community which some literary Parsis tried to project to the British.

Naturally these educated authors made substantial use of western academics and writers (Framjee 1858: 51; A. S. N. Wadia 1912: 21, 58, and Ch. 2; Masani 1938: 93, 99). Naoroji is an exception which is surprising because his political speeches, discussed below, were characterized by extensive collections of British opinions. As his Liverpool paper was given in 1862 it predates much of the western scholarship, but unlike Framjee before him, he does not refer even to the western travellers' accounts. Despite his involvement in community affairs, both in Bombay and London, it seems likely that his own explanation is correct: that he did not know a great deal about the study of Zoroastrianism. This impression is reinforced by the fact that his 1908 paper still displays little knowledge of western scholarship on the subject.

The writers are concerned to stress Zoroastrian monotheism. This is evident in Framjee (1858: 51) coming as it does only fifteen years after Wilson's attack (p. 250), and in the first years of K. R. Cama's religious education programme. Framjee argues that Ahriman should be understood in an allegorical sense only

(p. 255), a very early example of rationalist demythologizing. He stresses monotheism even more in his 1884 volumes (Karaka 1884: ch. 10). Naoroji's starting-point is the ignorance of Zoroastrian priests, but in his exposition of Avestan texts the theme to which he gives priority is monotheism (1862. 19). Almost all reject the label 'dualism'. The exception is Wadia (1912: ch. 2), who accepts the interpretations of dualism given by the English writer Laing in terms of the polarity that he maintained science had discovered at the heart of matter in the positive and negative forces of magnetism and electricity. Masani, who also uses Laing but in this instance on the 'sweet reasonableness' of Zoroastrian worship (1938: 93), rejects dualism as part of later 'corrupt' Zoroastrianism and not part of the abstract teaching of the prophet (pp. 49–103). Like Framjee eighty years earlier, Masani interprets the traditional mythology as allegory: 'Heaven is simply the best life or the region of best mental state, and hell the worst life or the region of the worst thought' (p. 111). The abstract interpretation of myth is clearly seen in accounts of the purity laws which are said to have symbolic significance and hygienic practicality (see e.g. Kapadia 1905: 33, and above on Dhalla and Modi). All of the writers are keen to deny the Muslim and missionary label of Zoroastrians as fire worshippers (Framjee 1858: 257; Naoroji 1862: 23; 1908; Karaka 1884: ch. 5; A. S. N. Wadia 1912: ch. 1; Masani 1938: ch. 7). Masani, for example, quotes (p. 80 without acknowledgement) Laing and Carnegie's demythologized account of the fire as the natural and sublime representation of Him who is Eternal Light (see above, p. 26). The common emphasis, therefore, of these writers is on Zoroastrianism as an abstract monotheism, that is, a religion worthy of respect in the modern West.

Some of the writers, notably Framjee and especially Naoroji, are vehement in their castigation of what they consider to be priestly ignorance. Thus Naoroji writes: 'Far from being the teachers of true doctrines and duties of their religion, the priests are generally the most bigoted and superstitious, and exercise much injurious influence over the women' (1862: 2). Partly he was reacting to the priests' inability to respond to Wilson's attacks; partly he was, as a westernized reformer, antagonistic towards the strict maintenance of the purity laws (hence his comments about the influence on women); and partly he may well have been reflecting the impact of Protestant influence on Parsi attitudes to priesthood. It is doubtful if Framjee and Naoroji would have been so contemptuous of priestly ritual concern had they experienced educational influences from the Roman Catholic tradition. These writers working in the West were concerned to present a mythologically sanitized religion, one free of the priestly 'superstitions' they thought unacceptable in Protestant Britain.

A strong theme of all who wrote for the British was the emphasis on positive links between Parsis and Britain: Karaka emphasizes not only loyalty (1884: ii. 272–95) and devotion to the monarchy (indeed, the last words of Karaka's two-volume book are 'God bless the Queen!') but he is also keen to emphasize any example he can of royal interest in the Parsi community (I. 325–27). They all stress what they perceive to be the common ethical values (Framjee 1858: 252; Naoroji 1862: 22 f.; 1908; Karaka 1884: ii, ch. 3; Kapadia 1905: 49; A. S. N. Wadia 1912: 170–80; Masani 1938: preface). Kapadia seeks to reinforce the parallels between the two religions by comparing the appearance of Zoroaster at court with the appearance of St Augustine at the court of King Ethelbert (p. 18). But perhaps his most rousing call is for British people to follow the Zoroastrian ethical code, for:

Then the nation will be rewarded by the sight of the sons of the soil, marching in distant climes for the glory and honour of the British flag, as soldiers of God and King, and pioneers of the ever-extending British Empire, as did their heroic brethren in Persia of old under the victorious flag of illustrious Gao [a legendary hero]. (p. 51)

In short, these (mostly) politically active writers, all western-educated and westernized, stressed Zoroastrian monotheism and the abstract nature of the religion, particularly with regard to worship before the fire, mythology, and the purity laws. They were concerned to present their religion as in accord with modern science and sentiments. In particular they stressed that their value–system meant that they had fundamental accords with the British which marked them out from the other religions of India. They were, therefore, deeply loyal subjects. Naoroji emphasizes this point least of all, which is odd since it formed an important element of his political message. Presumably he did not relate it to religious issues. This one theme apart, the conclusion for his 1862 paper sums up how Parsis presented their religion to the British:

A handful of persecuted exiles living in a foreign land, surrounded for 1200 years by idolatry, and persecuted at times by religious fanaticism, it is rather a matter of surprise, as with the Jews, that the Parsees have preserved their national type and character, and their original worship. Though they have not altogether escaped contamination, and have adopted many superstitious ceremonies and notions of the Hindoos, they have always recoiled from degenerating to the worship of idols, and have tenaciously clung to the idea that they were worshippers of the invisible Hormuzd. Believing in the existence of Angels and their delegated powers to assist and benefit man, the Parsee centres his prayers and his hopes above all, on Hormuzd, the Lord of the Spirits; his whole morality is comprised in three words—pure thoughts, pure words, and pure deeds . . . (p. 28)

(d) *Conclusion*

British Zoroastrians, specifically the Parsis, are conscious of a long pioneering history in Britain. Most came to learn, either formally or informally, and some came for business. Although the majority of early settlers were single men, a number came to stay with their wives and families. It was usually the educated, westernized individuals who came, but it must not be assumed that they all left their religion behind in India. The Wadias, for example, were industrial pioneers in India with their innovative use of western technology, but they still brought their servants to prepare their food and carefully avoided interdining even in the course of a two-year stay. What the Parsi travellers enjoyed were the features of British society which were famed in India—industry and pageantry. What they liked less were the harsh realities of social and religious life.

Typically the Parsis considered that they were liked and respected by the British whom they encountered—the lower orders apart that is. They believed they were recognized as distinctive by the British, for they were conscious of the honours they were given (three baronetcies and sixty-three knighthoods; Katrak 1958: app. K); they were the first Indians to be formally presented at court (A. S. N. Wadia 1840).[9] They were also very

---

[9] The first Indian woman to be presented at court was a Parsi, Shirinbai M. Cursetjee, 20 June 1865 (*PP* II. 157). The *Parsi Prakash* lists eight more presentations at court in the 19th c.

proud of being the first Indians to be elected to membership and office in western societies and bodies. For example, Maneckji Cursetji Shroff was elected to the Royal Asiatic Society in 1835, even though the Society's Bombay branch had rejected him because he was a 'native' (*PP* I. 277[10]). Six years later he was refused membership of the Masonic lodge in Bombay, again because he was a 'native', but in 1842 he was admitted to the Order in Paris. On his return to Bombay he was again refused membership of the lodge 'Perseverance' (No. 546) and as a result he was active in establishing a lodge in 1843 with the specific intention opening it to 'natives' (A. S. N. Wadia 1912: ch. 1). Parsis are proud of two aspects of this sequence of events: (*a*) that a Parsi was the first Indian Mason, and (*b*) that he showed such determination in establishing the first 'native' lodge. It again illustrates the difference Parsis found between the British in India and in Britain, for Cursetjee was admitted to the Royal Asiatic Society in London but not Bombay, and he was admitted to the Masonic Order not in India but in Europe (practical concerns led to this taking place in Paris rather than London).

Parsis also considered that their achievements were being publicized nationally for there were numerous instances of biographical sketches and photographs of Parsis in the British press, especially the quality magazines. The first to publish such material was the *Illustrated London News* in 1849 (Cursetji R. Wadia on 6 January and Jijibhoy Dadabhoy on 4 August). The *Parsi Prakash* lists nineteen such articles during the nineteenth century; most were in the *ILN*, but they also appeared in the *Graphic* and the *Daily Telegraph*.[11] The Parsis, therefore, had

[10] Four more Parsis joined in the 1830s: B. H. Wadia, 1836 (*PP* I. 294); A. C. Wadia, A. H. Wadia, and Cursetji Jijibhoy in 1837 (*PP* I. 300).

[11] *ILN*, 6 Jan. 1849, C. R. Wadia (*PP* I. 911); *ILN*, 4 Aug. 1849, Jijibhoy Dadabhoy (*PP* I. 911); *ILN*, 6 Dec. 1856, Sir Jamesetji Jijibhoy (*PP* I. 721); *ILN*, 20 Aug. 1859, Sir Cursetji Jijibhoy (*PP* I. 800); *ILN*, 28 Feb. 1863, Dosabhoy Sorabji Munchi (*PP* II. 57); *ILN*, 16 Nov. 1867, Maneckji Cursetji Shroff (*PP* II. 234); *Graphic*, 10 Oct. 1873, Sir C. J. Readymoney (*PP* II. 459); *ILN*, 12 Apr. 1887, Sir D. M. Petit (*PP* III. 217); *Graphic*, 25 June 1887, Sir D. M. Petit (*PP* III. 223) see also 23 Apr. 1891 — (*PP* III. 368)); *Daily Telegraph*, 20 May 1893, M. C. Murzban (*PP* III. 426) *Daily Telegraph*, 17 Aug. 1893, P. M. Mehta (*PP* II. 437); *ILN*, 3 Feb. 1894, M. C. S. Langda (better known in Parsi circles under the pseudonym 'Mansukh') (*PP* III. 470); The *Commerce*, 28 Feb. 1894, C. D. Kharas (*PP* III. 473); *St James' Budget [Gazette?]* 6 Feb. and 2 May 1895, M. M. Bhownagree and C. D. Adenwala (*PP* III. 518 and 530); *Vanity Fair*, 19 Nov. 1897, M. M. Bhownagree (*PP* III. 659); *Black and White*, 17 Nov. 1898, Dastur Dr J. M.

reason to believe that the British recognized them as worthy of public respect. In order to reinforce that image they produced publications which gave an account of their tradition which would be likely to commend them to the British. From the early days down to the Second World War, they also saw Britain, or some of its poor, as in need of their charitable benefactions. In addition to the earlier examples cited mention should also be made of the substantial sums of money, and number of men, given to the British cause in the First World War (sixty-one lost their lives). Most of the support went to the Medical Corps (*PP* V. 17–60). In the Second World War the Parsis gave in excess of seven million pounds and more than twenty men died.[12] So there is a legitimate sense of Parsis having given not only their wealth to Britain, but also their lives.

Some Indianized Parsis and a few outsiders, speak of the Parsis in British India as craven in their attitudes to the British. This is not wholly just. The travellers and the community back in India considered that the respect was mutual and that the Parsis had much to be proud of. Some of the travellers gave critical assessments of Britain, be it of the poverty or Parliament. In the years before Independence several Parsis were active in the Congress party and were opposed to British policy, for example Khurshid Dadabhoy, granddaughter of Dadabhoy Naoroji; Dr M. D. Gilder, who was Gandhi's physician; Minoo Masani, who became a prominent politician after Independence; and Feroze Gandhi, who married Indira Nehru. All spent some time in Britain.[13] Naoroji, Bhownagree, and Saklatvala were each critical in Parliament of aspects of British policy (see Ch. 5). Had the Parsis been as craven as sometimes suggested, then there

Jamaspasana (*PP* III. 717); The *Sketch,* and The *Queen,* 20 Oct. 1899, Mrs R. J. Tata (*PP* III. 765); The *Graphic,* 7 Jul. 1900, C. D. Adenwala i.e. the Cowasji Dinshaw discussed on p. 63 above (*PP* III. 796); *Daily Chronicle,* 10 Jun. 1902, Sir Jamsetji Jijibhoy (*PP* IV. 82); *Tatler,* 14 Oct. 1902, K. M. Baliwala also on that date in the *Graphic* and *ILN,* N. M. Wadia and B. D. Petit (*PP* IV. 92). The list consists mostly of individuals who had visited Britain, but not exclusively so. The first Sir Jamsetji Jijibhoy did not come, nor is Mansukh particularly associated with Britain. The Petit family visited Britain, but is again not associated with the UK. Dastur Jamaspasana is noted for his scholarly work, for which he was awarded an honorary doctorate by Oxford University. He is the ancestor of Dastur JamaspAsa to whom this book is dedicated.

[12] For the Second World War the *Parsi Prakash* gives details annually instead of together. The reports are in VII. 510–27; VIII. 22, 53 f., 95, 138, 170, 224.

[13] See *PP* VIII. 9, 51, 72 and VIII. 47. For Masani, see his biography, Karanjia 1970.

would have been far more anti-Parsi agitation in India than there was. (The only example was in 1921 when the Parsis stood out in Bombay in their support for the politically unpopular visit of the Prince of Wales (*PP* VI. 36 ff.)). There were, however, sections of the Parsi community which were uncritical in their attitude to Britain. Karaka and A. S. N. Wadia, quoted above, are two examples. An extreme example is the editor of the Ladies' column in the Bombay magazine, the *Parsi*. In June 1905 she wrote:

> I do not suppose that I need to labour to assure you that we are a white race, and that the dark skin of a portion of our community is foreign to us, and is the result of our prolonged stay in this country, and of a close intercourse with the natives . . . socially, politically in every way, we *must* suffer if we cease to be a fair race.

In the August issue she commented:

> The closer union of the Europeans and Parsis is the finest thing that can happen to our race. It will mean the *lifting up* of a people who are lying *low*, though possessing all the qualities of a European race. It will make our men more of 'men' than they are at present and will make our women better women. The complete Europeanization of the Parsis is now a mere matter of time . . . Imagine 100 well-to-do Parsi families settled down in England and bringing up their children in English schools and colleges! What a glorious day that would be for the race! (pp. 324 f.)

Obviously this editor did not represent the views of all the Parsis who came to Britain before the Second World War. But she was giving, in extreme form, something of the attitude with which many came: they were different from other Indian religions and coloured races, they saw themselves as being closer to the British, and thought that the British shared that opinion (as they had indicated in India—see Hinnells 1978*a*; Firby 1988) and that the settlement in Britain could be a positive force for good in the history of Zoroastrianism.

Perhaps the seven books written for the British on Zoroastrianism are more representative of Zoroastrian attitudes than the *Parsi*'s lady editor. They are obviously a limited corpus and written by a particular type of person, who was not only western-educated but usually politically active as well. It is noticeable that none of the opponents of British rule produced a book on

Zoroastrianism, presumably because they considered themselves primarily Indians.[14] The link between political allegiances and religious commitment is a theme in Parsi history worthy of greater study (Langstaff 1983). The value of these books is that they may be presumed to represent the kind of image which London Zoroastrians sought to give to their British contacts in personal meetings as well as in formal publications. That image was of a religion which shared western values in theology, ethics, and worship, one which marked the Zoroastrians as different from all other communities and moreover inspired loyalty to the Empire of these like-minded people. Precisely how such Zoroastrians fared in western society is the subject of the following chapters.

[14] The writers on the occult were objecting to western secular reasoning being applied to religion, not necessarily to western political rule. Under Annie Besant the two merged in the Theosophical Society, but Zoroastrian occult movements have not linked repudiation of western scholarship and rejection of British rule.

4

A Century of Zoroastrian Associations in Britain (1860s–1960s)

(a) *The Founding of the London Association*

The Zoroastrian Association was the first Asian religious association founded in Britain, and because it has kept many of its records it provides a unique opportunity to study the developments in the trajectory of settlement over a long period.[1] It is remarkable how many records have been preserved. But they are not complete. For some years there are Annual General Meeting records, for others correspondence files, for others there is only the copy-letter book. It is, therefore, not possible to write a connected history, but it is possible to give what is appropriate in this book—namely an account of episodes and problems which enable an understanding of how the community has evolved.

The oldest document relating to the Association's history is a letter dated 15 August 1861 from Muncherji Hormusji Cama, countersigned by Dadabhoy Naoroji, inviting Zoroastrians in Britain to attend a meeting to form an Association. Its historical significance justifies full quotation:

To Zoroastrians of England

Sirs,

Our people go to several countries for business. There each person gives according to his means for religious (charitable) purposes and

---

[1] Thanks are due to numerous people for making this chapter possible: to successive Association committees for allowing me access to the files and for generous practical help (and much coffee!); to Burjor Avari, Cyrus Mehta, Dr (Mrs) S. S. Kutar, Ervad Keki E. Kanga, Mrs Ruby Contractor for help with the Gujarati sources; to Rusi Dalal and Mr Mistry for clambering through the attics of Zoroastrian House for the papers; to Shahpur Captain for his help during his period of office; and to Malcolm Deboo while librarian at Zoroastrian House.

thus performs meritorious deeds. This enables them not only to perform good deeds but enables them to live in harmony with one another and be with one another in good times and bad.

Currently by the grace of God we are about 50—including students (who come here for higher studies) and our number is likely to increase year by year. For this reason it is essential to consider this matter urgently.

If you think my idea is good, we can then arrange to meet at some place, listen to each other's views and reach a satisfactory conclusion.

It is worth noting that this reference in 1861 to students coming 'for higher studies' dates the trend earlier than the figures quoted from the *Parsi Prakash* in the previous chapter. Cama chaired the meeting at his home on 22 September 1861. Fifteen people attended,[2] and copies of a draft constitution were posted to Zoroastrians resident in Manchester and Liverpool. A redrafting committee, including Naoroji, was formed at the next meeting on 13 November, when Cama was elected chairman and Naoroji a trustee. Donations were also collected to start the funds. The Association was actually called the Religious Funds of Zoroastrians of Europe. Six funds were established: to bury the dead; to help destitute Zoroastrians stranded in Europe; to purchase books about Zoroastrianism; to help 'scholars dealing with research in Zoroastrianism [and] to help intelligent and suitable Zoroastrians for research work in Zoroastrianism'; to establish a 'House of Prayer'; and finally to organize a general fund for miscellaneous expenditure.[3] The funds were seen as having a European perspective and were not simply for Zoroastrians in Britain. The charitable concern for the poor, the religious orientation of the group, and the emphasis on scholarly learning are typical Zoroastrian qualities, as is the formal administrative structure of the small group (comparable to the associations which were established in China and East Africa in the nineteenth century). Some details of the constitution illustrate precisely how business-like the proceedings were: funds were to be invested in British or Indian government stock and

---

[2] Those present were: A. L. Wadia; D. Naoroji; Dr B. Dorabji; E. Nusserwanji; J. Burjorji; A. U. Engineer; Dr M. B. Colah; R. K. Engineer; P. Pestonji; D. K. Ratnagar; B. S. Umrigar; B. M. Modi; F. B. Cama; N. C. Poachji; M. H. Cama.

[3] The details of the funds are taken from pp. 6–8 of the minute book. Gujarati was used until the AGM on 25 Sept. 1889 when English was adopted.

could only be sold with the general body's agreement; books were to be kept with the secretary until there was a house of prayer; accounts were to be rendered at an Annual General Meeting; any six donors could summon a Special General Meeting and a quorum of eight was required for any General Meeting. There was a restriction on voting and office-holders to 'any Zoroastrian living in the main centre city who has donated a minimum of £5 to one or more of the funds' (p. 11). That effectively excluded Zoroastrians in Manchester or Liverpool who had been circulated. References to Zoroastrians in those cities indicates that the community was more widespread than is recorded in the files.

Inevitably problems arose. The first was that reports circulated in Bombay (specifically in the Parsi paper, *Rast Goftar*, 3 November 1861) suggesting that the London Zoroastrians were planning to build a fully consecrated temple. The London committee reassured Bombay that this was not their plan, but the issue foreshadows debates in later years when Bombay Zoroastrians expressed concern at what they considered the questionable religious practices of the diaspora communities who, it was feared, were taking unauthorized steps. The problem was, and remains, who authorizes what in the Zoroastrian world?

A matter demanding early attention was the provision for funerals, since Zoroastrians could not be buried in a Christian cemetery. Agreement was reached on 28 September 1862[4]. The minute book records (p. 16) that there was unanimous approval for the proposal that 'the site selected by the Managing Committee in the grounds of London Necropolis Company at Woking be accepted'. The agreement, or indenture, was for 5,500 square yards of the Company's unconsecrated ground 'solely for the bodies of such deceased members of the said Society and such other persons of their religious persuasion as the said Society shall permit'.

Naoroji was elected chairman at the AGM in 1864 in succession to Cama who left Britain for India on 28 February of that

---

[4] The first recorded death of a Parsi in Britain was D. H. Hakim, 3 Nov. 1862 (*PP* II. 50). He joined Cama's firm that year from Singapore. There is no explanation of the cause of death, nor what happened to the body, nor whether the death was a factor in hastening plans for a funeral ground.

year (*PP* II. 101). The funds do not appear to have been very active. There are no records of social functions. The numbers were small and fluctuated. At the AGM on 1 September 1865 Naoroji Fardunji reported that the funds had incurred no expenditure because: 'Currently several merchants are not doing well and the number of Zoroastrians living in Europe has declined considerably.' The problem was the stock-market crash in Bombay following the share mania and many businessmen, including Parsis, lost their fortunes. In 1866 the AGM had to be postponed because it was not quorate and the constitution had to be amended to allow people to hold more than one office (there were not enough volunteers). Subscriptions were lowered and plans were made to involve more Zoroastrians. In 1890 an appeal was launched for donations from the Parsis who, it was anticipated, would be visiting the Paris exhibition in some numbers. Whether any of these ventures proved successful is not known. Clearly the Association was struggling to survive.

The AGM on 14 September 1891 was notable for two reasons. It was the first meeting attended by Muncherji Bhownagree who was to dominate the funds from 1909 to 1933. It was also the first time that the community faced a debate which would continue into the 1990s, namely the attendance of non-Zoroastrians at Zoroastrian funerals. Some Christians were present at the funeral of Mrs D. P. Cama. Three months later a member raised objections to their presence and from the chair Naoroji proposed that the related correspondence be discussed at the end of the meeting, 'and once for all it will be necessary to decide . . . whether any persons not Zoroastrians should be admitted in our chapel at the time of the funeral or not'. But the minutes record: 'This subject raised great discussion which for want of time was left undecided.' It was raised again at the AGM for 1892 (11 October) and by a majority it was decided 'that in future non-Zoroastrians may be freely admitted into the Chapel in the Parsee burial ground in Woking at the time of the funeral'. The difficulty of observing Zoroastrian purity laws away from the old country was already proving a problem which was to recur. A question for many was, and is, how can one exclude the majority British population among whom one lives, and with whom Parsis especially (and it is the Parsis who are most vocal in wanting to exclude non-Zoroastrians) have repeatedly, publicly, and forcefully expressed a strong sense of kinship, particularly if the British person is married to a Zoroastrian? For others, however, the problem is how the few living in the diaspora can jettison the powerful traditions of strict boundary-markers in the old country, which had undoubtedly been a factor in the preservation of the religion and the community for a millennium. In fact, most Zoroastrians are themselves emotionally and intellectually ambivalent over the issue and experience great anguish, especially about events affecting their family and friends. It would be simplistic to divide the community into two clear camps.

(b) *London and the Iranian Zoroastrians*

The London Zoroastrians sought, in collaboration with Indian Parsis, to ease conditions for their co-religionists in Iran through deputations and petitions (see Ch. 2, Sect. (*a*)). They were acting from a sense of being at the heart of an imperial power and, by implication, having greater political influence than, say, the Zoroastrians of Canton or Sind. The first deputation was in 1873 when four Parsis, including Dadabhoy Naoroji and Naoroji Fardunji, waited upon the Shah when he visited London. They had also solicited the help of Sir Henry Rawlinson (former ambassador to Tehran) and E. B. Eastwick MP. The Shah indicated that he would 'give this subject his best attention on his return to Persia', but when nothing happened the Parsis made further representations through the British embassy and some small relief was given (Karaka 1884: i. 75 f.). On a further visit in 1899 the Shah again received a deputation of Parsis while visiting Europe. The AGM report of 16 January 1901 refers to an address of welcome drawn up by Bhownagree and presented by Naoroji to the monarch at the Royal Palace Hotel in Ostend. They had been asked to approach the Shah by Bombay Parsis, notably Sir Dinshah Petit, who defrayed the cost of the illuminated and bound volume of the address, and by one of the leaders of the Iranian Zoroastrians, Ardeshir E. J. Reporter. It was not, therefore, simply that London Zoroastrians presumed that they held a useful political position; they were seen by both their Bombay and Iranian co-religionists to do so.

In addition to these personal deputations the London Zoroastrians also submitted various petitions to the Persian authorities. It is worth documenting them because of the implications for London Parsis' self-perception, as an indication of their attitudes to Iran, and because these actions have disappeared from the light of history, not having been published elsewhere. The meetings records at Zoroastrian House report a special gathering on 26 June 1907, when, at Bhownagree's instigation, a reception was given to the Persian ambassador to announce the new Shah's accession to the throne. Under the new Shah a parliament, the *Majlis*, was established and a Zoroastrian, the wealthy and influential banker Jamshid Bahman Jamshidian, became a member. Sixty-six Parsis gathered at the Criterion restaurant in London to present the address for the amelioration of the Iranian Zoroastrians, asking specifically:

that he may grant to our co-religionists, who are subject to his sovereignty, the same rights, privileges, and protection which His Majesty has evinced his desire to extend to the Persian nation under the constitution which has been recently inaugurated in his Empire.

We are deeply sensible of the assurances conveyed to us and the unquestionable proof already given by His Imperial majesty of the interest he and his government feel in the welfare of our co-religionists. The privilege of representation granted to them in the new Persian parliament and the nomination of Arbab Jamshid to a seat there has, as Your Excellency is doubtless aware, evoked sentiments of gratitude from all Parsees. We trust that this is an earnest of the genuine solicitude for the welfare of the Zoroastrian subjects entertained by the Persian Government and we beg humbly to represent through you to His Imperial Majesty that every measure of justice, of generous kindness, and above all assured protection of their lives and property will be gratefully repaid by their increasing loyalty and devotion to His Majesty's throne and august person.

At the AGM on 15 August 1907 the community renewed its thanks to the Shah and sent a congratulatory message to Jamshidian conveying their best wishes 'for his success in safeguarding the interests and promoting our welfare in that useful and responsible position'.

The meetings file for 13 October 1919 refers to another presentation of an address drawn up by Bhownagree and of a casket similar to the one presented in 1907. This was evidently appreciated by Zoroastrians in Iran, for on 17 May 1920 a letter of thanks was received from the Tehran *anjuman*. However, this occasion was not as momentous as that which triggered the next petition agreed unanimously at a meeting on 18 May 1926. The occasion was the coronation of the new Shah of the Pahlavi dynasty after the last Qajar had been deposed. The Association's letter books contain copies of correspondence between the secretary, Spitama Cama, and Bhownagree, who was then in India. The Association evidently wanted to cable the new Shah but in a letter to K. P. Kotwal, dated 21 April 1926, Bhownagree objected, saying: 'we are ignorant of the circumstances causing the succession'. In a letter of the same date Cama regretted Bhownagree's attitude and said that it would be 'a great mistake if Parsis here did not send an address to the Shah, who is reported to be well inclined to the Parsis. I believe his right hand man, guide, philosopher and friend is our Parsee Arbab Ardeshir.'[5] Cama repeated the arguments four days later in another letter to Bhownagree, saying that had he been at the discussion Bhownagree would have agreed with the rest of the Association, although they were 'staying their hand' until they had heard from him. He argued that:

the reasons for deposing the ex-Shah are known to all of us and he is rightly deposed, instead of looking after his country he has been living in Europe and squandering money. This Shah is expected to be very well intentioned to our community, this was told to me by Sir Hormusji Adenwalla when last in London, therefore if we sent him a letter of congratulation in the shape of an address it would please him and perhaps make him take a deeper interest in the Parsees.

Bhownagree eventually agreed and his name was at the head of the address:

RESOLVED that at this the first Meeting of the Committee of the Parsee Association of Europe, London, since the coronation of His Imperial

---

[5] Parsis of this period commonly used the term 'Parsi' to denote Iranian Zoroastrians; the correspondence does not concern Indian Zoroastrians living in Iran. It is worth noting, however, that some Iranian Zoroastrians did adopt the term 'Parsi' for themselves. In a letter dated 10 Apr. 1907 to Bhownagree, the leading Iranian Zoroastrian Kaykhusrow Shahrokh (Kermani) described himself as 'a pure Parsee from Kerman' and goes on to explain that the book he had written in Persian and was sending Bhownagree, was for Parsis in Persia. I am grateful to Malcolm Deboo for drawing my attention to this letter in the Zoroastrian House files.

Majesty Riza Shah Pahlavi as Shah-in-Shah of Persia the Committee beg leave to convey their congratulations upon his accession. It is their fervent prayer that he may reign long and prosperously over the country with which they have cherished ancestral associations and whose peoples include some thousands of their co-religionists. They rejoice in the many evidences of virility, justice and wise statesmanship which were afforded by His Majesty during the years of his Prime Ministership. They trace to this cause in large measure the restoration of good order and prosperity to the country, and in particular they beg to convey, with their felicitations, warm appreciation of the paternal interest His Majesty has shown in the welfare of their fellow Zoroastrians in Iran.

In a letter dated 23 June 1926 the Persian chargé d'affaires promised to take the necessary steps to have the address, which he considered 'beautifully executed' and a 'charming work of art', presented to His Imperial Majesty in Tehran and on 9 July he attended a reception arranged by the Association.

These audiences and petitions illustrate not only the concern of London Zoroastrians for their co-religionists in Iran, and their perception of their potential international influence, but also their concerns that they should not do anything to further endanger their vulnerable fellows; hence Bhownagree's hesitations in 1926. Such a tiny minority has to avoid alienating the majority population. The incidents also highlight the fact that even at the time of their peak of influence in British India, the Zoroastrians were deeply conscious of their Persian ancestry.

(c) *The Incorporation of the Association*

At the Annual General Meeting on Friday 14 August 1908 it was announced that Naoroji's resignation from the Association had been received from Bombay, where he had retired owing to ill-health, and that Bhownagree had been elected in his place. Bhownagree changed the Association in two significant ways: (*a*) he established it on a more formal, legal, basis, and (*b*) he changed its nature from what had been essentially an informal burial club into a high-status social body. Both changes merit discussion.

The lawyer Bhownagree considered that the formulation of the trusts was inadequate to deal with the growing number of

Zoroastrians in Britain in the twentieth century. He employed the parliamentary lawyers, Messrs Bull and Bull, to draw up the Memorandum and Articles of Association which resulted in the legal establishment of the Incorporated Parsee Association of Europe, formally dated 29 May 1909. The stated objects correspond roughly to those of the 1860s in terms of charitable help with funerals, support for the indigent, money for academic research on, and the purchase of books about, Zoroastrianism. But they extended the caring role of the Association and reiterated the commitment to owning their own House (by this date they were leasing a property in Cromwell Road, as detailed below). But such a formal document required definitions previously avoided, above all: who is a Parsi? Paragraph 4 of the Articles of Association states: 'Parsees of the Zarathushtrian faith only shall, subject to election as hereinafter provided, be qualified to become members of the Association.' The very name of the Association ('the Parsee . . . ') indicates that the focus is India orientated because there was no prospect of Iranian Zoroastrians settling in Britain. The document does not address the question of intermarriage. The records did not indicate clearly whether spouses and offspring of intermarriages were allowed to be members and so an amendment was introduced by the lawyers, on the motion of D. P. Cama, 'limiting the Society's membership and beneficiaries to Parsees of the Zoroastrian faith' (Meeting Report, 16 May 1908). The problem of non-Zoroastrians being buried at Brookwood emerged at an AGM in 1923 (11 August), when it was reported that the Association had approached the secretary of the Bombay Parsi Punchayat, Sir J. J. Modi, for guidance on who could be buried there. He replied:

Our practice is (*a*) not to permit the use of the Tower of Silence, fire temple and funds by the non-Parsee wives of Parsee Zoroastrians even though in their lives they may profess the Zoroastrian faith but (*b*) to permit the use of the same by the child of Parsee fathers by non-Parsee mothers provided such children have been brought up as Zoroastrians. This practice is in accordance with the terms of our Trusts as was decided by the Bombay High Court some years ago, in a well known case, Original Suit No. 689 of 1906.

So the Association secretary reported to the AGM that 'these rules have been approved and made applicable to the Necropolis ground in the charge of this Association'. What is significant here is not simply who can and cannot be buried at Brookwood, but rather the precedent of the diaspora community turning for, and accepting, the guidance of the Bombay Parsi Punchayat. A line of authority from the old country to the diaspora community was implied, a precedent for future debate concerning reform.

From 1908 the AGM records refer to social events in the Association. So, for example, at Pateti in that year, 'a large number, about 60 ladies and gentlemen spent the afternoon on the river in a specially chartered steamer followed by a dinner'. On another occasion a banquet was held at the Criterion restaurant to which the Rt. Hon. Lord Ampthill and Harold Cox MP 'were invited as the guests of the Community in appreciation of the valuable services they had rendered to our, among other, Communities of India in advocating their rights and better treatment in South Africa'. The political interests of Bhownagree are evident (his concern for Indians in South Africa is discussed below). But at subsequent meetings maharajas and Muslim leaders as well as MPs and noblemen (e.g. Field Marshal the Earl Haig and Countess Haig) were invited. Occasionally scholars, such as L. H. Mills, are recorded as present but generally the aim was to project the image of Parsis as belonging to the higher social echelons, as well-to-do, a sophisticated, loyal, and splendid body. The standing of the community was aided by the appointment of a Parsi, Sir Dadiba Dalal, as Indian High Commissioner in London (he attended some meetings and contributed to causes).[6] Another social luminary who helped develop this community image was Sir Dhunjibhoy, who with his wife, Lady Bomanjee, lived in Windsor in what was said to be one of Britain's most expensive homes, with grounds so extensive that they included a full race-course and visitors travelled around them in cars.[7] To the same end of projecting an image of high social standing, meetings were held not only in sump-

---

[6] Congratulatory letter sent by the Association, 24 Feb. 1923.

[7] An article on him appeared in the *Windsor, Eton and Slough Express*, 24 Mar. 1922 and see his obituary in *PP* VII. 35 for 1 Apr. 1937. He made his fortune as a government supplier in the Boer and First World Wars and purchased the estate from the Duchess of Sutherland. He was knighted for his charitable work, much of which was targeted to victims of the war. A brief cyclostyled history of Bomanji was produced by the late Jamshed Pavry of Vancouver, a Parsi who devoted much of his life to garnering information about his co-religionists.

tuous restaurants such as the Criterion and the Ritz but also at the National Liberal Club (rather surprising during Bhownagree's presidency!) and at Caxton Hall (e.g. a lecture by Dastur Dhalla in 1915). The Association made occasional use of Ratan Tata's mansion, York House, at Twickenham, which was large enough to be sold off as a town hall some years later.[8] Any 'Parsi watcher' of the period would have formed an impression of a 'good class' of people, which is just what Bhownagree wanted. The Parsis were seen to different from the Lascars and the undesirable aliens who were the subject of adverse comment and legislation at the turn of the century (see Ch. 1, Sect. (*b*)).

(d) *The Parsi Social Union*

It was, perhaps, inevitable that the emphasis given to the Association by Bhownagree should provoke a reaction, and this seems to have found expression in the formation of the Parsi Social Union. The Union was said by a later chairman (J. C. Coyajee, 1909; *PP* IV. 50) to have been formed to help people studying in the UK. Under its regulations four of the seven managing committee were to be students and: 'There shall be, when available, three additional members to be appointed by the Committee, and to be called corresponding members to represent the Union at the Universities of Oxford, Cambridge and Edinburgh.' A passing reference in the records also suggests that there may have been a branch in Manchester.[9] These seem to have been the universities towards which Parsis gravitated. The leading figures included persons of standing: Dorab J. N. Tata as vice-president, B. D. Petit as president, and S. A. Kapadia the lawyer-author of the book on Zoroastrianism discussed above (Ch. 3, Sect. (*c*)). Naoroji was vice-president and presided at one of the Union's functions before he left the country in 1907. The four stated aims and objectives were:

(1) To promote and increase social intercourse and goodwill among members of the Parsi community. (2) To bring Parsis into closer touch

---

[8] The Report of the AGM for 18 Sept. 1911 speaks of 100 guests at such occasions.
[9] Letter book, correspondence of 1 Mar. 1922 to A. D. Jilla of 'The Parsee Union of Manchester,' Gorton House, 421 Rochdale Rd., Manchester'.

with Europeans and other nations of the East. (3) To hold debates and read papers on social, legal, scientific and literary subjects. (4) To afford every possible assistance to Parsis who come over to Europe either for study, on business or health, or any other purpose.[10]

There is clearly some overlap with the Association, specifically with regard to points (1) and (2). It was noted earlier how Bhownagree introduced social events into the proceedings from 1908. The formation of the Social Union implies that there was a perceived need for such contacts before he took over and that the informal 'burial club' had not been meeting the social needs of the Parsis. The student group evidently saw itself as a westernized social club, for in its first year the lectures were on very British topics, one on Lakeland poets and another on 'Cumnor, An Historic English Village'. Although it was a student-led body, it nevertheless sought to be fairly high status, so that at an at-home on 23 July 1907 there were 100 guests who included a member of the Persian legation and two prominent political figures, Sir Thomas Barclay and Sir Curzon Wyllie. The Union's records state that it had seventy members so one assumes there must have been more dual memberships than just that of Naoroji (Annual Report, 1906/7).

The fact that such a group was organized at all, when it had such complementary aims and some dual membership with the Association, suggests an element of rivalry and indeed there were evident tensions with the Association from the outset. The first Annual Report (1906/7) says the Union was started:

> by a small body of Parsis who were actuated by the desire to promote a better social intercourse among members of the community. The idea did not find favour in certain quarters, from which hostile manôeuvres were set on foot to nip in the bud this excellent and much-desired idea of a Club in a country where club life is an essential thing. Thanks to the sagacity and broadmindedness of your committee it took very prompt measures to disarm the opposition. An informal conference was held on July 2nd, 1906, between your committee and Sir Muncherjee Bhownagree, who was acting on behalf of the Committee of the Zoroastrian Fund. To show that the Union was not started in opposition to the Zoroastrian Fund, your Committee acceded to Sir Munch-

---

[10] *Rules and Regulations of the Parsi Social Union*, published in 1907, p. 3.

erjee Bhownagree's request and changed the name 'Parsi Club' into 'Parsi Social Union'.

The Annual Report of the new Social Union then relates how the Association had dissuaded the Northbrook Society from letting the student body use its rooms in Piccadilly, but the Social Union had the decision reversed and it was put on the list of Privileged Associations. The records do not exist to facilitate a coherent history of the student body, but it seems clear that what lay behind its inception was a clash of views between the different generations on what was needed by members of the small diaspora group. In 1922 there was a burst of correspondence in the Indian press, in *The Times of India*, the Bombay *Sanj Vartaman*, and the Karachi *Parsi Sansar*, where an article appeared (7 August) saying that the young people thought that 'the Parsi Association of Europe is too much under the control of elderly people and tends too much towards entertaining personages at expensive banquets . . . The object of the Union seems to be to create a rather less august and more sociable centre for Parsis in London'. The leaders, notably Bhownagree, quickly responded by presenting the Social Union as 'a very small body of very small means'. This was a foretaste of community debates in Zoroastrian groups around the world, where the younger generation consider that the elders do not understand their needs and the elders consider the young to be 'presumptuous upstarts'.[11] Gaps between generations can be a problem in any community, but especially in small ones where the resources do not exist to provide a wide range of options for different interest groups.

(e) *Broacha House, Edinburgh*

It was, perhaps ironically, a student need and initiative from the Parsi Social Union which led to the first Zoroastrian property in Britain. Edinburgh had been a common destination for Parsis studying in Britain, especially medical students, from the early

---

[11] See the meetings file for 6 Sept. 1922; 12 Jan. 1923 (correspondence with *Sanj Vartman*) 12 Mar. 1923 regarding a rival New Year party and an article in the *Times of India*, 14 Aug. 1922.

days of such travels. On 26 June 1909, the Parsi Union in Edinburgh agreed with Sir Shapurji Broacha, while he was lecturing in the city on finance, to establish a house in the city named after him which could be run as a hostel and club for Parsis (Dadachanjee 1928). The charitable endowment consisted of the house (38 Chalmers Street), the furniture, and shares which Broacha gave to fund its maintenance. The trustees were Broacha himself, Sir Muncherji Bhownagree, R. H. Appoo (a Parsi student at Edinburgh), N. J. Mulla, and an Edinburgh law firm, L. & T. Cumming. There are only two recorded contacts between Parsis in Edinburgh and the London Association: the subscription paid by Edinburgh to the London Association and a gift of a silver cup sent from Edinburgh to Naoroji on his departure. (It may be that there was more contact with the London branch of the Parsi Social Union, whose records have not survived if they were ever formally kept.)[12]

The problem with Broacha House was that adequate supervision could not be given to the maintenance of the property and to its use. By 1937 the only surviving trustee was Appoo, who was then living in India. In 1930 it was leased to a Mrs Robertson for fifteen years with the agreement that she would maintain it as a hostel for Parsi students. On 21 January 1936 the solicitors attempted to evict her because she had informed them that she was not willing to take Parsi students, even though it was known that there were some seeking accommodation in the city, because, as she told the Association's secretary (Spitama Cama), 'She was not keeping Parsees for if she had kept them then the police would be after her.' As she was known to have taken French, German, and Belgian students it seems clear that the basic problem was one of colour-prejudice. She maintained that she had the lease for fifteen years and could not be moved. Cama pursued the case and in 1947 the property was sold and the money donated to the trust funds in London.[13] Thus the first attempt to buy a Zoroastrian property in Britain ended in the frustration of its intention by a clear example of prejudice.

[12] Records of the AGM for 15 Aug. 1906 and 19 Sept. 1907 respectively.
[13] The account of Broacha House is based on a collection of notes filed at Zoroastrian House, London, under the heading 'Broacha House'. The sale of the property and transfer of funds was originally discussed at a committee meeting in London on 19 Sept. 1936.

(f) Growing Numbers, Problems, and the Need for a Zoroastrian House

Numbers grew slowly in the first half of the twentieth century. There are no precise figures but records suggest that attendances were about a hundred at various functions (other than AGMs, when fewer attended). In 1911 there were ninety-five individual subscribers, most of whom had a family. But in the years during and after the war, and with the slump in the 1920s, increasing numbers of members needed help in returning to India, and the funerals of Zoroastrians living alone in Britain had to be funded by the Association. The situation is illustrated by correspondence in the letter book for 6 June 1917 in response to an appeal for money for a temple in India:

> The committee regret that your request for subscription to your fund has not much chance of being complied with, for the bulk of Parsi residents here are students living on the allowances made by their parents for their education. There are very few here ... [the writing is illegible] older residents, the calls upon whom for various purposes are so frequent and numerous especially in the present troubled and distressed times, that you can easily understand their inability to give any appreciable money help elsewhere. We ourselves have to support the funds of this association for the benefit of distressed cases here and for maintaining the burial ground and other necessary communal expenses ... the burdens of even living expenses owing to the war and the urgent calls made for subscriptions in various ways for help to soldiers and charities connected with the war.

The splendid mansions and glittering banquets which evoked the image of the community which Bhownagree and his committee sought to project among London society were, therefore, only one side of the story. So on 30 March 1922 the London secretary, Desai, wrote to Modi, the secretary of the Bombay Parsi Punchayat, explaining that the Association did not have the money to meet its demands. They had an income of £150 but in the previous eighteen months had had to pay out £120 for three individuals to be returned to India and they currently had a lady with two sons who were helpless and were applying to the Association for support. The Association intended, he said, that 'in this country no Parsee should be allowed to resort to begging or to be a charge upon the rates and thus tarnish the name and fame of the community in the Metropolis of the

Empire'. He explained that when the funds were started it had been envisaged that firms would flourish and so there would be a need to help people to return to India only about once in five years, but now with the slump in the British economy, numbers were greater than the Association could manage. Desai visited Bombay later that year and went to the Punchayat to seek funds to assist with repatriations. He reported to Bhownagree: 'I had a little hot discussion with Sir C. J. Readymoney who began to criticise your turning the Association into a Limited Company [a reference to the formal Incorporation discussed above]; ultimately they assured me that they would be willing to help us in the repatriation of any Parsis when a demand is beyond our means.'[14]

The Association was indeed active in its stated commitment not to allow a Parsi beggar nor any member to be a cost upon the rates. It is worth illustrating this statement with a specific example from the early 1920s. For obvious reasons the following account preserves the anonymity of the family. A married lady in Bombay sought help in tracing her father in England. He was known to be in the Manchester area, so the London Association sent letters to the superintendent of the Union Workhouse Hospital, Manchester, to Withington Hospital in Chorlton, to Hope Hospital in Salford, and to the Salford Union Infirmary in Pendleton. In the last letter the secretary commented: 'I beg to point out that the gentleman referred to is a Parsee residing in England for nearly 60 years, and although as you say "coloured" he is whiter than a good European in every respect.' Clearly the secretary felt it necessary to stress that Mr 'X' was not like an Englishman's stereotype of an Indian. Eventually Mr 'X' was traced and the Association gave him £50 plus the second-class fare to help him return to Bombay. The search was, therefore, extensive, effective, and charitable. The need for such support grew as the slump worsened and as Zoroastrians continued to stress their difference from the 'undesirable aliens'.

The growing membership numbers meant that at the same

[14] Letter dated 12 Aug. 1922. At the AGM on 11 Aug. 1922, it was reported that 'the Committee wish to have it broadly known that in future they will be able to extend such help in only extreme and absolutely deserving cases, when it is found the inability to pay the passage home has arisen through unforeseen recent circumstances'. The minutes indicate that on some occasions the Association's costs had been covered by one of the wealthy benefactors, notably Sir Dhunjibhoy Bomanji.

time that the Association was dealing with the economic problems attendant upon the war and the slump, it also decided that action had to be taken to implement the intention expressed in the founding trusts, to open a Zoroastrian building. Discussions began in earnest at a meeting on 16 December 1914, when Mr F. Ilavna proposed that they should seek 'a House in London for the offices of the Association and the provision of rooms for religious and ceremonial functions and a resting place for dead bodies prior to the funeral, for temporary accommodation of strangers who might need it'. Ilavna explicitly stated that 'the want of [a house] had been growingly felt in recent years, owing to the increasing number of Parsees in England'. The concept of the House had grown from the original idea of a religious structure to an administrative base and a hostel for Parsis visiting London.

Originally it was decided to keep the funds in a separate account in the Bombay Parsi Punchayat, an Indian link which would not have been established at the end of the century and one which presumably reflected the assumption that most of the money was likely to come from India. In 1919 the Association decided to sell its Government of India bonds and to invest the proceeds in Britain, partly in order to avoid paying tax twice. In May 1920, Sir Dhunjibhoy Bomanji promised £5,000 to the fund and Dr E. J. Khory £1,500. It was then decided to make a general appeal, but before the document was circulated premises were found and purchased—168 Cromwell Road, South Kensington, the road on which Bhownagree lived. It was a large house, so a club was planned from 1922 (the records make no further mention of this, so one may presume it was not a success) and in the same year the committee considered dividing it into maisonettes. The problem was that the house was too large for the Association's needs; it needed substantial renovation and while awaiting such attention it was depreciating in value. Further, it was too far from central London for many people and rather than being a social success the correspondence files suggest that it caused divisions within the community.[15]

[15] Correspondence files, letters from the secretary, Cama, to Bhownagree dated 20 Feb. 1925; 27 Feb. 1925; and 13 Mar. 1925; letter to solicitors Bull and Bull, dated 7 Mar. 1925; letter to Col. S. H. Dantra, 27 Mar. 1925. In a letter to some estate agents, dated 3 Apr. 1925, Cama said the Association was looking for a property, freehold or long lease, 'containing 8 or 9 rooms, of which 2 must necessarily be large reception rooms

After turning down an offer to buy the (leasehold) Cromwell Road property from a local hotel in 1923, the Association disposed of it in 1925. In the correspondence there is a reference to Bhownagree doubting the need for a house[16] but within four years another property had been purchased—11 Russell Road, Kensington. As a freehold property it could be considered a permanent base and it was smaller than the previous one. Different people funded rooms for specific purposes which highlight the perceived needs of the community: Banjee ritual room; Sir Dhunjibhoy and Lady Bomanji room for social functions; Khory Benevolent room 'for temporary shelter to indigent Parsees stranded in England'; and the Cowasji Adenwalla room for billiards.[17] The building was evidently seen as multipurpose: in part it was a social centre or London Club for Parsis (with the billiards), in part a hostel (or traditional *dharmsala*) which was evidently, in the light of experiences discussed above, needed by a growing number of impoverished British Zoroastrians, and in part a ritual centre. The opening, by Bhownagree, was reported in *The Times* (10 August 1929) and was attended by community leaders from Britain and Bombay (Sir Dhunjibhoy and Lady Bomanji; from Bombay Sir Jamsetji Jijibhoy, Sir Ness Wadia, Lady Dorabji Tata, i.e. the social élite of Bombay Parsis) as well as by people from outside the community, for example the Maharajah of Burdwan and Princess Sophia Duleepsingh. The event replicated in the new community-base the sort of social gathering Bhownagree had organized in splendid restaurants. The success of the new house was commented on in the AGM on 28 October 1931:

Up to recent years the Association's objects were confined mainly to the maintenance of the Community's burial ground, the proper disposal of remains, and the repatriation of any indigent member stranded in Europe . . . In recent years there had been a welcome addition to the activities of the Association . . . the establishment of the House where they had now assembled had opened out what might be regarded as the social side of the Association . . . its amenities and

---

somewhere between Strand and Victoria and definitely not south of the river'. In a letter to the same firm on 8 May 1925, he explains that the old property was too large and the tax and ground-rent were too high.

[16] Cama to Dantra, 28 Feb. 1925.
[17] See the *Rules and By-Laws* of the House, published in 1937.

functions [attracted] a larger and more frequent attendance at its Communal gatherings.

In short, the Association became a community.

(g) *Personalities and Politics within the Community*

Two of the first three presidents of the Association were MPs, and a third MP, Saklatvala, had an active, if chequered, history of relations with the Association. When Parsis were part of Indian political deputations to London they called upon the Association, for example, the three Parsi delegates to the Round Table Conference on the future of India in 1931, namely Sir Maneckji Dadabhoy, Sir Pheroze Sethna, and Sir Cowasji Jehangir, attended the AGM. Important politicians were, therefore, deeply involved with the community. What is more, they were politicians of very different 'colours'. In public the Liberal Naoroji, and especially his supporters from the INC such as Wacha and Mehta, were very critical of the Tory Bhownagree. Bhownagree was deeply opposed to the Socialist Saklatvala. Their respective political contributions will be discussed in Chapter 5, but the point here is how they interacted as community members.

Within the Zoroastrian community, relations between Naoroji and Bhownagree appear to have been at least correct and their political differences were set aside. Thus Bhownagree chaired a dinner to honour Naoroji on his election to Parliament and gave the first hint that he was thinking of treading where Naoroji led, albeit from the opposite political benches. In his speech he said:

And let me venture on your behalf a hope that the day is not far distant when our friends on the Conservative side may find a fellow subject from India of their own way of thinking, and see fit to elect him as representative of their own constituencies in the British Parliament.[18]

The two acted together in deputations to the Shah, though these may be considered simply diplomatic collaborations. Perhaps a more significant incident took place on 10 June 1907 when fifty members assembled and Naoroji led the plea to Bhownagree to

---

[18] *Indian Spectator*, 21 Aug. 1892, quoted in Mellor (1985: 45, 52).

withdraw his resignation from the Managing Committee (the cause of the dispute is not clear, but the context suggests a debate over the Parsi Social Union and the deputation to the Shah). In his speech Naoroji said:

I am sorry that Sir Muncherji proposes to resign from the Committee of the Fund—He has done much active and valuable services [sic] to the Fund and I agree with the Hon'ble Secretary that Sir Muncherji be asked in the name of the Managing Committee to reconsider his resignation and to withdraw it. As to the matter connected with Persia I consider that Sir Muncherji has hitherto adopted the best course and that he be requested by the Managing Committee to follow it up.

The meeting then unanimously adopted a resolution expressing concern that the matter was likely 'to create a false impression regarding the reputation and harmonious relations of the community in England'. After affirming the Association's 'high appreciation of the many services rendered by Sir Muncherji Bhownagree to the Parsee community both in England and the East' the resolution expressed members' 'continued and unabated confidence' in him. Bhownagree withdrew his resignation. In his turn Bhownagree chaired a General Meeting on 19 September 1907, which Naoroji could not attend for health reasons, and it was then that Bhownagree proposed the resolution of thanks to Naoroji on his return to India. Although leadership battles within a small community can be fierce and bitter, there are times when personal differences have to be, and are, set aside.

Bhownagree was evidently a powerful personality, but with Naoroji he was definitely the junior party. With others in the Association his relationship seems to have been more complex. While visiting Zoroastrian House during his London Round Table Conference visit in 1931, a leading figure of the National Liberal Association of India, Sir Pheroze Sethna, paid generous tribute to the work Bhownagree had done.

Sir Mancherji was regarded as the one to whom not only their Community but their countrymen looked for advice, guidance and help, in difficult situations. The constitutional security of the Association and its funds were his conception, and it was the confidence which he had inspired in the community, and especially among its leaders . . .

which had induced large hearted benefactors . . . to endow the Centre in which they had met. (1931 AGM records)

It is probably no coincidence that it was during Bhownagree's presidency, not Naoroji's, that the separate student body, the Parsi Social Union, was formed; Bhownagree evidently attached considerable importance to community occasions involving high society and he appears to have had an imperious manner. On one occasion even the friendly secretary commented on Bhownagree's dismissal of an application for a few pounds from a totally destitute student: 'This seems to me a very high-handed proceeding' (letter file, 19 January 1915). It is always difficult to know how much value to attach to speeches made at banquets held in honour of an individual, for they are obviously not going to contain damning criticism. But it is interesting to note some of the points emphasized at a banquet to honour Bhownagree in London on 27 July 1927 (reported in *The Times of India*, August 1927). It was the sort of social occasion Bhownagree evidently enjoyed—eight peers of the realm, a Maharaja and a princess, as well as leading Parsis from India and Britain, were present. The toast was proposed by one of the luminaries of Bombay Parsi society, Sir Dinshah Petit, who praised the work Bhownagree had done in India for female education, for vocational and technical training, and for social reform. The address asserted: 'you have been the guide and friend of every compatriot, more especially of the student class, who has sought help and counsel from you'. It also emphasized the campaigning work Bhownagree had undertaken 'to remove the disabilities of Indians in South Africa'.[19] Most of these roles are evident from other sources, as discussed in Chapter 5 on Bhownagree's political work, but it is worth noting the particular reference to help for students. There is simply no way of knowing if this element of the speech was simple flattery, or whether he undertook more quiet work than is recorded, or indicated, by contacts with the Parsi Social Union. The report notes that the Association had made several previous efforts to honour him and that he had blocked them all, but on this occasion the plans had been made and presented to

---

[19] *Presentation of an Address and Portrait to Sir M. M. Bhownagree* by his friends and admirers, (1928), 4 f.

him as a *fait accompli*. One interesting element in Bhownagree's reply to the toast was his account of his relations with Naoroji:

In respect of my career in another place, it was a privilege, which I have always cherished, to follow—doubtless at a long distance and by methods which, in spite of some of them seemingly different, were yet designed to arrive at the same goal—the course pursued by that venerable patriot of India, Dadabhai Naoroji, whose friendship I had the honour to enjoy from early years.

It is also, perhaps, significant that at such an occasion he should make a point of seeking good relations with other races in their common Indian 'motherland':

While thankful for the security and prosperity enjoyed under the Pax Britannica, it has ever been the aspiration of the Parsee race to work hand in hand with Hindu and Mahommedan compatriots for the development and well-being of the common Motherland of them all . . .

I express the conviction that when the tasty dish of a common nationhood which is now in process of preparation is ripe for digestion, there will be detected in it a savour of that pinch of salt and spoonful of a sauce which the Parsees are pouring into it.[20]

In so far as one can use speeches from such occasions as evidence for people's thoughts and contributions, the suggestions are that Bhownagree did more for the Association, and for students, than is commonly acknowledged; that his political campaigns for women and for technical education, as well as for Indians in Africa, are undervalued by historians and that at least by 1927 he foresaw Indian nationhood as a goal Parsis should work for alongside other communities. The Association's records thus throw light on some of the issues to be discussed in the chapter on his political work. They further show that although Bhownagree had little contact with the INC politicians (on whom most Indian histories of the period focus), he had a number of friendly relations with several of the leading politicians from other parties, notably the Western (and National) Liberal Federation, the retreat for the old moderates of the INC when the more radical Tilak and his followers came to power. His friendships with some of the foremost Parsis of the day, the families of the

[20] Ibid. 6.

Jijibhoys and Petits, with Sir Cowasji Jehangir and Sir Pheroze Sethna, show that he was not as marginalized in the Indian community as he is generally portrayed, (e.g. by Kulke 1974).

Bhownagree's relations with the third Parsi MP, Saklatvala, were less good. One might have expected that Saklatvala would have had few contacts with the Association because the Communist party of which he was a member viewed membership of a religious organization with hostility. Further he was married out of the community and he had been baptized. Books on him rarely mention his Zoroastrian links, but the Association records indicate that there were contacts and these reveal the depth which community ties often have even in the most apparently distanced members.[21] This unpublished material merits discussion because of the light it sheds on the personalities of the two MPs and to some extent on the running of the Association. The earliest reference to Saklatvala in Association records is a letter in the correspondence file dated 20 April 1910 (by which time he had been in England five years) in which he complained to the secretary about the upkeep of Brookwood, a theme he pursued in successive letters for three years. There is silence in the records about relations between him and the community over the next seventeen years. Oral tradition coincides with the one known published reference to suggest that Saklatvala did attend functions but was commonly snubbed by Bhownagree, to the point where some members walked out.[22] What the cause was, especially in the earlier years, is mainly guesswork. Probably at a fundamental level it was a personality clash with totally opposed political views fuelling the fire.[23] Clearly there were specific incidents which triggered the antagonism, for the Association

---

[21] It is, unfortunately, difficult to reconstruct a full picture of Saklatvala's relations with the Association because the main extant records are the copy-letter files of outgoing mail. Few incoming letters have survived.

[22] *Indian National Herald*, 15 Jun. 1929, quoted in Hancock (1990: 12), relating to events in 1923 and 1925.

[23] Squires (1987: 26 f.) relates an incident (reported also in personal community contacts) that once, during the war, when Saklatvala, Bhownagree, and friends were in a restaurant, Saklatvala said in a loud voice that they should poison London's water-supply with cholera. Throughout his life he was a man of highest integrity, a quality testified to by friends and parliamentary foes alike. It is inconceivable that there was any seriousness in the suggestion, but it is not a joke that the Tory Bhownagree would appreciate!

secretary, Spitama Cama, says in a letter to Saklatvala (copy letter file, 14 July 1927):

I greatly appreciate your sentiments about Sir Muncherji Bhownagree and I am forwarding your original letter to him. I do personally wish the past be forgotten and peace and harmony reign among all Parsees here. We might disagree in politics and in the past Parsees have disagreed even with the policies of the great Dada of Hind [Naoroji], but in social life we all ought to make no difference.

On the same day Cama wrote to Bhownagree: 'I enclose letter received today from Mr Saklatvala. He has expressed very good sentiments about you and hopes the unfortunate occurrences of some years back will never recur.' Whatever the causes of the disagreement, the initiative for reconciliation appears to have come from Saklatvala.

The initiative coincides with Saklatvala's approach to the Association seeking agreement for his children to have their initiation performed. It took place on 22 July 1927, in Caxton Hall in the presence of many Parsi and non-Parsi dignitaries, including among the former Sir Muncherji Bhownagree, Sir Dinshah and Lady Petit, and Sir Dadaba Dalal (*PP* VI. 325). Shortly afterwards there was further correspondence seeking permission for Saklatvala and his family to be buried in the Parsi cemetery at Brookwood. The main issue was not his marriage out of the community, nor his politics, but whether by undergoing baptism while at the Catholic school of St Xavier's in Bombay he had thereby for all time renounced his Zoroastrianness. Cama wrote to Saklatvala:

Now coming to your own relationship with the Association and that of your children, I am glad you gave me a good opportunity of discussing the same with you at length the other day. I conveyed the purport of our interview to Sir Muncherji [he and other committee members] . . . think if you send us a sworn statement that you are a Zoroastrian, you always were a Zoroastrian and you hope to continue in the same faith would be quite sufficient for us till some one else proves to the contrary. If you like you can add that your children were, of course, born Parsis of a legitimate marriage and have been recently naujoted here and taken into the Zoroastrian fold. (Copy Letter File, 26 October 1927)

The committee met and Cama wrote with their conclusions to Saklatvala on 31 October 1927:

The Committee of this Association were pleased to note your statement 'I assure you emphatically that there is no truth whatever that I have ever renounced or given up Zoroastrianism and I emphatically deny that I have accepted any other creed as my religion' . . . they are prepared to accept your assurances . . . but cannot understand how they would be asked not to give this statement of yours any publicity.

Some of these issues are elucidated further in the report of a committee meeting on 20 July 1928:

Mr Saklatvala denied he has ever been converted to Christianity. In his young days he had taken part in a Baptism ceremony just to gain personal knowledge of the ritual but there was no God-Father certificate issued to him. He cannot say if any such certificate was recorded by the Church. The attack in *Navsari Prakash* and *The Times of India* made on him about his religious belief were inspired by the Tata family who are trying to deprive him and his children of money left by late J. N. Tata in trust . . . The committee thereupon came to the conclusion that 'Mr Saklatvala's written statement of 28 October that he had never renounced the Zoroastrian religion and also his emphatic declaration made before the members of the Committee meeting held that day that he is a Zoroastrian is quite satisfactory for our purpose.'

The family memory of Saklatvala is that he consistently perceived of himself as a Zoroastrian, but that he was not much enamoured of the ritual expression of religion; that he had the *naujote* performed for the sake of his family, but that he did not want publicity because the affirmation of a religious commitment might cause problems with the Communist party (which in due course, it did). Eventually a small endowment was made on the children for their education from the Tata will.[24] Discussion of Saklatvala's motivation in seeking these Zoroastrian links is best delayed until after discussion of his political work in Chapter 5. When Saklatvala died a special meeting of the Association was called (26 January 1936) when a 'large number of members and others' passed a resolution which 'paid tribute to the lifelong disinterested work in various spheres of the life of the deceased'. Five hundred people are said to have

---

[24] Information from his daughter, Sehri Saklatvala; see also her book (Saklatvala 1991: ch. 6); Hancock 1990: 13 f.; and Saklatvala's obituary in *PP* II. 142 for 14 Nov. 1933.

attended the cremation at Golders Green and the ashes were interred at Brookwood cemetery by a Zoroastrian priest. So the rather tumultuous relationship between Saklatvala and the Association ended harmoniously.

(h) *London: An International Centre*

From its inception the London Association has seen itself not only as based at 'the centre of Empire' but also as an international centre, as a political base from which to plead the cause of Iranian Zoroastrians but also one particularly concerned with Europe. This concern involved mainly burials, although Bhownagree affirmed that returning indigent Zoroastrians was also a continent-wide responsibility of the Association.[25] In a letter from the Association secretary dated 6 December 1919, D. S. Cooper in Paris was informed that he had been appointed the Association's honorary agent in France, though there are no records of any consequences of this appointment. The Association was responsible for a burial ground in Berlin, where five graves were maintained for sixty-three years because the families in India did not care for them.[26] Responsibility for the graves was taken over by a church in Germany in 1986, very much against the wishes of the Association, which threatened legal action (letter file, 31 December 1980) because of the tradition that Zoroastrians should look after their own; the German church ignored the threat.

This sense of being an internationally significant Association re-emerged in the 1980s with the formation of the World Zoroastrian Organization based in London (to be discussed below). In practice the contacts between the London Association and the more informal group in Paris have been closer than

[25] The first burial of a Zoroastrian from outside Britain was that of Mrs Dorabji Saklatvala, whose remains were brought from New York in 1908 (AGM Report, 14 Aug. 1908), and from Europe, that of Ardashir Patel from Paris on 29 Oct. 1919. In a letter (correspondence file, 6 Nov. 1916) to the British Vice-Consul in Monte Carlo funds were given to cover the costs of transporting the body of E. Manckjee Sethna to London.

[26] The earliest traceable record is to a meeting on 24 Feb. 1923, in London, when it was agreed to fund the building of a wall around the plots which had been purchased. In 1938 efforts were made to contact the Bombay families to persuade them to fund the maintenance; these were unsuccessful in four cases.

any links with other overseas Zoroastrian associations, although links with America are growing at the end of the millennium.

(i) *The Post-War Situation*

From the late 1930s and through the 1940s the Association's records are not full and it may be assumed that its activities were curtailed by the war. The end of the war was greeted with real joy and a letter was sent to the King's private secretary:

> The Parsee community of London assembled at Zoroastrian House ... to celebrate their New Year, take this opportunity to send their humble and respectful duty and sincere congratulations to Your Majesty at the successful conclusion of the World War and the unconditional surrender of Germany and Japan. (Letter file, 2 September 1945)

Numbers increased in the post-war period (although no precise figures are known), mainly as a result of people who had been in the forces settling in Britain, especially those involved in the medical corps joining the new National Health Service, but the consequence was not a better financial position despite the increase in subscriptions. The Association's members suffered, along with all other Londoners, in the war and many of them, as well as the new settlers, needed help. Its finances were depleted by the funds it had helped raise for the war effort. Further, its investments had been in government securities whose value the War Cabinet had been forced to reduce. Income tax had been doubled and the revenue did not cover expenses, so the Association had to eat into capital and depended on the help of some of its wealthy patrons. The situation was transformed in the 1960s and 1970s, first by a change of investment policy in 1962 and secondly when the Association became a registered charitable institution in 1979 and thereby became exempt from tax. Membership numbers had increased but the increase in subscriptions did not affect the finances significantly. In the 1980s and 1990s the Association has been on a sound financial footing despite having extended the burial ground, purchased and expanded a new House (Captain 1984), and supported the initial launching of the World Zoroastrian Organization (WZO).

The significant increases in numbers occurred in the 1960s and early 1970s, first when Zoroastrians migrated along with others from India and Pakistan, then as a result of the exodus from East Africa from the late 1960s, and finally as a further exodus took place from Iran in reaction to the Iranian revolution and the establishment of the new Islamic Republic. The nature of these various groups and the consequences of their arrival will be discussed in Chapter 6 (for London efforts to help Zoroastrian refugees, see Sect. (*m*) below on the WZO, and generally see Writer 1994: 224–37).

(j) *The London Funeral Ground*

Since one of the main reasons for starting the Association was to provide burial facilities, and because it has in diverse ways been a major focus of community concern, the history of the cemetery at Brookwood needs discussion.

The Trust Funds negotiated a burial area in the cemetry at Brookwood, near Woking, with the London Necropolis Company in 1862. The facilities at Brookwood have grown over the years. In 1863 a hedge was grown around the site to provide privacy and two stone pillars with English and Gujarati inscriptions were erected to mark the entrance.[27] In 1865 discussions began on the erection of a 'chapel' or *sagdi*, where prayers and purifications appropriate to funerals could be said. This was eventually opened in 1901, along with other developments funded by Mrs Jerbai Wadia, widow of N. N. Wadia. Because this was the first attempt to create a distinctive Zoroastrian space in Britain, it is worth quoting a contemporary account of the event:

The fire was kindled and some Avestan prayers were recited by Mr Kekobad B. Dastur MeherjiRana and Mr Ardeshir M. Masani. Sir George Birwood delivered a lecture on the Parsis and the history of their religion. Then Sir M. M. Bhownagree CIE, talked on the life of late Mr Wadia and then Mr Nusserwanji Naoroji Wadia, one of the sons of the deceased, requested the Zoroastrian Fund Committee of London to take over the building in their care which was accepted by

---

[27] Agreed at a management committee meeting, 7 Oct. 1863 (see also AGM Report, 23 Oct. 1863). Completion of the work was confirmed at the AGM, 4 Sept. 1864.

its President, Mr Dadabhoy Naoroji, on its behalf. The building and mausoleum are built on the style of the Persepolis palace, the Astodan in the centre resembles the Astodan of Cyrus at Pasargadae with seven steps from where four paths lead in four directions at the end of which a door is proposed to be built. A beautiful gate has been built outside the cemetery by Mrs Shirinbai, widow of Mr Meherwanji R. Dalal, in his memory... (*PP* IV. 35)

The evocation of architectural motifs from Persepolis is an indicator of the consciousness of the Persian ancestry of the community, though this is not specific to the British Zoroastrians since Achaemenid symbols in general (but not the *Astodan*) were commonly employed on Indian fire temples built in the nineteenth century. Persepolis was a royal palace and in one sense a secular site, but it came to represent the artistic inspiration for much Persian and later Parsi art and architecture.[28] The funeral ground was consciously designed to represent a Zoroastrian cosmos, according to the ancient royal designs. Early gravestones simply reproduced western designs, but later monuments followed more Asian forms, using the motif of the fire and a picture of the deceased. The dead were, therefore, laid to rest in a space clearly designated as a Zoroastrian place apart.

As the community grew, so did problems with the funeral ground because of the need for more space. It was extended in 1908 with help of Mrs D. J. and R. J. Tata (AGM, 6 May 1908). One solution to the problem was proposed in 1938, namely the use of crematoria in order to economize on the amount of burial space required. The then president, Jilla, tackled at the AGM the religious questions such funerals pose (see above, Ch. 1, Sect. (*g*)). Modern crematoria, he argued, are different from traditional (Indian) forms of cremation and cause less religious offence:

Disposal by exposure to Electric Radiant Heat Rays serves the same purpose as solar rays and does away with the gruesome idea of access

---

[28] This paragraph rather simplifies the question of the function of Persepolis, the purpose of which is keenly debated by historians (see Boyce 1982). It is also questionable whether one can draw a clear line between a royal palace and a religious site in that era. But whatever its function, it was not simply a temple or a burial ground. The sites for the royal burials were clearly in a separate place. The London imagery was drawn more from Bombay temples, yet the use of the *Astodan* shows that there was some direct study of Persepolis in the search for a distinctively Zoroastrian symbolism at Brookwood.

to birds ... Science teaches that fire can never be defiled for it consumed all impurities but ultimately retains its integrity and remains pure by itself. (AGM, 12 September 1938)

He explained that he thought members should consider cremation to save ground and because so many families, especially those overseas, failed to maintain the graves properly. In this context, however, what is interesting is the example of how a diaspora group has to rationalize and justify the changes of practice which are pressed upon it when the members seek to live their religion in a different culture. Jilla foreshadowed later debates which are discussed below.

Cremation has become common in Britain. Nevertheless the demand for space at the funeral ground grew and it made the Association vulnerable to pressure from the owners of Brookwood. There had long been arguments about the increased charges, despite the company's failure to maintain the grounds as agreed.[29] In 1974 the new owners of Brookwood, Maximillian Investments Ltd., linked an agreement to extend the *sagdi* to a demand for the Association to purchase more land for £40,000 and to increased charges for funerals. Although apparently having few negotiating powers the Association fought the proposal and eventually a compromise was reached whereby the land was to be bought for £2,000. However, the company did not instruct its solicitors and the Association took the matter to court. At this point (letter dated 28 May 1976) the company said that no further funerals would be permitted unless a new scale of charges was accepted. The matter was taken to the High Court in London (2 April 1981) and an out-of-court settlement was agreed in which the Association was given freehold of what was already purchased; three-quarters of an acre of adjacent land was purchased for £1; the Association's legal costs were reimbursed and excess burial charges were to be returned. The extension to the *sagdi* was allowed and was funded by Iranian Zoroastrian benefactors, Arbab Rustom Guiv, and Mehraban and Faridon Zarthoshty.[30]

[29] See e.g. the records of the AGM for 8 Oct. 1890 and the AGM for 1955 on the question of maintenance. The question of charges came to the fore in 1944–46 when (31 Mar.) a new agreement was reached after arbitration.

[30] Captain 1984: 5; meetings files relating to 13 Jan. and 24 Feb. 1974; 9 Mar. 1975; 27 Apr. and 8 June 1975; 28 Mar. 1976. Rustom Guiv was a wealthy Iranian Zoroastrian who in the 1960s foresaw the need for support for diaspora Zoroastrians. He and the

Small minority groups can be vulnerable to pressure from powerful outside bodies for some of their fundamental requirements but the Association, led by its vice-president (who was both an accountant and a lawyer), Shahpur F. Captain, stood its ground. The incident also demonstrates the determination with which Zoroastrians characteristically fight for their cause (see also below, ch. 5).

The funeral grounds highlight other problems of being a minority religion, particularly how the purity laws are to be observed in another culture where the outside world is perceived as impure. The issue has become a matter of intense, indeed acrimonious, debate, concerned in particular with whether non-Zoroastrians can attend Zoroastrian funerals and even more with whether non-Zoroastrians (including spouses) can attend the annual ceremonies for the souls of the dead (known as *muktad* by Parsis, *Farvardigan* by the Iranians).[31] For decades the British Zoroastrian practice had been to allow non-Zoroastrian spouses to attend funerals and *muktad* ceremonies. But in 1985 this was challenged. Death is a time where impurity is potently present and therefore a time when the purity laws have to be strictly observed (see chs. 1 and 6). When the souls of the dead are thought to be present it is essential that the place of worship is maintained in purity. The reassertion of the traditional purity laws caused distress to many, not least the friends of the people excluded. This debate has not been confined to Britain but has erupted in America and Canada also (and elsewhere, e.g. in Hong Kong). Traditional rites of purity conflict with the traditional Zoroastrian values of family ties. It is a tension which has not been resolved. Both exclusions from ceremonies and *juddin* admissions to them have caused distress. It was easier to define the physical space of the funeral ground than it has been to draw the family boundary of the community.

---

trust he established have funded most of the Zoroastrian buildings in America and Canada. His work will be considered in more detail in the subsequent Katrak volume. The Zarthoshty brothers (one lives in Iran and one in Canada) have several times funded projects in Britain, sometimes anonymously.

[31] The following discussion is deliberately vague, although there have been specific instances, details of which are known. They are not related because of the sensitivities of many of those who have been involved and are still alive.

(k) A New Zoroastrian House and Community Religious Needs

At the AGM on 28 October 1931 mention was made of the large numbers present at functions and on the increased use of the House for social purposes so that 'At times the House proved too small for our purposes, and the Committee would be glad to consider the question of moving into a more commodious and conveniently situated house.' And so began a process which was to last for twenty years—the search for a new House—which was to cause acrimony and grief before a happy conclusion was reached.

Little could be done during the war years and the Association's finances thereafter were so meagre that an Emergency Meeting had to be called in 1954 (28 November) because of the problems of decay both at Brookwood and at Zoroastrian House and because the Association could not fund the return of the numerous indigent Parsis to India. These difficulties need emphasizing in order to appreciate the immense courage it took to decide to seek a new Zoroastrian House. The great inspiration behind the initiative was the then president, Jehangir D. Moos. The Iranian Zoroastrian Khodad Rustom Mehrabi was also active seeking donations and land. The search was difficult. Because Association funds were involved, a committee had to be convened. This not only caused difficulties in timetabling visits to potential properties, and the inevitable conflict of views on priorities, it also meant that vendors increased the price when an Association was seen to be involved.

The raising of funds from a relatively small and not very wealthy community was the greatest difficulty. A six-page appeal document was written by Mr Moos in 1959 for use not only in Britain but also India, from where it was assumed much of the funding would come (as in 1914, see Ch. 4, Sect. (*f*)). It merits consideration because it reflects the Association's perceptions of its needs and priorities, the dangers it faced, and the values it wanted to preserve. It provides an unusual and clear account of a group's self-perception at a time when wider South Asian migration to Britain was in its early phase.

The document begins with a brief history of the Association and records some of the early charitable benefactions. With the new arrivals, a House which had accommodated functions with about seventy people now needed to cater for up to 175 and as a result 'members of our Community are reluctant to go to a crowded Zoroastrian House after their first visit and they stay away'. The document then notes the religious needs of the Association (para. 20): 'A Zoroastrian cannot live by bread alone. The spiritual side of life is of vital importance to any Religious Community.' This marks a changing perception of the needs of members. In the early years the Association was simply an informal burial club. Under Bhownagree it became a high social-status group. The appeal document explains why the religious needs of the community were seen to be increasingly important:

In the midst of highly organised and liberally subsidised Proselytising Religions, we Zoroastrians are fighting a losing battle . . . As our people are naturally inclined towards religion, they inevitably drift into one or other of the highly organised religions which keep open doors and receive you with open arms. They have so much more to offer with their powerful resources in the way of highly paid, learned lecturers and priests, wonderfully furnished and well appointed Churches and places of worship . . . In the absence of religious instruction in our own institutions, our children naturally learn and adopt other religions in Schools and in social contacts. The first generation of Zoroastrians who come to live in Europe, generally have the necessary training and knowledge to follow their own religion. The second generation is rarely properly instructed, and the process of merging with others becomes evident. The third generation is almost completely lost to our religion. This process has been going on for the last Hundred Years and we have lost some of our best sons and daughters to other communities. (para. 22)

The document continued with the religious theme at some length, arguing that:

Our Great Religion has contributed very largely to the subsequent religions including Judaism and Christianity; and the Greek Civilization owes a great debt to our Religion . . . We are, therefore, naturally anxious to preserve our heritage for prosperity. . . All Great Religions have a common purpose, but owing to our different backgrounds, we all feel more at home in our own religion and further we are more likely to make quicker progress, ethically and spiritually, by following our own religion in which we are born. It is part of our make-up, therefore we must preserve and not destroy that which is of spiritual value to us.

And so, the document concluded, 'A spacious House, a large Assembly Hall, a proper place of worship worthy of our tradition is a real necessity' (para. 38). The threat of proselytizing religions, the lure of good facilities, the danger of conversion through religious education at school and the erosion of knowledge and identity over successive generations were the problems envisaged. The document also highlights two further typical and strong Zoroastrian convictions, namely the great historical significance of the religion and the idea that individuals should remain within the tradition into which they are born.

The quest to raise funds started with a visit to India by the president, Jehangir Moos, in 1959 and he obtained the support of leading Parsis both in Bombay and Karachi. But with the debates over a suitable property, the slow rate of donations, and the other financial pressures in the post-war period, many lost heart and the leadership had difficulty in maintaining the credibility of the proposal as a few people began to demand the return of their money. When the right house was found in 1967, events moved swiftly. No. 88 Compayne Gardens is reasonably central, large, and close to an underground station but because it needed renovation the price was not too high, so the property was bought without a loan by selling the Association's investments.

The building was opened on 6 September 1969 by the president of the Bombay Parsi Punchayat (Nadirshah Mulla), with 350 members assembled, and a *jashan* was performed by eight priests, led by Dr Sohrab Kutar who then carried out 'the age old ceremony of "Boi-Maachi" in the Keeblah. Thereafter Members in turn offered their Prayers in the presence of the holy Fire created by Dasturji Sahib'.[32]

This does not conclude the story of the Zoroastrian building in Compayne Gardens because from the outset there was an awareness of a need for a large hall for major gatherings. Obviously financial security had to be maintained and to aid this the secretary, Shahpur F. Captain, pressed successfully for the Asso-

---

[32] The quotations are taken from an unpublished document duplicated by the Association to record the event.

ciation to be made a registered charity. But there was also a sense of needing a place where new members could be welcomed and where there could be a club atmosphere with a bar and discos for the young. The president, Dr (Mrs) Shirin Kutar, urged the committee that they 'should try and enlist people from Africa who are still strangers'. At a further meeting Captain also commented that there were many Zoroastrians in Britain who were not members of the Association: 'They were mostly Zoroastrians from Africa.'[33] The sense of distance between the earlier settlers who came from the subcontinent and those who came from East Africa was a problem which was to grow, as will be seen in Chapter 6. However, the money was raised to build an extension, mainly through the charitable benefactions from two Iranian Zoroastrian sources, Arbab Rustom Guiv and the Zarthoshty brothers, the people who had helped fund the Brookwood development. It was opened on 20 March 1983 and has proved a great success for a whole range of proceedings, lectures, and initiations as well as on numerous social occasions.

There have been various attempts to obtain the services of a full-time priest, but difficulties of funding and finding a suitable person (not least one wishing and able to observe the purity laws in Britain) have thus far proved insurmountable. But one priest has stood out, and has been respected by all, in his work to sustain the spiritual life of his people: Dastur Dr Sohrab Kutar. At the time of writing he is the only person outside the subcontinent to have been formally recognized as a High Priest by the religious authorities, including the traditional Dasturs, in India. He graduated as a medical doctor in Bombay in 1939, though during his vacations he had worked as a priest at a temple in Poona. (This Indian temple experience is rare among diaspora Zoroastrian communities.) He arrived in Britain just before the start of the Second World War and volunteered to join the Royal Army Medical Corps, serving for over five years with the Eighth Army; he was decorated with the Star of Africa by Field Marshal Montgomery for his work in North Africa. The first recorded instance of his priestly activity was the performance of a *jashan* at Jamshedi No Ruz in 1938 and he then began to conduct the nine-day *muktad* prayers for the departed. Not only did he steadfastly

---

[33] Meetings files for 31 Jan. 1970 and 4 Jun. 1978.

refuse all remuneration (even the payment of expenses), he and his wife gave substantially to the religious requirements of the Association, for example the equipment for the prayer-room (the *Setyash Gah*). Discussions and consultations with Bombay regarding his dasturship began in 1963. Bombay confirmed that his medical duties need not debar him from the high priestly office. Although the medical profession is traditionally a holy one in Zoroastrianism, for it is concerned with caring for God's good creation of the body, doctors necessarily are involved with dead matter, not only corpses but also in pathology. Some, therefore, asked whether this honourable profession might not, in practice, have to be separated from the holy priestly profession, where purity is essential. The judgement in Bombay was that Dr Kutar embodied the ideals of both professions and could legitimately be formally installed as a Dastur. He was formally presented with the shawl as a token of his authority on 17 January 1965, a position he held until his death on 20 April 1984. He was a quiet, shy man but one whose integrity and sincerity was so evident that he was widely respected and during his dasturship there were no acrimonious religious debates. Unfortunately deep religious divisions did break out after his death.

In 1985 new leaders were voted into the secular offices of the Association—president, secretary, and so on. In part this was the outcome of personality clashes. The new officers also represented some people who felt that the traditional Zoroastrian beliefs and practices, particularly those relating to the purity laws and the place of non-Zoroastrians at death˙ ceremonies, were being set aside. They sought to expand the level of religious knowledge through new religious classes and seminars and there was an increased drive to involve the youth and increase the membership. One factor, among others, in this reassertion of tradition was the involvement of East African Parsis who like other East African Asians, tended to preserve a more traditional religion.

(l) *Zoroastrian 'Boundaries'*

A significant feature with any group is how it defines its own boundaries. The debate on this matter in the London Association has been over two main issues: the place of non-Zoroastrians (*juddins*) at religious ceremonies and whether the name of the Association should indicate a religious (Zoroastrian) or an ethnic (Parsi) group.

The question of the attendance of non-Zoroastrians at ceremonies for the dead at Brookwood has already been discussed above (Ch. 4) and was a focus of disagreement in the change of leadership in the 1980s. But the question was not a new one, nor restricted to events at Brookwood. It has also arisen over attendance at ceremonies at Zoroastrian House. The meetings file for 24 April 1954 shows there was a lively debate on the subject then, but the details are not recorded. In the 1960s, interfaith dialogue and a growing interest in comparative religion resulted in an increased number of requests from outsiders to visit Zoroastrian House. Advice was sought from the Bombay High Priest, Dastur Dabu, and he advised that such attendance was acceptable providing the *juddin* was kept at least 3 feet from the fire.[34] There was unhappiness, however, expressed by a priest when a *juddin* was invited to sit in the front row at a *jashan* to mark *Zarthost-no-diso* Festival in 1976 a foretaste of clashes to follow in the later 1980s when the protest was voiced particularly by East African Zoroastrians. The problems of boundary lines to mark off the pure sacred space require that Zoroastrians define where the outside world begins and ends, so that all may know where non-Zoroastrians can, and cannot, enter. The doctrinal aspects of this issue are discussed further below.[35]

The second boundary has to do with name of the Association and at a deeper level with self-perception. The original funds used the term 'Zoroastrian' (i.e. a religious description) but with the formal incorporation in 1909 the racial term 'Parsee' was used. There were then no Iranian Zoroastrians in the community, so the label was not divisive at that time. At a meeting on 21 July 1957 the appellation was discussed and 'Parsee Zoroastrian' was confirmed. For the Indian community the terms 'Parsi' and 'Zoroastrian' are often used interchangeably, but Iranian Zoroastrians feel excluded and insulted by such an identification.[36]

---

[34] Report in meetings file, 11 Feb. 1962.
[35] Meetings file, 20 Jun. and 8 Aug. 1976.
[36] This point was made by Bailey Irani, a Zoroastrian of Iranian extraction brought up in Bombay, at a meeting, 13 Aug. 1960.

When the new House was opened it was called Zoroastrian House and the following year the president, Mr Moos, proposed that the name of the Association should be changed to 'the Zoroastrian Association of Europe' in order to emphasize the religious aspect of the Association's work.[37] This was accepted in 1971 and was further modified in 1979 to allow for the newly acquired charitable status, to become 'the Zoroastrian Trust Funds of Europe (Incorporated)' (hereafter ZTFE). Much lies in a name, in this case both a sense of ethnic and national pride and an indication that the boundary identifies a religious group. The timing of the change of the name at the end of the 1960s indicates both an increasing consciousness of the religious dimension of the Association, which has already been noted, and a growth in the number of contacts with Iranian Zoroastrians. The original Association used the title Zoroastrian, but its membership was wholly Parsi. One hundred years later the Association had become more international in its membership and outlook.

(m) *The World Zoroastrian Organization (WZO)*

From its inception the London Association has seen itself as having an international standing because of its place at 'the heart of Empire' (see p.132). That broader picture has been mostly Europe-wide. From the 1960s London Zoroastrians have been at the forefront of a larger international project, the World Zoroastrian Organization, and Iran has been prominent both in the leadership, the funding and the concerns. The earliest reference in the London files is from 1962 (21 January meetings file) when Messrs Irani and Mehrabi reported on the World Zoroastrian Congress they had attended in Tehran as representatives of the London Association. They had been sent with a list of recommendations which merit attention because of the way in which they anticipated debates of coming decades, including: the use of a concept simply of 'Zoroastrian' and not 'Iranian' or 'Parsi'; support for the priestly class; to give full support for the formation of a permanent World Zoroastrian

---

[37] Meetings file, 17 Jan. 1970.

Organization; 'to consider the question of Zoroastrians living singly or in very small groups in various parts of the world and thereby being lost to the community; to recommend to the Congress to study the question of outsiders to our faith, and in particular children of mixed marriages'. London offered to host the next World Congress, but this offer was not taken up because of the problems of obtaining foreign currency in India for delegates to travel. Nothing happened regarding any of the suggestions and in 1965 Bailey Irani pressed the London Association to start moves to create such a body; he visited Iran, Pakistan, and India in an effort to raise international support.[38] By 1970 impatience with the inactivity was growing in the London Association and so it was resolved that an account be opened in the Association's books for WZO.[39] A further impetus was given to the initiative in the early 1970s by the concerns for the East African Zoroastrians, especially in Uganda. A special General Meeting was convened to launch the Organization and it was decided to base the working committee in London but to appoint representatives in various countries and to involve not only India, Pakistan, and Iran but also the North American continent, Hong Kong, indeed anywhere where there were Zoroastrians.[40] The inaugural meeting of WZO was held on 18 July 1980 in London (Captain 1984: 33f.)

A crucial motive in the establishment of WZO was to seek a protective umbrella for a community so microscopic that it was vulnerable, as it had been in East Africa and it was feared it might be in Islamic Iran. The early hope had been to seek recognition by and therefore protection from, the United Nations and UNESCO.[41] From late 1978 concern grew over the fate of Iranian Zoroastrians because of the political developments in that country and the new London president, Shahpur Captain, urged that in view of the potential troubles the establishment of a

---

[38] Meetings file 25 Sept. 1965 and 8 Oct. 1966.
[39] Meetings file, 22 Aug. 1970; 27 Mar. 1971.
[40] Meetings file, 17 Apr. 1971. Despite concerns over costs, a report of a meeting on 7 May 1978, records: 'But enthusiasm prevailed and the following proposition was passed unanimously "That steps be taken to form a WZO in London, properly constituted and properly financed."'
[41] Various efforts have been made over the years for such recognition, though without success, an outcome foretold by Dr Jal Bulsara who had worked in South East Asia for UNESCO (meetings file, 7 Apr. 1977).

world body was a matter of urgency, a move supported by a leading Iranian Zoroastrian, Farhang Mehr, an oil minister, deputy Prime Minister and Chancellor of Shiraz University in Iran under the Shah. At a succession of meetings in early 1979 appeals for Iranian Zoroastrians were made, to Ayatollah Khomeini, to the Iranian leader Bazargan, to Amnesty International, and to the British Home Secretary. The fears appeared to be justified when it was reported that two Zoroastrian girls had been abducted and forcibly converted to Islam, but the worst fears were not realized and an assurance was received from Bazargan saying that 'the rights of the religious minorities would be safeguarded'.[42] The position of Iranian Zoroastrians regarding political asylum and refugee status has not been clear. In addition to WZO appeals numerous individuals in Britain, the Indian subcontinent, America, and Canada have laboured quietly and sometimes effectively to help Zoroastrians (see above all Writer 1994: 185–98), but the threat has left many conscious of a need for a unified international voice and this has been a factor in the development of WZO.

In 1983 WZO was put on a firm financial footing with an anonymous donation of £150,000 towards the capital of the World Zarathushtrian Trust Fund, a separate body established to 'meet the expenses of WZO, or other Zoroastrian welfare institutions'. Three people were appointed trustees of the Fund, all London-based and involved in the London Association: Dr (Mrs) Shirin Kutar (chairperson); Shahrokh Shahrokh (secretary) and Shahpur Captain (vice-president). Bailey Irani was the president of WZO.[43]

Although Iranian Zoroastrians were leaders in, and a major concern of, the early WZO, it was not a body with a single focus. Its Memorandum and Articles of Association resemble those of the original London Association projected on to a global canvas. They include 'the advancement of the Zoroastrian faith ... provision of burial grounds ... relief of poverty among persons of Zoroastrian religion ... establish and maintain charitable homes ... publish ... literature relating to the religion and

---

[42] Meetings file 11 Feb. 1979; 14 Feb. 1979; 18 Mar. 1979 (report of girls' abduction received); 3 Jun. 1979 (Bazargan's reply tabled).
[43] *World Zoroastrian*, 2, (1983) is dedicated to the subject of the endowment.

history . . . promote the study of, and research into, the Zoroastrian faith . . . provide a place of worship' and then a series of concerns focusing on identifying and meeting the various needs of Zoroastrians around the world. One feature of WZO activity has been the organization of a series of seminars, mostly in Britain but also in America and India, the proceedings of which have subsequently been published. Typically these are academic in nature, although some have been specifically for the concerns of the youth (see Ch. 6). It also publishes a newsletter, *Hamazor*, which circulates information taken from local association newsletters around the world and keeps members informed of the achievements of Zoroastrians. The Trust Fund has also supported scholarly research, including some of the work for this book. In the 1990s it has increasingly been involved in charitable work among poor Parsis in Gujarat.

Such an initiative, almost inevitably, provokes opposition. Some of this has undoubtedly been personal, although the extent is difficult, and inappropriate, for an outsider to quantify. There have been underlying issues. The main clash has been with the Bombay Parsi Punchayat. The substantive issue, as aired in public, has been the question of membership and whether bodies such as *punchayats* or *anjumans* (two types of communal management structures in the Indian subcontinent) should have greater voting power than individuals. From the Bombay perspective, WZO is seen as a self-appointed body, lacking credible power, and as a usurper of traditional authority, notably that of Bombay where achievement, learning, religious institutions, and trusts are based. From the WZO perspective, Bombay has said a great deal but done little about the needs of Zoroastrians internationally and seeks to impose its specifically Parsi perspective on diaspora groups, composed of Iranians as well as Parsis (as well as young people born in the West), whose needs and problems it does not understand. The argument has developed into strife at international congresses, not least at the World Congress in Bombay in 1981 when the Congress resolved to work to strengthen WZO, and in 1985 when an invitation was issued to the then president of the Federation of Zoroastrian Associations of North America (FEZANA), Rohinton Rivetna, to produce a proposal for a federated world body, a process still under discussion at the time of writing. Another underlying issue is the authority of the old country and the changing needs of the diaspora. In 1993 relations between the WZO (still led mostly by earlier leaders of the London Association) and the present leaders of ZTFE deteriorated further over the acceptance of non-Zoroastrians (e.g. intermarrieds) as members. Possibly because of its international network and contacts with American and Australian, and even Indian (specifically Delhi) associations where intermarrieds are accepted, WZO has decided to extend the boundaries of its membership to include such families. The leaders of ZTFE have condemned the move in very strong terms, for they see this as inevitably leading to the erosion of the Zoroastrian identity, and as a marker of the reforming trends of the older leaders, the 'settlers' of the 1960s and 1970s. The problems of boundary-markers for a tiny diaspora community wanting to be a part of, yet distinct from, wider British society are increasing, not diminishing.

(n) *Local Zoroastrian Associations*

Balancing the international perspective of WZO there have also been moves to bring Zoroastrians together at the local level. There have been very informal family meetings, mainly at the time of New Year, in Leicester in the 1970s and in Newcastle upon Tyne in the 1980s. But more formal groups have also been established, mostly in London, because the difficulty of travel across the city has discouraged many from going to Zoroastrian House. A proposal for a 'zonal plan' was first discussed in 1973.[44] The first such local association was the North London Zoroastrian Association (NOLZA) which was formed on 2 May 1982 to 'meet the local needs of the Zoroastrian community in the context of Ethnic Community Development in North London and is in no way a rival body competing with the long established national organization'.[45] The constitution of this body emphasizes educational and social concerns more than religious activities. It is distinctive in stressing its role as a

---

[44] Meetings file, 6 Dec. 1973, again referred to on 14 Mar. 1982. In one sense the Parsi Social Union discussed above, with its branches in Edinburgh and Manchester, operated such a plan.

[45] Personal letter from the first chairman, Faredun Madan, 15 Oct. 1989.

'voluntary self-help ethnic minority Community Group' and is therefore eligible for local authority ethnic-minority funding. In becoming affiliated to Haringay Community Relations Council, NOLZA has identified itself with the wider Indian community in a way which other Zoroastrian associations have not.

A similar group was set up in the nearby district of Harrow on 21 March 1983. Both groups number about 200 but as their memberships overlap with each other and with Zoroastrian House, their numbers cannot be put together to give an accurate idea of the total Zoroastrian population. Whereas NOLZA has had an Iranian Zoroastrian office-bearer, Harrow is an India- and Pakistan-originated group (with relatively few East Africans). The Harrow and NOLZA groups share social visits but Harrow concentrates more on educational and debating issues, including involvement in interfaith dialogue. Two of its founder members, Zerbanoo Gifford and Thrity Shroff, have been involved in local and national politics (discussed below).

A smaller group (approximately 150) was established in south London in 1986. This group harmonizes its activities with the calendar of events at Zoroastrian House and tends to leave the main religious activities to that body. The south London group meets on a monthly basis for social events, day trips, bingo, whist drives, dinners (especially No Ruz and Christmas), but also cultural events—Indian music, Gujarati songs, and Parsi *Nataks*. There has been the occasional lecture on Iran and two visits have been made to see the Persian collection of the British Museum. The food provided is mostly Indian, reflecting the dominant constituency. In 1993 charitable work was added to the list of activities specified in the constitution, naming Indian Zoroastrians as the target of the charity. The association is, therefore, predominantly Parsi in nature.

The most recently founded body and the only formal one outside London, the North West Zoroastrian Community, was formed in Manchester in 1987. It is a mixed group with its original office-bearers coming from Iran, East Africa, and India. Its first circular emphasized the religious intent more than other groups:

In an increasingly complex and plural world [Zoroastrians] and their offspring need a sense of bond and identity. We belong to a very ancient faith, and we must cherish and preserve our heritage. We have to give our children pride in belonging to our faith.

The Community has sought to address the question of intermarriage. As a previously scattered group (one member had not met a Zoroastrian for thirty years), intermarriage is not uncommon. Non-Zoroastrians (spouses or not) are welcome to functions and may become associate members, although only full members are invited to the prayers beforehand. The Community has had lectures and debates but most of its functions are of a social nature with preliminary religious prayers. Bringing fellow Zoroastrians together, especially the young people, is seen as a necessity in the preservation of identity; indeed for some it is at least as important as religious ceremonies as a strategy for survival.

(o) *Conclusion*

Although the size and number of associations have increased from the 1861 conception, several of the original concerns have been achieved and preserved, notably the burial ground, the charitable work, and a permanent religious centre. The international perspective has been expanded with the work of WZO. One aim which has not been consistently realized is 'to live in harmony with one another'. Allusions have been made in passing to personality clashes, and to tensions between groups from different countries (e.g. East Africa and India), and to different interest groups (e.g. the Parsi Social Union and the London Association). In fact there have been many more conflicts than have been indicated. There have, unfortunately, been several law-suits against fellow Zoroastrians and tensions have existed between Iranian Zoroastrians and Parsis (see Ch. 6, Sect. (*g*)). One reason for glossing over such debates in this book is, obviously, a wish not to exacerbate problems, another is to respect the confidentiality of the materials to which access has been granted and a sense that these internal fights are not the concern of the outside world. But they cannot be wholly ignored for they are reflective of real difficulties. In part the difficulties are associated with varied backgrounds, but they are not untypical of leadership struggles in many, if not all, minority groups. It would seem that where groups feel restricted in their promotional opportunities in the wider society, then the acquisition of status within one's own community becomes especially important in terms not simply of prestige but also of personal fulfilment. A further factor aggravating these divisions within the Zoroastrian community is that such a high proportion of the members (62%, as discussed below) have had a higher education and aspire to leadership and authority roles. In a sense, they are 'all chiefs and no Indians'! Another major factor is the sense of being under the threat of extinction. Whereas this might have been expected to unite them, it has in practice intensified the arguments because each side argues that the other is threatening the long-term survival of the community.

London Zoroastrians have always seen themselves as having an important position within the global Zoroastrian population: there were three Parsi MPs at Westminster; Association leaders considered that they had a status which might give them influence with royal policies in Iran; they had a sense of a European perspective and of being at the heart of Empire; they hosted delegates to the Round Table conferences; they held high-society functions; and there was a perceived connection between a period of London residence and subsequent success. Since the 1970s London Zoroastrians have also pointed to the fact that they have constituted the largest Zoroastrian population in any city outside Iran and the subcontinent. They do not, therefore, see themselves as 'just another' Zoroastrian community and it is not mere coincidence that it was in London that a world body was founded.

It is difficult for members of a majority group to appreciate the significance of some of the physical resources and apparently trivial activities for a small minority. The obvious example is having a building to facilitate mixing with people of a shared heritage, where self-explanation is not necessary; a place where, as one interviewee in Toronto put it, 'I can go and be myself'. Having a Zoroastrian space in Britain has a significance far beyond merely pragmatic concerns. Ordinary social functions, dinners, or trips on a river steamer are important because they bring people together and reinforce the sense of identity, and provide opportunities for young people wanting to meet a

Zoroastrian spouse. These needs are particularly acute for Zoroastrians because their numbers are so small and they are scattered around the outskirts of London and through the country, with little contact apart from Association functions. The small numbers also make it difficult to provide some of the necessary resources, either material (such as buildings) or human (for example priests and religious teachers). There is, perhaps, a critical mass necessary for community survival. The London Zoroastrian Association has not merely survived but extended and diversified over 130 years, but the difficulties have, at times, been considerable. Strategies have had to be developed for coping with a considerable range of issues: the management of funds and care for the needy; the balancing of interests between generations or different social groups and various nationalities; the resolution of personal conflicts; the delineation of community boundaries; the tensions between being part of British society yet distinct from it; the management of change with the growth of numbers; the reconciliation of an international perspective with local needs; the definition of lines of authority between Britain and the traditional centres in India; and not least of how to develop a religious tradition that can both meet the changing needs of a dynamic community yet function without the extensive resources available in the old country. These and other issues have developed significantly as the end of the millennium approaches and will be discussed in Chapter 6.

It is obvious that a community is not a static phenomenon. The nature of the Zoroastrian Association has been seen to change from that of an informal burial club, to a group seeking high social status, to a larger and more religiously conscious body. The importance of religion among diaspora communities has generally been neglected in the plethora of studies on ethnic minorities in Britain. The case of Saklatvala highlights what is almost certainly a common phenomenon, namely that however secular and distanced from the community someone may appear to be, a communal and a religious contact often matters, especially where children are involved and as old age approaches. The 1959 appeal document asserted that a knowledge of the religion is essential for the preservation of the community over three or more generations and that some of 'the best sons and daughters' have been lost because they have not been provided with the necessary religious support. The sense of that need has increased in the community in succeeding decades and merits further discussion (Ch. 6).

An important point to emphasize from this overview of the associations' histories is the Zoroastrian sense of distinctiveness. There have been minimal contacts with other South Asian groups. Occasionally Bhownagree invited an Indian prince to a function, but that was a recognition more of his royal status than his nationality. Like Parsis in Dar es Salaam, British Zoroastrians have seen themselves as closer to the British in terms of value-systems, ethical concerns, social standing, and religious ideals. NOLZA has been the only association which has engaged in activities with other Asian and race-relations groups. That is a bridge relatively few Zoroastrians have been willing to cross. By contrast the Persian heritage is emphasized at various points in the Association's history: the deputations to the Shah, the design of the cemetery, the 1959 appeal document, even the Dar es Salaam appeal, are obvious examples. There has, therefore, been more stress on the Persian than the Indian origins despite the difficulties between Parsis and Iranian Zoroastrians.

The question of identity is, therefore, a complex one, with numerous internal divisions and tensions. These are so widespread and fundamental to the individuals involved that the question has to be asked: 'Is there any such single phenomenon as the Zoroastrian community in Britain, or are there several?' The answer depends on the definition of 'community'. If that term is meant to indicate anything approximating to a clearly defined homogeneous body of people with a common background and agreed set of aims and policies, then there is no such single entity in existence, however commonly the term 'community' may be used by Zoroastrians. There is a common stress on a Persian heritage, but how that ancestry is seen as affecting contemporary identity, how it is thought to affect the individual's life, and how it determines relations to those beyond the boundary walls, indeed how it conditions the perceptions of those very boundaries, differs enormously. Various strategies have been developed over the 130 years of the Association's history in terms of funds, education, social events, and religious activities, aimed at facilitating and enhancing an internal network of relationships which would otherwise remain inactive. Material resources and what may seem to outsiders to be insignificant activities can be important facilitators. But the problems of bridging the gaps between generations or different social groups, and especially between Zoroastrians who have been nurtured in different continents, are manifold. How this diversity within the Zoroastrian community is reflected within its religious life as it approaches the third millennium will be discussed in Chapter 6.

5

Zoroastrians in British Politics

Unlike other South Asian groups in Britain, Zoroastrians have never, because of their small numbers, constituted a significant electoral group which candidates at election time have had to canvas (for other groups, see Werbner and Anwar 1991). In that sense, therefore, they have never had political power. They have, however, held political office. Five Zoroastrians are known to have achieved office in local government. On 6 December 1901, Naoroji D. Allbless was elected president of Hampton District Council and in 1904 a member of Surrey and Middlesex County Council.[1] Mr N. M. Taramchand, who first practised as a medical doctor and changed to law in 1905, was elected to Mansfield Town Council in 1906, and was then re-elected for thirteen years. In 1918 he stood for parliament but was unsuccessful.[2] A. R. Kapadia, after serving as editor of Hansard was elected to Ilford Urban District Council: he died in 1927.[3] In the 1980s two Zoroastrians were elected Liberal members of Harrow Council, Zerbanoo Gifford (who will be discussed below) and Thrity Shroff. In national terms, however, the major figures have been the three Parsis who were the first Asians to become MPs at Westminster: Naoroji, Bhownagree and Saklatvala. Because of their significance they merit individual consideration.

Where parliamentary speeches have been reproduced in compendia (usually of Naoroji's speeches), these have been cited because they are generally more accessible to Parsi specialists working outside Britain than the main source, Hansard (*Parliamentary Debates*). Access to the last source can easily be obtained through the dates given.

[1] *PP* IV. 47, 55, and his obituary, 15 Nov. 1935, *PP* VII. 258. See also the account in The *Parsi*, May 1905, pp. 177 f.
[2] *PP* VI. 224 with the obituary following his death on 10 Oct. 1925.
[3] *PP* VI. 315.

(a) *Dadabhoy Naoroji (1825–1917, MP 1892–1895)*

Much has been written about Naoroji's work in India with the INC,[4] but relatively little has been published on his campaigning in Britain, even at Westminster. That will, therefore, form the main focus of this section, although a brief account of his wider activities is necessary first.

Background

Dadabhoy was born into a priestly family in Mandvi (Gujarat) in 1825. In what might be considered the first stage of his life, until 1855, his energies were channelled into educational and social reform. He studied in Bombay and became the first Indian professor (of mathematics) at the prestigious Elphinstone Institution at the age of 28. During his academic years he was a pioneering campaigner for female education, against infant marriage, and for the remarriage of widows. Within the Zoroastrian community he started the liberal society *Rahnumae Mazdyasnian Sabha* and helped start the newspaper *Rast Goftar* ('Voice of Truth'). This was intended as an anti-establishment mouthpiece specifically targeting the Bombay Parsi Punchayat and the conservative newspaper *Jam-i Jamshid*, but it later turned against Naoroji and the INC. He was also instrumental in the formation of the Bombay Association, one of the first Indian political bodies to seek to reform British rule. In this period, therefore, Naoroji's interests ranged widely, but in all areas he was a radical and pioneering reformer.

The second phase of his life, from 1855 to 1874, might be described as the wilderness years. His concern was to persuade the British of the problems faced by India, as he saw them, but at this stage he does not appear to have a long-term personal strategy. He was based mainly in Britain and in 1855 helped

[4] The main studies are, in date order, Seal 1968; Mehrotra 1971; Dobbin 1972; Johnson 1973; Masselos 1974. The standard work on Naoroji, full but rather uncritical, is Masani 1939. The major collections of his writings and speeches are Parekh 1887 and Natesan 1906. An important collection of Wacha's correspondence to Naoroji (which kept him informed of developments in India) is Patwardhan 1977. It is a pleasure, as well as a duty, to record my gratitude and indebtedness to my former students, Mrs Candida Riley (née Monk) and David Mellor for what they taught me during their postgraduate studies on the work of Naoroji and Bhownagree in Parliament; see Monk 1985 and Mellor 1985.

start the first Indian firm in Britain, with the Cama brothers, based in London and Liverpool. After that collapsed he started his own company in 1859. But he was not primarily a businessman; business was simply a way of supporting himself in Britain while he conducted political campaigns. His main concern in this period was the foundation of the London Indian Society in 1865, which was remodelled as the East India Association in 1866 and started by Naoroji in India two years later. The aim of this body was to spread knowledge about Indian concerns among influential, mostly political, figures in Britain. One of Naoroji's basic convictions was that the British were fundamentally just, but were also ignorant about India and therefore the focus of political activity had to be to inform the British about the condition of India. He commented in a speech as late as 1904 (when his patience with the British was diminishing):

We Indian people believe in one thing, and that is that although John Bull is a little thick-headed, once we can penetrate through his head into his brain that a certain thing is right and proper to be done, you can be quite sure that it will be done (Natesan 1906: 262).

It was during the 1860s that he began to elaborate his 'drain' theory (arguing that Britain 'drained away' India's wealth and talent, as will be discussed below) which led to the publication of his first book, *Poverty of India*, in 1873. He sought to influence Parliament through the Committee on East India Finance and in supporting the Ilbert Bill (1873).

In 1874, at the age of 49, he began the third phase of his life when he returned to India to become Dewan (Prime Minister) of Baroda. He resigned after a few months in protest at the prince's corruption and became a member of Bombay Municipal Corporation and Town Council. At this point it seemed that his future lay in India, so in 1881 he closed his London office and started campaigning in the subcontinent. He sought in vain to have Ripon's period as Viceroy extended; more successfully he started *Voice of India*, a newspaper which collected and disseminated Indian opinion on political matters in order to inform the British who did not read the native press. In 1885 he was instrumental in the foundation of another important political reforming body, the Bombay Presidency Association, and in the same year, the Indian National Congress. It was during these

India years that he began to emerge as a major political figure on the subcontinent, but he was becoming frustrated at the Indian inability to influence British political opinion and decided that this had to be done in Britain. So on 12 December 1884, he declared his intention to seek a parliamentary seat at Westminster.

At the age of 60 Naoroji embarked upon the fourth and most significant phase of his life. From 1885 to 1907 Dadabhoy became essentially London-based, visiting India only occasionally. This was the period of his greatest prominence and most intense activity, involving three parliamentary campaigns, one of which was successful and led to five years in Parliament; he made several important speeches to the East India Association and gave countless lectures around the country; he submitted evidence to, and was a member of, a Royal Commission; he published two books (one with Wedderburn on the INC, the other *Poverty and Un-British Rule in India*); and he led the calls for self-government. All of these activities increased his stature back in India and he was unique in presiding over three meetings of the INC, all of them in this period (1886, 1893, 1906). As a man of international stature his guidance was sought by leaders of various political colours, both English and Indian, Gandhi being one. It is this fourth stage of his life which will be the focus of the next section of this chapter.

The last period of his life, 1907–17, was spent in India where he retired in ill health. In view of his achievements there were various moves to honour him—with a knighthood, a decoration from the Shah—but the only one he would accept was an honorary doctorate from his old university, Bombay.

It is important to note that although Naoroji publicly asserted that he was an Indian first and a Parsi second, in his private life he was consciously a Parsi. While still a young man he started a religious reform group which remains active in Bombay over a century later. His articles show that his link with the reforming wing of the community was ideological and not simply a matter of communal politics. He was very critical of the priests and the liturgical traditions they stood for, and firm in his assertions that the truth of his religion was to be found in the abstract ethical monotheism whose ideals could be summed up simply in the values of good thoughts, words, and deeds (Naoroji 1862 and

1908). In the preceding chapter he has been seen to have been active as an elder statesman of the community, wanting to see his fellows to meet together, conscious of the need for a funeral ground, and representing his people to the Iranian government, but there is little indication that he was involved in religious functions or undertook serious reading on his religion.

Naoroji's Parliamentary Candidatures

Naoroji's campaign to enter Parliament was fraught with difficulty. His first attempt was for the Holborn constituency in 1886, but as it was a snap election he had only two weeks to canvas in what was a safe Tory seat and inevitably he was unsuccessful (Mellor 1985). In 1887 the long process began of his adoption as the Liberal candidate for the Central Finsbury constituency. At a meeting in August he received the most votes of all those standing for the seat and was congratulated by the secretary of the Liberal party on his election. But the result was not confirmed and a rival Liberal candidate, Mr Eve, was proposed. The National Association failed to support Naoroji and the local party was divided, but when Eve withdrew in August 1890 another candidate came forward, C. A. Ford, who continued to divide the party until June 1892. Despite this period of almost five years of local divisions, when the general election was held on 6 July 1892 Naoroji was elected, though only by three votes. His Tory opponent, Captain Penton, demanded a recount and as a result the majority was increased to five. Penton then alleged irregularities in the campaigning, specifically of bribes being offered, and a scrutiny was fixed for 5 December 1892. But Penton withdrew at the last moment and costs were shared. Naoroji's election to Parliament was, therefore, a lengthy contest with much acrimony (Masani 1939: ch. 20; Mellor 1985: 24–58). Racial and colour prejudice played their part. The notorious example of this was when the then Prime Minister, Lord Salisbury, sought in a speech in Edinburgh (30 November 1888) to explain the reduction in a Tory majority by explaining that the previous candidate

> was opposed by a blackman [Naoroji]; and however great the progress of mankind has been and however far we have advanced in over-

coming prejudices, I doubt if we have yet got to the point of view where a British constituency would elect a blackman. (Masani 1939: 263)

There was widespread public sympathy for Naoroji, which included a public rebuke for the Prime Minister from Queen Victoria. As a result he was projected into the public limelight and his campaign was boosted. He was, therefore, seen to be viewed by the monarch herself as different from the Lascars and 'undesirable aliens' whom many were concerned to exclude. One theme which his supporters pressed was that in appearance and values he was British (Masani 1939: 243 f.). Even so, after his election various newspapers chided the voters of Finsbury for having elected a 'fire-worshipping Asiatic' (Masani 1939: 278). The reason for the local party divisions are not clear; perhaps the best interpretation is that it was thought that an Indian was less likely to win the seat than a White Anglo-Saxon. However, in 1901 when Naoroji tried to re-enter Parliament and sought the candidacy of North Lambeth, he again found himself opposed. Having been proposed by the Liberal Club, he was opposed by the Liberal Association. This time it was argued that he was too old (by then he was 80) and that his remaining energies would be dedicated to India. He refused to stand aside for a compromise candidate (Sir John Peel) and at the election the official Liberal candidate was elected, the Tory came second, and Naoroji received only 733 votes, only a third of those polled by his Liberal opponent. The suspicion must remain, possibly at Lambeth, but more particularly at Finsbury, that racial/colour prejudice was at work. At least in Finsbury he overcame that prejudice. There is no evidence that such discrimination was a factor in the loss of his Finsbury seat, for he was one of many Liberals to fall to a swing to the Tories and he seems to have been respected and popular in his local constituency (Monk 1985: 90–101).

Naoroji's Political Message

In the early years of his campaigning in Britain, in forming the East India Association (EIA) and in Parliament, Naoroji's aim was to inform the British of what he saw to be the truth concerning the condition of India so that the rulers would reform their policies. Thus, in a speech to the EIA in London (2 May 1867) he commented at length on the blessings of British rule, citing as examples the removal of 'oriental despotism', of violence, of the poor material condition and of the superstition which he believed characterized pre-British India and which he contrasted with British rule:

> Law and order are its first blessings. Security of life and property is a recognised right of the people . . . To the enlightenment of the country, the results of the universities and educational establishments bear witness . . . In material progress it can easily be seen what impulse will be given to the natural resources of the country by railways, canals, public roads . . . The social elevation of the people, their rescue from some of the most horrible rites ever known to mankind, and the better sense of domestic, social and religious duties awakened in them are boons of the highest importance . . . The last but not the least of the benefits which India is deriving at the hands of the British is the new political life they are being inspired with . . . The freedom of speech . . . is another invaluable lesson. (Parekh 1887: 27 f.)

Later in the same speech he remarked:

> During my pretty long residence in this country I have observed that the English public as a body are very ignorant, and even to some extent misled, on Indian matters; but that whenever any subject is fairly and fully put before them, their decision is certain to be on the side of fair play, justice and honour.

He carried these fundamental convictions into his parliamentary career, despite the traumas of the campaign. So in an interview given to the INC newspaper, *India*, in January 1893 (Monk 1985: 23) he spoke of the friendly reception he had experienced on his entry to the House of Commons:

> I feel surrounded by many friendly to India and I hope and trust that with such a spirit and desire on the part of the British nation, the day for India's amelioration and justice to her, and the conversion of her present evils into blessings, both to Britain and India is not far distant.

In his maiden speech on 9 August 1892, he spoke of the 'the spirit of British rule, the instinct of British justice and generosity'. After three years in Parliament he still asserted: 'I, for one, desire from the bottom of my heart that the British rule and connection with India may last for a long time' (21 February 1895; Natesan

1906: 166). Even after his parliamentary life, in his presentation to the Welby Commission (1896), he could affirm: 'It has been the faith of my life, and it is my faith still, that the British people will do justice to India.' Throughout the 1890s, therefore, Naoroji consistently emphasized his faith in British rule and his support for its preservation despite calling for its reform. How his goal changed in the early years of the twentieth century will be discussed below. First it is necessary to give an account of his assessment of British rule and the reforms for which he called.

Naoroji spoke fifty-three times in his three years in Parliament, on twenty occasions on the condition of India; eight times on the Indian Civil Service (ICS); five times concerning the Royal Commission; four on Indian Councils; four on the Indian currency; two on the Indian opium revenue; and he was involved in the presentation of ten Indian petitions.[5] It is obvious that his concern was Indian affairs rather than local British issues. In addition he established the Indian Parliamentary Party (IPP) which, within twelve months, had a membership of 120 MPs. Members were not committed to any view or policy and were drawn from all sides of the House. The aim was simply to encourage an interest in Indian affairs so that debates were better attended and listened to more carefully.

The main thrust of his paramount concern, the condition of India, was that although Britain invested some money in India (e.g. into roads and railways) she nevertheless 'drained away' much of the wealth of what was fundamentally a poor nation. A major 'drain' was the heavy taxation imposed to fund British military adventures undertaken for her own imperial concerns and not for the sake of India. Thus, in his submission to the

---

[5] In 1892 he delivered only his maiden speech, but in 1893 he spoke on twenty-nine occasions; eleven times in 1894 and twelve times in the six months prior to the election of 1895. That is a very active record (most of his speeches, in the custom of the time, lasted approximately two hours). Masani (1939: 369) provides the figures for Naoroji's attendance in the House, which show him to have been particularly diligent. On his concern for non-Indian affairs: he delivered eight speeches on British topics, mostly concerning London: Lincoln's Inn Field Transfer Bill (1 Feb. 1893); Land Values (Local Authorities Taxation) Bill (11 Mar. 1894); officers' pay (20 Apr. 1894); London County Council Powers Bill (29 May 1894); Parliamentary expenditure (23 Aug. 1894); the Post Office and electric lights (8 Apr. 1895); Speaker's retirement (9 Apr. 1895); Locomotive Acts and street cars (2 May 1895); Post Office employees and politics (20 May 1895).

Welby Commission in 1896 (Natesan 1906: 330–59 at 354 f.) he pointed out that India provided £16 million of the total cost of £21 million for the Afghan Wars and that all of this was 'exacted out of the poverty stricken Indians, and all for distinctly avowed Imperial and European purposes'. Since Indians had also to fight he protested they were made 'to shed blood for Imperial purposes and to pay the whole cost also!', just as they had been made to die and pay in the Abyssinian campaign when Britain went to war simply to save her face after a public insult.[6] He questioned whether Indians should have to fund the British navy, since 'There was not a single Indian employed in the navy... There was not a single ship from or to India which belonged to India... there is every inch of the British navy required for the protection of these blessed islands.'[7] Indian taxes, he argued, not only funded British expenditure, they also paid the enormous salary bill of British officials working in India, money which was then drained away from India because the officials invested that money back in Britain for education, for savings, or for pensions. Naoroji estimated that in this way £1,600,000,000 had been transferred from India to Britain. He concluded that:

In a way the great mass of the Indians were worse off than the slaves of the Southern States [of America]. The slaves being property were taken care of by their masters. Indians may die off by millions by want and it is nobody's concern. The slaves worked on their master's land and resources, and the masters took the profits. Indians have to work on their own land and resources, and hand the profits to the foreign masters.[8]

As early as 1867 (in a speech to the East India Association, May 2nd) he asserted that the consequence of imperial rule was that Britain grew richer while India grew poorer.[9] India, he maintained before the Welby Commission, was being treated differently from other Colonies. Britain should pay honestly for what it took and India should only have to pay for what benefited her, all other charges being the imposition of tyranny:

[6] Paper to the East India Association, London, 2 May 1867 (Parekh 1887: 29).
[7] Parliamentary speech, 12 Feb. 1895 (Natesan 1906: 159 ff.).
[8] East India Association lecture, 2 May 1867; see n. 6 above. The same point was made in the 1895 speech (n. 7).
[9] See also his speech in Parliament, 12 Feb. 1893 (Natesan 1906: 161).

I would be, therefore, asking nothing unreasonable under the Reference to this Commission, that what is entirely for the British purposes must in justice be paid for by the British people, and the Indian people should not be asked to pay anything. Notwithstanding that the European services, in their present extent and constitution, are India's greatest evil and cause of all its economic miseries and destruction, and the very badge of the slavery of a foreign domination and tyranny, that India may consider itself under a reasonable arrangement to be indirectly benefited by a certain extent of European agency, and that for such reasonable arrangement India may pay some fair share of the cost of such agency employed in India. As to all the State charges incurred in this country for such agency, it must be remembered that, in addition to their being entirely for British purposes, they are all, every farthing, earned by Europeans, and spent every farthing, in this country. It is a charge forced upon India by sheer tyranny, without any voice or consent of India. No such charge is made upon the Colonies.[10]

Naoroji further argued that the drain from India was not only of money but also of talent, as Indians were deprived of important responsibilities.[11] He protested that the cost of training British officials was an unreasonable demand on the Indian taxpayer (he estimated that each official cost £18,000 per annum to train); it meant also that educated Indians were effectively being barred from running their own country. He repeatedly quoted an 1833 Act regarding the rights of Indian citizens and in particular Queen Victoria's proclamation on becoming Empress of India in 1858:

We hold ourselves bound to the natives of our Indian territories by the same obligations of duty which bind us to all our other subjects; and those obligations, by the blessing of Almighty God, we shall faithfully and conscientiously fulfil . . . And it is our further will that, so far as may be, our subjects of whatever race or creed be freely and impartially admitted to offices in our service, the duties of which they may be qualified, by their education, ability and integrity, duly to discharge.[12]

---

[10] Natesan 1906: 339.
[11] 28 Feb. 1893; 2 Mar. 1893; 13 Apr. 1893; 2 Jun. 1893; 23 Jun. 1893; 3 Jul. 1893; 30 Sept. 1893; 14 April . 1893. 1893 was Naoroji's busiest year in Parliament and it was the year in which, as will be seen, he supported a motion in the House on the subject of the Indian Civil Service, but it is remarkable that he did not return to the subject more often in following years. The figures in notes 5, 21, 22, 24 suggest that his speeches on different topics tended to be blocked into relatively short periods.
[12] Submission to the Welby Commission (Natesan1906: 420); here he collected all parliamentary pronouncements on the topic. See also his proposal to the Indian National

Naoroji's argument was that as far as entry to the ICS was concerned, this promise was blocked by several measures (see ch. 3, Sect. (*a*)): the examinations were held only in Britain thus subjecting Indian candidates to the difficulties and costs of a long voyage; the tests were set on the English public-school syllabus; and a minimum age was set which did not give Indian students time to make up for their more restricted educational opportunities. He was convinced that these measures were deliberately employed to block Indians. In a parliamentary speech in 1893 Naoroji quoted from a confidential minute of a former Viceroy, Lord Lytton, acknowledging that the educated people of India had been deceived with false promises of good opportunities by an 1833 Act of Parliament which had assured them of responsibilities and opportunities for promotion:

No sooner that the Act was passed than the Government began to devise means for practically evading the fulfilment of it. Under the terms of the Act, which are studied and laid to ear by an increasing class of educated natives, whose development the Government encourages without being able to satisfy the aspirations of its existing members, every such native if once admitted to Government employment in posts previously reserved to the covenanted Service is entitled to expect and claim appointment in the fair course of promotion to the highest post in that Service. We all know that these claims and expectations never can or will be fulfilled. We have had to choose between prohibiting them and educating them and cheating them and we have chosen the least straightforward course. The examination system as conducted in England, and the recent reduction in age at which candidates can compete, are so many deliberate and transparent subterfuges for stultifying the act and reducing it to a dead letter. Since I am writing confidentially I do not hesitate to say that both the Government of England and India appear to me up to the present moment to answer satisfactorily the charge of having taken every means in their power of breaking to the heart the words of promises they had uttered to the ear.[13]

Congress, Bombay, 1885 (Natesan 1906: 111 f.); his speeches to the East India Association, 13 Aug. 1867 (Parekh 1887: 345–54) and 17 Apr. 1868 (Parekh 1887: 76); and to the North Lambeth Liberal Club, 4 Jul. 1901 (Natesan 1906: 248).

[13] *PD* 13: 112 f, 2 Jun. 1893, and see Natesan for his use of the quotation on another occasion.

Naoroji went on, in the same speech, to quote a later public assertion by Lytton, where, despite this private acknowledgement of British injustice, the Viceroy still maintained the public protestation of just treatment for Indians, and that they:

> have a recognised claim to share largely with your fellow subjects according to your capacity for the task . . . The claim is founded on the highest justice. It has been repeatedly affirmed by British and Indian statesmen, and by the legislation of the Imperial Parliament. It is recognised by the Government of India as binding on its honour and consistent with all the aims of its policy.

Whatever public affirmations of equal treatment Queen Victoria or ex-Viceroys made, Naoroji, in an earlier speech outside the House, listed the practical objections to having Indians in the ICS which had been presented to him. They were:

1. That the natives are not fit, on account of their deficient ability, integrity, and physical power and energy.
2. That Europeans would not like to serve under natives.
3. That native officials are not much respected by the natives, and that when a native is placed in any position of eminence, his fellow countrymen all around him are ready to backbite and slander him.
4. That natives look too much to Government employment, and do not show sufficient independence of character to strike out for themselves other paths of life.
5. That though natives may be good subordinates, they are not fit to be placed at the head of any department.
6. That natives who seek admission into the Civil Service should be Anglicized.
7. That natives ought not to be in positions of power.
8. That the places obtained by the natives will be so many lost to the English people.
9. That the natives are already largely employed.[14]

Naoroji does not document precisely where or when he heard these allegations. They may be credible, but without documentation they must be considered speculative. However, what they do show are the sort of charges which he considered he had to answer. He also pointed out that no Indian, irrespective of background, education, or experience could (in 1867) enlist in

---

[14] Speech to the East India Association, London, 17 Apr. 1868 (Parekh 1887: 75).

the forces at any other rank than private.[15] In a letter in 1884 to senior officials (mainly Viceroys, both past and present) he argued: 'The whole problem of India is in a nutshell. Never can a foreign rule be anything but a curse to any country, except in so far as it approaches a native rule' (Parekh 1887: 501).

In the House Naoroji declared: 'Brute force may make an Empire, but brute force would not maintain it; it was moral force and justice and righteousness alone that would maintain it.[16] Similarly, he argued before the Welby Commission that the British government should, in its own interests, as well as in the cause of justice, take account of Indian concerns: 'You must remember that you as an alien people will have to rule over a large number of people in the Indian Empire, and if you do not consult their feelings, you will make a very great mistake.'[17] Naoroji and his allies appeared to gain a significant parliamentary victory in 1893. A member of the IPP, Mr Paul MP, put forward a resolution, supported by Naoroji, to the effect that all entrance examinations for the ICS be held simultaneously in India and England, that these examinations should be identical, and that the final results be in one list classified according to merit. The government opposed the motion but, confident of their success, did not make the normal arrangements to 'pair off' enforced absences from the House. However, the interest in the subject raised by the IPP resulted in 160 MPs remaining in the chamber for the debate. The result was described in the *Manchester Guardian* of 3 June 1893:

The members streamed in large numbers into the opposition lobby. Still nobody thought of a defeat. But when Mr Ellis, the energetic junior whip, came hurrying into the House with a nervous, anxious look and a flushed face in the place of the usual calm smile with which he returns from counting the Government majority, the House began to wonder. A moment later the Clerk handed the paper to Mr Paul showing that he was the victor. Cheers and laughter hailed the result. The motion was carried against the Government by a majority of eight, and Lord Salisbury's 'blackman' had shown himself able to defeat the Govt. which Lord Salisbury and all his confederates and allies attack in vain.[18]

[15] Speech to the East India Association, 2 May 1867 (Parekh 1887: 38).
[16] 12 Feb. 1893 (Natesan 1906: 159).   [17] 21 Feb. 1895 (Natesan 1906: 166).
[18] Quoted in Monk 1985: 42.

The Indian press was delighted at the outcome, but its joy turned to despair as the Prime Minister decided that the matter was of such importance he must consider it further and referred it to the Indian government who declared the decision impractical; the resolution was ignored. Naoroji reported to the House in a later debate that 'feeling in India among the educated was nearing despair. It was a very bad seed that was being sown in this matter.'[19]

This theme of British injustice provoking growing Indian resentment recurred in his speeches on other Indian themes. In his four speeches on the subject of Indian Councils[20] Naoroji objected that the large, consequently expensive, membership of the Councils was appointed by government and not elected, although the Indian taxpayer had to pay. Naoroji called for smaller, more economic, and elected Councils. Government refused. In his three speeches on the Indian currency[21] Naoroji argued for exchanging the Indian silver-based currency for the gold standard rather than trying to link the rupee both to a silver-and gold-based currency (bimetallism). Eventually the government held an inquiry (at the Indian taxpayers' expense), closed the mint, and propped up the falling value of the rupee out of Indian taxes. Naoroji's basic complaint was that the real problem lay in the excessive charges laid upon India for British administration and in the absence of Indian political power:

> It is just because the poor Indian has no vote that there is so little heed for him. He is truly helpless and crushed down with every possible burden . . . Remove the yoke of the stranger and make it the rule of the benefactor.[22]

Naoroji had long spoken out against the curse of opium (it was a factor in the breakdown of his relationship with M. H. Cama in their British firm), but he only spoke on the matter twice in Parliament.[23] Apart from his fundamental objection to the abuse of the drug, the question he asked in the House was: 'How could that which is a poison here be harmless in other portions of the

---

[19] *PD* 28: 1065, 14 Aug. 1894. Monk (1985: 44) details some of the Indian press reaction.
[20] 9 Feb. 1893; 8 Sept. 1893; 11 Sept. 1893; 20 Feb. 1895.
[21] 16 Feb. 1893; 28 Feb. 1893; 16 Mar. 1893; 8 Aug. 1893.
[22] *PD* 10: 1390 f., 28 Mar. 1893.   [23] 30 Jun. 1893; 30 Sept. 1893.

Empire?'—for government banned its use in Britain, yet not only permitted it elsewhere but fought the Opium Wars with China to press the trade upon that country.[24] It is difficult to explain why he raised the subject so rarely when he clearly felt strongly. Presumably he did not wish to deflect attention from what he saw as his overriding concern, the condition of India.

Naoroji's Impact on British Politics

Patwardhan (1977: p.xxix) includes a number of letters from Indian leaders written to Naoroji before he stood for Parliament, urging him not to seek election and so work in England. Wedderburn wrote (13 September 1886) 'From this distance it is difficult to judge, but for the most part we regret your determination to remain in England. There is much work to be done here and no one so well fitted to do it as yourself.' Similarly Malabari informed him 'Mehta and Telang do not like the idea of your staying in England . . . Telang has no belief in your mission to England.' Similar sentiments were expressed in the Indian press, for example in the *Mahratta*, 8 May 1892:

> The services of Mr Dadabhai are urgently needed in this country . . . The need in India far outweighs any advantages that are to be gained by having our own countryman in Parliament. The call of his own country ought to persuade Mr Dadabhai to abandon a hopeless pursuit and return to India where his services would be much better appreciated.[25]

The question has to be asked: 'Were they right?' How successful was Naoroji in Parliament? At one level he was very successful. It was a remarkable achievement to become an MP in the first place and once he took up his seat he was very active; he started the IPP; successfully campaigned for, and became a member of, a Royal Commission on Indian finance; was deeply involved in a successful resolution opposed by government. It is generally assumed by scholars that it was Naoroji becoming a Liberal MP which provoked the Tory party to select an Indian candidate (Bhownagree), so Naoroji might be thought to have been responsible for more than just his own election. He was widely seen as the representative for India, though there were attempts

---

[24] *PD* 14: 632, 30 Jun. 1893.
[25] *Indian Spectator*, 15 May 1892 quoted in Mellor (1985: 34).

to undermine his position by questioning his right to speak for his fellow countrymen. So, for example, Sir George Chesney argued:

I would venture to remind the House that the Hon. Member who speaks with such confidence and assumes such knowledge has spent only a small time in India, and that in only one corner of the country . . . Many of us have lived in almost every part of India. We have thus had an opportunity of knowing intimately the races with whom the Hon. Gentleman is entirely a stranger . . . I would remind him that as regards the people of India he belongs to an alien race which has spread over that country solely and only as a result of British supremacy. . . they are no more natives in the proper sense of the word than Englishmen. They are aliens separated from the people of India by religion, by race, by caste, by tradition and by history. If English domination, as it is called, or English government, in India were to come to an end then that community would be driven out of India at the heels of the latter. So much, therefore, with regards to the claim for the Hon. Gentleman to pose as a member representing India.[26]

His position was secure, however, because of the overwhelming support he received on his visits to India (particularly in 1893 when he went to chair the INC congress at Lahore), in the Indian press, and from such notable figures as Wedderburn and the former Viceroy, Lord Ripon.

The problem for Naoroji was that MPs were generally more concerned about issues which affected their own constituents and not with the problems of 250 million people thousands of miles away. Even after the formation of the IPP, attendance at debates on Indian matters was sparse, the newspapers took little interest in Naoroji after his early curiosity value, and even when he was successful with the resolution regarding simultaneous examinations the government ignored the vote. The establishment of the Royal Commission raised many hopes, but Naoroji and Wedderburn were in a minority in their recommendations and their separate report carried no influence. Effectively, therefore, his arguments both in Parliament and in his other speeches in Britain were ignored. It is difficult to point to any significant impact Naoroji achieved through his work in Parliament—a sad comment when hopes had been raised so high by his election.

[26] *PD* 17: 1773, 20 Sept. 1893.

The consequence of his failure to influence government (even his own Liberal government) policy seems to have had its inevitable effect on Naoroji. In the early years of the twentieth century he began to move increasingly towards the political Left, notably towards the Labour party and the Socialists. This is illustrated in quotations from private correspondence published in Masani (1939: 393–428). Although he resisted the Socialist Henry Hyndman's calls for more active agitation, the two of them began a long spell of mutually supportive correspondence. Despite no longer being in Parliament, Naoroji undertook various lecture tours around Britain in order to stir the British public and the tone became increasingly critical of government policy. For example, at a meeting at North Camberwell Radical Club on 23 April 1901, he declared:

You have not spent a shilling in the formation of the Empire. The blood that was shed was also Indian blood. You have been regularly draining and bleeding us of millions of money . . . These millions do not go to make you any better off, they go into the pockets of capitalists. Britain claims that Britons shall never be slaves, is it her intention that she should make others slaves? (Masani: 1939: 420)

By 1904 Naoroji was making public calls for self-government. On 1 June he addressed the London Indian Society and proclaimed:

I earnestly press upon the Indian people to claim unceasingly their birthright and pledged right of British citizenship, of self government. When this one fundamental remedy will be accomplished, every other evil or defect of the present system . . . would right itself. (Masani 1939: 428)

But the occasion which is generally referred to as the first public call made for self-government occurred at the International Socialist Congress at Amsterdam, 14–20 August 1904. The fact that Naoroji attended the Congress indicates his move towards the Socialists (although he was at the time seeking nomination for the Liberal candidacy of North Lambeth). He condemned the way powerful Britain was treating weaker India:

Imperialism of brute force is barbarism. The Imperialism of civilization is the Imperialism of equal rights, equal duties, and equal freedoms. The remedy is in the hands of the British people. They must compel their Government to fulfil the promises that had been made to India. The remedy is to give India self-government. She should be treated like the other colonies. (Masani 1939: 432)

The Congress unanimously supported the proposal, but Naoroji's Socialist links caused some concern in India. He refrained from calling for violent agitation, but warned that his disillusionment with British promises was shared by a growing number of younger politicians who were not likely to be as restrained as he and his colleagues. Naoroji's growing disenchantment and concerns can be seen in a speech in 1904 to honour Sir Henry Cotton on his departure to preside at the INC in Bombay. His main emphasis was the desirability of retaining links between the British Empire and India, but he concluded on a sombre note of prophetic accuracy:

My principle has been from the beginning based on the necessity of the continuance of the connection between England and India. I hope I may hold that view to the end of my life. I am bound, however, to mention one fact, and I will do so without comment. Leaving aside the general system of Government, which we condemn, there have been during the past six or seven years repressive, restrictive and reactionary methods adopted, and there has been further, a persistence in the injustice of imposing upon India the burden of expenditure incurred for purely Imperial purposes. What I want to point out is that the rising generation of Indians may not be able to exercise that patience which we of the passing and past generations have shown. A spirit of discontent and dissatisfaction is at present widely spread among Indians in India, and I wish our rulers to take note of that fact and to consider what it means. An Empire like that of India cannot be governed by little minds. The rulers must expand their ideas, and we sincerely hope that they will take note of this unfortunate circumstance and will adopt measures to undo the mischief.[27]

---

[27] Natesan 1906: 264 f. The increasing sense of despair is expressed in a series of letters to Indian contacts quoted in Masani (1939: ch. 30) Their location is not indicated and they have not been published elsewhere, so they cannot be checked or set in full context. Masani indicates that the italics quoted below are original. To Romesh Dutt, 5 Jul. 1903: '*The time is come when an agitation must be begun for self-government under British paramountcy.*' In a letter to Wacha, 12 Jan. 1905, he wrote of co-ordinating the spread of information both in India and Britain: 'The co-ordination of both is necessary to evolve the required revolution—whether it would be peaceful or violent. The character of the revolution will depend upon the wisdom or unwisdom of the British Government and action of the British people.' On 27 July in the same year he wrote to Wacha again: 'The demand that we must have self-government must be ever present and roaring all over

Of course, government did not heed Naoroji's warning then, or at any time; the 'militants' came to power in the INC three years later, bloody conflict broke out in India, and many lost their lives. The moderates, led by Naoroji, were left impotent because they were ignored by Government.

His presidential speech to the 1906 INC meeting at Calcutta is technically outside the compass of this study of his work in Britain, but it is interesting to see how in the last major public speech of his life he addressed the issues in which he had been involved for half a century. The full text of the speech (Natesan 1906: 65–95) raises most of the themes that he had pursued consistently, notably: full rights of British citizenship; reasonable opportunities for Indians to enter the ICS through simultaneous examinations; a just taxation system; constitutional representation and self-government. At one point he commented: 'Since my early efforts, I must say that I have felt so many disappointments as would be sufficient to break any heart and lead one to despair and even, I am afraid, to rebel' (Natesan 1906: 82). But although he explicitly supported the calls for self-rule, for Swadeshi, and he condemned the partition of Bengal, he nevertheless vowed to persevere, believing that there was a '"revival" of the true old spirit and instinct of liberty and free British institutions in the hearts of the leading statesmen of the day'. Although he called for agitation, it was specifically vocal agitation. To the end of his political life he refused to support violence. Again with prophetic insight he made a particular call for unity with the Muslim population. The aim of India

India . . . Another object it will accomplish is that the mass of the people will be trained in agitation and be educated in the evil and the remedy. *We need to move the masses* to an appreciable extent . . . '. Before the 1906 Congress, which he chaired, he wrote to Wacha (12 Jul.): 'I hope the next Congress will make a strong pronouncement as to the absolute necessity of self-government as the only remedy for all India's wrongs and needs. Congress should make a clear distinction between two aspects of its duties. The one, *a complete change of policy* as speedily as possible in the most suitable way, leading to self-government—this is Congress's main work—and the second the hatefulness of the vagaries and failures of the existing administration. The most important of the two is the first . . . The whole movement of the Congress must be managed to be backed by the masses.' And again to Wacha (19 Oct. 1905): 'I hope the Bengalees will keep up the Boycott Movement—and will now be awakened to the necessity of taking their Industries in their own hands and by their own capital.' In each of these quotations, as in those quoted in the main text, Naoroji stopped short of calling for violent action, but the calls for agitation became ever stronger.

he defined as 'the thorough union of all the people of India without any obstruction . . . In Self-government lies our hope, strength and greatness' (Natesan 1906: 95).

The End of his Life

The visit to India for the Calcutta congress drained Naoroji's health considerably and after his return to England he effectively withdrew from public life before returning permanently to India in 1907. He lived quietly, advising some visitors and many correspondents. To the concern of some of his supporters (e.g. Wedderburn) he moved yet closer to the Socialists and especially to the Home Rule League, accepting the post of president in September 1915 (Masani 1939: 530–35). Nevertheless he refused to oppose Congress, and still refused to condone violence. He remained a determined and courageous, but peaceable, campaigner for self-government until his death on 30 June 1917. Even if his campaigns left governments unmoved, from a Zoroastrian point of view he had projected an outstanding and favourable image of his community on to the international political stage at practically the highest level. As an example to the outside world, and as a role model within the community, he was one of the most outstanding Zoroastrians for centuries.

(b) *Muncherji Bhownagree (1851–1933, MP 1895–1905)*

Background

Muncherji Bhownagree was born in Bombay in 1851, the son of a wealthy merchant. After a short career in journalism, he succeeded his father in agency work in the state of Bhavnagar before studying law in London, where he was called to the Bar in 1885. In 1887 he returned to India and was responsible for drafting a constitutional for Bhavnagar. Constitutional matters appear to have been his early interest, for while still a student at Elphinstone College he had written a dissertation on the constitution of the East India Company, which he subsequently (1872) published as a book. He was also involved in social issues, notably female education, working for a ban on infant marriage, and campaigning for the remarriage of widows. He was one of the commissioners of the Indian and Colonial Exhibition held at South Kensington in 1886, for which he was made a CIE. He moved to London permanently in 1891 and within four years was the undisputed Tory candidate for North-East Bethnal Green (he faced none of the constituency difficulties encountered by Naoroji). His wife lived in India, finding the English climate unhealthy. He made occasional visits to the subcontinent but essentially lived in London until his death on 14 November 1933. His role in the Zoroastrian Association of Europe has already been discussed in ch.4. He was also a leading figure in London Indian society, but the main focus of interest here is his work in Parliament.[28]

Bhownagree in Parliament 1895–1905

Studies of Bhownagree typically emphasize the strength of his pro-British views, indeed his craven attitude to the imperial rulers (Kulke 1974: 225; Visram 1986: 94). In doing so they reflect the comments made by contemporary leaders of the INC notably Wacha, who gave various reasons for this attitude in his correspondence with Naoroji.[29] Bhownagree, he alleges, obtained his posts by intrigues and misrepresentations (letter dated 20 May 1883). Sometimes Bhownagree is said to have supported Congress, at other times he attacked it (Patwardhan 1977: 346). The INC rejected his right to speak for India:

Mr [Pherozeshah] Mehta laughs Bhownuggree to scorn for his presumption to pose as India's representative when he represents absolutely nobody ... I give the sentence in his own words 'The pretensions of Mr Bhownuggree to depose Mr Dadabhai in the hearts of his countrymen of all classes and degrees could only be received in India, as they actually were received, with amused shouts and roars of laughter.' (Patwardhan 1977: 469)

[28] Much less has been written on Bhownagree than on Naoroji. The main published accounts are: Natesan 1930: 475–88; Kulke 1974: 224–8; Visram 1986: 92–7. In addition there is his entry in *DNB* for 1931–40 (pp. 75 f.) and an account in *The Times*, 14 Nov. 1895 on his election and his obituary in the same newspaper, 15 Nov. 1933. I wish to reiterate my gratitude to my former student, Candida Monk, whose unpublished thesis (1985) remains the only substantial study of Bhownagree's parliamentary work.
[29] Patwardhan 1977: ch.1. See, in addition to pages cited below, pp. 267, 417, 426, 450, 454, 508, 525, 528, 545, 549, 613, 627.

According to Wacha Bhownagree gave unquestioning support to British imperialism. For example Wacha to Naoroji, 16 January 1897,

> Our contention . . . is not that he is a Conservative but that he is a tool of the Anglo-Indians and does harm to India's cause by his abject slavery to them. If as a Conservative he could do real service to India, India would not care from which side of the House he conserves her interests. (Patwardhan 1977: 550)

Wacha was dismissive of Bhownagree, writing for example to Naoroji on 22 July 1899, 'That pomposity of "Bow and agree" will try to do his best although we need not care two straws for him' (Patwardhan 1977: 713). He, together with Mehta and other Congress Parsis, sought to undermine Bhownagree's credibility whenever possible. On one occasion they persuaded influential people to stay away from a dinner organized in honour of the new MP:

> As to this busybody Bhownaggree he is determined to play the grand role. Possibly a Jubilee Knighthood is in store for him next year. So the more actively he falls in with the views of the rabid Anglo-Indians the greater will be the advancement of his personal ambition. I am glad to say that our agitation so far has had its desired effect.[30]

More damaging to Bhownagree's standing was a campaign in which they collected adverse Indian press-cuttings and sent them to Naoroji and other leaders in Britain and finally published them in 1897 under the title *The Indian Political Estimate of Mr Bhavnagri: Or the Bhavnagri Boom Exposed*.[31]

How justified were these attacks on Bhownagree? He was a strong supporter of the British Empire and fulsome in his praise of what he described as 'the blessings of British rule in India';[32] he often spoke of 'our Indian Empire'[33] and considered that the aim of education was not to remove British rule but to educate and instruct the Indian people in order that they might appreciate and profit from being part of the Empire.[34] He attacked the IPP on the grounds that its members were not well informed

---

[30] 24 Oct. 1896; Patwardhan 1977: 520.
[31] No editor or author is indicated. For Wacha's comments on this to Naoroji, see Patwardhan 1977: 521, 525, 528, 549.
[32] *The Times*, 14 Nov. 1895.   [33] e.g. *PD* 52: 477, 5 Aug. 1897.
[34] *PD* 57: 932, 7 Jun. 1898.

about India and they rarely attended debates.[35] The INC and its supporters, especially Wedderburn, were often the objects of criticism, sometimes in intemperate language in debates which according to the *Daily Telegraph* and *Manchester Guardian* were not conducted according to the gentlemanly traditions of Parliament.[36] He could be seen, on occasions at least, to be unquestioning in his loyalty to Tory policy, changing with party policy even when it turned back on itself, for example with regard to the annexation of Chital (1898–9, Monk 1985: 142–5). But that is, for better or worse, part of the discipline of the British party system, particularly with the Tories (and with the Communists, as will be seen below). It is worth examining his career and speeches to assess the validity of this image of Bhownagree.

How Bhownagree came to be nominated as a parliamentary candidate is not known. He was the third-choice candidate for the constituency of North-East Bethnal Green, but after the others had declined, he was elected without opposition. The other candidates had rejected the seat because it appeared to be unwinnable, having a strong, established Liberal tradition with a popular sitting MP, George Howell. *The Times* did not help Bhownagree's cause by saying that he was likely to withdraw at the last moment, a point he vigorously rejected (14 July 1895). How he managed to overturn that established majority is unclear. He stressed his involvement in British and not just Indian issues: for example he opposed both Home Rule for Ireland and the disestablishment of the Church of England. He was a good orator, received support from prominent Tory statesmen, and presented himself as a good constituency man. These factors, plus a good campaign, some Liberal complacency, and a national swing towards the Tories provided the combination

---

[35] See the reports of parliamentary debates in The *Manchester Guardian*, 27 Jan. 1897 and the *Daily Telegraph* of the same date. On the venom of Bhownagree's attacks on Wedderburn, see Monk 1985: 155 f., 161 f., 190 f. Other examples cited of his attitude to Britain are his account of the constitution of the East India Company in his published thesis on that subject and his translation into Gujarati of Queen Victoria's *Leaves from the Journal of our Life in the Highlands*. In his reply to the toast at a dinner to honour him after his election he not only praised the blessings of British rule but also dismissed those who 'tried to sow discontent'; he expressed the thought that most of the Indian population was loyal and patriotic and that he could, therefore, survive the wrath of the agitators (Monk 1985: 110).

[36] See e.g. *PD* 58: 926, 7 Jun. 1898; *Daily Telegraph*, 27 Jan. 1897 and the *Manchester Guardian* of the same date (Monk 1985: 189).

of factors which yielded the surprising success.[37] Howell expressed incredulity at the outcome in a personal letter: 'After ten years hard labour in Parliament . . . I was kicked out by a blackman, a stranger from India, one not known in the constituency or in public life' (Leventhal 1971: 212). This reference to a 'blackman' occasioned no public outcry as Lord Salisbury's had, because it was in a private letter and is the only known example of colour prejudice to surface in the campaign. Otherwise Howell's bewilderment at Bhownagree's success is understandable.

Although India was not featured in his election campaign, once in Parliament Bhownagree focused mostly on Indian affairs, making 182 of his 267 interventions (including both speeches and questions) on that topic, with 44 on Indians in South Africa and 41 on British topics (including 25 on local Bethnal Green issues). Bhownagree spent twice as long in Parliament as Naoroji and intervened more frequently on a wider range of subjects. It is, therefore, more difficult to summarize his points briefly. The focus here will be on those issues which might affect the assessment of his overall contribution to the debate on India.[38]

The subject on which Bhownagree spoke most in Parliament was the Indian economy. Despite the INC's criticisms of him, Bhownagree in fact pressed similar questions to Naoroji, even using his phrase 'the drain of the wealth of India'.[39] He questioned the justice of making India pay for such a high proportion of military expenditure. For example, with regard to expenditure for the annexation of Chital he said:

---

[37] Ibid.: 106–8. She also studied the local press reports of his campaign, notably *Bethnal Green News* (see 29 Jun. 1895 for his fluency) and *Mercury* (see esp. 18 May and 13 Jul. 1895).

[38] See his campaign statement, *Mercury*, 13 Jul. 1895 (Monk 1985: 107). The breakdown of Indian topics is as follows: Indian economy—24; famine and disasters—22; technical and industrial education—20; military expenditure—20; railways—9; administration—9; Imperial Institute—9; plague and Poona—8; education of Indian labourers' children—7; Lascars—6; promotion of Indian trade and industry—6; native troops—6; Indian riots—5; Royal Commission on Indian expenditure—5; Indian communications—4; Cooper's Hill (an engineering college for people going to work in India, but where restricted access was given to Indians)—4; miscellaneous Indian topics—18.

[39] *PD* 53: 695, 15 Feb. 1898.

Some plan will have to be arrived at, some principle established, as to how the Frontier policy, pursued alike by the Conservative and Liberal Governments, imposed on the Indian Exchequer, should be shared by the Imperial Exchequer . . . The patience and fortitude of the people in India were severely put to the test. More even than their bodily sufferings, their mental condition was one of extreme strain and anxiety.

Political firebrands, he warned, could take advantage of the situation to stir up discontent. The best way to combat this would be to give a 'handsome contribution' to the Indian finances, which would strengthen loyalty to the 'beneficent' British rule.[40] He objected to Indians having to finance costs of the campaign in Africa, waged solely in the interests of Imperial concerns (and where he argued that Indians were very badly treated—see below):

To have made India pay for a portion of a garrison in South Africa, which was really provided for African purposes, would have resulted in not only imposing on her a cruel burden, but inflicting on her an indignity by forcing her into relations for mutual help with a country that has treated her shamefully.[41]

Similarly he argued that making India bear costs for the Tibet campaign, again conducted solely for British purposes, was unjust to India:

But I regret to say, although it is unpleasant to say it, I feel I should not be thinking, and acting, Imperially, if I refrained from frankly telling you that in the adjustment of your financial relations with her [India], you have been parsimonious.[42]

But, like Naoroji, it was not only foreign military ventures he objected to funding, but also the costs of the British army in India. For example, in 1903 the government decided to increase the pay of the military and, without consultation, to charge the India taxpayer for that increase. Bhownagree objected:

The people of India regard this imposition of the new Army charges as a flagrant act of injustice . . . India has paid all along every penny of the huge cost of maintaining a large military establishment, twice as

[40] *PD* 86: 1398, 26 Jul. 1900.
[41] *PD* 127: 1243, 13 Aug. 1903. See also *PD* 125: 973 and 1443.
[42] *PD* 140: 454–61, 12 Aug. 1904

large in respect of British troops as her own requirements warranted. In the last twenty-five years, and more, she has lent thousands of her troops, both British and native, for purely Imperial necessities, and when occasionally you have reimbursed her the cost of the men for the time they were actually employed on expeditions abroad, you have taken endless credit for being just to her . . . But even then you have not repaid your full debt to her, for you give not a penny piece to the credit of the enormous outlay she makes, year in and year out . . . India is as quiet and devoted to the British Crown as any other portion of the Empire . . . if any emergency arose, why should not India be then allowed to draw upon the army in other quarters of the British dominions, just as her Army has been drawn upon for Imperial service abroad?[43]

Bhownagree developed a further economic argument, different from those of Naoroji, namely the moral duty and economic wisdom of investing in technical and scientific education so that India could develop her own industries and not be exploited by British industry or so vulnerable to drought, famine, and plague. He believed that the existing policy of providing an education in the humanities produced too many intellectuals who were mere 'spouters and writers',[44] people who were overly critical of Imperial British rule (clearly an attack on the leaders of the INC). He argued that every school should 'be provided with workshops and scientific laboratories', because 'making the people literary scholars . . . is right enough in its due proportion, but a nation of literary scholars is not one that is likely to advance in the paths of prosperity'.[45] As a nation India needed an education which would develop her economy because her imports were nine times greater than her exports. In various questions and speeches in Parliament he challenged government to declare how much was spent on technical, industrial, and art schools in India.[46] In a five-point plan submitted to the Viceroy, Lord Curzon, he called for forestry schools; polytechnic and

---

[43] *PD* 126: 123, 13 Aug. 1903. Similarly *PD* 99: 1224–35, 16 Aug. 1900; he pointed out that in that year's review the Indian economy was seen to be on a better footing because of the absence of troops in Africa and China and so the budget was reduced by 1¼ million pounds. Their departure for other countries established that they were stationed in India for Imperial not Indian purposes and therefore that Europeans, not Indians, should pay for them.
[44] *PD* 58: 925–34, 7 Jun. 1898.   [45] *PD* 86: 1398–1405, 26 Jul. 1900.
[46] *PD* 81: 1104, 3 Apr. 1900; *PD* 76: 230, 8 Aug. 1899; *PD* 112: 464, 31 Jul. 1902.

industrial schools; an industrial exhibition to give Indian manufacturers and artisans knowledge of their fellows' industries; encouragement for internally produced manufactured goods; grants, scholarships, and awards to enable Indians to study practical and technical subjects both in India and Europe.[47] He estimated that India paid out £33,000,000 per year for imported goods and that:

> 90% of the population of India subsists on agricultural pursuits, and that if we succeed in withdrawing say, even 10% from this occupation, we at once reduce by so much the burden on the soil, and increase the productive power of that 10% by teaching them to turn raw material into articles of domestic use, every one of which nearly they now import from foreign countries ... The mission of the British Government in India is absolutely a paternal one, and it places an obligation upon them to guide the people of the country.[48]

He objected to the government preventing the expansion of some Indian industries. For example, the sugar-cane industry was not allowed to expand into rum production although it was a natural product of the refining process. He also protested against the imposition of taxes on Indian products, such as tea, so that exports were restricted.[49] The redirection of labour into export markets, he maintained, would mean that 'famine would to a large extent disappear'.[50] Further, he argued by implication that the government was not using justly some Indian investment in research. Various Indian benefactors (including Bhownagree, though he did not allude to his own involvement) had invested in the Imperial Institute in London and he wanted to see Indians benefit from the scientific research pursued there. So in 1904 he begged to

> ask the Secretary of State for India whether in consideration of the contribution made by Government, princes, and people of India to the Imperial Institute, and of the annual payment now made by India, he will move the Board of Trade to arrange for the reception and training

---

[47] PD 76: 22 f., 8 Aug. 1899. See also PD 52: 48, 5 Aug. 1897; PD 92: 429, 15 Jul. 1901; PD 74: 1367, 1899; PD 86: 230, 1900.

[48] PD 86: 1398–1405, 26 July 1900. See also PD 81: 1104, 3 April 1900; PD 119: 1232, 17 Mar. 1903; PD 140: 449–61, 12 August 1904.

[49] PD 118: 546, 5 Jun. 1902; PD 41: 292, 2 Jun. 1896; PD 86: 1315 and 1401, 26 Jul. 1900; PD 126: 535, 28 Jul. 1903; PD 97: 431, 15 Jul. 1901.

[50] PD 86: 1405, 26 Jul. 1900.

of three or four graduates of Indian universities in the laboratories of the Institute in such chemical research work as is now performed there for Indian purposes.[51]

His proposal was ignored. As part of this campaign for industrial development Bhownagree also called for the development of the railways, to facilitate trade, to ease the transportation of supplies at times of plague or famine, and to unite the peoples of India.[52]

Bhownagree's campaign concerns differed at several points from Naoroji's. Naoroji had opposed the building of the railways because he thought the loans involved would further drain Indian resources. Nor did Naoroji support the building of technical schools. But these differences are questions of individual policy-issues, not long-term strategy. In these campaigns Bhownagree was not being craven in his attitude to the British— he was seeking financial and industrial independence for India. What he was condemning was the sort of arts education pursued by most of his INC opponents. His campaigns for technical and scientific education were not unique in India. Wacha's correspondence with Naoroji indicates that several others held similar views: Dosabhoy Framji [Karaka], B. M. Malabari, Sir Jamsetji Jijibhoy, N. M. Wadia, (of Petit Mills), Sir Cowasji Jehangir, N. N. Wadia, and Sir Shahpurji Broacha.[53] J. N. Tata held similar views but remained close to the INC, as did Malabari, but the others were industrialists and businessmen, not politicians.[54] The *Indian Spectator* generally supported Bhownagree's initiative, though it questioned his fervour and suggested more modest reforms in the educational programme might be considered— a pointer to Bhownagree's radicalness in some matters.[55]

Another aspect of government's financial policy which Bhownagree condemned was the combination of executive (revenue and police) with judicial duties, because he feared this would undermine people's faith in the administration of justice.[56] He

---

[51] Monk 1985: 126 ff.; see also *PD* 138: 267 f., 18 Jul. 1904.
[52] *PD* 52: 480, 5 Aug. 1897; *PD* 136: 1119, 24 Jun. 1904; *PD* 58: 927, 7 Jun. 1898; *PD* 64: 987, 11 Aug. 1898; *PD* 41: 439, 2 Jun. 1896; *PD* 44: 485 and 786, 11 Aug. 1896; *PD* 52: 481, 5 Aug. 1897; *PD* 108: 539, 26 May 1902.
[53] Patwardhan 1977: 417, 508, 532, 623, 658.
[54] *Indian Spectator*, 16 Oct. 1898 and Harris 1958: chs. 6, 7.
[55] 6 Dec. 1902; see also 11 Sept. 1898; 2 Oct. 1898; 27 Aug. 1899; 9 Sept. 1900 (Monk 1985: 128).   [56] *PD* 44: 786, 13 Aug. 1896.

noted with concern that there was an increasing tendency to withhold complaints regarding miscarriages of justice from consideration by higher authority. So in 1884 two-thirds of the petitions to the Secretary of State were forwarded and a third rejected, whereas by 1896 only one-sixth were forwarded and the rest rejected. He said that he did not wish to suggest that there was a wish to prevent justice, but it might be that officers considered the complaints trivial. However, he pointed out, to the person concerned they were important. In short he was arguing that justice should be seen to be done.[57] One area where he was convinced justice was not done concerned the blocking of the promotion of Indian medical staff to important offices; instead, they were being 'restricted to inferior posts with trivial salaries':

There has been a long standing and justifiable complaint that men trained in India for the medical profession who enter public service have no prospect of promotion. Capable men of long experience have to relinquish their posts, or retire, after a service of more than thirty years without having had any appreciable advance in pay and position from where they began early in life. I trust, therefore, that in the contemplated increase of officers in the medical service, the Government of India will make some provision for the inclusion of men of tried and long careers as a reward for work which has hitherto been ill-requited.[58]

Such racial considerations, he argued, 'were inconsistent with the traditions of British rule in India' and against the assurances of the Empress's proclamation.[59] These were issues pursued by Naoroji in similar language. Both MPs believed that the ideals of British rule were for the good of India but that these were not always effectively implemented, and both sought to bring them into effect by an information campaign. They even agreed on what many of the issues were: the drain of India's wealth through unjust charges and the blocking of reasonable Indian aspirations to higher office when appropriately qualified. To the issues discussed thus far Bhownagree added further arguments, namely that the British investment in education had been misdirected towards the humanities when it should be more scienti-

---

[57] *PD* 147: 1293, 5 Jul. 1905.   [58] *PD* 99: 1224–35, 16 Aug. 1900.
[59] *PD* 44: 790, 13 Aug. 1896.

fically and technologically orientated, that there should also be more investment in industrial infrastructure (the railways), and that the government was being seen increasingly to neglect legitimate enquiries into grievances against the justice system.

Justice was a far greater concern of Bhownagree's than is generally reflected in previous studies, not only in terms of a just balance of charges between the countries, but also within India. An example of this is his concern with the salt tax. He argued that although famine costs meant that in some years there was a negative balance with the Indian budget, in many years there were large surpluses. As the labours of Indian people had facilitated these surpluses, so, he believed, they should benefit from them; one way to acheive this would be to lower the salt tax, because this financial burden affected most those who could afford it least.

The next and perhaps more pressing obligation for relief in taxation is with respect to the duty on salt. The small reduction made last year was received throughout the country with feelings of gratitude . . . I regret that anticipation [of further reductions] has not been realised. I account for it on two suppositions. One is that the Government are apprehensive that if they reduced the tax appreciably they would find it difficult, if not impossible, to increase it again should it be found necessary to do so. The second is that it is the only tax which reaches certain classes of the people who are otherwise immune from all public burdens.

With regard to the first supposition he commented that he hoped that government would never be in such financial need, but he was sure that if they were, the Indian public would not grudge a necessary increase. He went on:

As regards the second assumption, I would point out that the very poorest classes, who feel the weight of this tax to be intolerable, are in a condition of existence which can be likened to that of those who seek Poor Law Relief in this country. By their toil and thrifty ways of living they contribute to the wealth of agricultural and trading interests, so that, after all, if not in coin, certainly in kind, they contribute to those sources from which the public revenue is derived, and I think they should not be subjected to any further exaction by the state, except under the most imperious necessity.[60]

[60] *PD* 140: 449–61, 12 Aug. 1904.

The government did reduce the tax the following year (1905), but Bhownagree wanted it abolished. He also sought reduction in land revenues especially in the areas which were worst hit by poverty, and he proposed increasing the income allowable before the payment of tax, to aid the poor.[61] He raised other issues in Parliament concerning justice for Indians which have been ignored by commentators. Monk (1985: 164–8) gives three further examples. Bhownagree protested that Cooper's Hill Engineering College (for people going to work in India) was closed because there were insufficient students, yet suitably qualified Indians were refused places; he argued that labourers' children should receive education and medical care; and he sought to protect the rights of Lascars working on P. & O. liners. Bhownagree's concern for the poor of India was therefore greater than is commonly implied in references to his work.

The main campaign with which he is identified is the fate of Indians in South Africa. Yet even on this point it may be doubted whether he has fared justly at the hands of historians. He raised the subject on forty-four occasions in Parliament: it was the main theme in his second period in the House of Commons. His basic point was that Britain was not honouring the pledges given regarding the equality of all her subjects. The Indians had been forcibly expelled from the Transvaal region during the Boer War. He argued that under the German African authorities conditions had deteriorated but when the British regained the territory conditions were not improved; if anything, he argued, they worsened. For someone labelled 'Bow and agree' his condemnations were strong. He argued that Indians were treated differently from people in other colonies:

When in our own colonies, as well as in foreign countries, Indian subjects of Her Majesty—not only coolies, but merchants, men who helped to make British settlements—were treated in a manner that was a disgrace to the Empire, were robbed of the rights that belonged to them not only as citizens of the Empire, but as human beings, without a word of protest from statesmen who have the direction of foreign and

---

[61] *PD* 140: 450, 12 Aug. 1904. See also *PD* 147: 1235, 21 Jun. 1905.

colonial affairs, no wonder this talk of care for Indian interests was regarded as hollow by the whole community of India.[62]

The government's attitude can be seen in an unpublished letter, dated 23 August 1897, from the Prime Minister's office to Bhownagree in the early days of his campaign. Chamberlain, through Lord Ampthill, expressed sympathy for the cause of the Indians, but said:

> It is impossible to disregard the strongly expressed wishes of Colonists who have been given all the local autonomy which is implied in Responsible Government.
> It would be idle for him to seek to disguise the fact that there exists in Natal a strong feeling against the influx of immigrants from Asia in such large numbers as to threaten to outnumber the European population; but he has been and still is sincerely anxious that Her Majesty's Indian subjects should not be placed under special disabilities by any legislation which is the outcome of the policy dictated by that feeling.
> He has therefore endeavoured to secure that the legislation should be of a general character and not directed against any particular race or nationality.[63]

Ampthill was essentially saying that government was not taking effective steps. Bhownagree felt that such proclamations of good intent were of little value because the government was treating the white colonists of South Africa differently from his fellow countrymen in the degree of autonomy granted them, and he objected to such racial and colour prejudice. So he said in the House that:

> If . . . Imperial statesmen were to throw up their hands and argue that, because they are a self-governing administration, they could not be touched even when they trampled underfoot the noblest traditions of the British constitution, then the right to govern India from here would

---

[62] *PD* 42: 846 ff., 6 Jul. 1896. See also *PD* 37: 345, 14 Feb. 1896 and *PD* 99: 1224–35, 16 Aug. 1900, where he referred to the scandalous treatment of the people of India in other domains: 'the people of India have well nigh lost hope of all redress'.

[63] I was fortunate to learn of a collection of papers relating to Bhownagree being auctioned for sale at Sotheby's (Lot 273, 19 Jul. 1990) while researching this section of the book and wish to record my sincere thanks to staff at Sotheby's for permitting Dr Writer to study the papers on my behalf and allowing me to quote from them. This collection will hereafter be referred to as Sotheby's 1990.

be seriously impaired not only in the eyes of the people of India, but in the sight of foreign nations.[64]

He accepted that there should be substantial local autonomy in Natal, but British Indians asked for little—merely for:

> freedom for those that are now settled and those that may be allowed to come in future to trade, to move about, and to hold landed property without any hindrance, save the ordinary legislative requirement. And they asked for abrogation of legislation that imposes disabilities on them because they wear a brown skin. The white inhabitants, or a portion of kin do indeed ask for drastic legislation against Indians, and they are strong. The Indians are weak. But the British Government has always been known to protect the weak . . .

In the same letter he pressed the view:

> If four years ago, Lord Lansdowne held it to be politically injurious for it to be known that the British Government was powerless to secure redress of grievances of Asiatic subjects of the crown 'at the hands of a small South African state' how much more injurious must it now be, to British prestige, in the 'brightest and greatest dependency of Britain' for the people to learn that more than three years after the State was incorporated within the King's dominions the grievances of their fellow-countrymen not only remained unredressed, but owing largely to the enforcement of laws that were inoperative under the Boer regime have been aggravated?[65]

His points were commented on favourably by officials, and by sections of the press, and Bhownagree expressed optimism, but the stark truth is that nothing effective was done (Monk 1985: 182-87). Bhownagree became deeply dissatisfied with the government's excuses which 'while indulging in vain regrets at the situation' merely justified the 'hideous vigour' of the treatment of Indians on the grounds of 'intense hostility' from the white population and the 'necessity of protecting the new territories against the apprehended invasion of Indian traders'.[66]

---

[64] *PD* 42: 846, 6 Jul. 1896. See also 114: 554, 10 Nov. 1902; *PD* 113: 555, 31 Oct. 1902; *PD* 138: 823, 21 Jul. 1904.

[65] From a letter written by Bhownagree and published in a blue book by the Colonial Office containing 'correspondence relating to the position of British Indians in the Transvaal', House of Commons Papers, 1906, LVI.

[66] *PD* 147: 1300, 21 Jun. 1905.

An assessment of Bhownagree

Because published accounts of Bhownagree have been so heavily critical it is worth beginning this assessment with some contrary contemporary appreciations. Private correspondence indicates that there was sincere appreciation of Bhownagree's efforts at a high level in Indian society. Thus Gandhi, as honorary secretary of the Indian community in South Africa, wrote formally to him on 6 August 1898, saying:

> The Committee of the British Indians resident in Natal having heard of work done by and on behalf of the British Indians in South Africa hereby places on record its thanks to Sir M. M. Bhownagree, KCIE, MP for the splendid support extended to the cause of the British Indians in South Africa and hereby directs the Honorary Secretary to convey this resolution to Sir M. M. Bhownagree.[67]

Gandhi was Bhownagree's main informant regarding the situation in South Africa. The first letter I have been able to trace is dated 16 August 1895. On 23 October 1903, Gandhi expressed dismay at the prospect of Bhownagree retiring from Parliament: 'we in South Africa had begun to rely upon the fruits of your continuous labours in the House on our behalf'. When Bhownagree did lose his seat in the 1906 election, Gandhi wrote tendering his sympathy: 'It deprives us in South Africa of our greatest champion in the House of Commons.' Another unpublished letter from Naoroji suggests that Bhownagree undertook more quiet diplomatic work than is generally recognized, for on 16 June 1904 the Grand Old Man wrote:

> You are doing much work privately for the British Indians in Africa. It may be somewhat [writing unclear] desirable that this work should be made public. When [writing unclear] you think so, could you let me know. I would ask *India* to publish it.[68]

There can be little doubt that his work for Indians in South Africa was widely appreciated, even by his INC opponents such as Wedderburn and Bonnerjea, with whom he collaborated on this issue. But it is not easy to give a balanced assessment of Bhownagree's wider work. He was a very loyal Tory and supporter both of his government and of the British Empire,

---

[67] Sotheby's 1990.   [68] Ibid.

though he did not have the unquestioning adulatory attitude commonly implied. His speeches, especially after 1897, contained sentiments resembling those of Naoroji. He commented that the government was testing the patience and fortitude of the people of India; he spoke of 'shameful treatment'; accused the government of being 'parsimonious' and of flagrant injustice. He said that they were acting inconsistently with the proclamation of the Empress; expressed grave concern about their policy of taxing the poor through the salt tax; called for greater investment in education and technology and more opportunities for Indian students. However, his public image has been conditioned to a large extent not only by his flowery pro-British declarations but also by his vilification by some of the leading INC figures, notably Wacha. There are indications in the Wacha–Naoroji correspondence which suggest that Bhownagree sought greater co-operation across the party divide in the cause of India than is widely appreciated. Wacha refers to Bhownagree wanting to meet because he had been misunderstood, but Wacha refused.[69] Wacha was critical of Bhownagree's suggestion that India be kept out of party politics.[70] It is worth quoting one passage from a Wacha letter to Naoroji (16 October 1891) at length for it may indicate something of the bias not of Bhownagree, but of the secretary of the INC. The occasion behind the letter was a speech delivered by Bhownagree at the Parsi New Year (*Pateti*):

The Pateti celebration was all right but the community as a whole is rather offended by the fulsome speech in praise of Lord Harris by Bhownuggree. You cannot gauge the depth of the incensed feeling for all the rubbish and nonsense he has spoken. He is *dead* against the Parsis. He has all through continued to insult them. Even when Wadia's term in the Legislative Council expired he did not nominate another Parsi but appointed Naylor! It is a shame therefore for Bhownuggree to pose as an exponent of the community (which he is not) and deceive people into the belief that Harris was a friend of the Parsis. The general opinion is that he made the Pateti occasion an opportunity to promote his own selfish ends. This is the view I take too. I am really disgusted. Everybody knows that Bhownuggree is playing a high diplomatic game all for himself. I cannot write all that has

---

[69] Wacha to Naoroji, 31 Oct. 1896, Patwardhan 1977: 523.
[70] Wacha to Naoroji, 6 Dec. 1898, Patwardhan 1977: 539.

authentically come to my ears. I only hope you as a shrewd veteran will not be swayed by his sweet tongue. He is more dangerous than Dosabhoy Framji [Karaka] was in his days of influence.[71]

There are several issues in this letter which could be pursued (e.g. the place of Karaka discussed in Chapter 2 Sect.(*e*)) but the point here is the depth of personal antagonism Wacha felt for Bhownagree. The assertion that Bhownagree should not pose as an exponent of the community conflicts with all the evidence of his work in the London Association discussed in the previous chapter. Ironically, not even the hagiographic biography of Wacha in Natesan (1930: 283–329) can find any community activities to credit to Wacha himself. Wacha's criticism of Harris for not proposing a Parsi for the Legislative Council could be taken as an example of communal narrow-mindedness on the part of the secretary of the INC. A study of the records of the political body Wacha turned to after the militants took over the INC from 1907, the Western Indian Liberal Federation, shows that he was a man who would not tolerate views contrary to his own. On balance it seems that his views on Bhownagree are less just than those expressed by Naoroji and Gandhi in private.

The wider popular reactions to Bhownagree have been assessed by Monk (1985: 187–220). Where newspapers (e.g. the *Voice of India* and some of the vernacular press it quoted, such as the *Gujerati*, *Maharatta*, and *Kesari*) or politicians (above all Wedderburn) were linked to the INC, then their criticisms of Bhownagree were severe, especially in his early days in Parliament. In his second term in office when he focused more on the plight of Indians in South Africa, then the criticism became muted. But not all the Indian press was consistently hostile. The *Indian Spectator* had a more balanced perspective. It not only respected his work on behalf of Indians in South Africa but also recognized his contribution as a party politician. It denied his right to speak for all of India, was more critical of him than of Naoroji, and was opposed to his attacks on Wedderburn and Gokhale. But it was also critical of Wacha's booklet against Bhownagree. The more conservative Indian press, for example *Rast Goftar* (whose editor was friendly with Bhowna-

---

[71] Ibid.: 1977: 267.

gree), the *Hindu Patriot*, and the *Moslem Chronicle*, was not hostile to him. Within Britain also opinions were divided. *The Times* gave him the most coverage, though apart from major events and important campaigns, this consisted of reports of speeches with no editorial comment other than the occasional reference to him as a 'steady supporter of the government'. *The Times* also published some letters written by Bhownagree and wrote a supportive editorial leader on his campaign for Indians in South Africa. Obituaries are not the setting for critical analysis of people's work, but the one given in *The Times* fairly reflects that paper's perception of him:

Bhownagree was of a different mould to either of these compatriots [Naoroji and Saklatvala] and possessed a versatility they lacked. He had a practical outlook, and with great tenacity of purpose there was nothing quixotic or crusading in his temperament. To the mortification of the National Congress politicians of the day, he sat for North East Bethnal Green as a Unionist and helped Lord George Hamilton, then Secretary of State for India, to repel the attacks of Sir William Wedderburn and other members of a small group of radicals known as the 'Indian opposition'. . . . during his ten year membership impressed the House by the vigour and eloquence of his speeches on Indian subjects . . . It will always be to his credit that he originated and unflaggingly maintained, in and out of the House, the struggle against the disabilities of Indians in South Africa and other overseas possessions of the Crown . . . Bhownagree was also one of the first Indians to press forward the need of technical and vocational education.[72]

The *Guardian* was less positive and declared that his intention appeared to be 'to use his Indian name and birth against any native movement which was distasteful to the Government of India' (27 January 1897). The only issue on which it was supportive of Bhownagree was that of Indians in South Africa. The *Daily Graphic* wanted a Conservative victory in Bhownagree's constituency and was supportive of his 1900 campaign. His speeches were noted, although only those on technical education and South Africa drew explicit support.[73] In short, he was seen as consistent Tory supporter and opponent

---

[72] *The Times*, 15 Nov. 1933. For entries on Bhownagree in that paper, see the issues for 29 Jun., 1,3,4, 6,13,15,18,19,26 Jul. 1895 all on his election campaign; 15 Nov. 1895; 7 Jul. 1896; 5 and 29 Jul. 1897; 4 Apr. 1900; 29 Aug. 1904.
[73] See the issues for 15 Nov. 1895; 12 Aug. 1898; 3 Oct. 1900; 5 Aug. 1904.

of the INC, but recognized for his work concerning South Africa and to a lesser extent his campaign for technical education. His points regarding Indian finance and justice for India's poor seem to have been ignored.

Within the House of Commons attitudes to Bhownagree inevitably followed party lines. The Tories in general, and the officials in particular, inevitably welcomed his support whereas the Liberals, notably Wedderburn, spoke scathingly of him, and he in return replied in more vitriolic terms than was conventional for the day. As already noted, he was very critical of the IPP. But just as Naoroji modified his position over the years, so it seems did Bhownagree. His attacks on Wedderburn and the INC were at their strongest until 1897 and his visit to India. These, and his (then) unquestioning support of the Tory party, were the main cause of his unpopularity in India. But his changing emphases, as well as his oratory, gradually brought him more respect, albeit grudgingly, from some quarters. On 11 August 1901 the *Indian Spectator* reported: 'Sir Mancherjee is undoubtedly popular with all sorts and conditions of men. Those who do not see eye to eye with him in public life can yet appreciate him as a friend.'[74]

There are at least two dimensions to Bhownagree. On the one hand there is the side emphasised by Wacha with his allegations of intrigues, pretensions, and self-seeking are true (and there is no extant secure evidence to support them); and his evident attempts on occasions to secure the favour of Tory leaders (as do virtually all MPs) and of members of high society (through the Zoroastrian Association of Europe as well as in Parliament). On the other hand, he sought to use his influence to achieve substantial reform for Indian economic and social conditions; like Naoroji, he was convinced that Britain was not in fact treating India with the justice that she proclaimed in taxation, education, and career opportunities, or in comparison with other colonies. The study of the Zoroastrian House records suggests that he had a rather imperious manner, did not take criticisms easily, or extend much courtesy to those who opposed him personally. However, he was willing to change his mind, act decisively, and worked tirelessly for what he considered to be a

---

[74] Monk 1985: 194 f.

good cause. The subject of Bhownagree's personality will be raised again after a discussion of Saklatvala in the light of correspondence between the two MPs.

What, in conclusion, can be said of Bhownagree's attitude to Britain? In his early years in Parliament he was a strong supporter of Empire and an abrasive opponent of its critics. In the light of his parliamentary experience his criticisms appear to have grown until, by 1928 at the latest, he saw Independence as inevitable. There is an interesting exposition of his beliefs in a book he was commissioned to write to put the case for British India, in order to counter German wartime publicity attacking the British Empire and in particular the conduct of the British in India. *The Verdict of India* was published by Hodder and Stoughton in 1916. Bhownagree was obviously a good choice as an Indian known to be sympathetic to the government. But as Bhownagree rightly points out (pp. 19 f.) most people in the subcontinent supported the British cause in this war (the position was different in the Second World War). Bhownagree quoted from his Parsi compatriots Nauroji and Pherozeshah Mehta (48 f.), but he pointed to wider support, in particular to a meeting of a number of prominent educated Indians in a London club at the outbreak of war. Even though the group included militant INC leaders and opponents of the British, all signed an address to the King expressing both loyalty and co-operation (pp. 3–6). Bhownagree makes it clear in the book that he shared some of the doubts about the internal administration of the Empire: 'there have been many defects, avoidable and unavoidable . . . there are different angles of vision . . . There are legitimate aspirations, which remain to be fulfilled' (p. 19). But his main theme, inevitably in the context, was what he considered to be the advantages of British rule in India, especially the system of justice and technological investment (roads and railways). Bhownagree even felt able to identify with the Government's perspective on British rule 'that broad and judicious conception of the trust England accepted when the destinies of the country gradually passed into her hands' (p. 21). It is uncertain whether Naoroji, even in wartime, would have gone so far; certainly Saklatvala would not have done. In short, Bhownagree may have been critical of details of British rule, some of which he thought were very serious, but essentially he remained, to the last, positive in his appraisal of it.

(c) *Shapurji Saklatvala (1874 –1936 MP 1922–1923, 1924–1929)*

Background

Saklatvala has been neglected in previous studies of the Parsis, not least because he is commonly, though not wholly accurately, seen as having been distanced from his community. In addition to seeking a balanced perspective of his life, this chapter will focus on his work in Parliament with particular reference to his attitudes towards India and will discuss further his community contacts. It is impossible, however, to isolate individual issues within his overall philosophy. Whereas Bhownagree's political work was concentrated on Parliament, Saklatvala's was more diverse, with extensive campaigning both for the Independent Labour Party and later the Communist Party in Britain and overseas. Naoroji was mostly concerned with a single issue, the condition of India. Saklatvala had a basic platform, his conviction that Communism was the necessary basis for future civilization, but this led him to raise a plethora of questions. Whereas the previous two Parsi MPs tended to deliver speeches on single subjects, Saklatvala ranged widely, from local to international matters, from social to military questions, all within the same speech. It might be said that Naoroji wanted to change the British government's policies, Bhownagree wanted to modify their tactics, but Saklatvala wanted to change the world.[75]

Saklatvala was born in Bombay on 28 March 1874. His grandfather (also named Shapurji) was related to, and a crucial partner of, the founder of the Tata empire, Nusserwanji (father of the famous J. N.). There is a conviction within the Saklatvala

---

[75] The main studies of Saklatvala are, in chronological order, Saha 1970 (a rather uncritical partisan account but with useful appendices, notably Saklatvala's correspondence with Gandhi and his assessment of the Round Table Conference); Kulke 1974: 228–32 (a short and over-negative account); Visram 1986: 144–58, 215–21 (useful); Hancock 1990 (the fullest account at the time of writing); Squires 1990 (good on his political work and philosophy) and Saklatvala 1991 (written by the MP's daughter and therefore providing a personal insight into his life; also including many lengthy excerpts from documents). I wish to thank Ms Saklatvala for giving me files of papers relating to her father and for sharing her memories.

family (Saklatvala 1991: 2–8) that the Tatas excluded them from their due share in the companies. Jamsetji Tata did take the Saklatvala family into his home, Esplanade House, in 1902 and acted as a powerful benevolent patron for the young Shapurji, possibly favouring him to the detriment of his own son, Dorabji. This caused jealousy, which was to give Saklatvala considerable problems later on. J. N. was an extremely powerful personality and even turned the future MP against his own father in his formative years (Saklatvala 1991: 4–7). The Saklatvala–Tata relations were a crucial thread in his life.

Another formative factor in Saklatvala's life was his education at the Jesuit St Xavier's College, Bombay. His debating talents were widely recognized, but his academic achievements were not remarkable. He failed his degree, did not resit, and when later in life, he began to study law in London, he did not complete his studies. St Xavier's was influential in the value-system he developed. His religious interests and baptism have already been discussed. His daughter comments on the impression the disciplined austerity of the priests and nuns made on him, characteristics of his own developed personality in adult life.

Saklatvala joined Tatas in 1901 and a year later began prospecting for iron ore and coal in Central India, a quest he pursued until 1904, sometimes in the company of an American engineer, and at times with Dorabji and J. N. Tata. Eventually Saklatvala was successful to the considerable benefit of the company, but the struggles were immense: first in locating the resources in areas of jungle and swamp devoid of any material comforts such as clean water but threatened by tigers; second in the growing antagonism with Dorabji who had little commitment to the search; and third in the severe health problems Saklatvala experienced in the course of his work. In 1905 it was decided that Saklatvala should move to the Tata office in England, partly for health reasons, partly to put a distance between him and Dorabji, now head of Tatas, and finally because his political views were causing difficulties for the firm. J. N. Tata was a supporter of the INC, Dorabji was an anglophile, whereas Saklatvala, though still formally a Liberal, was moving further to the Left. It was feared that this might threaten the growth of Tata industries.

There is no known single event which triggered his political development. Two episodes are commonly related to illustrate his early interest in social issues. In 1902 bubonic plague afflicted Bombay. Saklatvala and some friends spent six years helping a bacteriologist, Professor Vladimir Haffkine, with a pioneering programme of immunization. Haffkine was a Russian Jew who had escaped from Odessa to avoid imprisonment and Tsarist surveillance of his radical political activity. Whether it was close contact with the terrible living conditions of the poor, or the views of Haffkine, or both, which sparked Saklatvala's socialist concerns is not known. The work made him ill and depressed. He went into a sanatorium, spending whole days walking and reflecting, but the trend of his thoughts is unknown. Another early indication of his social concerns was his treatment of the Tata workers for whom he was responsible. He paid them more than was customary and gave them a rest period in the afternoon, as the British had but the Indian workers did not. He also experienced their lifestyle, living in their huts.

Saklatvala thus arrived in Britain in November 1905 having spent what was to prove half his life working among the poor in both rural and urban India, a dimension to his experience that his critics ignored, choosing rather to question his socialist integrity on the grounds of his capitalist family connections and his Tata income.[76] It is reasonable to assume that the contrasts in lifestyles he experienced between the Tata home and the cholera-ridden hutments and extreme deprivation of the rural areas fundamentally affected Saklatvala's world-view. His conviction that he suffered grave injustice from the new head of this capitalist enterprise is not likely to have endeared him to the associated political perspective.

Within three days of arriving in London, depressed, ill, and on crutches, Saklatvala went to Matlock in Derbyshire to take the waters at this spa town. There he met, and fell instantly in love with a local girl working as a waitress at his hotel; Sarah Elizabeth, known as Sally, was renamed by Saklatvala, Seri. They married a year later and moved to London. They had five children. Everything points clearly to a stable marriage, though with little overt affection. His marriage out of the community produced some problems with traditional family

---

[76] e.g. *PD* 207: 1403, 17 Jun. 1927.

members, friends in Bombay, and the community in London. But it did not isolate him from Parsis, for his close personal friends were Kekoo Mehta and (Dr) Fram Gotla who was active in the Association, though married out of the community.

The story of his political allegiances is more complex. When he arrived in London he came with a family membership of the Liberal party and gave the Liberal Club in London as his first address. But his move through the spectrum of socialism was steady. In 1907 he joined the Finchley branch of the Social Democratic Federation (later renamed the British Socialist party), a Marxist group which in 1920 became the Communist party of Great Britain. Like others he was a member of several socialist groups, being particularly active in the Independent Labour party (ILP) and through that affiliated group became a member of the Labour party in 1909. He appears to have been somewhat unsettled in succeeding years, moving house between Manchester and London and within the capital. In 1912 he returned to India, apparently with a view to resettling in the old country, but when that did not prove satisfactory he returned to Britain. After the outbreak of war he became more politically active, mainly through the ILP. With the Russian Revolution, Communism became his overriding passion until he resigned from the Labour party in 1921 when Communist party affiliation was rejected nationally by the party. Between 1917 and 1921 he rose to national prominence as a popular orator, campaigning vigorously to overthrow capitalism.

Saklatvala's Parliamentary Years 1922–1929

The story of Saklatvala's parliamentary candidature is not as complex as that of Naoroji. Battersea North had a long history of Socialist and organized Labour activity, partly because of local conditions and partly because it had an anti-imperialist tradition, with a large Irish electorate. Battersea also had the first black mayor in Britain, J. R. Archer, who had a West Indian father and an Irish mother. Archer actively campaigned for Saklatvala. It was, therefore, a constituency with traditions appropriate for an Indian Labour/Communist candidate. In 1922 dual party membership was still accepted and Saklatvala publicly accepted the Labour manifesto. His candidature was unopposed in either party and he won the seat with a majority of over 2,000 (Squires 1990: 60–8).

Because successive governments lost votes of confidence there were three elections in the years 1922–4. Saklatvala won the first and third, but lost the second. His share of the vote varied by as little as 1%. In each of these elections he stood with Labour party backing; when he stood in 1929 without that support, he received few votes. He appears to have lost in 1923 because his Liberal opponent's vote (there was no Tory candidate) was no longer split by an Independent Liberal candidate. Saklatvala's return to Parliament in 1924 was remarkable because he won the seat in the face of a huge swing to the Tories which left the Liberals only forty-two and Labour fifty seats. Why one of those Labour seats was won by Saklatvala is not clear. The campaign had been marked by scaremongering tactics from the media targeted against Socialists generally and Communists in Battersea in particular. The strategy worked nationally, but not locally in Saklatvala's constituency (Squires 1990; Visram 1986: 144–58).

Saklatvala's parliamentary message will be discussed below. This was the most active phase of his life, with visits to Moscow and Copenhagen, a planned (but government-blocked) visit to America, and a particularly active campaigning period associated with the General Strike which culminated, for him personally, in imprisonment. He had been deeply involved in the public debate regarding the substantial growth in unemployment, the miners' strike, and later the General Strike, a period of considerable political unrest in Britain. Saklatvala was sent to prison on 26 May 1926 for two months because he refused to give the court an undertaking to refrain from calling on the army not to take up arms against the civilian population in the Strike, a call he had made at a public rally in Hyde Park on 1 May. The support of his immediate family was unquestioning (Saklatvala 1991: 307–13), but the reactions of his wider family in India and of the Zoroastrian community are unknown. In Parliament he had few supporters at any time. His speech to the House on his return was characteristic of his courtesy and his concern for the disadvantaged. Within one and a half hours of his release from Wormwood Scrubs prison he was justifying, in Parliament, Russian support for starving miners:

I hope the House will pardon me for any slips on this occasion, because I have only just returned to this House from a semi-socialistic institution in which I have been taken care of on a much better scale than the poor miners. I also beg at this juncture to express my gratitude for the many considerations which have been shown to me, and also for the happy impressions I carry away of some of the brighter sides of British character in regard to the treatment meted out to me by British prison officials . . . I have been permitted through the courtesy of Mr Speaker and the Home Secretary to follow the Debates that have taken place from day to day during my absence.[77]

After release from prison he continued to be subject to harassment. Throughout his career his mail was opened and he was subject to Secret Service surveillance. During the Strike and its aftermath his speeches were frequently cancelled by the police at the last moment when it was too late to make alternative arrangements. There were no violent disruptions associated with them, but it was feared that his oratory would stimulate political opposition. The longterm effect of the Strike was to give the Tory government justification for restricting trade union powers, and as they weakened so Saklatvala lost part of his power-base.

Saklatvala in India

The major event for Saklatvala in 1927 was his visit to India. This merits special attention here for several reasons. It clearly heightened his concerns for the land of his birth, as shown by the increased frequency and force of his subsequent parliamentary interjections concerning India. The visit also had a profound effect on his relationship with the Zoroastrian community both in India but more particularly in London, and was a factor in his decision to have his children's *naujotes* performed. It is often said, not least in the Zoroastrian community, that he did not enjoy widespread popular support on the subcontinent and it is worth asking if that is true.

The British government was slow to grant Saklatvala a visa to visit the land of his birth. He eventually wrote to the Prime Minister, saying that he was being restricted in his parliamentary work, that he was being denied due 'political opportunities when

[77] *PD* 197: 1163, 30 Jun. 1926.

logical and constitutional methods have no chance of destroying my political contributions'.[78] He was eventually allowed to go (although he was refused permission to call at Egypt *en route*, probably under British government pressure) and the visit lasted from January to April 1927. The delay in giving permission made advance planning difficult,[79] but nevertheless he had a crowded itinerary, starting with several meetings in Bombay, notably a public welcome given by 'the citizens of Bombay'.[80] One strong theme in his speeches was his call for Hindu–Muslim unity in the face of imperial force and to this end he addressed specifically Muslim audiences in Bombay and later in Calcutta. After four days of meetings in Bombay, including one organized by the Parsi Rajkiya Sabha in the Cowasji Jehangir Hall,[81] he proceeded to Navsari where he was greeted on arrival by the Parsi High Priest Dastur MeherjiRana and was given the freedom of the city.[82] While in Navsari he addressed a meeting in Gujarati and wore traditional Parsi dress. It would be difficult to imagine the anglicized Bhownagree expressing his communal roots so publicly! On 21 January Saklatvala arrived at Ahmedabad station, where he was garlanded by the Congress leader, Vallabhai Patel. He visited Gandhi's ashram, but the two did not meet until February. After returning to Bombay, and publicly criticizing Gandhi for looking backwards in industrial terms, he proceeded to Delhi, where Nehru attended one of his public meetings.[83] Once again Saklatvala stayed with Muslim leaders, doubtless as part of his policy to try to unite the communities.[84] From Delhi Saklatvala went to Nagpur, where he finally met Gandhi. The results of the meeting were not made fully public, though reports circulated that Saklatvala was affronted at the way Gandhi allowed himself to be venerated, or as Saklatvala put it, 'the resuscitation of the old Gurudom'. It is also said that Saklatvala's argument that Gandhi should support industrialization to improve the income of the workers of India was greeted with laughter, not with argument. The newspaper report concludes:

[78] Published in the *Daily Worker*, 21 Feb. 1926 quoted in Saha 1970: 22 f.
[79] *Bombay Chronicle*, 15 Jun. 1927.   [80] Ibid. 19 Jan. 1927.
[81] Ibid. 25 Jan. 1927.   [82] Ibid. 21 Jan. 1927.   [83] Ibid. 29 Jan. 1927.
[84] Saklatvala had in his parliamentary speeches condemned the British for dividing Hindus and Muslims, e.g. *PD* 198: 1110, 20 Jul. 1926.

The Comrade then made a final effort to persuade Gandhiji by agreeing to put on the Khaddar cap as a disciplinary measure if Gandhiji would bless the workers' programme. But this was also of no avail and so the Comrade finally left Gandhiji thoroughly disappointed in all his hopes of finding some via media with the author of the modern renaissance in India.[85]

This vain attempt at collaboration was followed by correspondence published by Saklatvala (Saklatvala 1927) which made public the gulf between their political philosophies . The hostility was thinly veiled and alienated Saklatvala from most people in the INC, even the Parsi who chaired and supported Saklatvala's meetings, J. K. Mehta,[86] expressed regret in the press at Saklatvala's attack on Gandhi. As far as Congress members were concerned, the MP was voicing a heresy that isolated him from their cause.

Saklatvala journeyed from Nagpur to Karachi (9 February), where the Parsi president of the municipality, Jamshed Mehta, presented the address of welcome.[87] By 20 February Saklatvala had crossed the continent to speak in Calcutta and then went south to Madras. In both cities he was given a Civic Reception and an Address. The *Bombay Chronicle* for 1 March reported that the Bombay Corporation debated whether it, too, should present an address to Saklatvala on his return to the city at the conclusion of his Indian tour. It decided not to do so. What is interesting in this context is how the Parsi vote divided. Sir Dinshah M. Petit, H. P. Mody, Byramji Jijibhoy, J. B. Petit, Honble Sir Pheroze Sethna, and several other less well-known Parsis, opposed the presentation whereas F. K. Nariman, K. E. Dadachanji, and two other Parsis supported it. The vote illustrates how Parsis did not function as a block in Indian politics, nor did they always support their own. Those who opposed the presentation included Bhownagree's allies (Petit and Sethna), and the supporters included one of Gandhi's allies (Nariman), and surprisingly Sethna's colleague in the Western Liberal Federation, Dadachanji. The vote was therefore mostly, but not wholly, on party lines. Saklatvala returned to Bombay in March. His Parsi chairman, J. K. Mehta, introduced him at a

[85] *Bombay Chronicle*, 29 Jan. 1927. [86] Ibid. 14 Mar. 1927.
[87] Ibid. 11 Feb. 1927.

meeting in Bandra as 'a great Indian, a great Parsi and a great Communist'. It would be unwise to assume that this list is in order of priority, but it is noteworthy that his communal identity was highlighted. It suggests that however strong his internationalism, he was seen, and presumably saw himself, as Parsi. His speech included a strong attack on the INC. He said that:

all the 40 years of work had been merely wasted. There was no effect of their propaganda on British Imperialism . . . The real work before the Congress was to organise the labouring classes and to make it impossible for a man to exploit another. Then Foreign rule would be an impossibility.

Yet, in his last speech in India delivered in Bombay, despite all his differences with Congress leaders, he called for support for the Congress:

All must get into the Congress, whatever might be their differences and exchange their views with one another. It was stupid to remain aloof and sulk and grumble, 'We should have a strong united National Congress, representative of all the classes and interests. Nothing can be national in India if the peasants and workers are not in it for they form the largest majority.'[88]

Clearly, for all his disputes with Gandhi, and his declared doubts about the Indian merchants and capitalists in Congress failing to concern themselves with the Indian workers, he still considered the INC to be the main instrument for the overthrow of British imperialism in India.

At his final meeting in the Cowasji Jehangir Hall the concluding speeches made much use of the term '*au revoir*' and emphasized the hope that he would soon return. Such hopes were vain, for the British (even the Labour) government refused him a visa to return to his country of birth and upbringing. The INC allegation that his visits to India were a flop would not appear to be have been shared by the government, who evidently thought him dangerous because his well–attended meetings aroused public interest and they feared he might recruit for the Communists.

[88] Ibid. 8 Apr. 1927.

Saklatvala's Last Years

Saklatvala's subsequent travels were confined to Europe and to Russia in 1934, when he determinedly spent time in Asian Russia in order to see what Communism could do for Asian peoples. He returned to Britain exultant, above all on what could be achieved in the field of mass education (Saklatvala 1991: 469–72).

After his defeat in Battersea in the 1929 election, he fought two further unsuccessful campaigns: Shettleston (Glasgow) in 1930 and Battersea North again in 1931. In each case he stood simply as a Communist, with no Labour support, campaigning on broad class issues, not on local concerns. With Saklatvala there is always a question of whether there were undocumented pressures upon him and what his unrecorded activities were. Squires (1990: 131) notes how his work was constantly supervised by the leadership of the Communist party, and how on occasions the most minute details of his parliamentary interventions would be worked out in consultation with the central committee. When he took actions or made speeches which were disapproved of, then he was reprimanded and his expulsion from the party was sometimes discussed publicly. This occurred when he commended the retiring speaker of the House of Commons, in June 1928; when he made a visit to Berlin that was not approved of in advance; and when he had his children's *naujotes* performed (Squires 1990: 125–8). One example of his unrecorded activities is his work to establish Communist groups on his tour of India .

After his election defeat he sought to remain active in politics. As well as making further attempts to enter Parliament he sought also, in vain, for a seat on the local council in St Pancras and Battersea; but his main concerns were broad ones of principle. He continued to travel around the country as a major speaker for the party, working as secretary of the Indian section of the Workers' Welfare League which he had helped to establish in the early stages of his career. He was active in the anti-Fascist movement from 1933 when, along with the party, he chose to revive support for the Labour party rather than see the right-wing forces evident in Germany come to power in Britain. The changing political scene of the 1930s required of Saklatvala, as of most politicians, that he modify his emphasis, if not his basic concerns. He died on 15 January 1936 of a heart attack.

Saklatvala's Message in Parliament

Saklatvala set out much of the broad picture of his political programme in his maiden speech on 23 November 1922 in a debate on the King's speech.[89] He began with what became a customary deferential reference to the proper traditions of the House, which he always observed punctiliously. His opening substantive issue was unemployment. First he pleaded with the Prime Minister to meet a deputation of the unemployed. He then addressed the causes of unemployment. A major factor he identified was the way in which investment was made in other countries. For example, new jute mills had been constructed in Bengal where local labour was used at a minute fraction of the pay in Britain, but people were compelled to work much longer hours and under far worse conditions. This therefore deprived the workers in Dundee of employment because they could not compete with such low labour costs, and the Indian workers of reasonable living standards, in order to achieve dividends for the capitalists of between 100 and 400%.[90] It was, he argued in his maiden speech, 'the spread of the cult of private enterprise by the political bosses in this country which is working the ruin of the workers of this land'. In the course of elaborating this point Saklatvala alluded, in passing, to an issue which he was to repeat frequently in later speeches, namely the unacceptability of one nation dictating governmental structures to other nations:

No Britisher would for a moment tolerate a constitution for Great Britain [drawn up] by people who are not British. In a similar way the constitutions for Ireland and India and Egypt and Mesopotamia should be constitutions written by the men of those countries, in those countries, without interference from outside.

He went on to argue that Britain had a poor record in preserving the interests of minorities. He started by citing the action of the Prime Minister in banning a Catholic procession in Westminster and then alluded to minorities in Armenia, Mesopota-

---

[89] *PD* 159: 110–18, reproduced in full in Saklatvala 1991: 150–7.
[90] A point he elaborated on 6 Jul. 1925; *PD* 186: 141–50.

mia, and to the unemployed in Britain. The last group, he said, the government had made into a criminalized minority simply on the grounds of their political allegiances. Standing courageously against the unified position of the House, he objected to the Irish Treaty, which he considered to have been imposed by Britain on Ireland. He argued that Britain should ensure justice for the citizens both in Ireland and South Africa if these countries were to be considered as part of the Empire. Finally he turned to the subject of British relations with Russia, specifically the fact that Britain refused to recognize and deal with the new leaders despite acknowledging Mussolini and the King of Serbia, even though they, too, had led revolutions. His explanation of the different attitudes to these regimes was that in Italy and Serbia it was the upper classes who had triumphed, whereas in Russia it had been the masses who were victorious. In Britain, he said, there was in-built class bias. The speech not only outlined his broad political beliefs, it also typified his wide-ranging style of oration.

He was an active MP throughout his time in Parliament, making many interjections in debates and committee discussions, (even though the Speaker sometimes refused to allow him to contribute).[91] The subjects on which Saklatvala made interjections in the House (both in debates and committee discussions) can be listed by year as follows:

1923: Ireland—15 times; India—14; individual cases—4; social issues in Britain—3; Local constituency issues—3; Sudan, Russia, China, Peru, and the police—1 occasion each.

1924-5: armed forces—11; India—11; Communism—9; social issues in Britain—6; individual cases—6; coal—4; Russia, Palestine, and Poland/Lithuania—3 each; China and Egypt—2 each; Morocco, Baltic Sea, Singapore, Indians in South Africa—1 each.

1926: General Strike—12 (on the related issue of the coal industry, a further 4); police—8; armed forces—5 (NB: both of the last two subjects he typically related to the General Strike); individual cases—5; Communism—4; India—4; social issues in Britain (other than the General Strike)—3; China—3; Russia,

---

[91] *PD* 185: 2139, 2150, 29 Jun. 1925. See also *PD* 181: 397, 16 Mar. 1925; *PD* 182: 1768, 3 Apr. 1925.

Africa—2 each; broad overseas issues —2; imperialism—2 (though obviously this theme lay behind many other interjections, e.g. on India).

1927: India—9; China—5; individual cases—4; Palestine —3; armed forces—3; Persia, Communism, trades unions, British social issues, local issues—2 each; Russia, South Africa, Egypt, Japan, the police, House of Commons affairs, imperialism, foreign legion—1 each.

1928: India—18; individual/local issues—15; Communism, armed forces, and parliamentary matters—6 each; Scotland — 5; Civil Service—4; Afghanistan, British social issues—3 each; Africa, Egypt, Russia, Japan, Kenya, Persia, Sudan, Iraq, coal, Kellogg Pact on disarmament, Empire—1 each.

He made four main personal speeches: on departure from prison, his protests over being refused a visa, on his treatment at Ostend (when the authorities impeded his travel to a political meeting), and an assurance given to the House that he had not received funds from Russia for his election campaign.

These listings are necessarily arbitrary at many points; for example, a speech on Russia and one on Communism may be focused on the same issue. Some interjections were only short questions which he did not pursue, but others were long, usually circuitous, speeches which are difficult to summarize. But however arbitrary these lists may be in detail, they serve the purpose of indicating his international perspective (which was greater than that of either of his Parsi predecessors), the range of his interests, and the changing emphases in his parliamentary work according to the political circumstances of the day. Thus he spoke on Ireland more than on any other subject in 1923 when the Irish Treaty was being effected. In 1924–5 he focused mostly on the build-up of the armed and special reserve forces when social unrest was growing and Saklatvala feared that the military was being mobilized to suppress the workers. In 1926 he was concerned above all with the General Strike, and in 1927 and 1928 with India after his visit to that country. Allowing for these changing emphases he pursued two main interrelated themes: (*a*) social issues particularly relating to Britain; (*b*) imperialism in general and British rule in India in particular.

The foundation of his arguments on social concerns was his conviction that 'the whole system, political, economic, social, is so constructed that there is no purity of justice, and that it is class justice all the time' in Britain and in any capitalist system.[92] The taxation system, he argued, was structured in favour of the rulers not the workers, but it was the workers who generated wealth.[93] He questioned the principles of private enterprise, commonly using housing as an example.[94] Landlords, he maintained, refused to improve housing conditions because there was no financial incentive as the shortage of housing enabled them to let properties in any condition.[95] He raised various social issues, for example he campaigned for women in the Civil Service, for the wives and children of criminals,[96] against means-testing the old-age pension,[97] and for better health insurance for the working classes.[98] He raised more individual cases than either of his Parsi predecessors had done, though most of these were related to the Irish question (particularly the problems of deportees to Ireland) and imprisoned Indian campaigners, so the underlying points still had broad implications.[99] He also raised a number of local issues.[100]

For Saklatvala the armed forces were an important aspect of the debate on social issues. He objected to the raising of the special reserve of the forces to preserve order, or as he saw it, to impose the will of the wealthy landowners on the masses of the poor at the time of the General Strike.[101] He did not call for violence by the workers, but rather that they should call on the

---

[92] *PD* 188: 2109, 1 Dec. 1925; see also *PD* 199: 599–605, 25 Oct. 1926; *PD* 200: 868–76, 29 Nov. 1926.
[93] *PD* 162: 1786–88, 16 Apr. 1923.   [94] *PD* 159: 1446–54, 4 Dec. 1922.
[95] *PD* 160: 2133–35, 27 Feb. 1923. See also *PD* 164: 2504–8, 7 Jun. 1923; *PD* 179: 500, 12 Dec. 1924; *PD* 181: 2602, 19 Mar. 1925; *PD* 191: 80–85, 2 Feb. 1926.
[96] *PD* 180: 914; 1117, 17 and 18 Feb., 1925; *PD* 183: 465, 30 Apr. 1925; *PD* 223: 1910, 11 Dec. 1928; *PD* 227: 2182, 9 May 1929.
[97] *PD* 181: 1872, 16 Mar. 1925; *PD* 185: 2703, 2737, 2758, 1 Jul. 1925.
[98] *PD* 185: 2703 f., 1 Jul. 1925.
[99] *PD* 162: 562, 28 Mar. 1923; *PD* 164: 866, 28 May 1923; 164: 1693, 1 Jun. 1923; *PD* 165: 14, 11 Jun.; 165: 1171, 19 Jun. 1923; *PD* 180: 2492, 19 Mar. 1925; *PD* 181:   2492, 19 Mar. 1925; *PD* 224: 1373, 4 Feb. 1929.
[100] *PD* 160: 2133, 28 Feb. 1923; *PD* 162: 506, 28 Mar. 1923; *PD* 181: 1303, 11 Mar. 1925; *PD* 223: 1899, 11 Dec. 1928; *PD* 227: 411, 9 May 1929.
[101] *PD* 181: 221, 3 Mar.; 181: 2092, 17 Mar. 2602, 19 Mar. 1925; *PD* 182: 231, 24 Mar.; 182: 1070, 30 Mar. 1925; 1695, 2 Apr. 1925; *PD* 188: 2120, Dec. 1, 1925.

troops not to shoot them when they were unarmed, and for this he was imprisoned. He declared in the House:

The ruling class always rules the world by physical means and not by common sense; not by moral persuasion but by terrorism ... The means of self-defence that we have suggested to the working class is not immediately to take up arms but to open the eyes of those who are likely to kill us and fight us and to say to them and appeal to them not to kill us and not to shoot the workers'.[102]

But his objections to the armed forces were fundamental and not restricted to this specific sequence of events. Essentially he argued that the air force, navy, and army were not used to help the poor nor even (as the government proclaimed) to safeguard food supplies. He pointed out that Britain did not import food from China but nevertheless maintained a substantial armed presence in the region.[103] In a few sentences in one parliamentary speech he brought together the themes of MPs' duties, the hypocrisy of the Church, the failure of the armed forces to meet the needs of the poor, and the evils of imperialism:

We are not here to afford to the country some amusement every night. It does not mean doing patriotic duty simply to jeer at minorities in this House. We are here to discuss problems which, in the hands of the older parties, have failed and have brought on the world misery, ruin, murder, degradation, unemployment, starvation and everything else that is evil ...

It is said that we of the Communist Party are the enemies of the Christian religion; that we are out to destroy all Christian Churches. I submit that the foundation stone of the Christian Church is 'Thou shalt not kill.' You who pretend to be the supporters and faithful upholders of that Church, come and tell the nation tonight that the biggest function of the Government and of the State is to organise the most efficient weapons for murder and killing ...

There is famine in Ireland today, and no aeroplanes are going over to the West of Ireland immediately with food for little children ...

[The Air Force is necessary] because you insist on maintaining your system of imperialism, of Imperial trade, of Imperial trade routes, and

[102] *PD* 188: 2109 and esp. 2120, 1 Dec. 1925.
[103] *PD* 192: 2738, 11 Mar. 1926.

your hereditary and God-given right to raw products growing in other nations.[104]

In Saklatvala's opinion the armed forces were not undertaking the important tasks in life: 'a powerful Navy and Army are helpless to defend the houses of the poor, who are living in slums, against the tyranny of the landlords ... or against wicked profiteers'.[105]

British imperialism was his major concern in the House of Commons. The basic point of his vehement attacks was the illogicality, or hypocrisy, of the arguments used by the British to legitimate their actions. For example, in one of his last speeches in the House he protested that the reason why the British government would not co-operate with the Soviet rule in Russia was because of the bloodshed in the revolution. But, he asked,

Was the British Empire founded without bloodshed? There was a hundred times more human blood shed in the founding of the British Empire than was ever spilled in Russia during the years of the Revolution ... This country has shed a hundred times more blood of people of all nations in the world. You have slaughtered Frenchmen, Spaniards, Dutch and Russians, you have slaughtered Turks, Persians and Afghans ... You killed in their own homes the Punjabis, Bengalis and the Mahrattas, and the Ceylonese, the Burmans, the Malayans and the Chinese. You murdered poor, primitive races, people who did not know the geography of where your country was situated as the Sudanese, the Zulus, the Bantus and the Swazis and you had not the remotest excuse that they were going to attack you and kill you. You have butchered them and murdered them in a wholesale manner. You have killed them in their own country. There is no nation in the world, no institution in the world, which has devoured more human lives and created more murders than the British nation and the British Parliament.[106]

---

[104] PD 180: 2302 ff., 26 Feb. 1925. In a speech on 19 Mar. 1925 (PD 181: 2599–2608) he developed a similar argument in connection with the proposed new base in Singapore. He argued that once it was built to protect British trade–routes in the region, then the government would argue for the deployment of yet more resources to protect the base itself. See also PD 179: 957 (re Sudan and Egypt), 1167 (Afghanistan), 968 (Baltic region), 1019 (eastern Europe) all on 17 Dec. 1924; PD 180: 258 f. (Egypt), 11 Feb. 1925.
[105] PD 181: 2602, 19 Mar. 1925.   [106] PD 222: 174 f., 7 Nov. 1928.

This was one of his strongest speeches, but the same theme ran through all his parliamentary career, especially with regard to British treatment of his native country. He returned to a theme of his maiden speech, that it was fundamentally wrong for one country to determine the structure of government and policy of a land thousands of miles away. The British would not accept the imposition of a constitution by the Chinese on their own country in the way that the Simon Commission was intending to do for India in 1927. Whatever government's proclamations, he argued, the motivation was in reality Britain's own interests: 'Everybody knows, whether it is put in black and white or not, that the first thing that will be put in the terms of reference is how this country can keep a stranglehold over India.'[107] He was forceful in his criticism of the government spending Indian taxpayers' money, and taking out loans on their behalf, without consultation, for projects such as railways. The British government directed the Simon Commission to draw up proposals to overcome the problems of the competing interests of different religions and castes in India. But Saklatvala's point was:

What is wrong in India is not the religious and social customs. What is wrong is the presence of British rule, which prevents the introduction of modern thought, modern evolution, modern education and scientific methods of evolving a people's political, economic and social rights. That is what we are suffering from . . .

Because the Mohammedans are a minority in India—80,000,000—that is a justification for 40,000,000 Britishers to enslave 220,000,000 Hindus. That is the logic of what the world is asked to believe.

What on earth is a British Commission to find out in India in regard to whether Indians should rule in their own country and more than if you had the impudence to send a commission to France tomorrow to see whether that country should be run by Frenchmen or whether the British should go there to take care of the minorities in Alsace-Lorraine.[108]

From his first year in the House Saklatvala argued that Britain adopted different policies among Whites and among her own people from those pursued elsewhere. He pointed out that the

---

[107] *PD* 207: 1387 f., 17 Jun. 1927. See also *PD* 166: 675, 5 Jul. 1923; *PD* 179: 1167, 17 Dec. 1924.
[108] See esp. *PD* 166: 668 f., 5 Jul. 1923, *PD* 167: 12 f, 23 Jul. 1923; 191: 80 f., 2 Feb. 1926; *PD* 207: 1391, 17 Jun. 1927; *PD* 222: 174 f., 7 Nov. 1928.

British government imposed one set of criteria on the parts of the Empire which were composed of White colonists (e.g. Canada and Australia) and different ones where there were coloured peoples, for example India and Africa. He protested against the hypocrisy that what was labelled the 'spirit of democracy' in Britain was called seditious in India. Other examples he cited of British inconsistency were the refusal to impose the Factory Act in India as in Britain and the blocking of a Trades Union Congress in India.[109]

In addition to his basic objection to the principle of British rule in India, he vehemently objected to the methods by which that rule was imposed and the consequences it brought about for the people of India. He not only attacked government but also merchants and missionaries who, he said, were getting 'the workers to live like vermin under the iron heel of foreign investors and exploiters'.[110] He went on to contest the British declaration that India was not prepared for self-rule, although they had done much to educate its people. He argued that even on British reckoning that 10% of the population were educated, there were 30 million people educated according to western standards:

which means a much larger population than many of the smaller European countries . . . as trustees [of India] you take jolly good care to see that the other 280,000,000 of people will remain ignorant, illiterate, uneducated with no freedom to call their souls their own . . . [they are treated as] so many animals or beasts of burden.

He argued that the majority of the population were not educated or politically free because the British did not want them to be. The Russians, he maintained, had shown what could be done, for they had given the franchise to agriculturalists and education to the masses. In contrast, he maintained, Britain imposed extremely harsh economic and political conditions:

I put it quite definitely that taking a comparison with any other Eastern country, you pay the most miserable wage, and give the most miserable conditions, and deprive the population which works for you and for the prosperity of your great Empire of their rights and inflict upon them political indignity and humiliation worse than can be found in any part of Asia.

[109] *PD* 186: 705 f., 9 Jul. 1925.   [110] *PD* 186: 141 f., 6 Jul. 1925.

The feature of the miserable living conditions imposed by British rule which he highlighted on this, and on other occasions,[111] was the infant mortality rate in Bombay and other industrialized Indian cities; these figures, he maintained, belied the British assertion that they were in India to 'save the people'.

In the Wards where the factory women live the annual death rate is from 600 to 700 per 1,000. You cannot attribute that to the climate or to insanitary conditions, because all over India in the agricultural areas without sanitation or education and with a hot climate the infantile rate is about 190. It is in the factory wards of Bombay, Calcutta, Allahabad, Delhi and so on, wherever there are modern factories, that the infantile death rate comes to between 600 and 700 infants, and we think that, if nothing else, that one inhuman item, that cannibalistic feature of your Imperialism, should be quite enough to make you come away . . .

You went there, you say, to save the people, but you have acted in a contrary direction, and in the name of the people here, in the name of the people there, in the name of the masses, in the name of world civilization, in the name of the necessity for world disarmament I appeal to you to Bolshevise your own minds and hearts and to determine once for all that Imperialism, with all its good talking points, has got behind it a trail of inhuman murder, brutality, negation of rights and degradation of human life, and must be dissolved. British Imperialism must go if humanity is to progress.

Saklatvala was outraged that government should impose such conditions, yet allow minimal discussion even in Parliament on the needs of so many people. He protested forcefully about this in 1927 when India was not mentioned in the King's speech even though a new Viceroy was going out, presumably with a plan for the future. Britain, he asserted, was simply and ruthlessly determined to hang on to India.

Why does Great Britain presume that, of all the savage people in the world who cannot manage their affairs, she must be the controller of India only? It is all nonsense to say that for the benefit of the Indians the British nation has got to be there and is performing some benevolent action. For goodness sake be honest, and say you are a nation of enterprise, and in seeking for enterprise to seek your own good, opportunity placed you in a strong position to throttle the country and the people of India—that you are there, and you are determined

---

[111] *PD* 167: 12 f., 23 Jul. 1923; *PD* 207: 1387 f., 17 Jun. 1927.

to remain there as long as you can get any good out of it . . . It is no use pretending as though a deputation had come to you from the Indians . . . and said 'Come and protect us; come and give us, military protection; come and teach us civil administration . . .'[112]

In short, Saklatvala concluded, British actions in India were 'of a very hideous character'[113] because Indians were 'held in bondage', taxed unjustly,[114] exploited industrially, deprived of freedom, and made to live in intolerable, indeed murderous, conditions and political bondage. Saklatvala considered that class-ridden Britain gave justice neither to its own working classes, nor to those in other nations.

An Assessment of Saklatvala's Influence

How effective was Saklatvala? Squires (1990) and Saklatvala (1991) refer to his brilliant oratory, as do the newspaper reports of his public speeches, especially on his India tour. But the transcripts of his parliamentary speeches do not carry that impression. They commonly ranged widely over a number of issues in a repetitive style. The Speaker of the House of Commons, or the Chairman of a House Committee, often asked him to keep to the subject. Mention has already been made of the fact that his opportunities to speak were restricted. When he did, then he was generally ignored.[115] Indeed it is difficult to find any example of the government making a direct response to his speeches (as opposed to the specific questions asked). One occasion when his speech drew comment was on 25 November 1927 (*PD* 210: 2272–9) when he again campaigned for the withdrawal of the British from India. Prime Minister Baldwin replied in patronizing tones which entirely ignored the substance of Saklatvala's arguments:

We are all very pleased to see the hon. Member for North Battersea back in his place. It is quite evident that during his absence he has made no speech against the Government of the country which he was visiting comparable to the one which he has delivered today, or we should most regretfully have had to do without his presence. When speaking of liberty, he must have lost for the moment his keen sense of

---

[112] *PD* 207: 1387 f., 17 Jun. 1927. [113] *PD* 191: 80 f., 2 Feb. 1926.
[114] *PD* 192: 2738 f., 11 Mar. 1926.
[115] *PD* 167: 7; 179: 1167; 180: 456; 185: 2740 and 2758.

humour. I felt that never had there been an exhibition more patent to this world of the height, depth, breadth and strength of British liberty than the sight of the hon. Member delivering that speech in the British House of Commons.

In one sense Baldwin was right: there were countries where such a vocal opponent of the government would not have been allowed to speak in Parliament. But despite the fact that the British government proclaimed freedom of speech so loudly, what Baldwin failed to mention was that Saklatvala had Secret Service Surveillance, his mail opened, his entry to America and later to his country of birth, India, refused; that his speeches were cancelled and he was imprisoned. Further, although Saklatvala was allowed to speak, he was not listened to. From the government's perspective, when Saklatvala spoke, he frequently gave a set lecture (acknowledged to have been determined by the Communist party), commonly ignoring the subject of the debate. That was not an effective way to debate with government. The two sides, therefore, failed to listen to each other. Essentially, Saklatvala was used as a public spokesman for the Communist party. There is little to suggest that he was expected to effect much change.

What of Saklatvala's relations with the INC? These lie somewhat outside the precise scope of this book's focus on Zoroastrians in Britain, just as much of Naoroji's INC work fell beyond the compass of this work. But they have some relevance because Squires (1990: 143–55) has shown that the Communist party of Great Britain, presumably under Saklatvala's influence, originally differed from Communist International on policy towards the INC. Originally Saklatvala had pressed for collaboration with INC leaders because they represented a strong move for freedom from British rule. On his departure from India in 1927 he urged everyone to unite behind Congress.[116] He enjoyed better relations with Nehru than he had with Gandhi. Nehru attended his lecture in Calcutta. In the debate on the Government of India Act Saklatvala pleaded for Nehru to be brought to the Bar of the House to give the Indian perspective on the government of that country. Nehru also sent a message to Saklatvala's funeral, unlike Gandhi. Basically, Nehru was more

---

[116] *Bombay Chronicle*, 9 Apr. 1927; *Forward*, 30 Apr. 1927.

sympathetic to the message of Communism. Saklatvala's main INC supporter, Nariman, was effectively removed from power in the early 1930s for daring to criticize Gandhi's invocation of religion in the nationalist cause.[117] In the longer term, therefore, Saklatvala was distanced from INC leaders and he became increasingly convinced that they were influenced by Indian capitalists whose interests were more allied to those of British capitalists than they were to those of the Indian workers. His relations with the Liberal Federation leaders (e.g. Sethna) were not good, as is illustrated by their vote against the Bombay Corporation presenting him with an address. Saklatvala was, therefore, dissociated from the main figures on both sides of the debate about India's political future. It may be assumed that he was much closer to the Socialist leaders on the subcontinent, but they had little access to the effective political discussions and Saklatvala did not provide such an opening.

Zoroastrian House files contain some interesting correspondence between Bhownagree and Saklatvala which sheds some light on the relations between them and their attitudes towards their critics. Saklatvala initiated the exchange with a letter written during his by-election campaign in Glasgow (23 June 1930). After excusing himself from attending Zoroastrian House the following week he commented:

My politics and standards of fights are otherwise at pole's end from yours, yet there are several factors that often make me think of you. When you first started breaking the Indian superstition that all Liberals are really liberal and all Conservatives were cruel you were considered to be the only 'fool among all wise men'! After 35 years the superstition still lingers. Now in Labour we have worse Impostors even than in Liberals, and in so-called Left-Wing I.L.Pers. [Independent Labour Party] we reach the maximum of political hypocrisy of present day. My last few years are spent in fighting this error, if injustice and oppression are to be fought. Our old-fashioned countrymen still adhere to this superstition. Gandhi seriously replies to Fenner Brockway, and he and old Punditji waste their time in giving long interviews to Slocomb. What a leg-pulling all round! Or is it the case of Birds of the same

---

[117] Kulke 1974: 201, though in a future publication (J. R. Hinnells and K. M. JamaspAsa,'The Parsis in British India: Their History and Religion') it is hoped to establish how much more of a factor Nariman's criticisms of Gandhi were in his downfall than is currently appreciated.

feather? When in between my whirlwind campaign work I give thoughts to these things, I think of you.

In his concluding sentence, Saklatvala adds that he realizes that 'in word and spirit my politics will be unacceptable to you'. Bhownagree, in his reply dated 30 June 1930, expressed appreciation of the labours of Saklatvala in writing during an election campaign and went on:

The couple of generations that have elapsed since my notions of men and matters political were taking shape, have not shaken the foundations of my beliefs; and as I have never cared to shift them in accordance with popular, that is mob, moods, I have been content to look on while groups of favourite leaders have enjoyed their transient day of fame, and passed into oblivion or been surpassed by others of their kind, feeling firm in the faith that I, or rather my beliefs, (for it is not persons, but principles that live) shall be in some remote future justified of . . . [writing unclear] . . . I have seen your election literature. It is not new to me. The goal being the same, namely the welfare of India, it is only in the methods of attaining it, lies the difference.

The letters are interesting for several reasons. Although at the extremes of the political spectrum, both politicians in private accepted that their goal was the same—the welfare of India. In the twilight of their respective careers it would seem that each had more respect for the other than for Gandhi. Saklatvala's perception of the hypocrisy in the Labour Party is as noteworthy as Bhownagree's perception of himself as one who refused to court popularity. This personal correspondence shows that relations, although somewhat frigid, were better in private than their political stances might suggest, as was the case between Bhownagree and Naoroji.

Even within the Communist party Saklatvala's influence waned towards the end of his life. While he was in Parliament he was, according to Squires, strictly under party control, as is shown by some public reprimands he received. After 1929 he was used as an orator but he was never, as far as is known, a policy-maker for the party, the only exception being his earlier pleas for the INC, which he himself was in due course to reject. When he could not visit India after 1927, he lost some influence through the party there and when the Tories weakened trade-union power in Britain his orbit of influence was again reduced.

The sad fact is, therefore, that by the end of his life his restricted influence had gone and if one presses hard the question 'What precisely did he achieve?', it is difficult to identify anything specific—not even the equivalent of the biased Royal Commission in which Naoroji was involved. It is said (Squires 1990: 119 f., 131) that if he had adopted a more moderate line acceptable to the Labour Party then he could have become Under-Secretary of State for India and he almost certainly would have been given a safe Labour seat. Like many politicians he was faced with a stark choice between principles and power. Saklatvala chose to campaign for what he believed in, and thereby never achieved real power.

On his death some sections of the press published tributes to him. The *Labour Monthly* (February 1936) said, rather extravagantly: 'The armed might of the British Empire feared this man as no other, whose only weapon was the truth.' The *Daily Worker* published messages from various people including Nehru, Clement Attlee, the Soviet ambassador in London, and the secretary of the Communist party in Great Britain. Even his parliamentary opponents recognized him as a man of unfailing courtesy, but they chose to ignore his arguments.[118] They rarely debated and never implemented them. He was sometimes referred to as the MP for India (Squires 1990: 118) but his impact on developments in the land of his birth is not discernible, though whether he had an undocumented impact through the Indian Workers' Welfare League and the trades unions is unknown. He condemned Britain for its colour prejudice, witness his remarks on the different treatment of 'white Colonies' (Canada and Australia) compared with 'coloured' (Africa and India), and he had some experience of such prejudice himself (Visram 1986: 151; Squires 1990: 87). His Parsi identity and family connections with the Tatas were used in Parliament in an effort to undermine his credibility as a spokesman for the Indian working classes.[119]

---

[118] I have been able to find only a single instance of Saklatvala launching a personal attack in Parliament, when he spoke at the time of the miners' strike of a Cabinet Minister 'whose family has flourished on the starvation, under-payment and over-production of the miners, whose family has made money out of the blood of the miners and are today crushing the miners that their future dividends may be higher than they ought to be under a just administration . . . The Minister . . . who is one of the worst inhuman exploiters, living on the blood-money and the sweat-money of the miners . . . (*PD* 200: 868 f., 29 Nov. 1926). [119] *PD* 207: 1387–1403, 17 Jun. 1927.

But it was his Communist affiliation, not his Indian origins, which was used by his opponents to render him politically ineffective. His own Parsi community did not know how to respond to him. Just as the London Zoroastrians were divided on this point, so too were those in India. On the one hand he was greeted by the senior Parsi priest, Dastur MeherjiRana in Navsari, and by some politicians, notably but not only Nariman; but he was rejected by others, especially those associated with the government establishment of the day—the Petits, Mody, and Sethna. He himself could criticize his community's capitalist tendencies, yet he chose on occasion to appear in Parsi dress. Despite recent studies, Saklatvala the Parsi remains an enigma.

(d) *Zerbanoo Gifford (1950–)*

The last Parsi politician to be considered is different from the others, not only on the grounds of gender, but also because she is still active and has not yet become an MP. However, she merits attention because of the work she has already undertaken. She was born in India but had her schooling at one of Britain's most prestigious girls' public schools, Roedean, and thereafter at Watford College of Technology, the London School of Journalism, and the Open University. She was brought up in a conscious Zoroastrian environment, for her father, Bailey Irani, was the leading figure in the establishment of the World Zoroastrian Organization (see Ch.4, Sect. (*m*), above). She is consciously Zoroastrian, as president of the Harrow Zoroastrian Association, and in her private life. She sees a line of continuity between herself, a Liberal Democrat politician concerned with women's rights, and her hero, Dadabhoy Naoroji about whom she wrote a book in connection with the centenary celebrations of his election to Parliament (Gifford 1992)—celebrations which will be discussed below. In 1973 she married Richard, a Christian, and thereafter experienced some of the problems faced by Zoroastrians who marry out of the community.

The earliest indicator of her social concerns was her work with Shelter, a charitable organization seeking to provide accommodation for the homeless, which she joined in 1971. She was elected a local councillor for the Liberal party in Harrow in 1982 (achieving a 42 per cent swing to the Liberals in what had been a safe Tory ward). A year later she came to national prominence when she was made chairperson of the Liberal party's Community Relations Panel and then chaired the party's Commission of Inquiry into Ethnic Minority participation (which reported in 1986). In 1983 she stood for election to Parliament in the Hertsmere constituency against the then Tory party chairman, and influential Cabinet Minister, Cecil Parkinson. She doubled the Liberal vote, pushing the party into second place and thereby receiving press interest.[120] The following year she was elected to the National Council of the Liberal party. She held office in local politics until 1986 and was there associated with campaigns concerning the rights of Asians, for example proposals for a Hindu temple and the plight of Ugandan Asians, as well as with purely local issues (parks, ponds, and wasteland). She stood again for Parliament, this time in her local Harrow East constituency, unsuccessfully, in 1986 and 1992 for Hartsmere again. As the *Liberal News* reported: 'She is the first Asian woman to be selected by any political party to fight the next election' (11 April 1986).

Zerbanoo Gifford has been identified with two particular political causes: women's rights and racial equality. In 1987 she was appointed to the Status of Women Commission, through which she was involved in discussions with the Home Office, mainly on rape counselling, well women's clinics and she campaigned for more women in political life. In 1984 she presented a paper on 'Women and the Law' to the Liberal Assembly. In that same year, she was invited to the USA to meet political and local leaders, being seen as herself a future policy-maker. But it is her campaign for racial equality that has attracted most attention. In 1987 she was given the Asian Times Award for Achievement and Service and in 1989 the Nehru

[120] *New Life* (a British Asian weekly) 15 Apr., 20 and 24 Jun.; *Harrow Midweek*, 19 Apr.; *Focus* 21 Apr.; *The Times* 18 Aug. The news was featured in India also: *Free Press Journal* (Bombay), 17 Nov.; *Blitz* (Bombay) 19 Nov.; *Parsiana*, Dec. (pp. 18 f.); *Eve's Weekly* (Bombay); *India Weekly*, 21 Apr. and 15 and 22 Dec. (a double-issue article). (NB: I wish to express my thanks to Zerbanoo for making her political files available for consultation—and for the generous hospitality she and Richard have always shown.)

Centenary Award.[121] She has been associated with the Centre for Research in Asian Migration at Warwick University and is an adviser in the Prince of Wales Youth Business Trust with a particular interest in youth employment. She has addressed the Liberal conferences on both of these themes. The two causes were united in her first book (Gifford 1990), an account of successful Asian women in Britain. As a result of her political and community contacts she has encouraged more Asians to support (Liberal Democrat) party politics.

She has herself, more than any of the previous Parsi politicians, been a victim of racial abuse—an indicator of the growth of the problem in Britain rather than of personal factors. Like Naoroji she faced at best non-cooperation, at worst opposition, at the local level in the Liberal party, manifest mostly in a reluctance to proceed with her nomination and help in her campaign, but she also experienced personal abuse. Again like Naoroji, she received little help from the national party with her local difficulties (on the grounds of the autonomy given to constituencies), though at a wider level she was supported, for example in her role on the Community Relations Panel. The fiercest racial prejudice surfaced in 1986. In February of that year she was provoked to walk out of local council meetings because of the Tory leader's refusal to act on racial prejudice.[122] A campaign of racial hatred had begun against her personally after she stood as a parliamentary candidate in 1983, but it attracted attention in the national press in April–June 1986, resulting in the then Liberal party leader, Sir David Steel, calling on the Home Secretary (Douglas Hurd) to give her police protection. The abuse involved not only obscene and threatening telephone calls to herself, but also threats against her children. Her property was damaged. Even the national tabloid Tory press, not normally associated with her causes, gave outraged front-page coverage to the campaign against her.[123] Fortunately she has also received more positive coverage in the national media, appearing on important radio and television programmes as a respected political campaigner

---

[121] 1986, *Asian Times*, 26 Sept.; *Focus*, 20 Sept.
[122] *Times and Post Newspapers*, 20 Feb.; *New Life*, 21 Feb.; *Observer*, 27 Mar.
[123] *Mail on Sunday*, 6 Apr. (front page coverage); *Daily Express*, 8 Apr. It was, also, in the local press: *Harrow and Northwood Informer*, 10 Apr.; *Asian Times*, 11 Apr.

on social issues, being recognized as an Asian woman ready and able to press the concerns of others.[124]

Zerbanoo Gifford has probably been seen less as a Zoroastrian (and more as an 'Asian') than have some of her predecessors.[125] This changed somewhat in 1992 when she was co-chair of the parliamentary celebrations to mark the centenary of Naoroji's election to Parliament, as well as writing her book mentioned above (see also Vajifdar 1993). As a consequence, the Zoroastrian community was brought into higher public profile, and in an appropriately pioneering way, than perhaps at any time in its history in Britain. This resulted in events not only within the community but within wider society also, in Naoroji's old constituency, at the Indian High Commission, and in Parliament. In 1994 Gifford was again prominent as a Zoroastrian when she said traditional prayers from the religion in a much-advertised public act of worship to give thanks for the multiracial developments in South Africa, which involved the prominent South African churchman, Archbishop Desmond Tutu. From the point of view of the history of Zoroastrians in Britain, it is to be hoped that there is much more work ahead of her!

(e) Conclusion

Allowing for their contrasting personalities and opposing political allegiances, are there any unifying factors between the programmes, principles, and lives of the Parsi politicians which may be identified as due in any measure to their shared Zoroastrian identity? The immediate impression is of such differences between them that it is hard to see any obvious connections. But it is difficult to believe that it is simply coincidence that each of the first three Asian MPs was a Parsi.

Evidently each of the three MPs focused much of his attention on the condition of India. In so doing they, and Gifford in recent

---

[124] *Sunday Times*, 'Day in the Life of Zerbanoo Gifford', 3 Nov. 1985; *Cosmopolitan*, 10 Apr. 1987; *Woman*, 30 Jan. 1988. She also wrote an article on the leader page in *The Times*, 8 Apr., 1987. Radio and television appearances include *Today, Any Questions, Woman's Hour, Newsnight*, and *Channel Four News*.

[125] Although in *Woman*, 1988, she described the *sudre/kusti* practices.

times, have been careful to avoid overidentification with a specific religious or racial group. When Naoroji was active in Parliament, Hindu–Muslim conflicts in the INC had not arisen as they did later in the time of Gandhi. It was not, therefore, necessary for him to make religion a central theme of his speeches. Nevertheless he is noted for his assertion that he was an Indian first and a Parsi second. His home in London was a meeting-place not only for Parsis but for any Indians in Britain. Bhownagree, likewise, addressed himself to all-India issues (e.g. technical education and industrial development) in Parliament, even though it was from a perspective which vocal leaders of the INC did not like. Similarly, on the issue of South Africa, he campaigned for Indians, not simply Parsis. At Zoroastrian functions he invited Hindu and Muslim as well as British dignitaries.[126] Saklatvala's vision was emphatically universal, global as well as pan-Indian. (It is interesting that it was the Tory Bhownagree who worked with Gandhi and not Saklatvala the great champion of Indian Independence—probably the problem had to do with personalities as much as politics.) Gifford's campaign brought out her Zoroastrianness at a relatively late stage; her primary concern has been for Asians and for women's issues. Because none of the four politicians have identified particularly with any one religious or ethnic group (such as Hindus and Muslims), they have not excited the anger of the other. Being a marginal group in society can facilitate political leadership roles both in Britain and in India (Kulke 1974: Part IV). The Zoroastrians have been seen as standing apart from communal tensions and have not, therefore, been thought of by other groups as having a narrow, selfish community vision; indeed they have been seen to vote against honours for one of their own community (in the case of the civic reception in Bombay for Saklatvala) and have attacked each other, as, notably Wacha did Bhownagree. The Zoroastrian identity has, therefore, been a factor in the broad acceptability of these politicians.

Equally, all had a sufficient regard for the British political system that they were prepared to work within it. Eventually

---

[126] Omar Ralph has drawn my attention to the fact that Bhownagree's attitudes became more sympathetic to Indian causes after his visit to the country in 1896–7.

Naoroji despaired of British justice and called for Independence, but he consistently saw constitutional measures as the only possible route and always eschewed violence. Bhownagree has been simplistically categorized as pro-British, in many ways he was, but he also offered more searching criticism than he has been given credit for. Yet, despite his criticisms of the system, he worked constitutionally. Even Saklatvala, by far the sternest critic of British rule, was nevertheless impeccable in observing parliamentary procedure and never called for violence—he was imprisoned for asking the military not to be violent towards strikers, not for advocating military revolution. Gifford is strong in her calls for change (within her party as well as in society) but wholly intent on working within the political and social hierarchy of Britain. The success of all four, therefore, is due in no small measure to their ability to relate both to other South Asian groups and to the British political system. As Parsis were middlemen in trade in nineteenth-century India, so these four have proved to be also in politics in Britain since the 1890s. Each of them has been seen to work for the benefit of India in their different ways, although Gifford is seen in a slightly different perspective, as working for Asians in Britain.

It may appear trite, yet it would be true, to say that each has campaigned vigorously for the central Zoroastrian virtue of justice. This is, perhaps, the basic Zoroastrian ideal dating back to the twelfth century BCE and the teaching of the prophet Zoroaster. Even secular Zoroastrians typically have a keen sense of justice and order. Whether it is in philanthropy, social reform, or political campaigning, the concept of justice is paramount. It is not, of course, a virtue specific to Zoroastrianism, any more than an emphasis on love is unique to Christians, but it is a characteristic point of emphasis which is part of practically all Zoroastrian conditioning. It is evident in different ways in the campaigns of the Parsi politicians. Naoroji's whole case concerning the condition of India was quite explicitly a call for justice. Bhownagree has not been presented in previous studies as having such a concern, but the omission is due more to the perspective of the commentators than to Bhownagree himself. Wacha and others may not have liked his campaign, but he was convinced that the weaker members of Indian society stood their best chance of achieving justice not simply through British rule, but through the western technical education which would enable them to rise above their deprived circumstances. Similarly, he campaigned with considerable vigour for the just treatment of Indians in South Africa. Saklatvala's perception of justice was undoubtedly different from that of his Tory forebear, but his focus was consistently on belief in the necessity of achieving the just rewards of all workers in the face of what he saw as capitalist injustice and imperialism. Gifford's campaign focuses on what she sees as two of the great injustices of contemporary British society, sexist and racist discrimination. Of course no politician would state that justice was not their concern, but what marks each of these Parsi politicians is the centrality they give to the issue, even (and consistently) to the detriment of their own careers—Saklatvala and Gifford especially could easily have enhanced their political prospects had they moderated their message or stood for a different party.

Anyone who has lived within a Parsi setting is inevitably and forcefully impressed by the tenacity, and courage, with which Parsis consistently fight for what they believe to be right, as warriors for what they perceive to be the truth. The point may be illustrated by a personal anecdote: a lawyer friend once commented to me that he liked to have Parsi clients because he could be certain that they would pursue their cause to its conclusion, regardless of how difficult the circumstances. This dogged determination has caused untold troubles within the internal history of the London Zoroastrian community, past and present. It has equally characterized the political campaigns of all four Parsi politicians, be it Naoroji's absolute refusal to stand aside for a compromise candidate, when his constituency party sought to revoke his election to stand as Liberal candidate; or Bhownagree's utter rejection of INC criticism and party disfavour over South Africa; or Saklatvala's straightforward refusal to be bound over to keep the peace, preferring prison to weakening his stand on military confrontation against the miners or Gifford's unwavering stand against the physical and personal attacks of the National Front. Again the virtue of determined courage is not unique to Zoroastrians, but it is characteristic of them, and each of the political figures has displayed it to a remarkable degree.

Books on the Parsis (e.g. Kulke 1974) typically emphasize their social mobility. In the case of Naoroji, Bhownagree, and Gifford this is based in part on their good education (professor of mathematics; a barrister; a leading public school as well as higher education). Saklatvala is the exception with regard to education, having failed to complete either his degree or his course in law. But in his case the facilitating factor was his place in Bombay's leading industrial family, from which base he had the opportunity to mix socially. As a result of their backgrounds, each has been able to move easily in British society and political life. It has helped that although none of them has been outstandingly wealthy, none of them has been poor (though Naoroji's financial resources were stretched at various stages of his life). It might also be added that each has, quietly, used what wealth they have with benevolence.

Although all four of these politicians have taken a public stand on behalf of all the peoples of India, they have also affirmed their community and/or religious allegiance. Naoroji had been an active religious reformer in Bombay. While still a student he founded the reformist group Rahnumae Mazdyasnian Sabha and he lectured on his religion while in Britain as well as presiding over the Zoroastrian Trust Funds until he left for India. Bhownagree dominated the Zoroastrian Association in London for three decades and pioneered many developments, including the acquisition of a property with a prayer-room. Saklatvala dressed as a Parsi while lecturing in India, pressed forcefully for the *naujotes* of his children despite the inevitable rebuke from the Communist party, and stipulated in his will that a Zoroastrian priest should say the prayers at his funeral. Gifford has presided at the Zoroastrian group in Harrow, written in the English press about her religion and its place in her life, and offered Zoroastrian prayers at public occasions. None of the politicians, therefore, have hesitated to assert his/her communal and religious ties. Each has seen him/herself as a Zoroastrian and has been referred to as such, not always in complementary fashion: Naoroji was labelled a fire-worshipper at the time of his election and Saklatvala's credibility was questioned in Parliament because he came from a wealthy family of a capitalist community. Even where it would have helped their cause to deny their community ties, each has steadfastly refused to do so. But because of the external perceptions of their community, these links have not formed a threat even at times of religious tension in India.

In short, their value-system, their marginality yet acceptability among diverse Indian groups, their social mobility and standing, their determination have all been powerful factors in common between the success of each of these politicians. The principles for which Parsis are accustomed to fighting with immense determination, while not unique to them are very typical of them. These factors, together with the position of the community and the individuals in British society, are the foundations from which each emerged to prominence as a consequence of his or her individual abilities and contribution. What is also distinctive of them are their individual talents—Naoroji's mastery of financial arguments regarding taxation which developed from his mathematical excellence and above all his universally accepted integrity; Bhownagree's competence as a constitutional lawyer and advocate (in both a technical and general sense); Saklatvala's vision of the needs of the working class, based on a closer acquaintance with the needs of the poor in Bombay and rural India than his critics acknowledged, plus his oratory and transparent honesty; Gifford's passionate crusade for two disadvantaged sections of society pursued with an energy and eloquence that command respect. Each has displayed different personal qualities as well as the shared values which form a prominent part of their background.

The popular images of the MPs have all been oversimplified. Naoroji is universally portrayed as gentle, meek, and unassuming. But his stalwart determination could easily become stubbornness: witness, for example, his refusal to stand aside for a worthy compromise candidate when he wanted to fight an election at the age of 80. Bhownagree's early eulogies of the British Empire have clouded images of his later criticisms and battles for justice. Saklatvala's criticisms were highly coloured, but the substance of many of them have become widely accepted decades later. The work of each of the politicians in Britain has certainly been neglected by earlier studies of Zoroastrian history and of Indian politics.

6

British Zoroastrians Approaching The Third Millennium: The Community and The Religion

(a) *Some Observations on Research Methods*

This chapter is based on three main resources: (*a*) a survey questionnaire circulated in 1985 (following a preliminary study conducted in the 1970s, published in Hinnells 1978*a*) with 562 responses, 37% of which were from non-Zoroastrian House contacts (there was a response rate of just over 30%); (*b*) 232 structured in-depth interviews conducted by a research assistant, Dr Rashna Writer, with some help from Ms Shirin Patel in 1986–7 and (*c*) close personal contact with London Zoroastrians stretching over twenty-three years, which involved numerous spells of staying with various families—representing a very pleasurable, but informal, dimension of 'participant observation'. In 1993–4 there have been a number of further focused studies of people within the community, monitoring developments since the earlier research. The first two studies yield hard figures whereas the other two provide a more personal impression. It is appropriate to give a brief statement of my own position on the debate concerning the validity of respective methods of study: participant observation, survey questionnaire, and structured in-depth interviews. Each has its limitations and its merits.

Participant observation enables close acquaintance. It is perhaps the approach most likely to result in the observer standing aside from his or her own presuppositions. But the intensive nature of the work may involve a small sample which can result in the acquisition of an unrepresentative perspective coloured by the views of those with whom one lives and works. It is important to recognize the bias within such a sample. In my case, although I have agonized with many younger Zoroastrians over personal problems and issues such as intermarriage; with young parents over whether their children should participate in the school Christmas play or whether the family should celebrate Christmas; with young people struggling with the traditional religious practices, such as funerals; yet most of my contacts have been with Zoroastrians of my own generation. Within that age-group my range of friends straddles the orthodox reform divide and includes close friends from East Africa, Bombay, and Karachi. Although I have some good friends of Iranian parentage, these are fewer in number and that is a weakness within my sample. I have closer friends among those who arrived prior to the 1980s than with more recent arrivals. Similarly most, though not all, of my contacts in Bombay, also over twenty-three years, have been with the orthodox sections of the community.

Postal surveys can overcome the problem of a balanced sample by studying a broad base across the different sections of the community. But any survey is dependent on the response rate. The representative nature of this survey is not beyond question because there is no way of knowing what the global 'universe' is of the community since there are no appropriate records of all British Zoroastrians. Instead a 'snowball' approach to collecting the sample was the only possibility—questionnaires were sent to the homes on the address list of the Association, to all Zoroastrians known to myself and friends, with requests for respondents to notify their friends and myself of others who had not been contacted. It is therefore possible that an unrepresentative sample was obtained. For example, it may be that it was the more highly educated, very literate section of the community which responded. But there was no other way to proceed and a sample of over 500, with more than one-third from outside the official Association, gives a reasonable base from which to generalize. The merit of such a survey is the breadth of the sample and the ability to identify general trends. The problems inherent in any postal survey still remain. The questions are framed by an outsider, often using the vocabulary of the outsider and generally demand a yes/no answer. Such responses can yield helpful demographic information on age, gender, and so on, but may be more problematic regarding religious beliefs and practices, since such matters are rarely reducible to one-word answers which can be analysed on a computer. How can one measure a person's Zoroastrianness? Sometimes in what follows such generalizations are made as: 'those who migrated from East Africa tend to practice their religion more traditionally than those from Bombay'; such judgements are based on a series of 'litmus tests'—the frequency of prayer; the manner of praying; the use of the sacred language, Avestan, rather than the vernacular; the wearing of the sacred 'badges' (the *sudre* and *kusti*); lighting a *divo* (or oil-lamp); attitudes to purity laws, affirmation of a belief in Ahura Mazda, and so on. Questions were asked about the observance of festivals, but this is less good as an indicator of the level of religious practice than others listed, because many Zoroastrians observe the festivals, especially New Year (No Ruz), much as the British celebrate Christmas, whether or not they consider themselves Zoroastrians. However, some assert that it is possible to be deeply devout and committed to the ideals of Zoroaster yet not follow the practices listed as litmus tests. The orthodox Zoroastrian might comment that these practices are essential aspects of being a traditional Zoroastrian, but they would recognize that someone can be religious in different ways. Behind the statements on the following pages lie many hundreds of charts arising from the survey and interview schedules mentioned in the Preface.

Questionnaires inevitably leave unanswered problems. However careful the preparation, subjects invariably emerge which were not foreseen (if everything could be foreseen, then the value of the questionnaire may be doubted). The danger of restricting respondents to predetermined vocabulary is considerable. The merit of a structured in-depth interview is that it provides the opportunity for interviewees to develop answers to questions in their own words, with their own emphases and to question the presuppositions of the researcher if necessary. In this instance the interview sample was balanced for age, gender, and country of origin according to the universal identified by the postal survey. The benefits of these interviews were enhanced by Dr Writer's own insights as a member of the British Zoroastrian community. It has to be recognized that an insider has their own distinctive perceptions but in this case they balanced my own outsider's perspective. The limitation of the structured in-depth interview, apart from obtaining the right structure and vocabulary in the first place, is that the sample is necessarily more limited by time considerations (e.g. time spent in travel) than a postal survey. One further difficulty is that surveys and interviews, even perhaps the very presence of an observer, however much he or she participates, is that the people studied can be confronted with issues which they have not previously articulated and would not have done so if the research had not been conducted. However, I hope that the combination of approaches deployed gives some validity to the observations below. My own opinion regarding method in the study of a religious community is that all three approaches are necessary in order to avoid the faults of each and derive the benefits of all.

The general aim behind the survey and the interviews was to try and identify patterns of community ties and religious practice among the obvious sections: youth compared with elders; male compared with female; different educational groups, and so on. The following discussions of the various topics will begin with broad generalizations which will then be discussed and qualified. It is sometimes worth stating what may seem to be the obvious, because people may differ on what they consider to be obvious and readers may wish to challenge what might otherwise remain a hidden assumption. In a full publication of such survey work it would be necessary to include all the tables and the questionnaire, but problems of space make that impossible in this overall study of British Zoroastrians.

(b) *A Broad Demographic Picture*

It is impossible to produce reliable figures for the number of Zoroastrians in Britain because the UK census data does not include information on religious or racial identity. If Zoroastrians do appear in reports, then they tend to be recorded as Iranians, Indians, Pakistanis, and so on. There is no common obvious Zoroastrian name, unlike Singh among Sikhs, so that neither electoral registers nor telephone directories can be used. The main source is the address lists of Zoroastrian House in London. In 1984 when the first survey was begun there were 629 addresses; 795 were counted in a follow-up study in 1989. This second list named 1,514 adults. These lists were administrative records of who had paid their subscriptions, and are more extensive than the published 1991 and 1994 Directories. The 1994 Directory lists 2,000 names, so as the Zoroastrians commonly assert that the formal membership probably represents less than half the number of Zoroastrians in Britain, the total number is probably in the region of 4,000.

A study of the addresses of the various membership lists indicates that 87% of members live in London and the Home Counties, with particular concentrations in Harrow, Wembley, and Wimbledon, but overall quite widely spread around the London region with very few in the immediate area of Zoroastrian House. There is, then, no single clearly identifiable geographical focus for British Zoroastrians. Nearly one-third of the 1994 Directory addresses are from outside London, mainly in the regions where it was noted above (Ch. 4, Sect. (n)) that local groups had occurred, notably Manchester and Newcastle. There are thirty-nine overseas addresses, from France, Portugal, Austria, Germany, America, and India. Unlike other Asian communities there are no Zoroastrians groups in Leeds or Bradford and only a few families in Birmingham or Leicester. Essentially the British Zoroastrians are a London-focused community.

The survey produced the following picture of the community. One in five are between the ages of 16 and 25; half are between the ages of 26 and 55; and almost one-third are over the age of 56 (put another way, just over 40% are over the age of 50). This gives a significantly younger community than in Bombay (Karkal 1983) but older than both the Zoroastrian community in America and the wider South Asian British population. There were almost equal numbers of men and women. More men than women migrated in the 1960s (though not in as disproportionate numbers as in other Asian groups) but more of the women were born here. There is not as strong a tradition as among other South Asians for British Zoroastrians to seek spouses back in the old country. There are more married than single persons (54% compared with 35%), with only 7% widowed and only 4% separated or divorced. Few married couples (11%) had no children and only 13% had three or more children; that is, three-quarters of Zoroastrian nuclear families consisted of three to four persons. Of the families surveyed, three-quarters belonged to an extended family network, but only 4% had grandparents in this country. One-quarter of the sample were born in Britain, one-quarter came before 1960, and the majority (78% of those not born here) came in the period 1960–79. Zoroastrian migration into Britain has virtually ceased. In the interviewing programme 46% had their education on the Indian subcontinent, mostly (36%) in India; 13% came from East Africa; only 6% were from Iran; and most of the rest (31%) had their education in Britain. A distinctive feature of the British Zoroastrian community is the level of education: 68% of those surveyed had a higher education, most studying for an arts (as opposed to a science) degree. This is a far higher proportion than would be found among a similar survey of White Anglo-Saxon respondents, higher than Jones (1993) found among the African Indian community, and higher even than among the Parsis in Bombay (18%—Karkal 1983: 54), but it is less than among American Zoroastrians (92% in New York and Chicago; Hinnells 1988). Although most had their higher education in the old country, one-third of the respondents had pursued higher studies in Britain. Where those higher studies included postgraduate education (23% of respondents), this generally occurred in Britain. The language pattern reflects something of this educational level. One in three described English as their mother-tongue and only 40% can undertake any reading or writing in Gujarati.[1] Career patterns also follow the educational levels. Fewer than one in twenty Zoroastrians are manual workers, whereas one in three can be categorized as executive class.[2] In short, the 'typical' British Zoroastrian has his or her roots in India, is young–middle-aged, belongs to a nuclear family which has settled here for over fifteen years, is well educated, and has a successful career. However, most respondents indicated that they had not yet achieved the career-status of their parents back in the old country, implying that it is the educated members of the well-placed families who migrated. It is interesting that a smaller proportion of those born here as compared with migrants went

---

[1] On the loss of Gujarati among British Zoroastrians and even in the Bombay community, see Writer 1994: 227–8. The problem is particularly acute with the reading and writing of Gujarati, less so with daily conversation.

[2] The figures are: manual workers 5%; clerical workers 30%; managerial 25%; executive 35%; 'other' 5%.

on to higher education, and when this study was undertaken fewer had the same level of career success. The Zoroastrian British population is, therefore, markedly different from the typical South Asian family described in the books considered in Chapter 1. This chapter, of course, provides only a very broad picture and later publication of the detailed figures will indicate other patterns. For example, the Zoroastrian groups outside London tend to be slightly older (having fewer students) and better educated and generally, therefore, have a higher proportion of their numbers in executive-class employment (for a global perspective, see Hinnells 1994a). The reason for this appears to be that those who have chosen to settle in the provinces are those who have benefited from promotion at work. Because they are not members of a clearly defined community there is a lower level of contact with fellow Zoroastrians and a correspondingly higher level of intermarriage and a lower level of (formal) religious practice. However, more East African Zoroastrians settled outside London and they have different trends, as will be seen below. The above is, therefore, only a general sketch of the community.

(c) *Religion and a Sense of Identity*

The overwhelming majority of interviewees described themselves as practising Zoroastrians (85% of the elders and 75% of the youth). Even the youth who did not describe themselves as practising mostly (80%) believed that religion was a part of their identity. Many of the elders expressed the conviction that they became more religious after migration than they were before. This belief may be untestable, but it is highly plausible. The great majority of Zoroastrians consider that their religion is fundamental to their sense of identity and it would be natural to reassert that identity in an 'alien' environment. If it be true, then it is all the more regrettable that religion has been so seriously neglected by so many writers on race relations.

In broad terms it would seem that the most religiously active groups are retired people; housewives; those who completed the education on leaving school rather than going on to university, especially those who had their schooling in the old country; those who continue to think in their Asian mother tongue (be that Gujarati or Persian); those who attend Zoroastrian House frequently; those who visit the old country more often and for longer and those who have fewer British friends; those who have migrated most recently; people from East Africa or from rural Gujarat (as opposed to Bombay); and those who have children. The obverse is also, generally, true. Those who express less commitment to the religion are the youth; those who do not have children; those who were born in Britain; those with a high level of education, especially those who studied in the West; those who think in English; those who do not attend Zoroastrian House; and individuals who do not intend to return to the old country. In short, the religion tends to be practised mostly by specific sections of the community and is less strong among those whose community ties are weak. However, these generalizations merit further reflection.

In this list of broad correspondences it is not evident which is cause and which is effect. Is it, for example, lack of contact with the old country and its language which is the cause or the consequence of weakened religious commitment? A comparable survey among the White Anglo-Saxon population might also find that university graduates practised their religion (whatever it might have been) less than school-leavers. But in the Zoroastrian community this point is particularly significant because such a high proportion of its members undertake higher education.

There appears to be a general pattern that young people are religious after the manner, and to the level, of their parents until they leave home. When they leave home for work, and especially for university, then they also commonly leave their religion until the time of marriage approaches, particularly if marrying a Zoroastrian. At that point, and in particular when they have children, many return to their religion. Religion is not, for Zoroastrians, simply a question of a set of beliefs: it is much more fundamental to their sense of identity. Although the majority of respondents and interviewees did link belief and religion, approximately two-thirds believed that there is a link between race and religion and that their identity was tied up with their history, in particular with their deep sense of being a tiny, persecuted minority. There is a strong pride not only in having survived oppression but also in having influenced major religions and contributed a great deal to the history of different nations. For many interviewees their identity was not expressed in terms of being British, or Indian or Parsi, but in being ultimately the true Persians—whichever continent they may have been born in (see Writer 1994: 229–33, 239–43). Even more respondents wanted to identify themselves as Zoroastrians, but this inevitably causes some problems because the term is so rarely understood by the outside world. How do you identify yourself if others do not recognize what you are? Zoroastrians themselves differ over what constitutes 'Zoroastrianness'. Science postgraduates tend to understand it in an ethnic sense of food, language, and music rather than in religious terms, whereas those who migrated in the 1960s tend to emphasize the belief dimension. The majority of all groups considered that a knowledge of the religion was important to them and to their preservation of their identity, but very few considered that they had a sufficient level of knowledge.

(d) *Zoroastrians and the British*

One important part of self-perception is the perception of others. A series of questions was, therefore, asked regarding the perceptions of the British. Of Zoroastrian elders, 84% said that they were not impressed by the British youth and hoped that their own younger generation would not grow up like their peers. The most common words used to describe the British were 'cold', 'distant', 'unreliable', 'patronizing', 'I do not trust them'. It was commonly thought that the British are sexually promiscuous—far more so than Zoroastrians—and neglectful of family responsibility, especially in the lack of care of the elders; they are generally perceived of as difficult to befriend. The greatest threats to the Zoroastrian community were thought to be those to the family, and from the secular nature of British society. A theme pursued in both the survey and the interviews was the perception of racial prejudice. In the global Katrak survey Toronto was the city where the highest proportion of individuals (48%) thought that they faced racial prejudice, but there it was considered to be something that was encountered only occasionally and not to a significant degree. However in London, of the 42% who considered that they had experienced prejudice, 39% thought they had done so frequently (in comparison to only 23% in Toronto). A higher proportion of London Zoroastrians than of those in the provinces thought that they had faced prejudice. Of those who considered they had experienced prejudice, 94% thought they had done so in education, mostly from their peers, but also from teachers and in the structure of the curriculum. Employment and housing were the other main problem-areas identified, but contrary to the media reports relatively few believed that they had experienced prejudice from the police.

This study cannot prove that prejudice was, or was not, faced. However, it is my opinion that the figures probably under- rather than overestimate the experience. Several respondents said that they had not faced prejudice, but had experienced 'Paki-bashing' (in analysing the figures such respondents still had to be counted as saying they had faced prejudice, otherwise one would be changing the evidence). A number of interviewees thought that they had not faced prejudice because they did not consider themselves coloured; that they were 'above that sort of thing' because they were so westernized. One young interviewee commented: 'I can't get excited about racism. I have integrated so well.' After the interview he objected to the inclusion of the question in the schedule. Racism is, then, something a number of Zoroastrians do not want to discuss. Most parents considered that their children faced less prejudice than they themselves had experienced, but a number of children commented privately that they had not related their experiences to their parents because they did not want to cause them distress. In order to test the hypothesis that being westernized, or integrated, lifted an individual 'above that sort of thing', the figures were compared for those who thought they had, and those who thought that they had not, faced prejudice. The groups most likely to sense prejudice appear to be housewives, retired people, and the elders in general; those who had arrived recently or who had been born in Britain rather than those who had arrived in the 1960s and early 1970s; those with children; those who continue to think in an Asian language; those who had completed their education at school, not university level, especially when that schooling was in Asia rather than in the West. It was also those who emphasized that race is a part of religion, that is those who are themselves conscious of racial issues, who tended to believe that they had faced racial prejudice. This was particularly true of East African Zoroastrians. The implications of this summary of the figures is that there are a variety of factors behind a perception of prejudice, but it would be simplistic to conclude that there is a 'type' which provokes the prejudice through not integrating, since some important groups, such as those born here, also have this perception. There is, then, no simple, single factor determining the experience. Being integrated does not necessarily help.

It is not possible to say definitively what the consequences of perceived prejudice are, but most respondents thought that the community would be more likely to draw closer together and reassert its identity than to assimilate in the hope of avoiding the prejudice. In order to keep a sense of perspective it is worth commenting that more respondents identified the main danger as being the threat to the family from British social values and the secular nature of that society rather than racism, although most of the younger generation saw racism as the main threat. There are two explanations for this difference between the generations: either the youth have acquired western family values and so do not see them as a threat, or they are more aware of White Anglo-Saxon prejudices. This study cannot determine which is the correct explanation.

In view of these perceptions, how do Zoroastrians in practice relate to White Anglo-Saxons? Two-thirds of Zoroastrians say that they have close Anglo-Saxon friends. This is especially true of the well educated and the career high-flyers and among those who settled in the 1960s rather than those who were born here. Those who have weaker ties with the religion and the community tend to be those who have most English friends. There is little difference between the genders, though more working women than housewives have non-Zoroastrian friends. The formation of friendships is therefore, probably a consequence of lifestyle rather than gender. Almost as many respondents said that Zoroastrian relations with the British were excellent as said that relations between Parsis were excellent (57% compared with 62%). Relations with other communities were seen as less good. In a special supplement, answered by 498 respondents, for the British section of the global questionnaire, there was a consistent pattern of Zoroastrians considering themselves to be equal with Europeans and superior to other races, notably Muslims, Hindus, other Asians, and the Black African community. When asked about their motives for migration most identified education as their first priority; career prospects came second and wealth was only third. Relatively few thought that the experience had failed to live up to their own personal expectations, though life in Britain does not appear to have fulfilled all the hopes of Zoroastrians at the start of the twentieth century (see Ch. 2). Many said they considered themselves materially better off, but felt that there was something lacking: the Anglo-Saxon population was thought to be not 'as genuine' as the Zoroastrians and less religious.

In the survey respondents were asked whether they identified themselves in terms of the old country (i.e. as Indian/Pakistani/Iranian), or in terms of race (i.e. Parsi) or religion (i.e. as Zoroastrian), or as British, or as a mixture. More described themselves in terms of the old country than as British. The answers break down, however. The elders tended to describe themselves in terms of the old country and the youth born here as British, though the majority in both cases still preferred the identification 'Zoroastrian'.

(e) *Does being Zoroastrian Conflict with being British?*

The question of the sense of identity leads naturally on to the question, of whether Zoroastrians feel 'caught between cultures'. This phrase was used in academic scholarship in the 1970s (Watson 1977) but has been questioned in the 1990s on the grounds that it implied clear and exclusive boundaries to cultures (Banks 1992). However, it is an expression that has entered popular parlance, including that of some Parsis. The interview schedule, therefore, asked people whether they considered themselves to be thus 'caught'. Less than half of those interviewed considered they were caught. The groups who did say that they felt caught tended to be the young, those who had recently migrated, those born here or whose secondary (or first degree) education was in Britain, the single rather than married people, and those who attend Zoroastrian House only occasionally rather than frequently. The last group provides the clue to the problem of who is it that feels caught; it is, essentially, those who do not feel closely identified either with their Zoroastrian tradition or with the British. Thus those who say that they are not caught between cultures tend to be the regular attenders at Zoroastrian House, those who describe themselves as Parsi not British, those who assert strongly that religion is part of their identity, those who interpret Zoroastrianness in terms of race, those who say they do not want to change religious beliefs, practices, and traditions. So on the one hand people do not feel caught between cultures because they feel closely identified with one culture—their Zoroastrian heritage. On the other hand, those who assert strongly that they are British; those who have had a postgraduate education, do not feel caught either, because they too have identified with one culture—the British. Those feeling caught are those without a clear base in either community (or in the case of single persons, without the same domestic base). But there is more to the question than this because some people felt caught in certain aspects of their lives and not in others. Some interviewees felt able to slide between different areas of their lives—between work and home, for example. The main point to emphasize, however, is that despite their self-proclaimed lack of religious knowledge, most interviewees and respondents were comfortable with their Zoroastrianness.

The above paragraph is, however, based on a straight counting of figures. The issues are complex and it worth quoting some of the precise words of some of the interviewees. A Karachi-born Zoroastrian commented: 'I am not totally British in attitude and thinking. But when I go to Pakistan I don't understand their everyday life, then I am stuck in limbo. I ask myself "where do I belong?"' A 34-year-old lady said: 'My mind says I should behave like a Zoroastrian, but my body says western. I feel a Zoroastrian but I have western attitudes.' One lady in her late twenties with a Parsi father and an Anglo-Saxon mother replied

Not caught between two cultures. Caught between two natures. There is definitely the English and the Parsi side of my nature. I do have more of a Parsi temper—fiery, argumentative. I have a very enquiring mind. All these Parsi attributes I suppress in Britain.

A teenage girl expressed succinctly a theme several elaborated:

When I started feeling that way [caught between cultures] I was frightened. I thought I was losing a grip on what I was. So I studied my religion and culture. Now I have no hesitancy at all in saying what I am. I am comfortable being a Zoroastrian in Britain. I would be comfortable being a Zoroastrian anywhere, even in Outer Mongolia.

I am not arguing that dated terminology should be restored, and accept the point of Jackson and Nesbitt (1993) that it is often those who are most fluent in English or competent with European musical instruments who are most happy with Indian languages and music; this research would nevertheless suggest that there is a substantial proportion of people who do have a sense of two parts to their persona. Perhaps we should refer not to being 'caught between cultures' but to a person's sense of having different, often undefined, aspects of their personality deriving from different cultural inheritances. These differing aspects of the personality may or may not live comfortably with each other. Generally most people have a sense of a clear identity and are comfortable with what they see as another part of their nature, but as they travel between countries, between the new and the old country, and sometimes between parts of their lives, then they can feel some sense of dislocation. An Iranian youth commented on the move between home and the outside world: 'It is two different worlds, English outside and at home fully Iranian.' But it is not only the Iranians who sense a distance from Britain; a 17-year-old Parsi said: 'We have no home really. We feel foreign wherever we are, foreign in India, foreign in Britain. Where do I belong? I don't belong in Britain, I don't belong in India.' This last remark typifies the views of many Zoroastrians, that their sense of self-identity is often expressed in negatives, not Indian/Pakistani/Iranian, not Hindu/Muslim/Christian. As mentioned above, it can be difficult asserting what you are if people do not recognise that identity. The identity problems of tiny minorities can be particularly difficult. It would be wrong to exaggerate these problems of identity. Most respondents and interviewees have a clear sense of who they are and are happy and proud of their Zoroastrianness, but it would also be mistaken to suggest that is a uniform picture (Writer 1994: 224–35).

(f) *The Country of Birth and the Preservation of Heritage*

Which groups tend to retain their Zoroastrian identity? The place of origin affects, to some extent, how Zoroastrians settle in Britain. Thus Zoroastrians from Gujarat preserve their language more, maintain closer ties to the old country and to Zoroastrian House, are more likely to read Zoroastrian literature, tend to look for fewer changes in belief and practice, wear the *sudre* and *kusti* more often, pray more frequently and more traditionally than do Zoroastrians who have migrated from cosmopolitan Bombay.

Zoroastrians from East Africa tend to be more traditional in terms of the practice of the religion (prayer, purity laws, affirming a belief in Ahura Mazda), the preservation of Gujarati, and in asserting the link between race and religion. Fewer of them are willing to assert that they are British and fewer are willing to maintain that they are Indian, because the links with that country have been weakened. They therefore have a strong preference for the name 'Zoroastrian'. Living a relatively isolated existence in East Africa, at a distance from Whites and Blacks alike, yet separated from India only by the Indian Ocean, and retaining emotional ties with the old country, they appear to have kept alive something of the nineteenth-century commitment to Zoroastrianism, relatively unaffected by the impact of Protestant scholarship or the seductions of life in the West.

In contrast, Zoroastrians who were born in Britain tend to describe themselves as British. Fewer British-born affirm that religion is part of their identity or consider that a knowledge of Zoroastrian history is important for preserving their culture; they more rarely keep in contact with Zoroastrians overseas and a smaller proportion pray daily. Fewer of them consider prayers or purity laws, death ceremonies, festivals, or *sudre* and *kusti* to be important.

Because there were not so many Iranian respondents and interviewees a direct comparison with the Parsis is not easy, but my personal impression is that typically Iranians preserve their mother tongue more, observe their own festivals more vigorously, intermarry less often and are less likely to consider themselves British. Many have a sense of grief at the loss of the homeland and a deeper sense of 'the myth of the return' than do Parsis, partly because they migrated more recently, and in particular because they felt compelled to migrate as a result of political pressures in the old country after the emergence of the Islamic Republic under Ayatollah Khomeini. A further factor is that Iranian Zoroastrians have an unequivocal sense of their 'Persian' ancestry, whereas the Parsis can move between Indian, British and Persian identities. There is, therefore, a greater resistance to the loss of identifying characteristics. Further, there is less of a sense of identity with Britain as there is nothing corresponding to the generally positive Parsi experience of British India. There are other broad religious differences between Iranian and Parsi Zoroastrians. Most British Iranian Zoroastrians incline towards the reforming wing of the community. Although the Zoroastrians of the Yazdi plain studied in Boyce (1977) have preserved the ancient traditions, many urbanized Iranian Zoroastrians were heavily influenced by Parsi reformists at the start of the twentieth century, owing to the zeal of Kay Khosrow Shahrokh who received his education in Bombay (Boyce 1978*a*: 219 f.; Shahrokh and Writer 1994; Amighi 1990). The Protestantizing influences resonated with the Islamic emphasis on the sole authority of the prophetic words in the holy book and with the repudiation of what was seen as the superstitious tendencies of priestly religion, trends which the weakened Iranian Zoroastrian priesthood could not withstand, especially in the modern urban centres. It is mostly (though not wholly) such urbanized Iranian Zoroastrians who have migrated. Generally, therefore, British Iranian Zoroastrians tend to emphasize the necessity of following exclusively the teaching of Zoroaster based exclusively on the *Gathas*, rather than the later priestly teaching which they tend to see as corruptions of the pure and abstract religion, just as they see complex rituals as superstitious. In contrast, many traditional Parsis emphasize the power of the rites performed by a pure and holy priest. As Iranian Zoroastrians have been affected by the Islamic spiritual environment, so Parsis have been influenced by the Hindu context in which they have lived for a millennium. Like most generalizations this statement merits qualification. Some of the westernized Bombay Parsis have a more Protestant-type emphasis on scripture and vernacular prayers; indeed, it was nineteeth and twentieth century Parsi reformists who influenced some educated Iranian Zoroastrians, and there are more traditional Iranian Zoroastrians. Despite these qualifications, however, there are broad patterns of difference between the religious emphases of Indian and Iranian Zoroastrians.

The Zoroastrians from Karachi tend to have higher levels of Gujarati and fewer of them went to university, but in the obvious litmus tests of Zoroastrianness Karachi Zoroastrians tend to be more traditional than those from Bombay, who have generally become more cosmopolitan, or westernized, as a result of the nature of that city and their high levels of education. It is not only the level of practice which is distinctive of Zoroastrians from Pakistan. The survey undertaken in Karachi suggests that in that city there is a stronger commitment to some of the traditional teachings, or myths, than in westernized Bombay; specifically, more of them believe in a life after death and the doctrine of the resurrection—beliefs shared, of course, by Islam (Hinnells 1994a and the forthcoming Katrak volume). Both the level of practice, and the traditional teachings, appear stronger in a setting where religion has such a high public profile. Karachi is the only Zoroastrian centre I visited in the course of this research where the older generation commented that the young people attended temple more often than they themselves had done in their youth. Something of this religious commitment has travelled with Karachi Zoroastrians into the diaspora.

(g) *Decade of Arrival and Religious Practice*

A comparison of the attitudes of people who settled in Britain in different decades and of those born here yields some interesting figures. Those who came to Britain in the 1960s tend to think in English rather than in their Asian mother tongue, whereas recent arrivals have a lower proportion of people thinking in

English.[3] More of the earlier settlers (at least when the survey was conducted) tended to be members of Zoroastrian House and attended more frequently. It was the recent settlers who tended to think of themselves as Parsi or Indian and the earlier settlers who thought of themselves as Zoroastrian (or one in ten thought of themselves as British). It was the new settlers who considered that they were caught between cultures, and many more of the newer arrivals described themselves as practising Zoroastrians. It was the newer arrivals who tended to identify Zoroastrian as a racial rather than a purely religious term, and it was the newer arrivals rather than the early settlers who affirmed a belief in Ahura Mazda. The level of prayer was higher among the recent settlers and the call for changes in traditions, beliefs, and practices were all strongest from those who came in the 1960s.

The global survey had a considerably higher number of responses (1,717) and the bigger sample permits more confident assertions. It was found that the newer arrivals keep in contact with the old country, wear *sudre* and *kusti* more regularly, and pray more often; fewer of them approve of intermarriage and fewer of them agree with allowing non-Zoroastrians into the prayer-room; more of them identify their country of birth, rather than the country of settlement, as their mother country. The pattern of figures suggests that recent arrivals are more traditional than those who settled in the 1960s. It might at first be thought that the 1960s settlers are more acculturated because of the length of time that they have resided in Britain. That may perhaps be a factor, but the fact that they were consistently less traditional in their attitudes to religious practice than those who had been born in Britain suggests that it not the only one; another appears to arise from their personalities. This may be confirmed by a study of the profile of the 1960s Zoroastrian settlers who were typically even more highly educated than later arrivals and would appear to have been particularly innovative, westernized, 'liberal' individuals.

---

[3] A cautionary note is needed: only eighteen individuals were interviewed who had settled in the 1980s, the sample is therefore too small for confident assertions on that group.

(h) Contacts with the Old Country

One means of preserving the tradition is contact with the old country, notably through visits there to renew ties, if not in search of a spouse. Of the Parsi youth interviewed, 88% had visited the old country; over half of them had done so three times or more and nearly half had stayed for periods of months rather than for weeks. There is, therefore, a closer link to the old country than many outsiders at first imagine. The reactions to these visits varied. Nearly half (41%) said they felt a stranger in the subcontinent and a third of them said that they found the experience a painful one, but more than half found it pleasurable. Many commented on 'the poverty and filth' of India and on the perceived corruption. Contrary to popular images, more of the youth (31%) than elders (18%) envisaged returning to the old country. One youth from a Pakistani family said: 'To go to an *Atash Bahram* ['cathedral' fire temple] gives so much pleasure . . . it was a recharging of batteries: a raising of self confidence, serenity.' Although some said that they felt at home there, others (quoted above) said that they felt foreigners in the old countries. Two-thirds of the elders thought that the young people were more likely to be practising Zoroastrians in the old rather than in the new country and most expressed positive feelings to the Indian Parsi community. It may be possible to identify some trends among those who felt strangers in the old country. More men than women, and surprisingly, more people born in India than in Britain, felt strangers there (a point discussed further below); so did single as opposed to married people; English rather than Gujarati speakers; those who describe themselves as 'British' (not Parsi); and those who do not attend Zoroastrian House. This suggests that distancing from the community had already begun in Britain. The evidence, therefore, implies that a visit to the old country reaffirms whatever trend is already developing regarding community ties. It rarely (though occasionally) acts as a (de-) 'conversion experience'.

Zoroastrians who have migrated from Iran and East Africa naturally find difficulties in visiting the old country, but in 1994 a religious pilgrimage was organized by Khojesti Mistree for young people, and this was a time of religious inspiration for those who went. Of the thirty on the tour, twenty were from India, the others from Britain. The close contact with fellow Zoroastrians, as hosts, guides, drivers, and cooks, inspired those who went on the search for their roots. Further visits are planned by both ZTFE and WZO for 1995. If the political circumstances permit, this could be a pilgrimage route followed by many British Zoroastrians in the future, just as some used to go from India in the 1960s and early 1970s. Because of visa difficulties for Americans, but also because of Mistree's influence, it is mainly the British diaspora Zoroastrians who currently follow that path. If such tours prove safe, it may give Iranian Zoroastrians some confidence to visit the old country also.

There is, however, another dimension to links with the old country, namely the chain of authority. If India, Pakistan, or Iran are the lands of the religious heritage and India is where the high priests, temples, madressas, religious scholars, and full-time religious professionals are, what is the standing of the established leaders there? For many of the elders the old country is understandably the land of religious authority, especially for those from India. But few of the western-educated, the youth, or those who settled in the 1960s and 1970s, accept that line of authority. Few, if any, Iranians would accept the authority of their own old country and certainly not of Bombay bodies. The same is true of Zoroastrians from Pakistan, however much they may enjoy visits to that country. There are no religious authorities in East Africa. The basic reason for the rejection of the authority of the old country is the belief that the priests 'there do not understand the problems faced by the youth in the West. But no clear western leader has emerged, so there is no widely accepted centre of religious authority to which to turn in disputes.

(i) *Differences between the Generations*

These issues naturally raise the question of the difference between generations. There are two White Anglo-Saxon stereotypes of the generation gap in Britain's Asian communities. On the one hand there is an image of the tightly knit family group where the father exercises strict control over the young, who are expected to submit to their parents' wishes regarding dress, recreation, marriage, and so on. On the other hand there is an image of rebellious young people, educated in Britain wanting to socialize with British contemporaries, to leave home and seek love rather than arranged marriages. It is assumed that the young often feel emotionally, as well as geographically, distanced from the old country as they drift inexorably towards assimilation and away from the practice of the religion. Jackson and Nesbitt (1993) have established how inappropriate that image is for many Hindu children. The question to be asked here is whether these stereotypes are in any way reflected in the British Zoroastrian community.

Among those interviewed, both elders and youth mostly considered that family relations would not deteriorate as a result of young people leaving home, and so they felt they would not be as upset as White Anglo-Saxons are at such turning-points in life. Both generations thought that sexual morals were stricter among Zoroastrians than in the wider community, both before and after marriage. But whereas the youth thought that there was a bigger generation gap within the Zoroastrian than in the wider community, the parents typically had the opposite opinion. Among the youth it was those born in Britain—especially the men, single persons, and those who think in English—who tended to think that there was a generation gap. Whereas all the parents interviewed attached importance to their offspring finding a Zoroastrian partner (a theme which will be considered further below) less than half of the youth interviewed thought that this was essential, and one in three thought it was of little or no importance. The qualities which the youth looked for in a marriage partner were (after love) education, a modern outlook, career prospects, a similar background, and wealth. There was one major difference between the genders among the youth: 73% of men attached importance to the partner's physical appearance, whereas only 37% of women did. Among those who attached importance to finding a Zoroastrian spouse, most (74%) thought they would find such a partner through family contacts, friends, or local social events. Relatively few favoured visits back to the old country to seek a spouse or the establishment of a marriage bureau, both of these solutions being advocated by leaders in India and Pakistan. Almost all parents said that they would accept the non-Zoroastrian spouse of their offspring, although most respondents said that they would feel hurt if their children married out of the community.

What has emerged is that stereotypes of young Zoroastrians as less religious than their elders are simplistic. It is true that young people tend to pray less often, less traditionally, keep in less frequent contact with Zoroastrians overseas and in Britain, and fewer stress the importance of festivals, and purity laws; and that most say they know less about the religion than their parents. However, these statements merit some qualification. It would be rash to assume that the Zoroastrian community is becoming less religious, because there is no evidence of the level of religion among the elders when they themselves were younger. In the global survey the different age-groups were asked whether they prayed daily/sometimes/infrequently/never. Of the youth, 56% affirmed they prayed daily and only 10% said that they never prayed (in contrast, the comparable figures for the elders were 79% and 4% respectively). It is unlikely that a survey among the White Anglo-Saxon population would have found such a high level of proclaimed religious practice. Although fewer young people than elders are members of Zoroastrian House, when young people are members, then more of them than the elders attend frequently (36% compared with 28%). This may be explained by difficulties of attendance caused for older people by responsibilities or health, but it nevertheless indicates that when young people involve themselves in their religion, then they can be very active. This is indicated by other figures: for example, more young people than elders envisage returning to the old country to settle. Fewer young people wanted to change their traditions or beliefs than did the elders; many more of them wanted to preserve the link between race and religion (78% of the youth compared with only 58% of the elders) and similarly, far fewer youth were willing to initiate non-Zoroastrian than were the elders (56% compared with 83%). The conclusion, it would seem, is that when the youth are involved in the religion or in the community, they are deeply committed to it. This is plausible, since religion maybe seen as part of a person's identity. The youth may be seeking their roots in a way that the elder generation is not.

(j) *Some Gender Issues*

Whereas the proportion of British Zoroastrian men and women obtaining first degrees is similar to that indicated in the global survey (Hinnells 1994*a*) the proportions are different for British Zoroastrian women at the extremes of the educational scale. So more British Zoroastrian women completed their education at school than did those in the global sample (42% compared with 25%) and fewer of them proceeded to post-graduate study (12% compared with 21%). Similarly, fewer British Zoroastrian men than in the global diaspora proceed to post-graduate study. Within the British community the number of men and women obtaining a first degree is roughly equal, but the figures suggest that in the 1990s the most highly qualified Zoroastrians are settling in America (which particularly attracts the scientists) and increasingly in Australia. But in Britain and elsewhere, a smaller proportion of women than men have undertaken post-graduate study (12% compared with 28%). The employment patterns are similar: whereas half of Zoroastrian men are in executive level employment, only 15% of the women are.

The distribution according to age is similar in the genders. Slightly more of the men are married than the women, with a slightly higher level of divorce for women (8% compared with 3%). Fractionally more men than women speak only English (64% compared with 59%) but the difference is minimal compared with other Asian communities. A study of the figures for comparative patterns of beliefs and practices indicates some variations. A slightly higher proportion of male interviewees compared with women belong to Zoroastrian House and more of them attend frequently, but with a variation of only 4% on a sample of 240 the variation is too small to be considered significant. Slightly more women than men assert that religion is important for their sense of identity and preservation of their roots, and a slightly higher proportion of women than men assert a belief in Ahura Mazda, but more men than women assert that they are practising Zoroastrians and fractionally more men than women assert that they pray daily. Since the variations are again only of the order of 4% one cannot assert, with any confidence, that there is a clear difference between British Zoroastrian men and women in general religious belief and practice. There is an exception: consistently more women than men call for changes in traditions, beliefs, and practices, yet appreciably more women than men affirm that they wish to preserve the link between religion and race (75% of women, 58% of men) and the purity laws. So although Zoroastrian women may be said, typically, to be more open to the idea of change than men, they appear to be stricter on some issues, specifically those relating to community boundaries.

There was something of a difference between male and female attitudes to Britain. Although there were more men who said that they had faced racial prejudice than women (41% compared with 36%), more men were still willing to advise their relatives to settle in Britain (30% compared with 20%). But in general, attitudes to the wider society do not appear to be different between the genders. There were insignificant differences in the figures relating to such issues as having close British friends; believing that the British are difficult to befriend; perception of the range and nature of the threats posed by British society to the Zoroastrian family and religion; and assessment of the long-term future for the religion in Britain. More women than men believed that there was a conflict between the British environment and their Zoroastrianness. But the overall figures are so low (15% and 6% of interviewees) that the basic point has to be that few Zoroastrians consider that there is a clash. In short, there does not appear to be any significant difference between Zoroastrian men and women in terms of religious activity or beliefs, or in their attitudes to wider British society. In this they differ from a number of other South Asian communities in Britain, but are being true to the age-old emphasis of Zoroastrianism on the equal and similar responsibilities of men and women. Consistent with these findings is the fact that women have held all the secular offices in the Association, including that of president.

(k) *Intermarriage*

The interrelatedness of the issues of intermarriage and conversion for Parsis was discussed in Chapter 1. It has been a subject of intense debate in Bombay (and other major urban centres, such as Delhi) throughout the twentieth century, as the westernized and educated sections of Parsi society have argued that there has been a paucity of suitable marriage partners within the community. In the diaspora the problem is more acute because the smaller the group, the greater the difficulty of finding a partner. Among the scattered groups which have no meeting-place of their own the problem is at its greatest. Intermarriage is, therefore, more common in these groups than it is in larger centres, such as London, and much more common than in India or Iran (see Writer 1994: 231–3, also Kharas Fraser 1993 and Amighi 1990). Which are the groups in the British Zoroastrian community that most strongly object to, and which accept, intermarriage? Is there an identifiable trend among those who marry out? What are the contrasting attitudes to the conversion of non-Zoroastrian spouses? It is unusual in any survey to find a 100% response on any issue, but all the parents interviewed placed a very high priority on their offspring finding a Zoroastrian partner. Even some of the intermarrieds hoped for a Zoroastrian partner for their children. Two-thirds of the youth wanted to find a Zoroastrian partner and the same proportion believed that the impact of intermarriage on the community was a negative one. The groups likely to think it unimportant were those born in Britain; the postgraduates; those who described themselves as British rather than Zoroastrian; those who do not have membership of, or attend regularly, Zoroastrian House; and those who have not been back to the old country. In contrast, those who thought in-marriage very important were Zoroastrians from East Africa; those who thought in Gujarati; those who were members of Zoroastrian House, especially the frequent attenders; those who envisaged a return to the old country; those who described themselves as Parsi or Zoroastrian; those who prayed daily; those who wanted to preserve the contact between race and religion; and those who thought that there is a conflict between their Zoroastrianness and the British environment. There was no indication that opposition to out-marriage was due to antagonism towards British society, because more of those who pressed for in-marriage said that they would recommend their relatives to settle in Britain than did those who were more positive about intermarriage; similarly, fewer of those who valued in-marriage said they thought they had faced racial prejudice (33% compared with 44%). The point would, therefore, seem to be that valuing in-marriage emerges from a positive attitude to, and close ties with, the Zoroastrian community rather than from a negative response to British society. Those who marry out of the community are precisely the groups who object to it least: the high-flyers in terms of education and career, those born here and/or those who are strongly identified with Britain through the language of thought; those who arrived in the 1960s; those who do not envisage visiting the old country; those with close British friends and those whose primary self-definition is British. Marginally more women than men are married out, but the difference is not great.

One theme which emerged in the interviews, and not easily conveyed through figures, was the intense communal pressure on the parents of intermarrieds, especially in the old country. One man brought up in rural Gujarat relayed the experience of his father: 'I have it in my family. It is a public shame for the family. The Parsi community ridicule you; "your daughter is married to a Hindu" was the taunt my father had to live through.' One Parsi woman married out felt that it would cause her family embarrassment if she returned for her father's funeral. On a later visit, her mother informed her that she was 'grateful I had spared the family embarrassment'. A number of young people said that they were so conscious of the wider family difficulties intermarriage would cause that if they could not find a suitable Zoroastrian partner then they would choose not to get married. One young Zoroastrian woman whose answers to other questions showed how deeply committed to her heritage she is, commented, sadly:

If I don't find a Parsi who is compatible, I don't think I would get married. Upbringing, background, language—you can mingle with the English outside your home to a point—when you come home you have to be comfortable. I have lived a certain way for twenty-seven years, I don't think I could adapt and change for an Englishman completely.

Others said that if they were to marry out, then the non-Zoroastrian partner would have to mean even more to them in order to compensate for the possible loss of the religion, since they realized that the priests would not perform any of the important higher, or wedding, ceremonies. Many of the young people commented that they thought that if they did intermarry then they would not practice the religion because of the 'hassle', because 'I would feel inhibited', because 'I would feel very hypocritical to practice. My child would be half-Zoroastrian. He would be very confused so I wouldn't worship any religion.' The Iranians interviewed were at least as hostile to intermarriage as Parsis, especially if the intermarriage was to a Muslim. Almost all parents indicated that they would accept the non-Zoroastrian spouse but that the experience would be deeply distressing. There was a general tendency among them to blame not the person marrying out, but themselves for not bringing the child up properly or the community for not providing the youngster with a suitable partner. When a community feels under threat of extinction, then it opposes what it sees as dangerous with particular vigour. Equally, of course, those associated with intermarriage argue that to reject spouses and offspring is going to drive people away from the diminishing community. They also argue that to oppose intermarriage looks like racism.

Twenty-five intermarried families were included in the interview schedule. Their experiences merit description. One middle-aged professional lady married to an Englishman had lived in Britain for twenty-eight years but still saw India as 'home' and expressed fondness for her religion. She voiced some hostility to the British: 'I have nothing in common with them . . . on a personal level I wouldn't have them [the British]. I don't have any loyalty to the British. Most to my Zoroastrianism.' She would not recommend intermarriage: 'For an Indian I am too liberal; for a European I am too conservative. I think like a westerner; I feel like an oriental.' Several intermarrieds commented on how they had been excluded by Zoroastrians, not only at functions at Zoroastrian House but also from private dinner parties in Zoroastrian homes. One 40-year-old intermarried lady seeking to maintain her religion had on a visit back to India wanted to visit the Atash Bahram, in Udwada, but had been required to take a purificatory bath and could only be smuggled in at night. She had resolved not to repeat the attempt and had begun to turn more to her husband's religion. One 37-year-old Zoroastrian woman married to an

Englishman commented: 'I cry for my community. I love being with my own people—the Parsis.' But the rejection meant that she did not feel able to socialize with Parsis, even though in the privacy of her home she continued the prayers and practices of Zoroastrianism. Some spouses, having originally attempted to learn about the community, felt hurt that they had been so rejected. One father spoke about the irony of teaching his children about the religion he respected, but which had rejected him. Many of the non-Zoroastrian spouses spoke with enthusiasm and admiration about the history and teachings of their spouse's religion, but most were embittered at their own rejection and treatment. There is particular distress to parents when their children are similarly rejected. Fearing such rejection, some intermarried interviewees had taken a conscious decision not to have children. Several children of mixed marriages have expressed immense surprise when I suggested to them that since their father was a Zoroastrian then according to British Indian law so were they (see Ch. 1, Sect. (*a*) on the 1906 test case). For some of them it was the first time anyone had put that idea to them. One 30-year-old interviewee, the offspring of an intermarriage, spoke of himself as 'a mixed race person' and commented that; 'There is no provision made for that. I can never be entirely British and neither entirely Zoroastrian, so I have to be something independent, in-between, but distinct. It is a question of identity. I don't see a way forward.' On the other hand one man, the offspring of an intermarriage, kept in contact with what he described as 'his Parsi side' through visits to his paternal grandmother in India and spoke of her idiosyncrasies and devotions with affection. A few others said that they felt at home with members of the community whom one said he found more 'genuine' than the British. There are three broad groups among the intermarrieds: (*a*) Those who migrated in the early years when it was extremely difficult to find a Zoroastrian spouse. When such families live at a distance from Zoroastrian House in London it is common for the expressions of their Zoroastrianness to diminish considerably. (*b*) More recent arrivals who have sought unsuccessfully for a Zoroastrian spouse and among whom there may well be a strong sense of their own Zoroastrian identity; these may be more likely to preserve Zoroastrian traditions, and who can therefore be all the more hurt at community rejection. (c) Those born and brought up in Britain who have chosen a non-Zoroastrian partner. As one young Zoroastrian put it to me when she married a White Anglo-Saxon: 'My parents told me that I should marry someone of my own background—well I was born and brought up in England, so I have done.' She was, and is, deeply hurt by the community's rejection of her.

(l) *Transmitting the Tradition: The Social Context*

Jackson and Nesbitt (1993) emphasized that a significant factor in the nurture of Hindu children was the variety of pleasurable experiences the children enjoyed within the community. If Zoroastrians are so concerned to encourage in-marriage, what pleasurable experiences flourish within their community? It is all too easy for an outside member of the majority population to ignore what may appear to be trivial activities, be they bingo or badminton. However, it does not matter what activities are arranged providing they offer a reason for Zoroastrians to come together. The happier the occasion the more effective it is as a means of transmitting the Zoroastrian ethos, providing it does not contravene Zoroastrian principles.

There is a range of social functions organized at Zoroastrian House and aimed at young people. Some are intended simply for pleasure, such as visits to Alton Towers leisure park or indoor sports occasions. There is a Zoroastrian cricket team, preserving the nineteenth century tradition (see Ch. 3, Sect. (a)), which competes in a London league. For a couple of years there was an international cricket match against the Canadian Zoroastrians but travel costs meant that the fixture did not continue. There are discos, barn dances, Valentine's evening soirées, Hallowe'en dinner dances, day trips to Calais, nature reserves, camping trips, and career days. Sometimes the young Zoroastrians prefer to meet away from Zoroastrian House and the watchful eyes of the elders and so at Christmas 1993 an 'Extravaganza' was organized in Leicester Square, the heart of London's West End. At other times, the occasions are ethnically focused: for example, Indian bhangra dancing or Iranian music, talks on Parsi and on Iranian cuisine.

One of the most common topics of Zoroastrian humour is food and rarely does a successful occasion pass without a meal. If a researcher on the Zoroastrian community thinks that food is an unimportant subject, it shows beyond doubt that he or she has not begun to understand the community! The menu associated with a function always figures prominently in the *Newsletter* publicity, and traditional Parsi *dhansak* is loved by most Zoroastrians of any age with an Indian connection. In recent years care has been taken at ZTFE events to include alternative Iranian dishes on occasions. In the survey respondents were asked which features of the heritage they thought it most important to preserve—religion, music, language, dress, and so on. The majority of all ages listed food as a priority (overall 96% identified food as important, 94% religion). In the classical (Pahlavi) texts enjoyment of alcohol is considered a virtue, though anything to excess is sinful (Zaehner 1956: Ch. 7). Modern Zoroastrians may not know these texts, but they happily preserve the principle. Anyone accepting a Parsi 'peg' of whisky should first appreciate that this is measured by stretching the index and little fingers far apart! The happy, noisy, chatter engendered at such occasions overwhelms any non-Zoroastrian newcomer.

In the mid-1990s there have also been occasional stagings of Parsi *Nataks*, plays in Gujarati, mostly characterized by a bawdy sense of humour (often reflected in Parsi novels in the modern tradition, e.g. Sidhwa 1978). Many Bombay Parsis, especially the younger generation, cannot read or write Gujarati, but it is sometimes used in conversation, heavily interspersed with English. In Britain also a number of Parsis who preserve their links with India use Gujarati in private conversation, and there have been occasional evenings of Gujarati songs at Zoroastrian House and a tape of them is quite popular with older Parsis. Persian language and music is central to Iranian Zoroastrian socializing in a way that Gujarati is not for Parsis. The point is that although Gujarati books may not be used, the young people have not lost all contact with the language, and its use is most evident in socializing. Iranian Zoroastrians meet once a month at

Zoroastrian House to enjoy their distinctive culture, language, music, and food.

There is relatively little restriction on young Zoroastrian men and women mixing and dating, unlike in many other Indian communities. The basic parental reaction is that they are relieved that the young people are mixing within their own community and not dating outside. The young Zoroastrians surveyed are not as opposed to intermarriage as some sections of the older generation, but it would be unusual for the non-Zoroastrian partner to take part in many Zoroastrian House events because the more orthodox atmosphere in the last few years has discouraged such contacts. The point of Zoroastrian social occasions is for Zoroastrians to meet each other. Outsiders, such as academics or interfaith groups, who are not seen to threaten the integrity of the community, are made very welcome and can be assured of a happy, if noisy, time. Intermarrieds tend to bring their partners more often in the scattered groups, where the phenomenon is more common, and where there are fewer Zoroastrians to come together. This is true internationally, not just in Britain.

Social life is, therefore, an important part of Zoroastrian House, and of meetings of the smaller local groups mentioned in Ch. 4, Sect. (*n*). But from the late 1980s the emphasis has swung more to social-cum-religious functions, notably the Jamshedi No Ruz, or New Year, in March and the six seasonal festivals or *gahambars*. These were part of the ancient Zoroastrian tradition, and have been dropped in urban India but preserved in Iran and in London, inspired by the Iranians. They combine a religious function, a *jashan*, in the hall, followed by a *boi* ceremony in the prayer-room, and a social one as they conclude with food and drink downstairs. Whether they are religious occasions or social functions is a redundant question. They are both. At New Year Zoroastrian House is bursting with over 400 people. Zoroastrians living at a distance from London will often have Zoroastrian friends to their home for dinner. It is the single most important time for Zoroastrians to meet. Before discussing religious practice, it will be helpful to turn to religious education because the classes can also be social occasions and the teaching relates to the understanding of what is done in the religious practice discussed below.

(m) *Transmitting the Tradition: Religious Knowledge*

Several authors writing on South Asians in Britain (see Ch. 1, Sect. (*b*)) have stressed the conscious need of British Hindus, Jains, and others to be able to articulate their religious faith. In view of the remarkable educational level (in western terms) of the Zoroastrians, this is even more true of them. The impact of western, largely Protestant, scholarship in India and Pakistan has already been noted (Ch. 2, Sect. (*e*)), inevitably this impact is also felt by educated Zoroastrians in Britain. As already mentioned, within traditional Parsi *baugs*, or colonies, in India, Pakistan or in Iranian Zoroastrian villages, there is little sense of a requirement to give coherent, logical explanations of beliefs and practices. Being Zoroastrian is a part of being within a community. In the western diaspora there is pressure to explain to outsiders the rationale for practices. Even in the well-intentioned atmosphere of interfaith dialogue there is an expectation that a 'believer' (the very term throws an emphasis onto one dimension of religion) can give an account of the doctrines. This same pressure is also felt within the family, because young people brought up in the West, attending religious education classes in schools, commonly feel a need for a more formal knowledge of 'the faith'. The consequence of these pressures is a greater emphasis in the diaspora on religious education than is typical in India. Only 18% of the interviewees in Britain thought that they had a level of knowledge necessary for them to preserve their religious heritage. Although the provision of such religious education is not on the scale of that provided in some of the American centres, nevertheless there is in London a growing emphasis on classes for adults as well as for children. These have been organized by both ZTFE and WZO. The lectures have been given by western Zoroastrians and by outside academics on topics ranging from the *Gathas*, to Middle Persian literature, archaeology, numismatics, and modern history. Sometimes speakers from India have been invited, although Parsis have done this much less frequently than many other South Asian groups in Britain have (Kalsi 1992: 166–189). London University (Birckbeck College) has organized extramural classes on Zoroastrianism at Zoroastrian House (initiated by Rashna Writer). Classes for children from 5 to 15 are given in one of the priests home (Ervad Rustom Bedhwa), focusing mainly on the prayers associated with the *naojote*, but often ending with stories from the great Iranian epic, the *Shahname*. While Ervad Bedhwa teaches the children, the parents socialize over coffee. The coming together both of parents and children is almost as important as the lessons. There are also classes for older children at Zoroastrian House, but many parents find it difficult to travel the distance every week. In addition an Iranian member offers classes in Farsi for the older Parsis in order to try and build a bridge of understanding between the two groups. There have been attempts to run courses on Avesta and Middle Persian literature, but after a few years these folded. Generally medieval literature has as little appeal for the Zoroastrian public as a course on Thomist philosophy would have for an average Christian church congregation. There is, therefore, a strong reform movement known by the others as 'the *Gatha-only-ists*'. Yet the impact of Mistree, whose teaching accepts the arguments enunciated by Boyce (see Ch. 1, Sect. (*a*) and Ch. 2, Sect. (*e*)) regarding the value of the later texts for an understanding of the prophet, means that the Pahlavi literature is taken more seriously in the 1990s than it would have been in the 1960s. The quest for personal roots by many young Zoroastrians involves gaining knowledge of their history and religion and as a result at the time of writing the youth (generally defined at Zoroastrian House as those under 35) have an active religious education programme.

Another means of education has been the production of reading materials, a newsletter, and a few books notably by Vajifdar (1993) and Gifford (1992), although both of these were on Dadabhoy Naoroji and not on the religion. The only London-produced book on the religion was by P. D. Mehta (1976), but he was not close to the community and his work does not reflect traditional Zoroastrian teaching. Much of the work for the children's book mentioned above (Mehta 1988) was drafted in London but my impression is that this Bombay publication is not heavily used in Britain. The largest London Zoroastrian publication activity is that of WZO, which has produced an annual set of conference papers since 1986. Over half of the papers are academic rather than religious in orientation, although three-quarters of the authors have been Zoroastrians, mostly from America.[4] It is the American communities which are the active publishing groups in the diaspora. There are no books produced within the British community which convey anything of a traditional spirituality. The book mostly used in this regard is Mistree (1982), published in Bombay; otherwise the focus is on historical studies (see also Writer 1994). There is therefore a lack of internally generated religious literature. This resembles the situation among 'non-sectarian' Hindus described by Jackson and Nesbitt (1993). Zoroastrian House in London does have a library to which increasing attention is being given but it is not heavily used by members. ZTFE sells books at diverse functions. The books which sell most are introductions to the history of the religion in the light of western studies.[5]

The British Hindu communities have the human resources and the materials to mount group cultural activities for children, notably dance, music, and drama. There have been occasional plays mounted at Zoroastrian House, but these also are rare. Indian films and videos are powerful teaching aids common in many Hindu homes. There is not the range of videos on Zoroastrianism that there is for Hindu communities, but those which exist are used in the homes and sometimes at the end of functions at Zoroastrian House. The best known is *On Wings of Fire* involving Zubin Mehta on his quest for his Zoroastrian roots (see Ch. 8, Sect. (*g*)). A video on the Parsis produced by the Bombay film-director Homi Sethna in 1993 is also quite popular. The Zoroastrians do, therefore, utilise some of the sort of teaching aids as the Hindus, but none of these has the teaching role comparable to the *Ramayana* videos. They are general programmes on the community which help a sense of

---

[4] Seven publications have appeared in seven years: *World Zoroastrian Souvenir Issue*, First World Conference, London, 1984; *World Zoroastrian Souvenir Issue*, one-day seminar, London, 1986; *World Zoroastrian*, Chicago conference, 1987; *World Zoroastrian*, London conference, 1988; *World Zoroastrian*, London conference, 1989; *World Zoroastrian*, London seminar, 1990; *World Zoroastrian Organization Seminar*, London, 1991. The 1993 publication was Vajifdar 1993. In 1993 an international conference was organized in London on the *Gathas*, to be published in 1995.

[5] I am told that the 'bestsellers' are Boyce 1984 and esp. 1975; Hinnells 1981 and 1985*b*, i.e. books by outsiders. The Zoroastrian authors whose books sell most are Mistree, Dhalla, and the radically reformist California-based teacher Ali Jafferey, i.e. mainly authors who have a western academic education. There are minimal sales of occult works and only one Iranian Zoroastrian author. Other sales include novels by Parsis and translations of the Iranian epic, the *Shahname* and especially Writer 1994.

pride but are used mostly for instructing non-Zoroastrian friends. Western studies play a much more important role in the edification of the community.

(n) *The Practice of the Religion*

It is inevitable that Zoroastrianism will be different in some ways in Britain from how it is in the old countries, just as Christianity has changed as it has been transplanted from one culture to another. The obvious difference for British Zoroastrians is the lack of material provision—no full-time professional priesthood, no fully pure and consecrated temple, and no Tower of Silence. Zoroastrian Houses in London have had prayer-rooms, and the one in Compayne Gardens has a sanctuary modelled on a Bombay prototype, with floor-to-ceiling walls to the sanctuary, and a large fire-holder purchased from India, as were the many implements used in the rites and others decorating the walls. Purity is maintained as far as possible by the removal of shoes before entry, the covering of worshippers' heads, and the exclusion of non-Zoroastrians during rituals. But it has not been possible to maintain total purity for various reasons: non-Zoroastrians have been employed as cleaners and the entry of non-Zoroastrian students or inter-faith groups would also nullify true purity. There has never been a full consecration ceremony, which for an *Atash Bahram* involves the collecting of different types of fire, including fire caused by lightning, and takes a full year. Unlike in the 1960s, there are now believed to be sufficient funds and priests to sustain the required pattern of five *boi* ceremonies to feed the fire at each of the five *gahs*. Finally, the priests are unable to attain the absolute purity necessary for major ceremonies because there is no totally pure precinct within which to perform the nine-day purification ceremony (the *bareshnum*). One consequence is that the 'higher' or 'inner' ceremonies cannot be performed, for example the *yasna*, which is an important part of the full death ceremonies and in many other contexts (Modi 1922: 73–81). Despite the devotion of many, and the generosity of donors, worshippers feel something of a personal and spiritual loss without a pure temple whose sanctity has been hallowed by the devotions of generations and without a permanently burning sacred fire and its aura of holiness. How different is the spiritual dimension of the religion in Britain?

The general opinion among the people I have spoken to at Zoroastrian House is that the level of interest in religious practice has increased in recent years.[6] Several explanations are given. One is the growing influence in the 1980s of East African Zoroastrians, who are generally thought to be more orthodox (just as academics tend to characterize other African Asians). A second explanation is that in the 1990s there is a growing search for a sense of identity, not least among the young, and that part of this is expressed through religion. Whatever the explanation, there is an active religious life at Zoroastrian House. The overriding impression gained by any outsider privileged to be present at such occasions is one of joy. Parsi ladies wear their splendid saris (Iranian ladies wear best western dress), there is food, much chatter, and laughter. If the community is able to realize its plans to establish a purpose-built community centre to house functions for up to 1,200, with parking and with a separate room for a permanently burning fire, then there will be yet more joyous occasions.[7]

Life-cycle Rites

An appropriate way to begin a consideration of the religious life among British Zoroastrians is with an account of the practices of the life-cycle rites. Within modern Zoroastrianism, either in the old country or in Britain, there are few rites particularly associated with physical birth, though recently in Britain young mothers have started asking the priest to perform the *nahn* ceremony of purification forty days after the birth, when the forces of evil which threaten life have departed. In this respect, therefore, there is a hint of a return to, rather than an eradica-

---

[6] This is, of course, one perspective. The former leaders also consider themselves to have been religious. The debate focuses on a variety of issues, especially intermarriage and the restrictions of the purity laws which exclude non-Zoroastrian spouses from various rites, notably those associated with death. What may be religious practice to one, can be bigotry to another. It is not the place of the outsider to judge between these views. There does, however, appear to be an increased demand for religious ceremonies and lectures or classes.

[7] The plans are outlined in a booklet, *The Unimpeded March of the Zoroastrian Spirit into the Twenty-First Century*, produced by ZTFE in 1993.

tion of, the purity laws. It is common to hold a *jashan* in celebration of the birth.

The specific life-cycle rites start with what may be translated as the second or rebirth, that is, initiation into the religion (pp.23f.). About half British Zoroastrian families have their children's *naujote* performed in the sub-continent if they still have close family ties with the old country. The reason is partly practical: in India (and Pakistan) the temple and *baug* authorities are accustomed to mounting such joyous occasions both liturgically and practically, catering appropriately for hundreds of people. It also means that elderly and distant relatives can share in the joy as the family priest initiates a new member into the army of God. In London the *nahn* ceremony often takes place at Zoroastrian House where there are facilities, but elsewhere in Britain it is performed in the home prior to the initiation and celebrations in such non-Zoroastrian centres as school halls or other communal rooms.. The priests and many parents still prefer to use the traditional *nirang* (cow's urine), but if the children object strongly then pomegranate or orange juice is used instead. The late High Priest, Dastur Kutar, a medical doctor, sent some *nirang* for pathology tests to assure his people that it was not harmful to them. When the results supported his contention he explained that the powerful spiritual forces of the consecration ceremony (an inner rite which can only take place in consecrated temples in the old country) rendered the harmful bacteria ineffective yet preserved its purifying properties.[8] Dastur Kutar thereby sought to integrate his spiritual heritage with his scientific training. But he recognized the sensitivities of many educated young people and did not press the use of *nirang* and in his instructional papers on initiation referred to the use of pomegranate and orange juice. The *naujote* is performed in Britain for the children of men who have married out, but not for the children of intermarried women. British Iranian Zoroastrians rarely have the *sedra pushan* performed, for the rite has not preserved the same significance in that country and the use of *nirang* is rejected by Liberal Iranis as it is by reformist Parsis.

---

[8] *Parsiana*, May 1969; see also *Parsiana*, Jun./Jul., 1977. It is noteworthy that the only other defence of *nirang* published in this Bombay-based but internationally circulated magaazine was written by a London priest, Darius Sethna (*Parsiana*, Apr. 1991).

Weddings are times of great communal joy when they involve marriage to fellow Zoroastrians. The traditional rites associated with engagement and the days leading up to the marriage are rarely followed nowadays in Britain or in India as much as they used to be. The emphasis is much more on the wedding day itself. Before the wedding the bride and groom separately take the ritual bath, the *nahn* ceremony, as for the initiation. After the formal legal ceremony at a Register Office the couple come to Zoroastrian House to receive the priestly blessing (though such a blessing may take place in the home and a few choose to travel to India for the religious part of the occasion). The full rite involves passing a length of wool seven times around the couple, binding them together in marriage. This is an Indian custom adopted as appropriate by Parsis, but is not practised by the Iranians. The latter have simply the concluding part of the Parsi rite which involves the priest satisfying himself that the couple agree to the marriage, obtaining their vows, and then showering the couple with divine blessings through prayer. The Parsi custom is for the priest to scatter grains of rice over the couple to represent the shower of blessings. Sometimes after a month a *jashan* is celebrated in the home, but most couples have this on their wedding anniversaries. In the case of mixed marriages the blessing does not take place at Zoroastrian House, though a *jashan* may be held later at the home. Marriages are sometimes held in Bombay, but less frequently than *naujotes* are.

Some Zoroastrians would like to have their funeral held traditionally at a *daxma* in India, but this is rarely done. The major problem for funerals in Britain is the purity laws (Ch. 1, Sect. (g)). The priests advise the bereaved to perform the *kusti* prayers as soon as possible after the death and if that occurs at home, then flowers are brought in (said to be symbolic of the soul, though in historical tradition the Good Creation should be kept at a distance from death) and an oil-lamp (*divo*) is lit so that its power may protect the living. The undertakers are asked to conduct the funeral with all reasonable speed (in India it would be held on the day of death if possible). If it can be undertaken within twenty-four hours, the body is washed, clad in a *sudre*, and wrapped in a white sheet. If the funeral has to be delayed, the undertakers take steps to preserve the body. If the body is to be cremated (the most common form of British Zoroastrian funeral) then the *gehsana* prayers are said at home, because there is insufficient time at a crematorium where funerals take place so quickly. But this is not ideal, as the prayers are necessarily recited at a distance from the funeral place. If the body is to be buried in the Zoroastrian cemetery at Brookwood, then the rites can be performed in the special building (*bungli*) there. For the first three nights, the period when the soul is thought to be meditating on its life before proceeding to the Bridge of Judgement (see Ch. 1, Sect. (*a*)), prayers are said in the home. The immediate period of mourning concludes with the *uthumna* prayers on the afternoon of the third day, when it is traditional for charitable bequests to be announced for the sake of the deceased's soul. The traditional teaching is that such bequests aided the soul on its journey, but they are now commonly interpreted as representing appropriate memorials for the deceased. Some British Zoroastrian families leave a box for donations to be made to a charity (often medical). In Britain gravestones have become a more common way of remembering the deceased, whereas in India they are rare and charitable endowments are the norm. The ceremony at dawn on the fourth day is rare in Britain but a *jashan* is held on that day. After that the soul is prayed for on the tenth and thirtieth days and then annually. However, the major religious rites to care for the soul (the *Yasna, Vendidad* and *Baj*) cannot be performed in Britain because there is not the necessary pure temple. Instead the family pay for these powerful rites to be performed in the old country on their behalf. While, therefore, the priests and family do all that is possible in Britain, it is recognized that this is restricted. Intermarried spouses are not excluded from the funerals, although they are requested not to attend the annual *muktad* and *Fravardigan* ceremonies when all the dead are remembered and their *fravashis*, or spiritual selves, are invoked. (Some Zoroastrians opposed to this exclusion have held separate ceremonies.) At these ten days (falling at the end of August according to the majority Parsi Shenshai calendar) Zoroastrian House is full, with as many as 250 attending at the weekends when up to 300 names are recalled in the *jashan*. The traditional practice of sharing food after the ceremony has been revived in London. Since the tradition is that flowers are brought to delight the souls and since the *fravashis* are joyfully invoked in the rite, the atmosphere in no way resembles the sombre occasion of a Christian All Souls' day.

Community Rituals

Nowadays, Zoroastrian House is full for any major religious ceremonies, especially the New Year festival and *gahambars* (discussed above), but religious rites are held on many other occasions also. Short community (*hambandagi*) prayers are said together before most events, even before a secular lecture, and a *jashan* can be held at Zoroastrian House on various occasions—when moving into a new house or even to mark a conference. Whatever the physical limitations on Zoroastrian worship may be in Britain, and however much the loss of treasured rites may cause grief on occasions, there is an active religious life which keeps the team of eighteen listed priests very busy. Some of the priests are young but the time-demands of travel to, and availability for, funerals means that the most active are those who have retired from their full-time careers. All of them have received some training and went through their priestly initiation ceremonies in India, and four have undertaken occasional periods of duty in a fire temple in India.

In the interviews people were asked what they considered important for the preservation of their Zoroastrian identity. The priorities identified were New Year (*No Ruz*), 97%; *sudre* and *kusti*, 96%; *jashan* ceremonies, 95%; seasonal festivals (*gahambars*), 95%; prayer, 94%; establish a fire temple, 91%; observe the death ceremonies, 85%; have a prayer-room, 76%; observing the purity laws, 58% and observing vegetarian days, 30%. It is noticeable that three of the first four priorities are congregational activities. This contrasts in many ways with traditional practice of worship in India. Devout Parsis go daily to the temple, make an offering to the fire, and say the set prayers. But the explanation given to me by several friends in Bombay accords with the Hindu practice of going on a pilgrimage alone (even if in the presence of others), to stand in the presence of the divine and receive blessing. In the Indian subcontinent and Iran there is rarely an emphasis on visiting the temple at set times, or as part of a group or congregation, as there is in Islam or much Christian worship. However, living as a scattered minority in Britain, Zoroastrians have different needs: to congregate together and through those communal meetings to give and receive mutual suppport, to establish and reaffirm social networks that will help in-marriage, and to be in a group where they can be themselves without the need for explanations. In Iran, and to a certain extent in Pakistan, the seasonal festivals are still important focal points for such meetings, but this is not so much the case in India. It may be significant that in Bombay the major communal activities are secular lectures and debates. In the diaspora the reaffirmation of these communal gatherings, feasts, and merrymaking serve as ideal, and truly Zoroastrian, ways of affirming identity. To give a sense of contrast, I suspect that had the same questions regarding priorities been asked in Bombay, most importance would have been attached to visits to temples, the purity laws, and the *sudre/kusti* with related practices. Congregational activities would not have had a high priority.

The fact that even more British Zoroastrians who were interviewed asserted the importance of the *jashan* rather than of the *sudre/kusti* prayers is significant. The *jashan* is an ancient liturgy, the main purpose of which is to honour and make present the seven Bounteous Immortals, and like almost all Zoroastrian acts of worship centres on the fire. It is normal for this to be a fire which is lit for the occasion and the permanently burning flame of the temple fire is not necessary (Modi 1922: 428–29, 354–84; Mistree 1982: 66–9). By the substitution of certain prayers it is a liturgy which can be used in a variety of contexts, as a communal petition (e.g. at a time of drought or famine); as an act of thanksgiving (e.g. at the time of a royal coronation, or for victory in war); and commonly as a form of blessing (e.g. on moving into a new home or at the public recognition of a High Priest). It can be performed in a temple, but also in the home or in a public place. It therefore naturally serves as the religious focal point of a social gathering. This liturgy is an important part of the living tradition in Iran (Boyce 1977: 42–3, 53–4) and Bombay, but my impression is that it has acquired an even more central role in diaspora devotions because of its particular appropriateness in meeting a community need, and because it can be properly celebrated without all the requirements of the full temple tradition. In short, what is happening is not the elaboration of new liturgies but the harnessing of those parts of the ancient tradition which most meet the needs of the new situation.

Interpreting Religious Practice

The understanding of those traditions, it may be assumed (no research has been done to prove this), is in the process of change. My impression is that the festivals have been secularized as Christmas has in many 'Christian' British homes. Something of the idea of charitable giving is preserved, because Iranian, and some Parsi, families endow the *gahambars*, but the strong sense of invoking the *fravashis* of the deceased to share in all occasions for happiness (Boyce 1977) is missing. For those close to the Indian tradition there is at the *jashan* a strong sense of the invisible spiritual power and force radiating from the sacred fire. On more than one occasion when I have been invited to attend, there has been concerned community discussion about the appropriate distance for me to keep from the fire. Partly this was because as a non-Zoroastrian (*juddin*) I do not observe the necessary purity laws and can therefore defile that which is ritually pure. But it was also because some were concerned that as a *juddin* I did not have the spiritual protection afforded by the prayers and the purity so I might be harmed by the divine energy. (Such an interpretation is more common among theosophically influenced Parsis than among Iranians.) In the technical Study of Religions sense of the word, the fire was *tabu* because it could be dangerous for the unprepared. Zoroastrians holding such views clearly have a strong sense of the presence of the holy in worship.[9] For younger Zoroastrians brought up in Britain, these ideas may not carry such conviction.[10] I have heard a number of them express support for such popular interpretations of the symbolism of the fire as the quotation from the British published book, (Masani 1938: 80): 'what ... can be a more natural and more sublime representation of Him, who is Himself Eternal Light, than a pure, undefiled flame?' This is an interpretation

---

[9] The situation is doctrinally more complex that the text implies. In India a *juddin* is excluded by the orthodox from all acts of worship, because his or her presence would vitiate the ritual. In the ancient texts (e.g. the Pahlavi literature and the *Rivayats*) there are directions on how far an unclean person should be kept from a sacred object. What London Zoroastrians are doing, in following the advice given from Bombay and lacking a permanently burning temple fire, is applying these traditions to the fire they light for a specific liturgy.

[10] It is not easy to find support in the older literature for the idea of impure persons being unprotected from the power of the sacred and this idea may be due to theosophical influence.

which places the emphasis on abstract symbolism, not on ideas of powerful divine energies. Another dimension to the symbolism is to see the fire as representing the warmth, or heat, associated with life in contrast to the cold equated with death. These symbolic interpretations may also be meaningful to those who prefer to emphasize the sacred power of the holy, but would not express what is the most significant feature for them. Dastur JamaspAsa's words, quoted at the end of Ch. 1, Sect. (*a*), reflect the interpretation of most Zoroastrians, however they may then explain them.

Inevitably there are many layers of symbolism regarding 'the holy' in Zoroastrianism as in other religions. Among traditional Parsis in India the sense of the holy is fundamentally integrated with the concept of purity. Whatever the theological origins of the doctrines of purity and pollution, as outlined in the Introduction, the emphasis is on maintaining a distance between the pollution of dead matter, be that a corpse or the blood of a menstruating woman, from the places and people (notably the temples and the priests) in direct contact with the divine presence. Non-Zoroastrians are strictly forbidden to enter Parsi temples because they would pollute the sacred. In some temple precincts this ban extends to the outer boundary of the encircling wall, in others to the building housing the sacred fire, but wherever the boundary is drawn entry within must always be strictly controlled. The priest who ministers to the fire must preserve his purity by living on the premises during his duty rota, and avoiding food cooked by the impure, even by Parsis who are not observing all the purity laws. Similar care must be taken with the sacred creation of water, so that wells, or drinking-vessels, in public places in Iran (Boyce 1977: 96) and wells charitably endowed by Parsis in India must keep impure *juddins* and Zoroastrian purity apart. In Zoroastrianism a sacred space is that within which purity is preserved and such areas are delineated by literal or metaphorical walls. An area for future research is how this concept of 'sacred space' translates from the old to the new country. This issue lies at the heart of countless debates among British Zoroastrians (referred to in previous chapters) on allowing *juddins* into the prayer-room, or to attend ceremonies focused on the sacred fire, and rites for the deceased either at individual funerals or the annual *muktad* ceremonies, where the souls of the dead are traditionally thought to be powerfully present.

The British Zoroastrians' difficulties associated with demarcating the religiously significant areas of pollution around a corpse have already been referred to (Ch. 4, Sects. (*j*) and (*l*)). How do they themselves understand the problems and deal with them? Nearly half of the respondents indicated that they would ideally wish for their remains to be transported to India for exposure in a Tower of Silence, a wish expressed particularly by the older generation. As few can afford the high costs of transporting the corpse and other expenses involved, most accept the inevitability of a funeral in Britain. Of those questioned, 90% said that they preferred cremation to burial though it is normal for the ashes to be interred at Brookwood, thus giving a Zoroastrian resting-place for the remains. What impact does this enforced change of practice have on the faith of Zoroastrians? This is a particularly sensitive subject to discuss with people not only because many find it difficult to talk about their own funeral, but also because it involves addressing directly the fact that they are not following the hallowed traditions which they have been brought up to believe are the necessary means of caring for the soul of the deceased. It was not, therefore, included in the survey questionnaires or the interviews. I have, however, discussed it with a number of Zoroastrians with whom I have a close friendship. The following comments are based on that unbalanced sample, and were made on occasions of grief shared with some particularly close friends and when I was living in a Zoroastrian home at the time of an unexpected family death. In such private conversations most have expressed the view that cremation involves less pollution than burial, for the latter results in years of the body polluting the sacred earth. I have heard even greater expressions of horror from Zoroastrians regarding worms in cemeteries than from outsiders about vultures in *daxmas* (though the Zoroastrians have been too discreet to publicize their feelings about Christian practices, see ch. 4). Typically, Zoroastrians feel a particularly deep revulsion against burial. Orthodox Parsis in India would argue that cremation also pollutes the sacred element of fire, but among British Zoroastrians, as among a few westernized Parsis in Bombay, the explanation preferred is that modern western crematoria do not involve a flame (unlike cremations in India) but intense heat generated by electricity and therefore there is not the same (or even any) pollution. Whether this logic convinces the outsider is irrelevant. It is an essential rationalization to enable devout Zoroastrians to cope emotionally with distress at being compelled to follow a practice condemned not only in ancient texts but also by the living senior priestly authorities in India. (In Iran, a Muslim country where burial is the norm, the interment of the body excites less opposition from Zoroastrians, although *daxmas* were used until the 1960s.) The problem is yet more complicated for British Zoroastrians because they cannot observe the 'inner' ceremonies to care for the soul, and which provide a catharsis for grief. My impression, based on the experiences described, is that the natural grief suffered on bereavement can sometimes be compounded by a sense of guilt that mourners are prevented from doing what they believe to be the right thing. The loss of the religious resources can be far more distressing than outsiders readily appreciate.

A study of theological belief in the diaspora was part of both the global survey and the interview schedule in Britain. Of those interviewed, 87% said that they believed in Ahura Mazda and a similar proportion wanted to assert that Zoroastrianism is a monotheistic religion—only 6% accepting the dualism as propounded by Mistree and which many outside scholars identify as characteristic of the religion. The beliefs regarding the power of God are less clear. Two-thirds thought that God is all-powerful. But contrary to Zoroastrian textual tradition more than half thought that he is responsible for death. The distinctive Zoroastrian teaching on the evil Ahriman as an independent being was not widely followed, only 5% being willing to accept any idea of a devil. Approximately one in ten thought that Ahriman was an aspect of human nature, but three-quarters of those interviewed had variant explanations, or simply said they did not know what they believed regarding evil. In short, there would appear to be a strong belief in God, though there is little or no engagement with traditional doctrine, but rather a general assertion of the sort of theology common in the Christian West. It should be added that the same is true of most Zoroastrians in Bombay. As Jackson and Nesbitt (1993) found with regard to British Hindus, religious knowledge focuses not so much on philosophy and cosmology but on what is considered appropriate social behaviour. Increasingly, however, western-educated Zoroastrians are demanding a different emphasis, a rational justification for belief and practice.

(o) British Zoroastrians in International Perspective

How different is the religion of British Zoroastrians from that of co-religionists in other countries? The subject has been raised in Hinnells (1994a) and will be explored further in the subsequent Katrak volume. The broad pattern is that the older established centres in Hong Kong, East Africa, and especially Pakistan are more traditional than the centres in the USA, Britain, and Canada. The most recent settlements, those in Australia, still show the features noted among the most recent arrivals within Britain, namely the retention of close ties with the old country and a higher level of religious practice. The most liberal are the scattered groups whether they are in USA, Canada, or Britain. Within the USA there are different patterns between different cities, with Houston being the most traditional and Chicago the most liberal (Hinnells 1988). The London Zoroastrians are in the middle of that broad spectrum, but the picture (inevitably) is complex. In some aspects of religious practice, notably wearing *sudre* and *kusti* and saying the associated prayers, attitudes to funerals, and prayers for the dead, they are more traditional. The maintenance of tradition in the last two categories is due, presumably, to the early establishment of a burial ground, which has resulted in the preservation of beliefs concerning death rituals.

Reference has already been made to the ties many British South Asian communities have with holy men from India who come to Britain. The British Zoroastrian community used to invite the more reformed high priests, notably Dastur Bode who was a controversial figure in Bombay and associated with a sectarian group in California. Another priest invited on a number of occasions was Dastur Minocher Homji who had a reputation (especially in the USA and Canada) for being sympathetic to the needs of diaspora Zoroastrians. The orthodox high priests from Bombay, Dasturs Mirza, JamaspAsa, and Kotwal, despite having academic links with Britain, were rarely invited, even though they were to America. This has changed in the mid-1990s, with talks from two of these three high priests. This fact confirms trends noted elsewhere of the move in some quarters towards the more traditional 'wing' of Zoroastrianism. In 1994 the senior Iranian Zoroastrian priest (*Mobed-e-Mobedan*), Mobed Ferouz Azargashasb, was invited to Zoroastrian House in London, the first time that such a visit had been made. Such visits by Iranian as well as Parsi priests represent an interesting move towards internationalizing British Zoroastrianism.

There are a number of ways in which the doctrinal orientation in Britain is different from that in Bombay. In the old country there has been a growing twentieth-century interest in the occult, mostly in Khshnoom and the teaching of Behramshah Shroff (Hinnells 1995*a*), but also in the nineteenth century Parsi priestly-miracle worker, Dastur Kookadaru and his twentieth-century follower, Dastur Aibara, whose advice on personal and miracle-working *manthras* has been widely sought. In India a number of Parsis follow non-Zoroastrian Indian holy men, notably the Babas. The global survey asked about veneration for such figures. The only one to attract any following was Sai Baba, and this was found most in the traditional centre of Houston and in the new centre of Sydney, which is still emotionally close to India in many ways. He had a minimal following in Britain. The British Zoroastrians, in so far as they resist the secularizing trends they criticize in British society, incline more to the western academic influenced, Protestantizing trends. Otherwise, among British Zoroastrians the figure most influential person in the religious sphere in the 1990s is Mistree. It is a significant indicator of the trends among British Zoroastrians that the religious inspiration is sought not from a trained priest, but from a devout layman who studied in the West and has an ability to communicate rational arguments with some charismatic authority.

There were some interesting doctrinal differences between centres: a belief in reincarnation was strongest in the traditional centres of Kenya, and India-linked Sydney, and least in liberal Chicago and London. The traditional Zoroastrian doctrine of the resurrection is now rarely accepted, especially in London, though it is more commonly accepted in Karachi, that is, in a

Muslim environment. (Although the resurrection is part of Christian tradition, it is not emphasized in liberal Protestant circles.) The mythical dimension of the religion appears to be stronger in the traditional long-established communities, so that belief in the coming of a saviour, a basic Zoroastrian teaching, is upheld more in Hong Kong, Karachi, and Kenya than it is in Chicago or London. The preservation of the tradition is affected both by the external religious and intellectual environment and by the internal composition and interests of the community.

Internal British Comparisons

Nevertheless, the differences are not simply between Zoroastrians in different countries. Associations in different cities within one country can have contrasting natures. Just as differences have been noted between Chicago and Houston, so they can also between, say, London and Manchester. The former has a large association with its own building, library, social and religious functions, and a team of priests. Despite its limitations in comparison with Bombay or Karachi, London still has a far more substantial Zoroastrian network than Manchester can provide. Until 1987 there were Zoroastrians in Manchester who had not met a co-religionist (family apart) for thirty years. Even since the formation of the Association, Zoroastrians rarely meet each other more than once a month even if they do not miss a meeting. Living on the periphery of Zoroastrian life makes the maintenance of the tradition less likely, especially for the young people at school who through assemblies and religious education come into contact with other religions more frequently than they do their own. The atmosphere within the meetings is different from that in London. This is affected partly by the personalities who founded the Association. The Manchester group is called not an 'Association' but a 'Community'. The motivation is to emphasize the friendliness of meetings between people who are conscious of having missed religious and community contacts. In comparison with London, the emphasis is, therefore, more on social than on educational activities or religious functions (despite the religious emphasis of the early document referred to in ch. 4, Sect. (*n*)). From the outset there was a conscious effort to link the Iranian, Indian, and East African experiences. The group had to address the question of intermarriage at an early date because so many individuals had married out, in-marriage being so difficult when living in isolation from other Zoroastrians. The solution has been to ask non Zoroastrians to respect the privacy of Zoroastrians (defined by lines of descent) during the prayers which precede many functions, but non Zoroastrians have been made very welcome during all social occasions and these have dominated proceedings. There has always been a conscious effort to give the children time and space to meet and play, whereas outside lecturers and library resources are low on the list of priorities. Inevitably some difficulties arose as individuals desperately keen to preserve the tradition felt more strongly than others about certain customs or ideals. The interests of the youth and the elders are not always easily reconciled when meetings are held in premises rented only for a short time on one day per month and when people cannot stay long because of the distances they have to travel. If the maintenance of the tradition is difficult in London, it is even more difficult in the scattered groups. Yet Manchester does have a Community. In other places, such as the north-east of England, even further from the London resources and priests, with very few families, the opportunity to meet is restricted to occasional dinner parties in friends' homes. These are very enjoyable occasions, but provide restricted opportunities within which to nourish the youth in the tradition.

(p) *Conclusion*

Religion is a strong force within the world-wide Zoroastrian diaspora, not least in Britain. How that religion is seen varies. For the great majority it is not simply a question of beliefs and practices associated with God, but encompasses also community ties and individual identity. Two-thirds of respondents and interviewees wanted to link religion and race. For many, religion is a question of blood and genes. The spiritual side is also evident, however, whether that is seen in terms of beliefs in God, life after death, or devotional practices and community worship. There are ways in which the religion cannot be practised as it is in the old country (temple traditions, for example). The young people sometimes struggle as they seek to balance their instinct to identify both with their heritage and with the religious assumptions common in the West regarding fundamental issues such as prayer. In Britain most people are brought up, especially through religious education, to assume that an essential dimension of prayer is dialogue with God in the form of petition, benediction, or penitence. All presuppose an understanding of the words of prayer; otherwise these are seen as 'mumbo jumbo'. In orthodox Parsi circles prayer is differently conceived (Ch.1, Sect.(*a*)). Ritual for such Zoroastrians is not simply symbolic, although symbolism is one part of worship. It is much more a powerful means of advancing the soul in righteousness, increasing purity in the world, bringing enjoyment to the spiritual forces, and making those forces really present in the material world. The rites must be performed by the son of a priest who has himself been duly initiated, offered in bodily as well as spiritual purity and in righteousness with proper intent. The *manthras* are dead when unspoken, but contain power which is activated when they are properly recited. The meaning of the words as expressed in limited human conceptual terms is insignificant; indeed it can obstruct the religious experience because it emphasizes human conceptual thought. It is not, therefore, simply that British Zoroastrians do not have physical resources such as temples; it is also that there is a different way of thinking and a different scale of priorities.

To what extent is change necessary, indeed inevitable? One-third of respondents thought that the religion in Britain must change, but this has the corollary that two-thirds thought that it need not, or should not, change. Contrary to popular images, it was the young rather than the elders (especially in contrast to the 1960s and 1970s settlers) who opposed change. More of the youth than elders wanted to preserve the link between race and religion. The people most likely to call for change are those who have pursued postgraduate education and the middle-aged, especially single people or those who have married out. Yet there are changes, other than the material losses already discussed. When interviewees were asked about the practice of prayer a number of students said: 'I pray before exams, in English: "Please God help me"'! Most Zoroastrians were more comfortable with the terms 'God' and 'the devil' than with Ohrmazd and Ahriman. This research cannot answer the substantive question which that statement raises—is it only the vocabulary that has changed, or does the change in terminology indicate a fundamental shift in the perception of the divine?

There is a complex range of factors which affects the extent and ways in which people assimilate or preserve the tradition: where they came from (Bombay, Karachi, or East Africa, rural or urban areas); when they came (1960s or 1990s); why they came (for perceived self-benefit or under the pressure of threatened persecution); who they came with (as part of an extended family or as individuals); at what stage of their lives they came (before or after schooling); where they came to (a centre or to live as isolated Zoroastrians); what they did after settling (education, career, marriage and having children, the preservation of links with the old country); who they are (gender, role in family, priest or lay person); and who they met (fellow Zoroastrians, secular or religious non-Zoroastrians). Further, it is wrong when studying small minority communities to underestimate the influence which individuals can have on the development of a group.

But in looking at factors for change it would be mistaken to ignore the very strong element of continuity in the lives of most Zoroastrians: the shared consciousness of their allegiance to the prophet and to non-Islamic Iran; the ideals generally valued even by those who do not think of themselves as religious, particularly honesty (even among Iranian Muslims, Zoroastrians have a strong reputation for integrity and reliability), generosity and charitable giving, hospitality, hard work, strong family values, tremendous emphasis on individual responsibility, immense determination, and an unashamed enjoyment of the good things of life. In their image of Zoroaster, as a determined warrior for the truth, they see their ultimate role-model.

Perhaps the last words of this chapter should be those of Zoroastrians. The following comments were made in the course of the structured interviews on the subject of being a Zoroastrian

... carrying on a long tradition. You feel, being so few in numbers, it is quite a precious thing. It is rare for people to belong to such a small group and not to have a sense of heritage ...

I feel a duty—I have been born into a religion which I find fascinating and beautiful, it has to be preserved. I am very thankful to be born Zoroastrian . . .

I feel very proud that it is the oldest religion . . .

It part of me, it is my past. Even though I may not be practising, it is part of my history and I am proud of it . . .

[Zoroastrianism] is the anchor. The children have to have that in this fast-changing world. The world is changing for the worse. This [religion] provides stability . . .

It is necessary for every human being to have an identity. This is my identity. I was born into it and I am most comfortable with it . . .

My religion tells me good thoughts, words and deeds are very important.

[Zoroastrianism] is my heritage. My heritage is my community which lives with its religion and I worship through Zarathushtra . . .

7

Conclusion

(a) *Zoroastrians in Britain: An Overview*

Although Zoroastrianism has been identified with one race throughout its history, the ancient Iranians and their descendants, it has nevertheless long been a religion in migration; it spread from north-east Iran to dominate the whole of ancient Iran and its empire by the sixth century BCE to the seventh century CE, and then from Iran to India in the tenth century CE. In the nineteenth century there was substantial migration from rural Gujarat to cosmopolitan Bombay, and in the twentieth century from rural Iran to the metropolis of Tehran. But also in the nineteenth century it spread around the world on a scale never previously experienced in the three millennia of its history, with Parsis following trade-routes throughout the British Empire. The community in Britain has a significant place in that history. It was one of the earliest of these modern diaspora groups. London, as the chief city of the Empire was, and probably still is, the largest Zoroastrian Association outside Iran and the Indian subcontinent. Further, London Zoroastrians have played an important role in Parsi history from the eighteenth century, when the status of leading Bombay families, such as the Wadias, was based in part on the wealth, knowledge, and standing acquired by some of their members through visits to Britain. Later in the nineteenth century many professionals came for their studies to British universities, law firms, hospitals, and industries. Others owed their status in India to experience gained in London, notably the three Parsi MPs, and above all Dadabhoy Naoroji, who was highly regarded in the Indian National Congress. From its inception the London Association has seen itself as having European-wide responsibility, indeed as having international significance because of its place at 'the heart of Empire', the most notable example of its activity in this sphere being the appeals made to the Shah of Persia for its co-religionists (ch. 2, Sect. (*a*)). Even at the end of the twentieth century movements and individuals in Britain have set something of the agenda for community debate world-wide, for example the London initiative in organizing a body to facilitate international collaboration between Zoroastrians—the World Zoroastrian Organization. The London community is unique in the Zoroastrian diaspora in its perception of itself as having an international and not simply local role.

The Zoroastrians, as the oldest of the Asian ethnic and religious minorities in Britain, should have an important place in the study of diaspora religion in this country. The early date at which the Association was founded in the nineteenth century, the existence of written records from those early days, indeed the existence of even earlier diaries so that the earliest background of the British Zoroastrians can be outlined, facilitates a historical perspective which is not possible with the other Asian religions in Britain. The diversity of backgrounds within the community makes it a good test case for the study of diaspora religion. Yet, as Holmes (1988) rightly observes, the community has been almost entirely neglected in the study of immigrant groups in the UK, and one might add, in the study of modern Zoroastrianism.

Zoroastrians have always had a strong sense of history—in Middle Persian literature, for example, the history of the world is important as the arena for the conflict of good and evil (Hinnells 1985*b*: 42–63). The sense of history still has a place among the modern communities. The Iranian Zoroastrians have a strong sense of their historical background, although the details are inevitably different from those of Parsi history because of their contrasting circumstances. They can, and do, justly take pride in the achievements they made once they were given even minimal opportunities in the twentieth century (Boyce 1977: ch. 14; Shahrokh and Writer 1994). But for them what is most important is their very strong sense of being the true, the original, Iranians untouched by the Arab invasion and culture. Zoroastrian communities generally, and Parsis in particular, keep good records in comparison with other groups from the Indian subcontinent. This may in part be due to their business practices, but it is also due to the strong sense of the religion's history among Zoroastrians, a sense which is not unlike that of the Jews. The members usually have a justifiable pride in their history (even if they are not personally aware of all the details) and in the substantial contributions they believe they have made to most countries where they have settled. As far as Britain is concerned, this contribution includes their perception of the role they played in the Empire from the China Seas to the North West Frontier, in Africa and in Britain itself, but above all in western India and the commercial capital of Bombay. Parsis do not see themselves as simply another insignificant and obscure minority group. Even though few British Zoroastrians know all the historical events summarized in Chapter 2, most have a strong sense that their forebears were collaborators with, not mere servants of, the leaders of the British Empire and Commonwealth. Bombay became central to the economy of British India and the Parsis were at the heart of its development, as they were in other centres, notably Karachi. One element of their success, which is pivotal to Parsi mentality, is the basic belief that there is a substantial range of religious and secular values which they share with the British: an image-free worship, abstract philosophy (at least among the modern liberals in the two traditions) and high ethical principles, a common work ethic, and a commitment to justice and education, to law and to care for the disadvantaged of society (Hinnells 1978a; Firby 1988). As a result of this widespread conviction that there was a common core of fundamental values and principles, a body of literature evolved which sought to explain Zoroastrian history and doctrine to the British, because it was thought that when the British, at the highest level, knew about the Zoroastrians, they would respect them (Ch. 3, Sect. (c)). Whether their perception of themselves, or of the British, is historically correct is in this context irrelevant. When the nineteenth-century Parsis came to Britain, as students, industrialists, or journalists they believed they were travelling to a country and culture with which they had much in common. There was no sense of 'visiting' an alien environment. Their wonder at British technology and royalty may have been tempered by their experiences of the prejudiced 'lower orders' in Britain, parliamentary deliberations may not have impressed them, nor the churches with their internal feuding, and they were shocked at the dirtiness of

London and extremes of wealth and poverty. But they were convinced that they were travelling to a country where they could be 'at home', indeed where they could flourish. Not all could aspire to a stately mansion like Sir Dhunjibhoy Bomanjee, but the experience of travellers since 1724 was that staying in Britain could bring wealth, professional standing, and social status.

Interestingly in the context of this book, a Parsi traveller in the late 1980s has also produced an account of his experiences (Kanga 1991). It cannot be simply compared with those from the nineteenth century because he writes from a personal perspective, as a disabled, gay member of a minority community. After the success of his first novel which was published in London (Kanga 1990) he visited Britain, liked it, and wanted to stay. His 1991 book is the account of that visit. He is an acute observer with a sensitive wit and is eager to talk to anyone about controversial subjects, such as race relations and Mrs Thatcher, (then declining in popularity as Prime Minister but for whom he had high regard). Yet despite all his individuality, there are ways in which his book can be seen alongside the earlier publications. Although he describes himself as an atheist, he frequently alludes to his Parsi identity and to himself as a Zoroastrian (p. 180). His humour is typically Parsi, with allusions to the size of the typical Parsi nose (a common focus of jokes in the community). He writes with affectionate amusement of the Parsi attitudes to British ways, Parsi women's sense of dress (p. 21), the Parsi love of British theatre and royalty (p. 17), and the strange mixture of Zoroastrian tradition and modern western popular music at weddings (p. 111). His own words neatly describe the book: he watched 'from one eye misted with anglophilia, the other clear and wide open' (p. xiii). He comments (p. 164) that 'at one level the Britain we imagine exists only in India, tennis and tea on the lawns served by liveried butlers'. His love of western drama, literature, music, and the visual arts, his pride in his good English, are typically Parsi. In contrast with Bombay, he valued the acceptance of homosexuality, particularly in London, and the consideration shown to the disabled. But he is aware of problems in Britain. He relates mixed experiences of racial prejudice; he found the churches mostly false; he thinks that the British do not value their families and that there is an intolerance of political views (especially of right-wing views among intellectuals). He therefore reflects some similar perspectives to the earlier travellers. Of course, this paragraph highlights features which may not be of paramount importance for the author. For him the climax of his visit is clearly his meeting with the brilliant and severely disabled Cambridge physicist, Prof. Stephen Hawkin, whom he refers to as 'an inspiration beyond cliché'. But there are ways in which, perhaps unknowingly, Kanga's book keeps alive a nineteenth-century Parsi literary tradition and its positive but not uncritical response to Britain.

Although some nineteenth-century Parsi leaders such as Naoroji and Pherozeshah Mehta referred to themselves in public as Indians first and Parsis second, this was not the usual self-perception of Parsis. Generally there was a sense of distance from Hindus and Muslims, but a conviction that they were so close to the British that they could represent them in Parliament. The sense of being more European than Asian was preserved in Britain as much as in Dar es Salaam (Ch. 2, Sect. (*a*)). It is not being simply light-hearted to point to the Parsi love of cricket as exemplified in the first Indian cricket tour of England undertaken in order to learn something of the 'noble and manly pastime' (Ch. 3, Sect. (*a*)). This 'Britishness' may not be the self-perception of all Zoroastrians, but it remains a part of the general community's self-image. For those who consider themselves to be British, the experience of racial discrimination is particularly difficult. Ironically, in view of Britain's contemporary image of itself as a 'liberal' country, it may be that some of the young British-born Zoroastrians at the end of the twentieth century feel themselves more distanced by racial prejudice from the majority population, than did their forebears in the Victorian era . There is, therefore a sense in which experience of life in Britain has not matched up to the expectations of the early travellers. But for all their fears about the threats posed by racism, by the secularism and declining moral standards of Britain, most Zoroastrians still consider Britain to be a land where there is fundamental security and a relative absence of corruption and persecution. Whatever emotional attachments there may be to India, Pakistan, or Iran, for most British Zoroastrians, Britain is a safe place in which to live and a country where the great majority consider they have a number of White friends. Relatively few Zoroastrians envisage leaving Britain.

The figure of 42% of British Zoroastrians who consider that they have experienced racial discrimination is high, viewed from the perspective of the nature and achievements of the community. But in the context of the race riots and the general situation in the 1980s, it is likely that a higher proportion of other minorities might have expressed such fears of discrimination. Although 1% of the community having such a perception may be considered 1% too many, it could be argued that more Zoroastrians see themselves as distanced from such problems than do other Asian religious groups. Partly this may be because Parsis do not live in the inner-city areas associated with the greatest deprivation and rioting. Many Zoroastrians believe that their education and social position distance them from other groups experiencing such problems. But the experiences of the educated youth born in Britain and of Zerbanoo Gifford (Ch. 5, Sect. (*d*)) demonstrate that discrimination is not confined to inner cities, nor to what the early travellers called the 'lower orders'. Those travellers and the early settlers would doubtless be deeply shocked by the perceptions of prejudice of many British Zoroastrians at the close of the second millennium. From the Iranian perspective, the main fears expressed were being confused with Arabs, which is offensive given the Zoroastrian experience in Iran, or simply being identified as Iranian and so associated with Islamic fundamentalism, also understandably distressing. Whether in Dar es Salaam or in Britain, Zoroastrians see themselves as adhering to a religion on a par with Christianity and to a value-system close to European jurisprudence. Indeed, a number of historically informed Zoroastrians take pride in asserting that their religion was a source of inspiration on early Christian doctrine (Ch. 4, Sect. (*k*)) and maintain that it is in accord with liberal enlightened attitudes to pure religion and respected by leading western scholars.

The long term survival of Zoroastrianism in Britain is widely seen in the community as dependent on a number of measures. The need for a Zoroastrian centre has been a conscious priority from the inception of the Association in 1861 and at the time of writing this book the ZTFE is actively trying to raise funds for a new centre, ideally with a fully consecrated temple. In all my conversations with Zoroastrians, young or old, of whatever background, there has been a deep sense of wanting a place where they could go 'to be themselves', where they do not have to explain themselves, where they can share food and fun, music and education, and enjoy religious and secular functions. But as Banks (1992) has commented the possession of such a place gives added bite to community power-struggles, it did in London in 1985 and has done several times before in the community's history. Power-struggles and structures are crucial features in the evolution of any ethnic minority community.

Also central from the time of the original founding document of the Association has been the concern with education. This is a common activity in most religious groups, but perhaps none stress it quite as much as the Zoroastrians. The original Articles of Association discussed in Ch. 4, Sect. (*g*) specified funds for research and publications. At the end of the twentieth century ZTFE are running classes, and weekend workshops with western academics and speakers from India. The library at Zoroastrian House is not heavily used by the majority of members, but it is a significant indicator of the community's priorities that resources have been allocated for a library and at various functions books on the religion are available for purchase. The fact that the sources existed for writing Chapters 3 and 4 indicates the importance attached to the community's history, which may be unique among British Asian groups. The level of religious education is stronger here than in India, though perhaps not as strong as in Karachi and America.

Despite this educational emphasis there has been relatively little internally generated literature on the religion. The books used have either been from India and Pakistan, or (a few) from North America, and most have been by western academics. The British Zoroastrians have, therefore, been more open to influence from western scholarship about their own religion than probably any other community from the subcontinent. Other writers have commented on how external perceptions of minorities, and the notion of, say, Hinduism as a world religion (with the attendant notions of the importance of coherently articulated doctrines and 'official' liturgies), are determining the shape of the communities' own religious practice. This has been even more the case with Zoroastrians, both in nineteenth-century

India and twentieth-century Britain. That raises serious questions for the outside scholar. One of my personal hobbies is plant photography. It would be wrong to damage the habitat being photographed. How much more should one be careful about the religious or community environment? Anthropologists often comment that their mere presence affects what they study. Because Zoroastrians are so educated and westernized, they read the books produced by outside academics about their religion more than other groups do, so the academic can be both lecturer and instructor. It is a heavy responsibility to affect that which you study, especially when the community concerned is already under the threat of extinction.

The majority of Zoroastrians surveyed said that in their own estimation they have inadequate religious knowledge to preserve their heritage. But what they count as *significant* knowledge is not what their great-grandparents in Bombay or Gujarat would have considered significant. Traditionally, the knowledge which then mattered was concerned with the directions for daily living, religious practices associated with worship, or the maintenance of a good Zoroastrian home. Philosophy, cosmology, and ancient history were not seen as significant, but it is now thought that such studies may help preserve Zoroastrianness among western-educated members who want to explain their beliefs and practices both to themselves and to outsiders. A serious problem for the British community is the ignorance among the rest of the population about Zoroastrianism. This difficulty was illustrated when I was in the final stages of writing this book. In June 1994 His Royal Highness the Prince of Wales said in a television programme that he wanted his traditional role as Defender of the (Anglican) Faith to become the Defender of Faiths, be they Roman Catholicism, Judaism, Islam, or Zoroastrianism. Few listeners knew who the Zoroastrians were. In the capital city's main evening newspaper, *London Evening Standard*, of 27 June 1994, there was an article on the Royal statement which all the Zoroastrians I know who read it found offensive: 'the notion of Charles being defender of faith . . . strikes me as bizarre. Take those Zoroastrians . . .'; and it goes on, after referring to them as a 'respectable people', to describe them as worshipping 'an evil god'; it alludes to them leaving the dead 'to be devoured in Towers of Silence by rats'; it states that the Muslims view

Zoroastrians as idolaters; and in the last paragraph it refers to 'the ceremony being conducted in the various dead languages favoured by the Zoroastrians'. The mocking tone was not only offensive; there were fears that it would undermine the religion in the eyes of the young and of non-Zoroastrian friends. Zoroastrians believe that because they are such a minority, they are prey to journalistic mockery and publishing insensitivity (see p. 17) in a way in which powerful groups such as the Muslims would never be treated. Education is, therefore, both an ancient Zoroastrian virtue and a modern political necessity.

Care for the public image has been an important concern for many British Zoroastrians, whether it took the form of the splendid banquets with which Bhownagree sought to impress British leaders, or the literature written by some nineteenth-century authors such as Karaka, Naoroji, and later Masani, or the books produced in association with the Naoroji centenary celebrations. In order to increase understanding of Zoroastrianism in Britain the community takes an active part in interfaith activities, seeking to explain its religion to others, and inviting them to attend functions at Zoroastrian House, even in the prayer-room. The priest most involved in these activities (Ervad Bedhwar) speaks with pride of standing in a crowded Westminster Cathedral and declaring the noble words of Zoroaster before the representatives of so many faiths. Similarly, the community took pride in the participation of its president, Rusi Dalal, in an interfaith activity in the presence of the Queen and Prince Charles, an occasion when a young Zoroastrian gave a solo flute recital prior to the act of congregational meditation (*Newsletter*, summer 1994, referring to an event on 14 March of that year). Interfaith activities generally are increasing in Britain in the 1990s and the Zoroastrians are taking a much greater part than they did at the end of the 1980s. Such experiences mean a great deal to a tiny community which carries memories of persecution in the homeland, and has been at times the victim of gross insensitivity. What the long-term effect will be on this, or any community, of interfaith meetings is not yet clear. It is to be hoped that greater knowledge leads to more understanding, but it may also be that it leads to a subtle form of syncretism, particularly a greater momentum towards Protestantization, at least in the participants if not in the community.

Similarly, it has always mattered to British Zoroastrians that they are not, and are seen not to be, dependent on the majority White population for support; hence the establishment of charitable funds from 1861 for the support and repatriation of destitute Zoroastrians. Indeed, Zoroastrians have given more charity in Britain than they have received, notably but not only, in the two world wars (Ch. 3, Sect. (*d*) and Hinnells 1985(*a*)). This concern has been a central tradition of Zoroastrianism from antiquity, but was commented on by (i.e. became publicly visible to) British travellers in India in the seventeenth century (Firby 1988). In view of British suspicions concerning the settlement of Lascars and impoverished seamen, and the change in laws in 1905, as well as the public debates from the 1960s, it was important that Zoroastrians were seen to uphold this charitable tradition. Because of White suspicions and stereotypes, British Zoroastrians typically want to stress not only the negative point that they have not been dependent on outside charity, but also the positive contribution which they believe they have made to British society. The most public Zoroastrian contribution to Britain has been through the three MPs. The argument in Chapter 6 that these individuals proved somewhat ineffective, because governments ignored them, does not undermine their pioneering role. Indeed, that chapter suggests that previous studies have not done justice to them. At the end of the twentieth century also, Zoroastrians are convinced that they make a contribution to Britain out of all proportion to their numbers. This was highlighted in 1992 by the centenary celebrations of Naoroji's election, with functions in Parliament, at India House, and at Zoroastrian House. But the MPs are not seen as the only contribution made by the community to Britain. In the early 1980s and 1990s there were several (Parsi) Zoroastrians whose public achievements were sources of community pride: Farokh Engineer, the Lancashire and Indian wicket-keeper; Farrukh Dhondy, the playwright and TV executive; Zubin Mehta, whose first professional conducting post was at Liverpool (Bookspan and Yochey 1980), and who conducted at the Royal Opera House, Covent Garden, and on television before the 1994 World (Soccer) Cup; Nicola Katrak, the prima ballerina at the Royal Sadler's Wells Ballet; the pop star Freddie Mercury, who though distanced from the community in his lifetime, put in his will that he wanted a Zoroastrian priest officiating at his funeral at Brookwood (which was done). There has also been public recognition of Zerbanoo Gifford for her work through the Liberal party for Asians and for women's rights; and of the role of the medical doctor Amroliwalla as leader of the team caring for the released British hostages, John McCarthy and Jackie Mann from Beirut in 1992. Amroliwalla was subsequently made Honorary Consultant Surgeon to the Queen. Three other Parsis have been honoured in recent years in the Queen's New Year's Honours list (Burjor Avari for community relations work, Roshan Sethna and Shirin Jasavala for their work as Civil Servants). There has also been a growth of Parsi secular literature published in Britain—a collection of stories about life in Poona by Dhondy (1980) and a number of novels, including those by Sidhwa (1983 and 1988); and Mistry (1987 and especially his book published in 1991, which was short-listed for the prestigious literary award, the Booker Prize). These are different from other books mentioned because they do not contain reflections about Britain and they will be the subject of a separate article published later. But Zoroastrians believe that they have also made a literary contribution in Britain. Such achievements are always noted in the Association newsletters to ensure that members can take pride in, and derive inspiration from, them. British Zoroastrians believe that they also contribute to British society in quiet yet important ways, because so many of them are high-flying professionals: doctors, lawyers, accountants, architects, university teachers. Whether Britain would have been different without the Zoroastrian community is not the point: Zoroastrians believe they have provided a positive input to society, and have not been the negative force or drain on society which many Whites throughout the twentieth century have alleged that Asians constitute. At a very basic level they do not see themselves as alienated persons in a foreign land. Typically, they do not feel any conflict between their Zoroastrianness and being British, though some see themselves wrestling with two sides to their lives or personalities.

Cama's original circular, which led to the establishment of the funds, refers to enabling people to 'live in harmony with one another in good times and bad' (Ch. 4, Sect. (*g*)). The social concerns of the Association have always been important. In the early years it functioned simply as an informal friendly burial club, meeting at Naoroji's home. Bhownagree worked hard to develop a stronger social life in the new formal Association with activities ranging from banquets to steamer trips. But he faced the problem of balancing the interests of different ages and groups and during his presidency the student-dominated Parsi Social Union was established which evidently reflected and reinforced some tensions. In the 1990s the different interest-groups' needs are met, sometimes with less conflict. There are now wide ranges of social and religious activities at Zoroastrian House, catering for the varied interests. The increasing numbers both arise from and facilitate these activities. The small, scattered groups experience far more difficulty in mounting such programmes. The emphasis on the type of activity varies according to community mood and the views of the president at any one time. One powerful external influence is the level of perceived racial prejudice, which can reinforce a sense of internal community solidarity. But the meetings are not only for what Cama described as 'the bad times'. Zoroastrians are typically a fun-loving people and enjoy good company and food.

The 'ethnic' Indian and Iranian functions, either at Zoroastrian House, or in rented halls or private homes, are important social occasions but in the 1990s the functions which attract the largest numbers are those which have religious connotations, especially the New Year festivals (there is more than one because of the different calendars in use, but *Jamshedi No Roz* in March is the most popular) when as many 350 will visit the House, even on a working day. Large numbers also attend for the other seasonal festivals and during *Farvardigan* (known as *muktad* by Parsis). The level of religious activity is generally said to have increased since the mid-1980s. Some explain this as due to the change of leadership and the assumption of power by East African Zoroastrians who are thought of as more orthodox. That may be a factor, but a change would not happen if it did not fit the mood of the community, and it would appear that there has been a surge in religious interest in the 1990s as there was in the 1960s. This time one cause is probably the widespread search for identity, and religion is seen as part of that identity. The concern with religion is evidenced not only by increased attendances at major functions. In the 1990s there has been more public concern over purity laws, monthly *hambandagi* (community prayers) have been started, and traditional Bombay high priests and religious teachers have occasionally been invited to meet the community. It is impossible to measure religious feeling, but there is certainly no sign of the weakening of religious interest at the end of the millennium and as the 'second generation' plays a larger part in community affairs. An outsider might ask whether it is the religion or ethnic links which are being asserted. But that may be an outsider's question. From a Zoroastrian point of view the two are inseparable. The calls for a ritually pure home for the fire in a new centre are probably stronger now than at any time in the Association's history. The advice of high priests has been sought, funds have been opened, and numerous events organized to raise the money. As far as one can judge from the records, the frequency of holding *jashans* and *boi* ceremonies, and certainly the numbers attending *muktad* prayers, is naturally higher than it was in the nineteenth century, when there was no Zoroastrian building, but higher also than when the community had its first two buildings. In the first there was no prayer-room, in the second it was a very small room. It is unlikely that such secular allocations of space would determine a building purchased or designed at the end of the twentieth century. My impression is that the sense of being Parsi or Indian may be giving way to being Zoroastrian as the next generation asserts its voice. In Britain there has not been the public acrimony between Iranian Zoroastrians and Parsis, despite the occasional tensions, that has occurred in America. There seems to be a growing consciousness of the Persian origins of the religion. That consciousness is expressed practically. Only a few Parsis learn Farsi, but there have been a steady number attending classes for a few years. The observance of the *gahambars* is an example of the Iranians reminding Parsis of an aspect of the religion they had neglected. Most *gahambars* are funded by Iranians, but some by Parsis also. Circulars advertising the *gahambars* and other ancient festivals preserved by the Iranians have begun to include explanations of the history and significance of the festivals, so that the Parsis may be able to participate in an informed manner. For example, the *Jashne Mehrgan* in October 1994, a festival in honour of Mithra, was explained in circulars incorporating sections from various books and the event was supplemented by an academic lecture on the festival. As the Iranian Zoroastrians settle down in Britain after the trauma of their departure from Iran, and as their English becomes more fluent, so the two groups interact more. One further illustration of this is the collaboration of the Parsi Rashna Writer with the Iranian Shahrokh Shahrokh to publish a translation of the memoirs of his grandfather, a member of the Iranian Parliament early in the twentieth century and adviser to the first Pahlavi Shah (Shahrokh and Writer 1994). Slowly, therefore, British Zoroastrians seem to be becoming internationalized as the Indian, Pakistani, East African, British, and Iranian Zoroastrians settle down together. The concept of what constitutes a Zoroastrian may be changing—but the will to assert identity is certainly no less than it was in the nineteenth century; if anything, it is even stronger.

Will a British Zoroastrianism evolve (Writer 1994: 231, 235)? Some of the features of diaspora religion noted by Knott (1986*b*) can be seen. In addition to the internationalization there is an institutionalization of the religion, though this had started in Bombay as the religion moved from the home to the temple in the nineteenth century (Hinnells 1985*a*). But the provision of religious education classes, community wide festivals rather than the domestic rites, and youth-group activities are all common. There is some pressure to abbreviate liturgies and a demand for clear articulations of the underlying theology (though perhaps not as strongly as in Canada and the USA); indeed, there is an increasing emphasis on articulating all aspects of the faith. Still evolving are the delineation of space defined as sacred by observance of the purity laws, relating particularly to the practices in, and access to, the prayer-room; the development of guidelines regarding the place of non-Zoroastrians with regard to the fire in the *jashan*; and practices associated with rites held at the funeral ground, Brookwood. The consensus would seem to be that the moments of particular holiness, such as worship before the sacred fire in the prayer-room, or prayers for the dead, should be restricted to the members of the religion. Membership continues to be defined in terms of descent from Zoroastrian parents, and that normally means both parents. Few Zoroastrian ladies will attend a religious function during menstruation. Most Parsis wear the *sudre* and *kusti* when attending a religious function, though very few wear them at all times. Religious practice is, therefore, being seen as something to be practised in a place apart at a set time. It increasingly has a congregational emphasis and that congregation has a racial boundary drawn around it. But it is important to emphasize the growing, not the diminishing, importance of religion at the end of the twentieth century. A president of ZTFE in the 1990s has to ensure the provision of more, not fewer, religious functions than Naoroji or Bhownagree did, both in the annual calendar and in the planning of a new centre.

As well as the internationalization within the community, there are also signs of international collaboration that could lead to the globalization of Zoroastrianism. There has, of course, been international collaboration between Zoroastrians in the past: the Iranian Zoroastrians guided the Indian community in a series of letters, the *Revayats*, from the fifteenth to the eighteenth centuries (Paymaster 1954: 66–84) and there was collaboration again in the late nineteenth and early twentieth centuries as Iranians escaped to India and there raised help for their oppressed fellows in Iran (Boyce 1978*a*: 209–10). In the 1990s there are moves to collaborate globally. There have been periodic world congresses in Bombay since the 1960s with delegations from around the globe, including from Iran, even after the establishment of the Islamic Republic. My impression is that the British, and particularly the American, voice has been increasingly influential in those congresses. The influence in London of the Bombay-based religious teacher Khojeste Mistree has been noted at several points in this book. The invitation to the *Mobed-e-Mobedan*, the senior Iranian Zoroastrian priest, in 1993 was a significant step in seeking global collaboration, for there had earlier been a sense among British Iranian Zoroastrians that the Parsis were neglecting the religious authorities in the religion's homeland. There is also a growing dialogue between the Zoroastrians in Britain, Canada, and USA. British delegations take part in the biannual Zoroastrian conferences in North America and a delegation went to the 1993 World Parliament of Religions in Chicago, where one of the organizers was the president of the Federation of North American Zoroastrians, Rohinton Rivetna. A delegation of British Zoroastrians took part in the First World Zoroastrian Youth

Congress in California, also in 1993, and the London community is to host the next such congress. This collaboration between the Associations, together with the work of WZO, and the moves to establish another world body (being negotiated by Rivetna with the support of the Bombay Parsi Punchayat) raises the hope that what small disparate groups cannot achieve alone, they may by acting in concert. One possible development could be an increasingly powerful voice of the diaspora groups in the development of the religion.

Scholarship has been valued by Zoroastrians for centuries. In pre-Islamic times priests were the learned men of society, some becoming judges and scribes. In Bombay in the nineteenth and twentieth centuries there have been some scholarly priests, but the emphasis has been on secular learning, with the widespread acquisition of western education. In London both ZTFE and WZO have attempted to develop a religious education programme. It is interesting that such an emphasis is not apparent in the smaller groups around the country. Even when these groups have been established in a city where Zoroastrianism is taught at the local university, as in Manchester, there has been little concern for formal classes or scholarly talks. The primary concerns of these groups is the coming-together of fellow Zoroastrians. Because this is a rare event and people come from considerable distances, they bring very young children, for whom an academic lecture would be a clear disincentive! But in London the community is large enough, and is minded, to stage formal scholarly lectures. One feature of London Zoroastrianism could, therefore, be its contemporary openness to western studies. This may be in contrast to modern Bombay where despite the nineteenth-century impact of Protestantism, nowadays Zoroastrianism at the popular level inclines more to occult traditions. There could well, therefore, be a trend towards doctrinal divergence between the old and the new countries. Liturgical differences are inevitable, both because of a lack of material provisions in Britain and because the social needs of the British Zoroastrians result in a more congregational emphasis than is characteristic of Indian Zoroastrianism. It is significant that what is happening is not the creation of new liturgies, but an emphasis on certain parts of the tradition rather than others, or a development of existing practices, such as the rediscovery of the *jashan*.

In short, British Zoroastrianism may be seen to be acting in accordance with its traditions; but by emphasizing specific ideals, social as well as liturgical, for example by supporting the weak and displaying a concern for the personal and educational needs of co-religionists, it is meeting the needs of a new generation in a different culture. The religion not merely survives but is actually an increasingly important part of the process of communal preservation. How that religion is understood intellectually and experienced emotionally is being modified as it becomes internationalized and increasingly institutionalized, but religion continues to be a binding force in the community and for many is an important part in the quest for self-understanding. The fact that its emphases change from the 1960s to the 1990s does not mean that it has been weakened.

If syncretism be understood as a dynamic process, interesting because of the significance of the forms in which one tradition has interacted with another when it could have done otherwise (Pye 1993), then British Zoroastrianism is a good case-study. It has interacted, or syncretised with, other religions in different countries, as will be noted below and discussed in the subsequent Katrak volume on the global diaspora. The process of syncretism should not be understood as a haphazard phenomenon. The outcome of syncretism is not accidental. It rarely involves the conscious imitation of alien traditions. But a variety of factors determine what is included and how. External influence commonly provokes reflection on the received tradition and affects which aspects are emphasized and how they are interpreted. Ideas develop under the impact of various stimuli as people wrestle with new problems in the light of changing experiences. Religions, like chameleons, change colour as they move from one colour of environment to another to harmonize with it. Whether it is the acceptance of burials in Muslim Iran, the preservation of myths shared with Islam in Pakistan, or the evolution of Protestant ideas (e.g. relating to religious education or worship) in Britain, it is natural that a religion assumes forms or expressions that are meaningful to its members in different environments. It is essential if that religion is to remain a living religion. To describe British Zoroastrianism as syncretistic is to recognize it as a dynamic process.

(b) *Zoroastrians and other South Asian Religions in Britain*

In the Introduction stress was laid on the importance of seeing the Zoroastrian community within the context of wider Asian migration to Britain. It is, therefore, right to ask in the Conclusion to what extent, and in what ways, Zoroastrians are like other groups mentioned. They share the same experience of legal restrictions on further immigration; they encounter something of the same perception of racial prejudice, though most (but not all) would say that they experience this to a lesser degree. The processes of institutionalization according to western, or alien norms, are similar, because each group is similarly affected by the experiences of its young people hearing about Christianity and being expected to be able to give comparable accounts of their own religion. This feature is probably more evident within the Zoroastrian community. Young Zoroastrians, like young Hindus, Sikhs, Muslims, or Jains feel the need to socialize with peers from within their own tradition. But because there are so few Zoroastrians and they are widely dispersed, this need is perhaps more urgent yet more difficult to meet for Zoroastrians, and so the young people may be more vulnerable to external influences. All groups face similar difficulties of transmitting the culture across the (potential) generation gap created by the different experiences in the old and the new countries. External forces, therefore, may be expected to generate similar strategies for survival between the religions, though different emphases may be expected.

The British Zoroastrians perhaps share more religious values with Hindus than with the other Asian religions, because a number of common attitudes derive from their ancient (Indo-Iranian) inheritance. Both religions emphasize the importance of the holy sound in worship and the precision considered necessary in rituals which generate power. The respective beliefs and practices associated with purity and pollution stem from a common historical source and both religions have similar ideas concerning auspicious days, foods, and numbers. All these are, of course, different presuppositions from those of western religious tradition. Parsis have also been subject to some influence from the Hindu majority in India. Zoroastrians, however, would want to assert their distinctiveness from Hindus, and not without reason. The contrasting histories in the old country, dissimilar doctrinal foundations, and value systems they would argue make them different in the subcontinent. But in Britain the two communities have a very different history. Zoroastrians have a longer, known history of travel, educational and literary ties, and strong convictions of shared values. They believe that they have always been seen to be like the British. From the outset education has been a more common motivation for Zoroastrian migration than it has for other communities. For Zoroastrians there was never a time when the community consisted simply of lone, single males undertaking manual labour and living cheaply in order to send funds 'home'. Britain was home for many Zoroastrians even in the nineteenth century. Zoroastrian women came either as visitors or settlers for a century before Hindu, Sikh, and Muslim women came. The 1960s Zoroastrian migrants benefited from an existing community infrastructure with an Association, burial ground, meeting-place, and social, educational, and religious resources. Zoroastrians also have a strong, and legitimate, sense of their contribution to British parliamentary history and a conviction that they live in harmony with the establishment.

Despite the religious values some Parsis share with Hindus there are some essential differences which merit comment. The religious ideal of the ascetic typical of the Jains and many Hindus has essentially no counterpart in Zoroastrianism. Few British Zoroastrians express allegiance to a miracle-worker, unlike the Hindu communities in this country, or Bombay Parsis. In comparison with Hindus, Sikhs, and Jains, or American Zoroastrians, there are few attempts to fund visits of holy men from the old country. This may be due partly to the more limited resources of British Zoroastrians (more limited even than among American Zoroastrians), but it may also be due in some measure to the greater emotional distance of British Zoroastrians from the old country and to the trend to the doctrinal divergences noted above.

In broad terms Zoroastrianism and Islam have much in common: a conviction of a revelation through a prophet, purity laws, and times of prayer; traditional Zoroastrianism and Islam share a similar eschatology and concepts of heaven and hell (it is quite likely that Zoroastrianism was a source of influence on nascent Islam). But as far as the communities in Britain are concerned, the contrasts are considerable. The obvious difference is one of numbers for it is estimated that there are approximately a million Muslims in Britain (Lewis 1994: 14). One consequence of this is the greater range of facilities. It is, for example, estimated that there are more than 450 Pakistani organizations (Lewis 1994: 198). There are Muslim radio stations, newspapers, journals, audio-tapes of popular music, even a Muslim board-game to replace Monopoly, where the target is not London property but Paradise (Lewis 1994: 180 f.). There is a Muslim Girls' School, two seminaries, many mosques, and religious hierarchies from the level of the *ulama* at the local mosque to the *Mufti* whose ruling is sought on proper conduct. Beyond this there is the Bradford Council of Mosques which has some national standing, and a self-proclaimed Muslim parliament to guide the faithful. There is an extensive supply of books from South Asia for use in the many supplementary schools. The consequence of all this is that Islam has a very high public profile, ensuring not merely that the Muslim view is not ignored, but that it is actively sought, for example by government in drafting the National Curriculum for religious education agreed in 1994.

There is, however, a different perception of Islam in Britain from within the community. There is little sense of affluence. The amount of money coming from oil-rich states into the British Islamic community has been exaggerated. Most mosques are funded from the earnings of a congregation consisting mainly of people on low wages and facing high levels of unemployment. There is also a common perception of facing an alien world that is actively hostile in terms of racial prejudice. Many Muslims, but especially the *ulama*, believe that the West is commonly anti-Islamic, that outsiders stereotype all Muslims as fundamentalists, and that the education system encourages a critical independence in the young, especially among its young women, which threatens to undermine Islamic values. Young and *ulama* alike are concerned that there is a gulf between the values of the mosque and outside society. Rarely fluent in English, the *ulama* see Britain as antireligious; devout parents fear that Islam now occupies only a very a small part of youngsters' lives. The educated youngsters are often concerned that the elders do not understand the pressures, or opportunities, which they encounter in Britain. If a British Islam is evolving, then it is evolving in a sense of tension with non-Muslim Britain in a way that few, if any, Zoroastrians feel. Zoroastrian leaders are not as mistrustful of western education or mores, and rarely have the sense of conflict with alien forces which many (but not all) Muslims express (Lewis 1994).

The Zoroastrian community has a different demographic profile from other South Asian groups, partly as a consequence of its history (see Ch. 1 sect (*b*)). Zoroastrians typically have smaller families, tend to be members of nuclear rather than extended families and intermarriage is more commonly debated and practised among them. There are not the same gender differences, either in the composition of the community or in male versus female religious beliefs and practices. The education and career patterns are also different from other communities, particularly in comparison with Pakistanis and Bangladeshis. Zoroastrians tend to be more highly educated, have more members in professional employment, and fewer self-employed. There are very few manual workers and almost no unemployed Zoroastrians. They approximate more to the East African section of the Asian community than to any other group.

The nature of religious leadership in the respective communities merits comment. Banks (1992) comments that many Jain leaders are successful businessmen or professionals not necessarily spiritual leaders, a feature which may be noted in other communities also. As Jones (1993) demonstrates, with the dramatically increasing proportion of highly educated young people within the Indian and East African Indian communities, it is reasonable to suppose that this secular leadership pattern will continue to evolve, in particular the growing influence of the educated professionals. Perhaps no other British group has its religion already under the direction of such a western-educated, professional, and secular leadership as the Zoroastrians. The greatest contrast is, clearly, with the *ulama* in the mosques, for only once in 130 years has a priest held the post of president of ZTFE (Ervad Zal Sethna, 1989–92). In ancient Iran kingship and the priesthood were closely linked, but in modern times lay people have administered the major bodies, for example the Bombay Parsi Punchayat. The influence of the priesthood on such bodies has declined (no longer are there automatically priestly trustees), in large part because of a lack of respect for the priesthood among the educated over the past hundred years. But that is not likely to be so true in Britain where the priests have worked part-time alongside their secular posts, which have generally been of high standing; for example Dastur Kutar was a medical doctor and Ervad Sethna is a qualified accountant. Few priests have held secular community office because they can rarely undertake both roles on a part-time basis. The Zoroastrian leaders have generally been highly educated people, successful in the outside world. The evidence of this research is that the older generation has an even higher educational record of achievement than the youth. This is in stark contrast to the other British South Asian communities. What is the consequence of this for the religion? My research for the subsequent Katrak volume suggests that educated professional, as opposed both to priestly and business, leadership leaves the Zoroastrians particularly open to the secular influences of British society. In so far as the Zoroastrians are a microcosm of the macrocosm of South Asian diaspora groups in Britain, this would suggest that other communities are likely to come increasingly under such influences as they follow the same trajectory. In the early 1990s Hindu, Muslim, Sikh, and even Jain leaderships are still heavily influenced by the less well-educated generation of 1960s migrants. The social and religious changes which it may be assumed lie ahead for these communities have been foreshadowed in the Zoroastrian community. It is to be hoped that some future research may be directed towards the changing nature of British South Asian communities following the significant increase in the numbers of those with a high standard of western education. But the Zoroastrians may be subject to more western influence also because of their interest in, and internalization of, western academic studies of the religion. It is noticeable that the Zoroastrian authors whose works are most popular in Britain are those who have pursued western studies, from Dhalla to Mistree.

It is important to appreciate the implications of the unique demographic crisis faced by Zoroastrians. If by some freak circumstance 200,000 Hindus, Muslims, or Christians disappeared from the world, the religion would not be fundamentally affected. In the old countries of Asian religions numbers are growing substantially. Such a loss of Zoroastrians would mean the end of the world's oldest prophetic religion, and Zoroastrians are well aware of their vulnerability. There is, consequently, a desperation in the appeals for unity or reform or the preservation of tradition. The disputes over such issues as intermarriage, and over authority, have a unique stress because the proponents of the various views have good reason to fear that if the wrong solution is adopted (leaving aside here what is the right or the wrong solution), then the imminent danger is communal extinction. The declining numbers give added urgency to strategies for survival. However, the Zoroastrians find it difficult to evolve a coherent strategy because of the internal differences of language, culture, and so on, and because there is no single authority to impose a solution. The fact that this tiny diverse community is so geographically scattered further compounds the problems. There is another dimension to this demographic dilemma. Whatever the future for British Hindus and Muslims, they are likely to remain only a small and probably marginal minority in the history of their religion. But with Zoroastrian numbers decreasing so dramatically in India and Pakistan, and the future uncertain in Iran, it is quite possible that the future of Zoroastrianism may lie in the diaspora, and British Zoroastrians could play an important role in the future of their religion.

The demographic problem also means, however, declining resources with which to implement chosen strategies. There are still Zoroastrian millionaires, even in the diaspora (but in Canada and the USA rather than Britain), and some large Parsi corporations in India, but the Zoroastrian world-wide community is nowadays characterized by middle-class professionals rather than by very wealthy benefactors who can facilitate costly strategies. So in comparison with Muslims and other religious groups they are considerably under-resourced, despite their past image of wealth. It is not only the funding resources that are depleted. The resources of 'person power' are also limited. The London Zoroastrian community may be larger than that in any other city outside Iran and the Indian subcontinent, but at c.4,000 it is minuscule compared with the number of Muslims, Hindus, or Sikhs in Britain. That has consequences for the number of priests, leaders, teachers, marriage-partners. It also means that there is only a small market for the production of religious objects, teaching aids, videos, and films. Their numerical insignificance means that Zoroastrians are easy prey for journalistic mockery. They not only lack the protection of numbers and vocal fundamental extremists, the size of their community also means most teachers and publishers think that they are not worth including in their planning. It can be difficult for Zoroastrian parents to convey their legitimate pride in the community to the younger generation if they find the outside world knows little about them, and does not want to learn. The stereotypes perpetuated by some of the (supposedly) better informed sections of society, such as religious education teachers and church leaders, are the links to the magi mentioned in the Gospel of Matthew. Hence children are cast in school Christmas plays as the people who bow the knee to Jesus, or the magi are identified with magic, a gross misrepresentation, naturally causing offence. Ignorance is not always bliss, it can be very damaging. Conversely, when reasonable newspaper coverage is experienced it merits reports in the community newsletter. Two reports which were unusual for their sensitivity appeared within three months of each other: a reasonable use of the magi connection in the *Guardian*, 24 December 1993, and an account of the joyful celebration of a *gahambar* by the London community in *The Times*, 12 February 1994. These produced immense joy and most Zoroastrian families proudly displayed copies to friends. The British Zoroastrians are, therefore, more heavily dependent on outside commentators than other Asian groups. In short, Zoroastrians are uniquely vulnerable in many ways.

(c) *Another Comparison*

A different comparison which many Zoroastrians would find more acceptable than the one with Asian groups would be with the Jews. The Parsis have often been referred to as the 'Jews of the eastern world' because of their business activities. But the analogy goes much deeper than that. The sense of the appropriateness of this parallel among British Zoroastrians is neatly illustrated by a function organized at Zoroastrian House in 1992 (*Newsletter*, January 1993) when an orthodox and a reformed rabbi dialogued before a full hall on the subject 'Can there be Orthodox and Reform in a Faith?' Both religions emphasize a belief in a creator God resulting in a sense of the theological significance of history. Although Zoroastrians do not use the term the 'chosen people' there is nevertheless in ancient Iranian tradition a strong sense of being a special people in the world. But more significant for modern communities than the parallels in their philosophies or eschatologies is the link each makes between religion and race, which causes intermarriage and conversion to be such sensitive subjects. Knott (1986*a*) and Jackson and Nesbitt (1993) discuss the appropriateness or otherwise of describing Hinduism as an ethnic religion. There can be no doubt that the term is appropriate for both Jews and Zoroastrians. Related to their broadly similar theological priorities are their comparable family and general ethical values. Partly as a consequence of these values they have similar community and demographic profiles: typically both communities are composed largely of well-educated professional people in small families, and have an ageing population. They also have parallel views on their respective modern histories. The Jewish communities in Israel and the diaspora cannot be understood without a full appreciation of the history of anti-Semitism and the horrors of the holocaust. Zoroastrians also have a vivid memory of a millennium of ruthless persecution, of being subject to public humiliation through dress regulations, of being excluded as *najesh*, highly polluting, by the majority socially, educationally, and at work (Amighi 1990; for earlier experiences, see Boyce 1992: 157–9). Unlike the Jews, Iranian Zoroastrians have had the opportunity forbidden the German Jews to convert (to Islam) and escape persecution, though Zoroastrian converts have still tended to be seen as second-class Muslims in practice. But for the Zoroastrians in Iran who chose to preserve their identity there has been a long history of oppression. Although this has not reached the depths of the holocaust, it has nevertheless left a deep communal scar which has conditioned much of Zoroastrian thinking about themselves and others. It is only in recent times that Parsis have become aware of the extent of the persecution in

Iran, but it has now made an impression on their communal consciousness also. A sense of external assault can often work to reinforce a sense of community, or religious boundaries. Many Zoroastrians would also favour this comparison with the Jews because they see it as making them more European than Asian.

But there are, of course, important differences between Jews and Zoroastrians. The demographic problem is far more acute for Zoroastrians than it is for Jews. Perhaps there is a numerical level, or a critical mass, below which a group cannot sink if it is to have the resources to survive. The Jews have not reached that level, but Zoroastrians perhaps have. Although the Jews have a global dispersion they have countries (e.g. USA and Britain) and cities (e.g. London and Manchester) where they are particularly concentrated. They are further concentrated within those cities because of the tradition of living within walking distance of a synagogue. A rabbi once commented in private conversation that 'ghettos are a bad thing'; but it depends on the ghettos and on one's perspective. Living as a community, within a geographically restricted area, facilitates the provision of community-support networks. Because the small number of British Zoroastrians are so widely dispersed around Britain, and even around London, it is much more difficult to develop all the activities which might otherwise generate a strong sense of a community. Further, Zoroastrians do not have an internal structure or religious education programme comparable to rabbinical organization and training, or the overarching institution of a chief rabbi whose authority is widely respected. Even within the various sections of the Jewish community: orthodox, reform, Ashkenazi, Sephardi, there are recognized internal leadership structures. One problem for Zoroastrians in their disputes is that there is little or no sense of who can arbitrate. The last, but not the least, distinction is that whereas the Jews have a clear, unified concept of the homeland, one that is now under Jewish rule, there is no hope of the return of the Zoroastrian homeland, and despite the trend suggested above towards an emphasis on Persian ancestry, there is still no clear sense of 'mother country'. There are, therefore, factors within the Jewish community which can aid its survival; these are lacking for Zoroastrians.

(d) *The Study of Diaspora Religions*

The study of diaspora religions seems to me to be an important and growing subject for comparative scholarly research, because of what it can reveal both of the religious groups and of wider British society. The members of the various religions may share a range of common experiences—being affected by the same legal directives, encountering racial prejudice, facing the impact of British society and western education—which result in their forming similar strategies, and studying those helps to understand the wider society as much as well as the individual religions. But the different reactions to some of those experiences can highlight what is specific to that tradition and therefore characteristic of it. In her studies referred to in the Introduction, Knott identified five factors which affect the preservation of a religion in migration: the home tradition; the host tradition; the nature of the migration process; the nature of the migrant group; and the nature of the host response (Knott 1986*b* and see Jackson and Nesbitt 1993: 169 f.). This analysis proved helpful in pursuing the present research, but in my opinion it merits some extension and I offer the following breakdown of factors which can affect how Zoroastrians, at least, settle in the new country and preserve their tradition.

1. Where people come. Earlier chapters found that there were differences between British Zoroastrians who had come from (Muslim) Pakistan or from (Hindu) India; from Iran or from East Africa; and those who were born in Britain. But the differences should not be thought of simply in national terms, or in terms of the dominant religion. These certainly are factors, but so are other considerations. People who migrated from a rural setting, be it in Gujarat or the region of Yazd, tend to be more traditional than Zoroastrians from a cosmopolitan metropolis, be it Tehran or Bombay.

2. How communities and individuals perceive of Britain prior to their migration. This affects attitudes and actions, at least in the early years. A positive image of wider British society can ease integration, but does it also lead to assimilation?

3. Why people migrated. Thus people who migrated because they felt impelled to do so for reasons of their own safety (e.g.

from East Africa or Iran) typically adapted less than those who migrated for their own self-perceived benefit (e.g. for education or career). The former group resent the new country more, may have a stronger myth of return, and so do not adapt or change as quickly as those who have chosen their new abode because they want to be there.

4. What people were before migration: whether they were educated, their career patterns, age, and family ties. Those who are well educated in western terms typically find it easier to settle and are more open to adaptation; people who were young when leaving the old country typically find it easier to settle in the new land than older people do. A crucial turning-point appears to be the level of education achieved—if people migrate after their formal education is completed then generally a mental set and cultural foundation has been laid down. Family background and aspirations are also clearly important.

5. When Zoroastrians migrated. This can be interpreted in two ways. Either: (*a*) The Zoroastrians who migrated in the 1960s (or before) were typically high-flyers in terms of education or career; they were the westernized or the more liberal or innovative people. (*b*) The figures in this research cannot prove but they suggest that people are typically more religious after migration than they were before their travels, that generally the higher level of traditional religiousness is maintained for ten to fifteen years and it is only after as long as twenty years, if then, that the signs of assimilation emerge clearly.

6. Who people migrate with. Thus people moving alone, either as manual workers or students or as high-flying executives, tend to assimilate more quickly than those who settle as part of an extended family, especially if grandparents are part of that family. People who are involved in chain migration tend to have a network of support and are therefore not as subject to external religious and cultural forces as the lone individual.

7. Where people migrate to. Hinnells (1994*a*) explored this theme internationally, and it is to be developed in the subsequent Katrak volume. But more than that, associations develop differently in different cities even within the same country, be it Chicago and Houston or London and Manchester. Maintaining the tradition when living in isolation from other Zoroastrians is very difficult in practice, whatever the theory about the ease of

transporting a religion which is essentially practised in the home. Diaspora religions may develop distinctive institutional forms in different centres.

8. What people do after they have settled: the level of education they pursue (e.g. whether they complete their education at school or proceed all the way to postgraduate research, and whether that education is arts- or science-based); and the sort of career they follow—the higher they proceed up the executive ladder the more open they become to pressures to assimilate (or is it the assimilators who progress?). Also crucial are the friendships that are made—how many are within the community and with whom in the group they are made; the frequency of contact with Zoroastrian friends in person or through correspondence; contacts with the old country; the amount of Zoroastrian or other religious literature that is read. But perhaps the two most important things are marriage and having children. The last can be the strongest factor in preserving the tradition if the spouse is also Zoroastrian. Bereavement may provoke some to learn about the religion, as also may the experience of discrimination.

9. At the most fundamental level, what determines how individuals preserve the tradition is who they are. There are some differences between the genders. The subsequent Katrak volume will advance the thesis that there are differences between business people and highly educated professionals. The latter typically feel the need to articulate and rationalize beliefs and as a consequence are more likely to become Protestantized. Typically, the business people tend to practice rather than rationalize their religion and successful individuals have the financial resources to facilitate more of the religious practice. Another important factor is, naturally, the extent to which a person was religious before migration.

10. All of the above factors are internal influences, but events external to the community can also be important: the impact of prejudice; the stereotypes propagated by the press, teachers, and others; legislation and events in the old country.

There is, then, a wide range of factors affecting the preservation of tradition. Since each of the above ten factors has a number of variables the total number of permutations is vast.

This merits emphasis because a danger in trying to identify trends is that the resulting conclusions can look very deterministic, as though every male, single, postgraduate scientist who migrated from Bombay alone inevitably cuts loose from the tradition. Human beings are not so predictable! Nevertheless it is possible to see some broad patterns.

These ten factors all relate to people who migrated. What of Zoroastrians born in Britain? Many of the factors also apply, notably where they come from. Young people brought up in a centre such as London evidently have more opportunity to meet co-religionists and enjoy the Zoroastrian experience. The family background, education, career patterns, social contacts are as important as for people who migrated. But perhaps the most significant factor for people born here is the urge to search for their roots and to preserve their identity. The trigger for this can take many forms: perceived external discrimination; the existence of role-models within the community; an appropriate form of religious education; personal crises; and the level of enjoyment of contacts with the tradition. A common theme in the comments of the young Zoroastrians I have spoken to is that being forced to follow the tradition in youth is likely to be a disincentive. Conversely, people cannot follow what they do not know.

No research project can be perfect or complete. It is, therefore, proper to point to gaps and failings. There were two areas of questioning that proved inadequate. In the survey and in interviews questions were asked to try and open up attitudes to 'mother tongue' and 'mother country'. Language is evidently a major feature in the transmission of a tradition. The questionnaires did not frame these questions effectively, partly because the wording evidently meant different things to different people (whether 'mother tongue' meant what people thought was their 'original' language or the language they now used most often). In the interviews, therefore, the question became: 'What language do you think in?' That was inadequate because many people think in different languages according to the subject-matter, the occasion, or the people they are talking to. For example, a Parsi who can speak in Gujarati may be likely to tell a bawdy joke to another Parsi in Gujarati, but talk to that same person in English about currency fluctuations on the Stock

Market. I contemplated framing the question: 'If you drop a brick on your toe, which language do you swear in?' But that language may be affected by who is present! It would be more helpful to ask a range of questions which brought out the various possibilities. The question of chosen means of communication merits further research. If the complexity of the language issue has not been fully appreciated, then it may well be that those associated with personal and community identity have not been either. A different, and possibly yet more complex area, but central to the study of religions, is the extent to which religious understanding evolves in the diaspora. Different Zoroastrian understandings of 'the holy' were discussed in Ch. 6, Sect. (*n*) and the question was asked: 'Does the use of "God" and "the devil" instead of "Ohrmazd" and "Ahriman" signify a change in patterns of belief?' Similar questions may be asked with reference to such terms as 'prayer', 'worship', and 'priest'.

(e) *The Future for British Zoroastrians*

The transmission of the appropriate knowledge and understanding of beliefs and practices, the communication of the experience and the consciousness of the identity, are complex processes affected by the internal workings of family, wider Zoroastrian social networks, and by the world beyond. The processes of change act more quickly than is at first apparent. The last two chapters have, for example, emphasized the changes from the 1960s to the 1990s. As the book reaches its final stages of writing, there may already be signs of further change and not only of personnel. Contrary to the images in the media, diaspora religion may strengthen rather than diminish as the third millennium approaches, at least if the Zoroastrians are in any way typical of the whole. British Zoroastrianism may well be different from the religion in the old country, or from what it was when it arrived, but the images of a linear progress towards assimilation, of a laying-aside of the old traditions, of an inevitable secularizing tendency, of a turning-away from the ancestral religion, are at least oversimple and possibly quite wrong. What is striking is how traditional Zoroastrian values and virtues derived from the teachings of the prophet, such as benevolence, determined pursuit of justice, individual responsibility, concern for the 'Good Creation' and the 'Good Life', have been maintained. Despite the lack of an extensive knowledge of the history of the religion, many of its practices—the prayers, the festivals, a sense of personal and community purity—remain a part of daily life for many and are important at major turning-points in life. Devotion to the prophet, pride in their very ancient religion, the sense of Persian ancestry, traditional family values, are important for many in their sense of identity. Whether or not comtemporary British Zoroastrians have a detailed or exact knowledge of the history of their religion, most of them maintain many of its important ideals. It is difficult to predict the future shape of British Zoroastrianism because of the many factors that can affect the dynamic process and because different aspects of the fine and complex web of a tradition have different degrees of significance for different individuals. For some people questions of language, food, and music will matter most; for others common principles, values, and friendships; for yet others it will be the maintenance of a distinctive persona or membership of a historic race and tradition; for others it may be a spiritual quest. The mixture of ingredients in the recipe of Zoroastrianness may vary from one individual to another, they may differ from Zoroastrianness in other countries both in the new world and the old, and the threats may be many and serious, but the indicators at the end of the second millennium are that there will continue to be a living history of Zoroastrians in Britain.

BIBLIOGRAPHY

Amighi, J. K. (1990), *The Zoroastrians of Iran: Conversion, Assimilation, or Persistence* (New York).
Anwar, M. (1979), *The Myth of Return* (London).
Arjomand, S. A. (1988), *The Turban for the Crown: The Islamic Revolution in Iran* (Oxford; repr. 1989).
Avery, P. (1965), *Modern Iran* (London).
Axelrod, P. (1980), 'Myth and Identity in the Indian Zoroastrian Community', *Journal of Mithraic Studies*, 3: 150–65.
Ballard, R. (1977), 'The Sikhs: The Development of South Asian Settlements in Britain', in Watson (1977), 21–56.
—— (1994*a*), 'What Should We Mean by Ethnicity?', Conference on the Census Volume, Leeds (unpubl.).
—— (1994*b*), *Desh Pardesh: The South Asian Presence in Britain* (London).
—— and Kalra, V. S. (1994), 'The Ethnic Dimensions of the 1991 Census: A Preliminary Report (Manchester).
Banks, M. (1992), *Organizing Jainism in India and England* (Oxford).
Banton, M. (1983), *Racial and Ethnic Competition* (Cambridge).
—— (1987), *Racial Theories* (Cambridge).
Barth, F. (1969) (ed.), *Ethnic Groups and Boundaries* (Bergen).
Barton, S. W. (1986), *The Bengali Muslims of Bradford* (Leeds).
Bhachu P. (1985), *Twice Migrants: East African Sikh Settlers in Britain* (London).
Bharati, A. (1972), *The Asians in East Africa, Jayhind and Uhuru* (Chicago).
Bookspan, M. and Yochey, R. (1980), *Zubin: The Zubin Mehta Story* (London; first pub. 1978).
Bowen, D. (1981), *Hinduism in England* (London).
—— (1987), 'The Evolution of Gujarati Hindu Organizations in Bradford' in Burghart (1987), 15–31.
—— (1988), *The Sathya Sai Baba Community in Bradford* (Leeds).
Boyce, M. (1969), 'Manekji Limji Hataria in Iran', in N. D. Minochehr-Homji and M. F. Kanga (eds.), *K. R. Cama Oriental Institute Golden Jubilee Volume* (Bombay), 19–31.
—— (1975), *A History of Zoroastrianism, i. The Early Period* (Leiden; corrected repr. 1989).
—— (1977), *A Persian Stronghold of Zoroastrianism* (Oxford; repr. Lanham, 1989).

—— (1978a), *Zoroastrians: Their Religious Beliefs and Practices* (London; 3rd revised repr. 1988).
—— (1978b), 'The Continuity of the Zoroastrian Quest', in W. Foy (ed.), *Man's Religious Quest: A Reader* (London), 603–19; repr. as *The Religious Quest*, 1988.
—— (1982), *A History of Zoroastrianism*, ii. *Under the Achaemenians* (Leiden).
—— (1984), *Textual Sources for the Study of Zoroastrianism* (Manchester; repr. Chicago 1990).
—— (1991), *A History of Zoroastianism*, iii. *Zoroastrianism under Macedonian and Roman Rule*, with F. Grenet and a contribution by R. Beck (Leiden).
—— (1993), *Zoroastrianism: Its Antiquity and Constant Vigour* (Costa Mesa, Calif.).
Brown, C. (1984), *Black and White in Britain: The Third PSI Survey* (London).
Brown, J. and Foot, R. (1994) (eds.), *Migration: The Asian Experience* (London and New York).
Browne, E. G. (1893), *A Year amongst the Persians* (London; repr. Cambridge, 1926; London, 1950 and 1959; New York, 1984).
Burghart, R. (1987), *Hinduism in Great Britain* (London).
Captain, S. (1984), '1861–1984 Zoroastrian Trust Funds of Europe and the World Zoroastrian Organization', *World Zoroastrian*, 1–8.
Cashmore, E. E. (1984), *Dictionary of Race and Ethnic Relations* (London: 3rd edn. London and New York, 1994).
—— and Troyna, A. B. (1983) *Introduction to Race Relations* (London; 2nd edn. London and New York, 1990).
Chehabi, H. E. (1990), *Iranian Politics and Religious Modernism* (London).
Clarke, C., Peach, C., and Vertovec, S. (1990), *South Asian Overseas* (Cambridge).
Clifford, J. (1994), 'Diasporas', *Cultural Anthropology*, 9 (3): 302–38.
Cohen, A. (1974) (ed.), *Urban Ethnicity* (London).
Coleman, D. A. (1982), *Demography of Immigrants and Minority Groups in the United Kingdom* (London).
Commissariat, M. S. (1953). 'The First Parsi in England (1724–25): Nawroji Rustom Maneck of Surat and his Relations with the East India Company', in R. P. Masani (ed.), *M. P. Khareghat Memorial Volume* (Bombay), i. 221–58.
Dadachanjee, M. H. (1928), *Life Sketch of Sir Shapoorjee Bharucha* (Gujarati; Bombay).
Darukhanawala, H. D. (1935), *Parsis and Sports* (Bombay).
—— (1963), *Parsi Lustre on India Soil*, vol. ii (Bombay).
David, M. D. (1973), *History of Bombay 1661–1708* (Bombay).

Desai, S. (1948), *A Community at the Cross-Road* (Bombay).
Dhalla, M. N. (1938), *History of Zoroastrianism* (New York; repr. 1977; Bombay, 1963, 1985).
────── (1942), *Homage unto Ahura Mazda* (Karachi; many repr.).
────── (1975), *Dastur Dhalla, the Saga of a Soul: An Autobiography of Shams-ul-ulama Dastur Dr. Maneckji Nusserwanji Dhalla*, English trans. by G. and B. S. H. J. Rustomji (Karachi).
Dhondy, F. (1985), *Poona Company* (London; first pub. 1980).
Dobbin, C. (1972), *Urban Leadership in Western India* (Oxford).
Fardunji, N. (1874), 'The Personal Bearing of Europeans towards the Natives', Lecture to the East India Association, London, 24 Jan.
Farquhar, J. N. (1914), *Modern Religious Movements in India* (New York and London, 1924; 1st Indian edn. Delhi, 1967; repr. New York, 1980).
Firby, N. (1988), *European Travellers and their Perceptions of Zoroastrians in the 17th and 18 centuries* (Berlin).
Fischer, M. (1973), 'Zoroastrian Iran between Myth and Praxis', Chicago, University of Chicago, Ph.D thesis, unpublished.
Framjee, D. (1878), *The Parsees: Their History, Manners, Customs and Religion* (London).
Fryer, P. (1984), *Staying Power: The History of Black People in Britain* (London).
Gainer, B. (1972), *The Alien Invasion: The Origins of the Aliens Act of 1905* (London).
Gavin, R. J. (1975), *Aden under British Rule, 1837–1967* (London).
Gazetteer (1909), *The Gazetteer of Bombay City and Island*, (3 vols. repr. Bombay, 1977).
Ghai, D. P., and Ghai, Y. P. (1970), *Portrait of a Minority: Asians in East Africa* (revised edn. Nairobi; 1st edn. 1966).
Ghods, M. R. (1989), *Iran in the Twentieth Century* (Boulder, Colo.).
Gifford, Z. (1990), *The Golden Thread* (London).
────── (1992), *Dadabhai Naoroji: Britain's first Asian M.P.* (London).
Glazer, N., and Moynihan, D. P. (1975), *Ethnicity: Theory and Experience* (Cambridge, Mass.).
────── and Young, K. (1983), *Ethnic Pluralism and Public Policy* (London; 3rd edn. Lexington, Mass., 1986).
Gregory, R. G. (1971), *India and East Africa* (Oxford).
Hancock, C. (1990), 'The Life and Works of Shapurji Saklatvala' *JCOI*, 57: 1–82.
Harris, J. R. (1958), *Jamsetji Nusserwanji Tata* (Bombay; first pub. London, 1925).
Helweg, A. W. (1986), *Sikhs in England* (Oxford and Delhi; 1st edn. Delhi, 1979).

Hinnells, J. R. (1978a), 'Parsis and the British', *Journal of the K.R. Cama Oriental Institute*, 41: 1–92 (four public lectures).
—— (1978b), *Spanning East and West* (Milton Keynes).
—— (1980), 'The Parsis: A Bibliographical Survey', *Journal of Mithraic Studies*, 3: 100–49.
—— (1981), *Zoroastrianism and the Parsis* (London).
—— (1983), 'Social Change and Religious Transformation among Bombay Parsis in the Early Twentieth Century', in P. Slater and D. Wiebe (eds.), *Traditions in Contact and Change* (Winnipeg), 105–25.
—— (1985a), 'The Flowering of Zoroastrian Benevolence: Parsi Charity in the Nineteenth and Twentieth Centuries', in *Papers in Honour of Professor Mary Boyce, Acta Iranica* (Leiden), xxiv. 261–326.
—— (1985b), *Persian Mythology* (London, new revised edn.; 1st edn. 1973).
—— (1987), 'Parsi Attitudes to Religious Pluralism', in H. G. Coward (ed.), *Modern Indian Responses to Religious Pluralism* (Albany, NY), 195–233.
—— (1988), 'Zoroastrian Migration to the American Continent', in M. Treasureywalla (ed.), *Proceedings of the 6th North American Zoroastrian Congress* (Toronto), 19–49.
—— (1989), 'The Zoroastrian Community of Bombay', *Encyclopaedia Iranica*, IV, iv. 339–46.
—— (1994a), 'South Asian Diaspora Religion: Comparative Parsi Experiences', *South Asian Research*, 14: 62–110.
—— (1994b), 'Zoroastrians in London', in Ballard (1994b).
—— (1994c), 'Modern Zoroastrian Diaspora' in Brown and Foot (1994).
—— (1995), 'Modern Zoroastrian Philosophy', in B. Carr and I. Mahalingam (eds.), *Asian Philosophy* (London).
Hiro, D. (1992), *Black British White British* (London).
Hodivala, S. K. (1931), *History of the Seth Family* (Gujarati; Bombay).
Hollingsworth, L. W. (1960), *The Asians of East Africa* (London).
Holmes, C. (1988), *John Bull's Island: Immigration and British Society 1871–1971* (London).
Jackson, A. V. W. (1906), *Persia Past and Present* (London; repr. New York, 1909).
Jackson, R., and Nesbitt, E. (1993), *Hindu Children in Britain* (Stoke-on-Trent).
Jessawalla, D. C. (1911), *The Story of My Life* (Bombay).
Johnson, G. (1973), *Provincial Politics and Indian Nationalism* (Bombay).
Jones, T. (1993), *Britain's Ethnic Minorities* (London).
Joshi, A. N. (1939), *Life and Times of Sir Hormusjee C. Dinshaw* (Bombay).
Kalsi, S. S. (1992), *The Evolution of a Sikh Community in Britain* (Leeds).

Kanga, F. (1990), *Trying to Grow* (London; repr. 1991; Delhi and Bangalore, 1990).
—— (1991), *Heaven on Wheels* (London and New York).
Kapadia, S. A. (1905), *The Teachings of Zoroaster and the Philosophy of the Parsi Religion* (London: 2nd edn. 1913; also New York, 1909, 1910, 1911).
Karaka, D. F. (1884), *History of the Parsis*, 2 vols. (London).
Karaka, D. F. (1935), *Oh! You English* (this author is the son of, not the same person as, the former author) (London; repr. Allahabad, 1940, 1949).
—— (1938), *I Go West* (London; repr. Bombay, 1941).
Karanjia, B. K. (1970), *Rustom Masani, Portrait of a Citizen* (Bombay).
Karkal, M. (1983), *Survey of Parsi Population of Greater Bombay—1982* (Bombay).
Kased, H. (n.d.), 'Parsee Lustre on the Emerald Isle of Zanzibar' (unpublished typescript).
Katrak, S. H. (1958), *Who are the Parsees?* (Karachi; repr. 1965).
Keddie, N. R. (1981), *Roots of Revolution: An Interpretative History of Modern Iran* (New Haven).
Khan, V. S. (1979) (ed.), *Minority Families in Britain* (London).
Kharas Fraser, H. (1993), 'Intermarriage among Bombay Zoroastrians', Manchester University Ph.D. thesis, unpublished.
Kincaid, D. (1938), *British Social Life in India, 1608–1937* (London; repr. London and Boston, 1973).
Knott, K. (1986*a*), *Hinduism in Leeds* (Leeds).
—— (1986*b*), 'Religion and Identity, and the Study of Ethnic Minority Religions in Britain', in V. Hayes (ed.), *Identity Issues and World Religions* (Bedford Park, South Australia).
—— (1987) 'Hindu Temple Rituals in Britain: The Reinterpretation of Tradition', in Burghart (1987), 157–79.
—— (1991), 'Bound to Change? The Religions of South Asians in Britain', in Vertovec (1991), 86–111.
Kothari, J. H. (1889), *Impressions of a First Tour round the World in 1883 and 1884* (London).
Kotwal, F. M., and Boyd, J. W. (1977), 'The Zoroastrian paragna,' *Journal of Mithraic Studies*, 2(1): 18–52.
Krausz, E. (1972), 'Acculturation and Pluralism: A Classification of Concepts', *New Community*, 1(4).
Kueppner, W. G., Lynne Lackey, G., and Swinerton, E. N. (1975), *Ugandan Asians in Great Britain* (London and New York).
Kulke, E. (1974), *The Parsees in India* (Munich).
Laing, S. (1887), *A Modern Zoroastrian* (London: repr. 1890; 2nd edn. 1898; repr. 1901, 1903, 1904).

Langstaff, H. (1983), 'The Impact of Western Education and Political Changes upon the Religious Teachings of Indian Parsis in the Twentieth Century', Manchester University Ph.D. thesis, unpublished.

Leventhal, F. M. (1971), *Respectable Radical* (London and Cambridge, Mass.).

Lewis, P. (1994), *Islamic Britain* (London).

Lofchie, M. F. (1965), *Zanzibar: Background to Revolution* (Princeton).

Lommel, H. (1930), *Die Religion Zarathustras nach dem Awesta dargestellt* (Tübingen; repr. Hildesheim and New York, 1971).

Lyon, M. A. (1972–3), 'Ethnicity and Gujarati Indians in Britain', *New Community*, 2(1): 1–11.

Macdonald, B. (1983), *Immigration Law and Practice in the U.K.* (London).

Malabari, B. M. (1893), *The Indian Eye on English Life* (Bombay; 3rd edn.1895).

Malcolm, N. (1905), *Five Years in a Persian Town* (London and New York; repr. 1907, 1908).

Mangat, J. S. (1969), *A History of the Asians in East Africa c. 1886–1945* (Oxford).

Marsh, Z., and Kingsworth, G. W. (1972), *A History of East Africa* (Cambridge).

Masani, R. P. (1938), *The Religion of the Good Life* (London; repr. 1958; also New York, 1938 and 1968).

—— (1939), *Dadabhai Naoroji: The Grand Old Man of India* (London; repr. 1960, 1970, and 3rd abbreviated edn. Mysore, 1968).

Masselos, J. (1974), *Towards Nationalism* (Bombay).

Mehrotra, S. R. (1971), *The Emergence of the Indian National Congress* (Delhi).

Mehta, A. (1976), *The Story of our Religion* (Bombay).

—— (1988), *The Story of Our Religion: Zoroastrianism* (Bombay).

Mehta, P. D. (1976), *The Heart of Religion* (London and Boulder, Color. 1976; Tisbury, 1976, and London, 1987).

Mehta, S. D. (1954), *The Cotton Mills of India, 1854–1954* (Bombay).

Mellor, D. (1985), 'The Parliamentary Life of Dadabhai Naoroji, the Great "Parsi Patriot" between 1885–1895; with Special Reference to the *Voice of India and Indian Spectator*', *JCOI*, 52: 1–113.

Menski, W. (1987), 'Legal Pluralism in the Hindu Marriage' in Burghart (1987).

Miles, R. (1993), *Racism after 'Race Relations'* (London and New York).

—— and Phizacklea, A. (1984), *White Man's Country* (London).

Mistree, K. (1982), *Zoroastrianism, an Ethnic Perspective* (Bombay).

Mistry, R. (1987), *Tales from Firozsha Baag* (London and Delhi, 1987; repr. 1993; London, 1989, 1992; Ontario, 1987).

—— (1991), *Such a Long Journey* (London, repr. 1992; Toronto, 1991, repr. 1993; New York, 1991, repr. 1992).

Mitter, P. (1977), *Much Maligned Monsters* (Oxford, repr. 1991; repr. with new foreword, Chicago, 1992).

Modi, J. J. (1922), *The Religious Ceremonies and Customs of the Parsees* (Bombay; 2nd edn. 1937; repr. from 1st edn., 1979; 1937 edn. repr. Bombay, 1984; repr. New York, 1980).

—— (1929), 'Rustam Manock (1635–1721 A.C.), the Broker of the English East India Company (1699 A.C.), and the Persian Qisseh (History) of Rustam Manock: A Study', in the collection of Modi's *Asiatic Papers* (Bombay), iv. 101–320 (paper read before the Bombay Branch of the Royal Asiatic Society, 27 Aug. 1928).

—— (1932), *K. R. Cama* (Bombay).

Mody, H. (1963), *Sir Pherozeshah Mehta* (Bombay).

Monk, C. (1985), 'Member for India: The Parliamentary Lives of Dadabhai Naoroji and Mancherjee Bhownagree', Manchester University M.Phil. thesis, unpublished.

Morris, H. S. (1968), *The Indians in Uganda* (London).

Morris, C. L. (1984), 'The Perceptions of Parsis in Nineteenth Century English Language Newspapers of Bombay', Manchester University M. Phil. Thesis, unpublished.

Moulton, J. H. (1913), *Early Zoroastrianism* (London; repr. 1926; Amsterdam, 1972, New York, 1980).

—— (1917), *Treasure of the Magi* (Bombay and Oxford; repr. 1971).

Murzban, M. M., (1917), *The Parsis in India*, 2 vols. (Bombay).

Nanavutty, P. (1980), *The Parsis* (New Delhi; 1st edn. 1977).

Naoroji, D. (1862), 'The Parsee Religon', *Proceedings of the Liverpool Literary and Philosophical Society* (lecture delivered in 1861).

—— (1901), *Poverty and Un-British Rule in India.* (London; repr. Delhi, 1962, 1969, 1988).

—— (1908), 'The Parsi Religion', in W. Sheowring and C. W. Thies, *Religious Systems of the World* (London; repr. Delhi, 1982).

Nauroji, D. (1909), *From Zoroaster to Christ* (Edinburgh) (not the same author as the above).

Natesan, (1906), *Speeches and Writings of Dadabhai Naoroji* (Madras: 2nd edn. 1917).

—— (1930), *Famous Parsis* (Natesan is the publisher, no author is indicated), (Madras; repr. Delhi, 1990).

Nusserwanji (1954), *Jamshed Nusserwanji: A Memorial* (no author) (Karachi).

Ogot, B. A., and Kieran, J. A. (1974), *Zamani: A Survey of East African History* (Nairobi; previously pub. Nairobi and New York, 1968).

Owen, D. (1992–3), *Ethnic Minorities in Great Britain*, National Ethnic

Minority Data Archive, 1991 census Statistical Papers, i–vi (University of Warwick).

Pailin D. (1984), *Attitudes to Other Religions: Comparative Religion in Seventeenth and Eighteenth Century Britain* (Manchester).

Panayi, P. (1994), *Immigration, Ethnicity and Racism in Britain* (Manchester).

Pangborn, C. (1982), *Zoroastrianism: A Beleaguered Faith* (Delhi).

Parekh, C. L. (1887), *Essays, Speeches and Writings of the Hon'ble Dadabhai Nauroji* (Bombay).

Parkin, D. (1970), 'Congregational and Interpersonal Ideologies in Political Ethnicity', in Cohen (1974).

Parry, C. (1957), *Nationality and Citizenship Laws of the Commonwealth and the Republic of Ireland* (London: repr. 1960).

Parsi Prakash (PP), Bombay, (eds. B. B. Patel, R. B. Paymaster *et al*. A multi-volumed collection in Gujarati of newspaper cuttings relating to Parsis, theoretically still in production, though no volume has appeared since 1962).

Patel, M. K. (1892), *History of the Parsee Cricket* (Bombay).

Patwardhan, R. P. (1977), *Dadabhai Naoroji Correspondence*, vol. ii, in 2 parts (Vol. i has never been published) (New Delhi).

Paymaster, R. B. (1954), *Early History of the Parsees in India* (Bombay).

Punthakey, J. H. (1919), *The Karachi Zoroastrian Calendar*, English trans. by F. H. Punthakey (Karachi, 1989).

Pye, M. (1993), 'Syncretism versus Synthesis', British Association for the Study of Religion, Occasional Papers (Leeds).

Rex, J. (1986), *Race and Ethnicity* (Milton Keynes).

Rich, P. B. (1990), *Race and Empire in British Politics* (Cambridge; 2nd edn.).

Robilliard, S. J. A. (1984), *Religion and the Law* (Manchester).

Robinson, V. (1986), *Transients, Settlers and Refugees: Asians in Britain* (Oxford).

Sachdeva, S. (1993), *The Primary Purpose Rule in British Immigration Law* (Stoke-on-Trent).

Saggar, S. (1992), *Race and Politics in Britain* (London).

Saha, P. (1970), *Shapurji Saklatvala: A Short Biography* (New Delhi).

Saklatavala, S. (1927), *Is India Different?* (London).

Saklatvala, S. (1991), *The Fifth Commandment: Biography of Shapurji Saklatvala* (Salford, private pub.). (Nb. the MP's daughter.)

Salvadori, C. (1983), *Through Open Doors: A View of Asian Culture in Kenya* (Nairobi, 2nd expended edition; revised edn. 1990).

Seal, A. (1968), *The Emergence of Indian Nationalism* (Cambridge; repr. 1971).

Shahrokh, S. and Writer, R. (1994), *The Memoirs of Keikhosrow Shahrokh*, (New York, Queenston, and Lampeter).

Sharpe, E. J. S. (1965), *Not to Destroy but to Fulfil* (Uppsala).
—— (1985), *Comparative Religion: A History* (London; 1st edn. 1975, repr. 1976; New York, 1976).
Sidhwa, B. (1978), *The Crow Eaters* (Lahore; repr. 1980, 1981, 1988; Delhi and New York, 1990).
—— (1983), *The Bride* (London).
—— (1988), *Ice-Candy-Man* (London).
Smith, G. (1879), *The Life of John Wilson D.D., F.R.S.* (London).
Solomos, J. (1989), *Race and Racism in Contemporary Britain* (London; 2nd edn. Basingstoke, 1993).
Squires, M. J. (1987), 'The Life and Influence of S. Saklatvala', Leeds University Ph.D. thesis.
—— (1990), *Saklatvala: A Political Biography*, (publication of the 1987 thesis (London).
Thernstrom, S. (1980) (ed.), *Harvard Encylopedia of American Ethnic Groups* (Cambridge, Mass.).
Tinker, H. (1976), *Separate and Unequal: India and Indians in the British Commonwealth, 1920-50* (London, St Lucia, Queensland, and Vancouver).
—— (1977), *The Banyan Tree*, (Oxford and New York).
Vadgama, K. (1984), *India in Britain* (London).
Vajifdar, F. (1993), *The Twist in the Rope: A Study of the Patriot Dadabhai Naoroji* (London).
Vertovec, S. (1991) (ed.), *Aspects of the South Asian Diaspora* (Oxford and Delhi).
Visram, R. (1986), *Ayahs, Lascars and Princes* (London).
Wadia, A. (1955), *The Bombay Dockyard and the Wadia Master Builders* (Bombay: 2nd edn. 1957).
Wadia, A. C. (1840), *Diary of an Overland Journey from Bombay to England* (London).
Wadia, A. S. N. (1912), *The Message of Zoroaster* (London; repr. London and Toronto, 1921).
—— (1913), *Reflections on the Problems of India* (London).
Wadia, D. F. (1912) *History of Lodge Rising Star of Western India No. 342 S.C.* (Bombay).
Wadia, J. N. and Wadia, H. M. (1841), *Journal of a Residence of Two Years and a Half in Great Britain* (London).
Watson, J. L. (1977), *Between Two Cultures* (Oxford).
Werbner, P., and Anwar, M. (1991), *Black and Ethnic Leadership in Britain: The Cultural Dimension of Political Action* (London and New York).
White, D. L. (1979), *Parsis as Entrepreneurs in Eighteenth Century Western India: The Rustum Manock Family and the Parsi Community of Surat and Bombay* (Anne Arbor).

Wilson, J. (1843), *The Parsi Religion as Contained in the Zand-Avasta and Propounded and Defended by the Zoroastrians of India and Persia, Unfolded, Refuted, and Contrasted with Christianity* (Bombay).

World Zoroastrian Souvenir Issues, Conference Papers for 1984, 1987, 1988, 1989, 1990, 1991.

Wolpert, S. (1984), *Jinnah of Pakistan* (Oxford and New York).

Wright, D. (1977), *The English among the Persians during the Qajar Period, 1787–1921* (London; repr. London and New York, 1985).

——— (1985), *The Persians amongst the English* (London and New York).

Writer, R. (1994), *Contemporary Zoroastrians: An Unstructured Nation*, Lanham, Md.).

Zaehner, R. C. (1955), *Zurvan, a Zoroastrian Dilemma* (Oxford; repr. New York, 1972).

——— (1956), *The Teachings of the Magi* (London; repr. London, 1975; New York, 1976).

——— (1961), *The Dawn and Twilight of Zoroastrianism* (London and New York, 1961; repr. 1975).

GLOSSARY

Achaemenids rulers of Iran from sixth to third centuries BCE, the empire founded by Cyrus the Great

Agiary Gujarati, 'house of fire', the common name for an ordinary fire temple (as opposed to an *Atash Bahram*)

Ahriman Middle Persian/Pahlavi form of Anra Mainyu, the source of all evil in Zoroastrian theology

Ahura Mazda Lord Wisdom, God, in the teaching of Zoroaster and his followers

Amesha Spentas the seven Bounteous, or Holy, Immortals whose presence is invoked in worship (see Table 1)

Anjuman the organizing body within Zoroastrian communities (see also Punchayat) but sometimes used to refer to the whole of a local community

Anra Mainyu the Avestan form of Ahriman

Asha Order or Righteousness in Zoroastrianism, one of the Amesha Spentas, protector of, and represented by, the creation of fire

Atash Bahram The third and highest grade of the ritual fires in Zoroastrianism, the temples housing such fires are sometime referred to as 'cathedral fire temples'. There are four such fires in Iran, eight in India and none outside these two countries

Avesta the holy language and the holy book of Zoroastrianism

Baag Gujarati, an open place, generally used to refer to compounds where such public functions as *navjotes*, weddings, and lectures are held. It is also used for a Parsi housing colony

Bounteous Immortals see **Amesha Spentas**

Boi ceremony the feeding of a ritual fire performed five times a day in temples, sometimes performed in diaspora prayer-rooms to evoke the temple tradition

Bungli in Parsi practice the building where the dead are taken to be ritually prepared for funerals

Chinvat Bridge the Bridge of Judgement in Zoroastrian belief

Dar-i Mihr literally, Court or Gate of Mithra, the traditional term for Zoroastrian temples

Daxma a round tower-like structure in which Zoroastrians have traditionally exposed the dead to vultures

Dastur the title for a Zoroastrian high priest

Dhansak a popular and traditional Parsi festive meal

Divo an oil-lamp kept lit for devotional practice, especially in the home

Ervad the title for a functioning priest, denoting that he has undergone the first level of priestly initiation

Farvardigan the annual Iranian ceremony invoking the dead

Frashokereti the Zoroastrian belief in the final renovation of the world

Fravashis the heavenly selves of all people

Gahs the five liturgical divisions of the day

Gahambars the six seasonal festivals

Gathas the hymns composed by the prophet Zoroaster

Gehsarna prayers Gujarati word for the funeral prayers

Getig Middle Persian/Pahlavi term for the visible and tangible world in contrast to the *menog*, that which is invisible and intangible

Guebre infidels, a Muslim term of contempt for Zoroastrians and others

Gurz the mace of Mithra, made of silver, the symbol of priesthood

Ilm-i Khshnoom a twentieth-century Parsi occult movement

Jashan a Zoroastrian ceremony which may be celebrated in temple, home, or other pure place, and in which the Amesha Spentas are praised and present

Jizya tax imposed on unbelievers by Muslims

Juddin a non-Zoroastrian

Khshnoomists followers of Ilm-i Khshnoom

Kusti the sacred cord tied around the waist by Zoroastrians and sometimes referred to as 'the sword-belt of the faith'

Maatchi see **Boi**

Majlis the Iranian Parliament established in 1906

Manthras holy words or prayers

Menog see *Getig*

Middle Persian a synonym for Pahlavi language, 'Middle' as opposed to 'Ancient' (cuneiform) or 'Modern'. The language in which much classical theology is expounded

Mithra an ancient Indo-Iranian deity, incorporated into Zoroastrianism as a *yazata*, and around whom a Roman mystery cult developed

Mobed a Zoroastrian priest who has undertaken the second level of priestly initiation and is thereby qualified to perform all Zoroastrian rituals

Muktad a Parsi term, *Farvardigan* among Iranian Zoroastrians, the annual ceremony when the dead are invoked and thought to be powerfully present

Nahn ritual bath of purification

Nasasalars corpse-bearers

Nataks Parsi Gujarati dramas

Naujote the Zoroastrian rite of initiation

Nirang consecrated cow's urine

No Ruz the Iranian Zoroastrian New Year festival

Ohrmazd Middle Persian/Pahlavi form of Ahura Mazda

Padan mouth-covering worn by Zoroastrian priests during rituals to avoid defiling the sacred fire with impure breath

Pahlavi see Middle Persian

Parthians the rulers of Iran from the second century BCE to the third century CE

Pateti Parsi New Year

Punchayat a traditional form of Indian community government adopted by Parsis

Qissa-i Sanjan a text dated 1600 CE relating the migration of the original Zoroastrians to India and their early history (although containing legendary and mythical material)

Sagdi the room set aside for prayers in Zoroastrian funerals before a ritual fire

Sedra pushun the Iranian Zoroastrian *sudre-kusti*

Shenshai calendar the calendar followed by most Parsis, in contrast to the Kadmi which follows Iranian Zoroastrian practice and the Fasli which is a twentieth century attempt to revise the calendar

Spenta Mainyu one of the Amesha Spentas, synonymous, in Pahlavi tradition at least, with Ohrmazd

Sudre the Parsi term for the sacred shirt worn by all initiated persons. The *sudre-kusti* prayers are the prayers associated with these garments and traditionally performed several times a day

Uthumna prayers prayers recited on the third day after death

Vendidad a Zoroastrian text and inner or 'higher' liturgy

Vohu Manah one of the Amesha Spentas

Yashts hymns from the Avesta, many of them pre-Zoroastrian

Yasna worship, and the term for one of the main 'higher' or 'inner' ceremonies. It is also the name of the text which forms the liturgy of the ceremony which includes the *Gathas*

Yazata a being worthy of worship, although Ahura Mazda alone is worthy of absolute worship

Zarthost-no-diso the anniversary of Zoroaster's death

Zoroaster the western form of Zarathushtra, the prophet of ancient Iran, generally dated around 1200 BCE

Zurvan 'Time' the focal point of a set of philosophical speculation generally referred to as the Zoroastrian heresy. Its history is unknown but it is generally thought to have flourished from Achaemenid times down to the early Islamic period of Iranian history

INDEX

abstract nature 11, 12
acculturation 46, 238–41, 244
  see also culture
Achaemenids 2, 321
Aden. Parsis 63
Adenwalla family, *see* Dinshaw, Cowasji
African Asians 43
  see also Natal; South Africa
African Parsis, *see* East African Zoroastrians
age, demography 5, 231, 249
agiary 12, 78, 321
  see also temples
Ahriman 8, 99, 271, 276, 321
Ahura Mazda 7–16 *passim*, 23, 25, 229, 241, 244, 249, 271, 276, 321
  see also God
Aibura, Dastur 273
alcohol 256
Alexander the Great 2
Aliens Act, 1905 (Britain) 34
Allbless, Naoroji D. 155
American Zoroastrians 5, 21, 133, 137, 145, 146, 148, 231, 249, 260, 272, 273, 285, 291, 293, 297, 301
Amesha Spentas 7, 11–12, 26, 267, 321
Ampthill, Lord 186–7
Amroliwalla, Dr 289
angels 12
Anglo-Saxon, *see* white Anglo-Saxon
Anra Mainyu, *see* Ahriman
Appoo, R. H. 120
Archer, J. R., Black Mayor of Battersea, 197
Ardeshir, Arbab 113
asceticism 13, 297
Asha 11, 13, 321
assimilation 47, 309
Atash Bahram ix, 245, 253, 261, 321
  see also temples
Australian Zoroastrians 5, 148, 249, 272
authority, religious 7, 19–20, 147, 152, 246, 273, 301, 304
Avari, Behram 59
Avari, Burjor 289

Avari, Dinshah 59
Avesta 6, 259, 321
Avestan language 23, 26
Azargashash, Mobed Ferouz 273

Baag 23, 321
Baba, Homi 58
Bahadurji, R. C., 82 n. 3
Baha'ism 3
Banaji, Limji N. 82
Bareshnum 261
Battersea North 197
Bedhwa, Ervad Rustom 259, 287
Berlin, Parsi burial ground 132
Bethnal Green North East 175, 177
Bhedwar, Jehangir 64
Bhownagree, Sir Muncherji 63, 120, 134, 191, 287; early life 174–5; Zoroastrian Association 110–15 *passim*, 118–19, 123 n. 15, 124, 125–7, 290; Parliamentary career 175–94; Indian interests: finance 179, technical education 180, industry and commerce 181–2, justice 182, Salt Tax 184–5; South African Indians 185–8, 190, 191–2; relations with Naoroji 125–6, 128, 169, 175, 189, 193; relations with Saklatvala 129–32, 215–16; character and work 176, 188–94, 222–6 *passim*
bimetallism 168
Birdwood, Sir George 134
Birmingham Zoroastrians 231
birth, pollution and purity 16–17, 262
'black' 31, 47, 197
blood 16, 17
Bode, Dastur 272
boi ceremony 25, 257, 261, 291, 321
Bomanji, Sir Dhunjibhoy and Lady Bomanji 116, 122 n. 14, 123, 124
Bombay 54
Bombay Association 57, 93, 156
Bombay Parsi Punchayat 19, 78–9,

Bombay Parsi Punchayat (*cont.*): 115–16, 121, 122, 123, 140, 147, 294, 300
Bombay Parsis 1, 4, 5, 54–8, 140, 194, 200, 201, 228, 229, 241, 242, 250, 256, 264, 267, 268 n. 9, 279, 281, 293, 294, 305; Cricket Club 85–7; funeral grounds 14–16; High Court decision (1906) 19; local politics 157; priests, high priests 143, 272, 291, *see also* Dasturs and individual names; relations with diaspora Zoroastrians 109, 143, 272–3, 291; temples ix, 78; Western education 56, 156, 195, 243; Zoroastrian studies 73; *see also* individual names and special topics
Bombay Presidency Association 57, 157
Bombay Rajkiya Sabha 200
Bombay stock market crash 1865: 85, 86, 110
Bombay University 81
Bombay Zoroastrians, *see* Bombay Parsis
Bonnerjea 188
Booker Prize 289
Bounteous Immortals, *see* Amesha Spentas
Boyce Mary x, 7, 73, 259
Bradford, immigrants 33
Breath 17, 25
Bridge of Judgement (Chinvat Bridge) 9, 15, 265, 321
Brier, Suzanne 19
Britain 5, 88–97, 193, 242, 243, 245, 246, 250, 258, 281–3, 287–9, 305
  see also Hindus in Britain; Islam in Britain; Parsis in Britain; South Asians in Britain; Zoroastrians in Britain
British, the 28, 74–5, 76, 153, 235–8, 239, 241, 244, 250, 251, 253, 254, 281
  see also British Zoroastrians; white Anglo-Saxons
British Empire and Commonwealth 29, 30, 32
  Parsi contribution 281
  see also immigration
British India, *see* India
British Nationality Acts 34, 35
British politics 156–226
  see also immigration; Parliament; Bhownagree; Gifford, Z.; Naoroji, Dadabhoi; Saklatvala

British Zoroastrians 1, 8, 74–6, 241, 242, 245, 272, 293, 295, 310–11
  see also Parsis in Britain
British Zoroastrians survey 227–78; research methods 227–30, 305–10; demography 230–3: residence, age marriage, family 231–2; education, language, occupations 232–4; religion and identity 233–5; youth 234; race 234; history 234–5; perception of British 235–8: racism 235–6, family values 237; youth 237, women 237; Zoroastrian and British identity 238–41; birth country and heritage 241–3; decade of arrival and religious practice 243–4; old country contacts 245–6; generation differences 246–8; gender issues 249–50; intermarriage 250–5; tradition, social context 255–7; tradition, religion 258–61; religious practice 261–2; life cycle rites 262–5; community rituals 266–8; interpreting religious practice 268–72; international perspective 272–4; internal British comparisons 274–5; conclusion 275–8; *see also individual topics*, e.g. intermarriage; young Zoroastrians
Broacha, Sir Shahpurji 120, 182
Brookwood burial ground 115, 129, 130, 132, 133, 134–7, 265, 270, 289, 292
bungli 14, 15, 265, 321
burial grounds, 16, 63, 109, 132, 133, 272
  see also Brookwood
business, *see* commerce and trade

Calcutta 174
California 272, 293, 294
Cama, Bai Bhikhaiji 85, 88, 110
Cama, D. P. 85
Cama, K. R. 69, 85
Cama, M. H. 85, 88, 107–8, 120, 169, 289, 290
Cama, S. C. 84
Cama, Spitama 113
Canada 5, 34, 137, 146, 272, 293, 301
Canton 4
Captain Shahpur F., 137, 140, 145, 146
caste 19
ceremonies 25–6, 270

see also liturgy; ritual
Chamberlain, Joseph 186
change 47
   see also diaspora, changes in belief and practice
charity 4, 16, 58, 74, 121–2, 147, 149, 265, 268, 288
   Parsi donations to British causes 79–80, 88, 104
Chesney, Sir George 170
Chicago 30, 272, 273, 274, 293
children 13, 139, 145, 254, 258–61, 263, 274, 275, 294, 308
China 4, 55
Chinvat Bridge, *see* Bridge of Judgement
choice, *see* free will
Christianity 2, 67, 76, 96, 97, 284, 296
   see also Protestantism
Christmas 149, 229
Colah, P. R. 85
commerce and trade 4, 5, 65, 84–5
communism 30, 194, 197, 203, 216–17
community 47, 274–5
   pressure, intermarriage 252
   rituals 266–8, 291, 292
   ties 230, 234, 245, 306
congregational worship 266–7, 293, 294
Conservative Party, *see* Tory Party
conversion 18–21, 45, 140
   see also intermarriage
Cooper, B. D. 85
Cooper, D. S. 132
Cooper's Hill Engineering College 185
cosmology 10
Cotton, Sir Henry 172
courage (a Zoroastrian virtue) 224
Cowasji family, Pakistan 59
Cowasji Dinshaw family, *see* Dinshaw, Cowasji
Coyajee, J. C. 117
Creation, Zoroastrian cosmology 8–9
cremation 14, 135–6, 265, 270, 271
cricket 56, 85–7, 255, 283
culture 296
   see also acculturation; diaspora, tradition transmission
Curzon, Lord, Viceroy 180
Cyrus the Great 1, 21

Dabu, Dastur 143
Dadabhoy, Khurshid 104
Dadabhoy, Sir Maneckji 125
Dadachanji, K. E. 201

Dalal, C. A. 84
Dalal, Si Dadaba 116, 130
Dalal, Rusi 287
Dantra, S. H. 84
Dar es Salaam 65–6, 283
Dara, D. D. 82 n. 4
Dar-i, Mihr 12, 322
   see also temples
Darukhanawala, R. M. 81
Darukhanawala Sorabji and Bomanji 63
Dasturs 272–3, 322
   see also high priests *and individual names*
daxma 14–16, 261, 264, 270, 322
death, dead 10, 13–17, 241, 261, 264, 269, 272
   see also burial grounds; cremation; *daxma*; funeral rites; *uthumna* ceremony
Delhi Parsis 148, 251
demography 4, 5–6, 230–3, 299, 301–2, 304
Desai, R. B. 81
destructive spirit, *see* Ahriman
Devil 276
   see also Ahriman
Dhalla, M. N. 70–1, 76
Dhondy, Farrukh 288, 289
diaspora (Zoroastrian) 5, 243, 246, 272, 279, 294, 305–9
   tradition transmission 255–61
   see also country and cities of settlement: America, Australia, Britain, Canada, immigration; intermarriage, *see* intermarriage
diaspora religion 37–41, 48, 146–8, 242–3, 257–71, 275–8, 292
   changes in belief and practice 23, 136, 148, 244, 250, 267, 268, 273–4, 275–7, 293, 294, 295, 309–10
   comparative study 152, 280, 293, 305–9
   education 258–61, 308
Dinshaw, Cowasji 62, 63
Dinshaw, Edulji 58–9
Dinshaw, Sir Hormusjee Cowasji 63
disabled 282–3
Divine, The, *see* Holy, the
divo (oil lamp) 229, 264, 322
divorce 249
dogs 15
Dorabji, Nanabhai 55
Dorabji, Rustomji 55

'drain' theory, British Indian finance 157, 162 ff., 178
dualism 100, 270

East Africa, Hindus 5
East Africa, Parsis 5, 6, 62–7, 145
  emigration to Britain 66–7
  see also East African Zoroastrians
East Africa, trade with South Asia 60–2
East African Indians 33, 36, 42, 299
  see also South Asians in Britain
East African Zoroastrians 74–6, 141, 142, 149, 228, 229, 232, 233, 234, 237, 241, 245, 246, 251, 262 272, 274, 290, 292, 305, 306
  see also East Africa, Parsis
East India Association (formerly London Indian Society) 157, 158, 160, 163, 165 n. 12
East India Company 56–7, 78, 80, 82, 174, 177 n. 35
Eastwick, E. B. 111
Edinburgh, Parsis 117, 119–20
education 299, 307
  and intermarriage 252
  technical and industrial 80–1; in India 180–1, 183, 191, 224
  western 4, 56, 80–4, 182, 225, 232–3, 236, 297, 298–9, 306–7; *see also* university education
  see also female education; religious education
employment, racial prejudice 236
end of the world, *see* world renovation
Engineer, Farokh 288
English language 234, 243, 245, 249, 252, 292, 308
enjoyment 13
  see also joy
environment and religion 295
eschatology 10, 298
ethics 13, 101–2, 277, 281
ethnic minority community groups 149
ethnicity 45–6, 291, 303
Europe, Zoroastrians in 110, 279
European race and Parsis 47, 65–6, 76, 105, 160, 238, 283, 303–4
evil 8–9, 10, 13–18, 22, 271
  see also Ahriman; good/evil
exposure of the dead, see *daxma*
extended families 232
  see also family

family:
  British 282
  British Zoroastrian Survey 231, 247
  groups, immigration 32, 67, 85, 306
  intermarriage 252; *see also* intermarriage
  values 237
Fardoonji (Fardunji) Naoroji 58, 93–5, 110, 111
Farsi 259, 291
Farvardigan, see *muktad*
fasting 13
Federation of Zoroastrian Associations of North America (FEZANA) 147, 293
female education 156, 174
festivals 21, 22, 229, 241, 242, 248, 268, 290, 293
  see also gahambars; jashans; New Year
Finsbury Central 159–60
fire, in Zoroastrian belief 15, 17, 24–7, 140, 262, 267, 268, 269, 271
  see also temples
  pollution and purity 14, 17, 143, 292; *see also* cremation
flowers (symbol of the soul) 264, 265
food 24, 256, 257, 265
Framjee, D. *The Parsees* 98, 99, 182, 190
  see also Karaka, D. F.
France 231
  see also Paris
frashokereti, see world renovation
Fravardigan 265
Fravashi 265, 268, 322
free will 9, 10, 13, 25
funeral grounds, India 14–15
  see also Brookwood; burial grounds
funeral rites 14–16, 264–5, 266, 272; *see also daxma*
  and non-Zoroastrians 110–11, 115, 142, 269

gah 12, 22, 322
gahambars 21–2, 266, 268, 291, 322
Gandhi, Feroza 57, 104
Gandhi, Indira, Sanchay, and Rajiv 57–8, 104
Gandhi, Mahatma 31, 39, 158, 188, 190, 194 n. 75, 222
Gathas 6, 8, 10, 169–70, 242, 258, 259, 322
gehsana prayers 265, 322
gender 24, 43, 230, 237, 249–50, 299
General Strike 1926 (Britain) 198–9

generation gap 247
  see also young Zoroastrians
getig 8, 322
Ghadialy, H. 58
Gifford, Zerbanoo 149, 155, 259;
  politician 218–21: background 218–19; Liberal Party 219–20, 289; political interests: Dadabhoi Naoroji 218, women's rights, racial equality 219, suffers racial abuse 220, 284; Zoroastrian identity 218, 221, 222 ff.
Gilder, Dr M. D. 194
Global Survey of Zoroastrians 244, 248, 249, 271, 273, 295
globalization 293
God 27, 271, 276
  see also Ahura Mazda
Godrej brothers 57
Golden Mean 13
good/evil 9, 13, 15, 17
Good Religion, the x, 7, 9
good thoughts *see* thoughts
Gotla, Dr Fram 197
Guiv, Arbab Rustom 136, 141
Gujarat, Gujaratis 1, 4, 14, 15, 27, 33, 37, 38, 147, 156, 234, 241, 252, 279, 305
  non-Parsis 33
Gujarati language 12, 232, 241, 243, 245, 251, 256, 308
Gurdwaras 33
gurz (mace) 12, 322

Haffkine, Vladimir, and Saklatvala 196
Hamazor 147
hambandagi prayers 266, 291
Haringay Community Relations Council 149
Harrow Zoroastrian Association 218
Harrow Zoroastrians 149, 155, 231
  see also Gifford, Zerbanoo
Haug, Martin 6, 69–70
Hawkins, Prof. Stephen 283
heaven/hell 9–10
high priests 291, 293
  see also Dasturs; priests
higher education 42, 232–3, 300, 307
Hinduism 30, 38–41, 242, 300
  and Zoroastrianism 4, 296
Hindus in Britain 32, 33, 37–41, 260, 296 ff., 300
history, sense of 280–1

History of the Parsis (Karaka) 70
Holy, the 16, 242, 262, 268, 269, 277, 296
Holy Immortals, *see* Amesha Spentas
Home Rule League 174
homeland, mother, 'old' country 75–6, 238
Homji, Dastur Minocher 272–3
homosexuality 282
honesty 277
Hong Kong:
  Parsis in 4–5, 6
  Zoroastrians 137
  World Zoroastrian Organization 145, 272, 274
honours, British 63, 102, 289
House of Commons 161, 192
  see also Members of Parliament; Parliament
housing, racial prejudice 236
Houston Zoroastrians 272, 273
humour 256
Hyndman, Henry and Naoroji 171

identity, Zoroastrian (includes Parsi) 76, 153, 233 ff., 244, 248, 251, 254, 262, 267, 278, 290, 293, 307, 308, 309
Ilavna, F. 123
Ilbert Bill, 1873: 157
Ilford 155
Ilm-i Khshnoom 72–3, 74, 273, 322
immigrants, African 29–31
  Asian 27–44; *see also* South Asians in Britain
  Indian 42–4; *see also* diaspora; Parsis in Britain
  Religion 280; *see also* diaspora religion
  stereotypes 29–30
immigration, UK 27–37, 296
impurity, *see* pollution; purity laws
in-marriage 251–2, 264, 267
Incorporated Parsee Association of Europe 115
  see also London Zoroastrian Association
Independent Labour Party 194, 197
India: British politics 156, 160 ff., 178–80, 185; British rule 4–5, 30, 177, 179, 193, 211–13; Hindu/Muslim relations, *see* India, Muslims; independence 193; industry and commerce 181, 184; Muslims 173, 200
  railways 182, 184
  Salt Tax 184–5
  Zoroastrians in, *see* Parsis
  see also 'drain theory'; politics

Indian Civil Service 83, 84, 164 n. 11, 165, 166, 167, 173
Indian Councils 168
Indian finance, Royal Commission 169, 170, 178
Indian Medical Service 84, 183
Indian National Congress 57, 125, 157–8, 164 n. 12, 170, 172, 173, 279
  Bhownagree and 175, 176, 182, 188, 189, 190, 193
  Saklatvala and 195, 200, 201, 202, 214
Indian National Liberal Federation 63
Indian Parliamentary Party (IPP) (Britain) 162, 167, 169, 170, 176–7, 192
Indian Political Estimate of Mr Bhavnagri, (The) 176
Indian Zoroastrians 232, 273–4, 274, 279–80, 290, 292, 293
  see also Parsis; Parsis in Britain
individual responsibility, *see* free will
Indo-Iranian heritage 22, 277, 296
  see also European race and Parsis
industry 80 ff.
infant marriage 156, 174
initiation (Naujote, Sedra pushun) 18, 23–4
  see also *Naujote*
institutionalization of religion 292, 295, 296, 307
integration 47
  see also diaspora, changes in belief and practice
inter-community (Zoroastrian) relations 150–4, 237, 291–2
inter-faith relations 261, 287
intermarriage 19–21, 45, 150, 196, 218, 228, 233, 239, 242, 244, 247, 250–5, 264, 275, 301, 303
  see also children; conversion; non-Zoroastrians
International Socialist Congress, Amsterdam (1904) 171–2
International Zoroastrianism 272–4, 292, 294, 295
Iran 1, 41, 145–6, 242, 292, 293; *see also* Persia, Ancient
  post-Revolution, 1979– 145–6, 242
  Zoroastrians in x, 3–4, 19, 22–3, 50–3, 111–14, 269, 293, 303–4
  see also Irani Zoroastrians
Irani, Bailey 143 n. 36, 144, 145, 146, 218
Irani Zoroastrians (i.e. diaspora Zoroastrians) 18, 23, 74–6, 136, 141, 143, 146, 149, 228, 232, 240, 241–2, 245, 246, 253, 256–7, 257, 264, 268, 274, 280, 284, 290, 291, 292, 293, 305, 306
Islam 2–3, 242, 274, 284, 295, 303
  see also India, Muslims
Islam in Britain 32, 33, 40, 297 ff., 302

Jains 297, 299, 300
  in Britain 37, 39, 40
JamaspAsa, Dastur Dr Kaikhusroo M. ix, 27, 269, 272
Jamshidian, Jamshid Bahman 112
Jasavala, Shirin 289
jashans 140, 141, 257, 263, 264, 265, 266, 267, 268, 291, 292, 295, 322
Jashne Mehrgan 291
Jehangir, Sir Cowasji 125, 129
Jerusalem 2
Jessawalla, Dosebai Cowasji 83
Jews 2, 21, 30, 34, 302–4
Jijibhoy, Byramji 201
Jijibhoy, Sir Jamsetji 56, 124, 182
Jijibhoy, Hon. Rustomji 82
Jinnah, Mohammed Ali 59
joy, religious occasions 22, 262
Juddins, *see* non-Zoroastrians
judgement after death 10, 15, 265
justice 223, 224

Kanga, F. 282
Kapadia, A. R. 155
Kapadia, J. P. 85, 117
Kapadia, S. A. 98
Karachi 5, 28, 58–60, 141, 201, 228, 239, 243, 273–4, 281, 285
Karaka, D. F. 83, 92–3, 98, 99, 100, 105, 287
  see also Framjee, D.
Katrak, Dr Nanabhai Naoroji ix
Katrak, Nicola 288
Kenya 33, 273, 274
Kerman 3
Khambatta, H. J. 82 n. 3
Khomeini, Ayatollah 3, 146, 242
Khory, C. F. 82 n. 3
Khory, Dr E. J. 123
Khory, R. N. 82 n. 3
Khshnoom, *see* Ilm-i Khshnoom
Kolah, Muncherji Behramji 82
Kookadaru, Dastur 273
Kothari, Jehangir H. 89–90
Kotwal, K. P. 113

kusti 22, 229, 241, 244, 266, 272, 293–4, 322
  see also sudre/kusti prayers
Kutan, Dastur Dr Sohrab H. x, 140, 141–2, 263, 300
Kutar, Dr Mrs Shirin 146

Labour Party 35–6, 171, 197
Lahore 60
Laing, S. 71, 100
Lancashire, Pakistanis 33
language 308
  see also English, Gujarati, mother tongue
Lascars 29, 160, 185, 288
Last Judgement 10
law, the legal profession 82
leadership 299–300, 304
  see also authority, religious
Leeds, immigrants 33
Leeds University Community Religions Project 37
legends, *see* myth
Leicester 33, 37, 148, 231
Liberal Democrat Party 218
Liberal Party 159–60, 171, 192, 219
  1986 Commission of Inquiry into Ethnic Minority Participation 219
  Community Relations Panel 219, 220
Liberal Zoroastrianism 7, 48, 74, 87–8, 263, 272
life after death belief 243
life-cycle rites 262–5
literature, secular, by Zoroastrians 289
  see also Zoroastrian literature (i.e. religious)
liturgy 294
  see also community rituals; funeral rites; *jashans*; ritual
Liverpool 85, 89, 91, 108, 109, 157
local government 36, 155
London 33, 89, 95–6, 97, 197
London, Imperial Institute 181–2
London Indian Society 157, 171
  see also East India Association
London, Parsis, *see* London Zoroastrian Association; London, Zoroastrian House; London, Zoroastrians
London University, Birkbeck College 258
London Zoroastrian Association 1, 5, 6, 107–17, 120–48, 150–4, 197, 250, 279 289–90; changes name 144, for later references, *see* Zoroastrian Trust Funds of Europe (Inc.); Charitable aims 121–2; International centre 132–3; personalities and politics 125–32; post-war 133–4; registered charity (1979) 133, 141; World Zoroastrian Organization 148
London, Zoroastrian House 49, 115, 121–5, 133, 138–42, 143–4, 192, 230, 234, 239, 241, 244, 245, 248, 249, 251, 253, 255, 256, 258, 259, 260, 262, 263, 264, 265, 266, 273, 285, 287, 288, 290, 303; prayer-room 142, 257, 261, 266
London, Zoroastrians 6, 151, 227, 231, 237, 251, 257, 273, 274, 279, 294, 301–2, 305; aid Zoroastrians in Iran 111–14; Zoroastrians in Britain Survey 227, 231, 272
Lytton, Lord 165, 166

mace (*gurz*) 12
Malabari, B. M. 89, 90–1, 182
Manchester 33, 81, 85, 89, 108, 109, 117, 122, 197, 231, 274–5, 294, 305
  see also North West Zoroastrian Community
Maneck, Rustom and family 53–4, 77
  see also Naoroji, Rustomji
Maneckji, E. 82 n. 3
Mansfield 155
manthras 273, 276, 322
Marker, Jamshid 59
marriage 13, 247, 249, 308
  see also infant marriage; intermarriage; weddings; widows, remarriage
Masani, Ardeshir 134
Masani, Minoo 57, 104
Masani, Sir Rustam 99, 100, 287
Master, E. N. 85
medicine 82
Meherhomji, P. M. 84
MeherjiRana, Kekobad B. Dastur 134, 200
Mehr, Farhang 146
Mehrabi, Khodad Rustom 138, 144
Mehta, Ava 73
Mehta, Jamshed, President of Karachi municipality 201
Mehta, Jamshed Nusserwanji 59
Mehta, J. K. 201
Mehta, Kekoo 197
Mehta, M. S. 82
Mehta, P. D. 259

Mehta, Sir Pherozeshah 57, 59, 75, 82, 86, 169, 283; and Bhownagree 175, 176, 193
Mehta, Zubin 58, 260, 288
Members of Parliament (Britain) 156
  see also Bhownagree, Sir Muncherji; Naoroji, Dadabhoy; Saklatvala, S.
menog 8, 322
menstruation 16, 17, 25, 269, 292
Mercury, Freddy 288–9
metropolitan Zoroastrians 305
  see also Bombay Parsis; London, Zoroastrians
Middle Persian (Pahlavi) texts, *see* Pahlavi
migration, *see* diaspora
Mills, L. H. 116
minority communities 234, 277
Minwalla, D. P. 58
miracle-workers and holy men 297
Mirza, Dastur 272
missionaries, influence on Indian Parsis 67–8
Mistree, Khojestee 73–4, 245, 259, 260, 271, 273, 293
Mistry, M. A. 63
Mistry, R. 289
Mistry, Sorabji 64
Mithra 12, 291, 323
mixed marriage, *see* intermarriage
Mobed-e-Mobedan 273, 293, 323
Modi, J. J. 71, 76, 115
Mody, H. P. 201
Mombasa 6, 64
monotheism 99, 271
Moos, Jehangir D. 138, 140, 144
Moos, Mrs Meher Master 73
mosques 33, 298
Motabhoy, N. R. 82 n. 4
mother ('old') country 244, 245–6, 272, 308
mother tongue 232, 242, 243, 308–9
Moulton, J. H. 67 n. 1
muktad 137, 141, 265, 269, 290, 291, 323
Mulla, N. J. 120
music 256
Muslims 253, 300
  see also Islam
myth 9–12, 17, 243, 274
mythical/abstract thought 11, 269

nahn purification 23, 262, 264, 323
Nairobi 6, 64–5
naojote see *navjote*

Naoroji, Dadabhoy 56, 57, 74, 81, 83, 84–5, 98–101 *passim*, 104, 114, 120, 218, 259, 279, 287, 288; M. P 156–74: background 156–9, Parliamentary candidatures 159–60, Central Finsbury, elected 159, political message 160–9, 183, impact on British politics 169–74, retirement 174, *see also under specific topics, e.g.* 'drain theory'; Zoroastrian Association 107–11 *passim*, 114, 135, 290; Zoroastrian identity and character 222 ff., 226, 283; and Bhownagree 125–6, 128, 176, 182 f.; centenary 287
Naoroji, Dhunjibhoy 83
Naoroji, Jehangir 80–1
Naoroji, Rustomji 77–9
Nariman, F. K. 201, 215
nasarsalas 14–15, 16, 17, 323
nataks 256, 323
Natal 186, 187, 188
National Indian Association, London 93
navjote 23–4, 259, 263, 323
  see also initiation
Navsari 200
Nehru 31, 200, 214
Nehru Centenary Award 219–20
New Year (No Ruz) festival 21, 149, 229, 257, 266, 290, 323
Newcastle upon Tyne 148, 231
newspapers and journals:
  British 103, 160, 167, 191–2, 217, 220 nn. 121–3, 221 nn. 124, 125, 286–7, 302, 303
  Zoroastrian (Parsi) and Indian 156, 157, 182, 190, 192, 201
nirang 23, 26, 263, 323
No Ruz, *see* New Year
non-Zoroastrians 110–11, 137, 143, 148, 150, 244, 247–8, 261, 265, 268, 269, 270, 275, 292
  see also funeral rites; intermarriage; sacred space
North America, *see* American Zoroastrians
North London Zoroastrian Association (NOLZA) 148
North West Zoroastrian Community 149–50
nuclear families 231

occult 294
  see also Ilm-i Khshnoom

occupations, professions 56, 65, 299
Ohrmazd, *see* Ahura Mazda
oil lamp (*divo*) 229, 264, 322
On wings of Fire (video) 260
opium trade 4, 168–9
orthodox (traditional) Zoroastrianism 7, 21, 48, 262
  see also traditional religious views

padan 25, 323
Padshah, C. J. 84
Pahlavi (Middle Persian) 6, 8, 258, 259, 322–3
Pahlavi dynasty, Iran 3
  see also Shah
Pakistan 5–6; immigrants in Britain 42–4; Parsis in 59–60, 267, 272, 295; WZO 145; Zoroastrians from 149, 239, 245, 246, 292, 305; *see also* Karachi
Palkivala, ambassador 57
Panday, Dinshawji 81
Panday, Furdonji Limji 81
Parekh, D. N. 82 n. 3
parental pressure, intermarriage 252
Paris 132
Parliament 96–7, 288, 297
  Committee on East India Finance 157
  see also House of Commons; Members of Parliament
Parsi Association of Europe 113, 115
  see also London Zoroastrian Association
Parsi identity 18–20, 113 n. 5, 115
  see also Zoroastrian, identity
Parsi Pakash 82, 83, 84, 103–4 n. 11
Parsi Religion as Contained in the Zand Avesta The (Wilson) 68
Parsi Social Union 117–19, 127, 290
Parsis 4–5, 18–25, 53–8, 77, 88, 148, 231, 232, 245, 251, 273, 293, 297, 305
  visits to Britain 4, 77–97: for commerce 77–9, 81, 84–5; for education 80–4; perceptions of Britain 88–97, 281–2
  see also Bombay Parsis; Delhi Parsis
  and the British: in Britain 102–6, 268, 279; in East Africa 60–7; in India 53–8; in Pakistan 58–60
  in Britain 5, 74–6, 103, 149, 239, 240, 264, 292; *see also* British Zoroastrians
  priests' objections to Adoption of Children Bill (1980) 46
  Zoroastrians' religious practices, variant 22; *see also* diaspora religion, changes
Parthians 2, 323
Patel, Shirin 227
Patel, Vallabhai 200
Pateti, *see* New Year
Patuck, Framji Pestonji 81
Penton, Captain 159
persecution 3, 20, 34, 287, 303–4
Persepolis style 135
Persia, ancient 1, 2, 21
  see also Iran *for Arab and modern Iran*
Persia, Zoroastrian heritage 75, 153, 235, 277, 291, 304
Persian language 256
  see also Pahlavi (Middle Persian)
personal responsibility, *see* free will
Petit, B. D. 117
Petit, Sir Dinshah 59, 111, 127, 130, 201
Petit, J. B. 201
pilgrimage 25, 245–6, 266
politics 4, 57, 125–32
  see also British politics
pollution 14–18, 24, 269, 270
  see also death; menstruation; purity and pollution; purity laws
pomegranate juice 23
Poverty and Un-British Rule in India (Naoroji) 158
Poverty of India (Naoroji) 157
Powell, Enoch 28
prayer 12, 15, 21–7, 241, 243, 244, 248, 249, 251, 254, 265, 266, 276, 277
  see also sudre/kusti prayers
prayer room 27, 142, 257, 261, 266, 269, 291, 292
priests, priesthood 7, 15, 17, 19, 24–7, 69, 101, 144, 158, 242, 264, 269, 276, 301
  British Zoroastrians 141, 252–3, 261 264, 266, 300; high priests' visits to Britain 272–3, 291
Prince of Wales 286, 287
  Youth Business Trust 220
professional occupations 5, 43, 299
Protestantism and Zoroastrianism 70, 71, 101, 241, 242, 243, 273, 274, 287, 294, 295, 307
Punthakey, Jehangir Framroze 58
purity and pollution 269, 296
purity laws 13–26, 137, 141, 142, 229, 241, 248, 250, 261, 263, 266, 268, 291

Index

Qissa-i Sanjan 4, 75, 323

race and religion 233, 234, 237, 238, 239, 241, 244, 248, 250, 276, 291, 293, 303
race, racism, racial prejudice 28–31, 35–7, 44, 92, 93–5, 219, 224, 235–7, 250, 252, 253, 282, 283, 284, 290, 296
   in British India 183
Race Relations Acts 27, 35, 45
Rahnumae Mazdyasnian Sabha 225
Rawlinson, Sir Henry 111
Readymoney, C. J. 82
rebirth 20, 273
reform Zoroastrianism 48, 158, 225, 242, 243, 263, 272–3
religious education:
   in British schools 286–7, 302
   Hindu 38
   Zoroastrian 73–4, 139, 258–61, 274–5, 285, 292, 294, 304
religious functions, social 257
   see also gahambars, New Year
Religious Funds of Zoroastrians of Europe 108
   see also London Zoroastrian Association
Religious Society of Zoroastrians 87
repatriation 248, 251, 288
   of Parsis to India 121–2, 132, 138
Reporter, Ardeshir E. J. 111
Reporter, M. E. 82 n. 3
resurrection 9–10, 18, 243, 273–4
Revayats 293
Ripon, Lord, Viceroy 157, 170
ritual 17, 22–7, 242, 261, 270, 276, 296
   see also ceremonies; community, rituals; funeral rites; life-cycle rites; liturgy; temple worship
Rivetna, Rohinton 147, 293, 294
Round Table Conference (1931) 125, 126
rural/urban Zoroastrians 305
Rustom Maneck, *see* Maneck, Rustom

sacred space 143, 269–70, 293
   see also space, Zoroastrian
sagdi 134, 136, 323
Sai Baba 273
Saklatvala, Shapurji 104, 125, 129–32, 152–3; *194–218*: background, early life in India, 194–7; marriage and family 196–7; children's *navjote* 199, 203; political life, parliament 197–9; General Strike 198, 206, 207, 208; Communist Party 197, 203, 218; Labour Party 198; Indian tour (1927) 199–202: criticizes Gandhi 200–1, 202, Bombay Parsis and Saklatvala 201; parliamentary message 204–13; political interests 204–6: social minorities 204–5, international perspective 206, social issues 207, against Imperialism, armed forces 207–10; British rule in India 211–13; assessment of influence 213–18: Indian National Congress 214–15; and Bhownagree 215–16; and Nehru 214–15; Zoroastrian identity 222 ff.; character 226
Salisbury, Lord 159, 167
Sanjan 4
saviour, future 10, 274
scholarship, *see* education; western scholarship
secularization 300, 309
Sedra pushun, *see* initiation; *navjote*
Sethna, Ervad Zal 299, 300
Sethna, Homi 260
Sethna, Sir Pheroze 63, 125, 126–7, 129, 201
Sethna, Roshan 289
sexual equality, mixed marriage children 19
Shah 3, 111, 112, 113, 280, 292
Shah Name 259
Shahrokh, Kay Khosrow 242
Shahrokh, Shahrokh 146, 292
Shanghai 4
shipbuilding, *see* Wadia family
Shroff, Behramshah 72, 273
Shroff, Cursetjee Maneckji 81, 82, 83, 85, 103
Shroff, Thrity 149, 155
Sidhwa, B. 289
Sidhwa, Justice Rustom 59–60
Sikhs in Britain 31, 32, 33, 300
Simon Commission (1927) 210
sin 23
Social life, Zoroastrian 255–7
Socialists 171, 174
Sorabji, Cornelia 83
soul 9, 10, 15, 265, 270, 271
South Africa 66, 179, 185–7, 188, 191, 224
South Asians in Britain 27–49, 296 ff.,

Index 335

see also Hindus in Britain; Parsis in Britain
South London Zoroastrians 149
space, Zoroastrian 135, 151, 270
  see also sacred space
Spenta Mainyu 11, 323
spiritual and material creation 8
spouses, non-Zoroastrian, see intermarriage; non-Zoroastrians
Sraosha 12
Steel, Sir David 220
students 127
sudre 15, 22–5, 229, 241, 244, 266, 272, 292–3
sudre/kusti prayers 21–4, 264, 267, 272
superstition 242
Surat 53, 54
Swadeshi 173
Sydney Zoroastrians 273, 274
symbolism 12, 22, 26, 269, 276
  see also fire
syncretism 287, 295–6

Taramchand, N. M. 155
Tata:
  company 57, 195
  family 19, 195
Tata, Mrs D. J. 135
Tata, Dorab J. N. 117
Tata, Dorabji 195
Tata, Lady Dorabji 124
Tata, J. N. 55, 81, 182, 195
Tata, Nusserwanji 194
Tata, Ratan 117
Tata, R. J. 135
Tehran 3, 22, 279, 305
Telang (Parsi) 169
temple worship 22, 25–7, 243, 261, 266, 292
  see also Atash Bahram
temples 12, 24, 26; in India 135, 141, see also Bombay, temples; in London 109, 265, 266, 285, 291
textile trade 80–1, 85
Thatcher, Margaret 28, 36
theology 292
Theosophical Society 71–2
theosophy 268 n. 10
thoughts, words and deeds, Zoroastrian belief 9, 10
three days after death 15
  see also funeral rites; soul; uthumna
tokens, see symbolism

toleration, religious 2, 4
Toronto 235–6
Tory Party 177, 192
Tower of Silence, see daxma
trade and commerce 4–5, 279
tradition, continuity of, Zoroastrianism 7, 18
traditional religious views 88, 142, 241, 243, 244, 272, 273, 277, 309–10
Transvaal, see South Africa

USA, see American Zoroastrians
Udwada 253
Uganda 33, 145
  Parsis expelled from 5
Ulama, Islam in Britain 298, 299
university education 81, 232, 234
urbanized Irani Zoroastrians 242
uthumna ceremony 15–16, 265, 324

Vacha, J. B. 85
Vajifdar, F. 259
vegetarianism 266
Vendidad, 265, 324
Verdict of India, The (Bhownagree) 193
Victoria, Queen 160, 164, 177 n. 35
videos, religious education 260
Vohu Manah 7, 11, 12, 324

Wadia, Ardashir Cursetjee 80, 89, 90, 93
Wadia, Ardasir N. 98, 105
Wadia brothers (J. N. and H. M.) British travels 89–92, 96–7; and East India Co. 93
Wadia, C. R. 84
Wadia, Dinshah 57, 175, 176, 182, 189–90
Wadia family 55, 88, 102, 279
Wadia, H. M. 80, 89
Wadia, J. B. 85
Wadia, Jehangir N. 80, 89, 90, 131
Wadia, Mrs Jerbai 134
Wadia, Lowji 55
Wadia, N. A. C. 81
Wadia, Sir Ness 124
Wadia, N. N. 134, 182
Wadia, Nusserwanji Naoroji (son of N. N.) 134
(Wadia?), Ookerji 81
Wadia, R. H. 83–4
Warwick University Centre for Research in Asian Migration 220
water, sacred 14, 24, 269

Wedderburn, Sir William, and Naoroji 158, 169, 170, 174; and Bhownagree 177, 188, 191, 192
weddings 264
  see also marriage
Welby Commission 163, 164, 167
Wembley Zoroastrians 231
West Indian Liberal Foundation 190
West Indies, migration 31, 33
Western Liberal Federation, Bombay 201
western scholarship 6–7, 30, 69–71, 74, 99, 147, 261, 273, 284, 285–6, 294, 300
westernization, influence 19, 20, 251, 272
white Anglo-Saxons 28, 47–8, 237, 246, 247, 248, 255
  see also British, the; European race
widows, remarriage 156, 174
Wilson, John 67–8, 83
Wimbledon Zoroastrians 231
women 33, 43, 297; rights 56, 207, 219, 224
  Zoroastrian: British Survey 249–50: dress 22, 262; education 83, 85; funeral prayers 15; in Britain, 19th century 298; intermarriage 252; and non-Zoroastrians 237; pollution and purity 16, 25; religious responsibility 250
Women and the Law (Zerbanoo Gifford) 219
'work ethic' 13, 281
Workers' Welfare League, India 217
World Parliament of Religions, Chicago (1993) 30, 293
world renovation (*frashokereti*) 9, 323
World War I and II 30, 31, 104, 193, 288
World Zarathustrian Trust Fund 146
World Zoroastrian Congress: Bombay, (1981–) 147, 293; Tehran 144
World Zoroastrian Organization (WZO) 132, 144–8, 218, 258, 259, 280, 294
World Zoroastrian Youth Congress, Calif. (1993) 293–4
worship 25, 296
  see also congregational worship; prayer; ritual; temple worship; yasna
Writer, Dr Rashna 227, 229, 293

Yashts 6, 324
yasna 261, 265, 324
Yazatas 12, 324
Yazd 3, 22, 242, 305

young Zoroastrians 119, 150, 230, 234, 238, 245, 246–7, 255–7, 259, 275, 276, 284, 294, 296, 308
youth, Asian immigrants 296, 298–9

Zanzibar 5, 6, 63
Zarathustra, *see* Zoroaster
Zarthoshti brothers 141
Zarthoshti, Mehraban 136
Zoroaster 1, 6–8, 21, 23, 69, 223, 229, 242, 277, 324
  see also Gathas; Zoroastrianism
Zoroastrian Association of Europe 192
  see also Zoroastrian Trust Funds of Europe (Inc.)
Zoroastrian Associations 107–54, 150–4
  local associations 148–5
  see also London Zoroastrian Association; North London Zoroastrian Association; North West Zoroastrian Community; South London Zoroastrians
Zoroastrian: contribution to British society 288, 289; identity 18–19, 221–2, 292, 310; literature: written for the British 97–102, 281, 287, written for Zoroastrians 241, 259, *see also* newspapers and journals
Zoroastrian centre 285, 291, 294
  see also London, Zoroastrian House
Zoroastrian Conferences in North America 293
Zoroastrian Fund Committee of London 134
  see also London Zoroastrian Association
Zoroastrian Trust Funds of Europe (Inc.) (ZTFE) 144, 148, 175, 256, 258, 260, 284, 285, 293, 294, 299
Zoroastrian studies, Bombay 73
Zoroastrianism: belief and practice 7–17, 22, 158, 271–2, 286, *see also special topics*; history 1–7, 279, 280, 295–6; and Christianity 67–74, 228; and Indo-European heritage 4; misrepresented in the West 17–18, 303; scriptures, 6–7, *see also Avesta*; *Gathas*; diaspora religion
Zoroastrians, declining numbers 5–6, 21, 301–2, 304; *see also* demography in Britain vii–ix, 36, 293, 294, 296–310; *see also* British Zoroastrians; Parsis, in Britain; *and under individual names and topics*
and South Asian Communities 296ff.

GENERAL THEOLOGICAL SEMINARY
NEW YORK

DATE DUE

HIGHSMITH #45230   Printed in USA